WILLIAM HENRY SEWARD

ALSO BY JOHN M. TAYLOR

General Maxwell Taylor

Garfield of Ohio

From the White House Inkwell

(WRITING AS RICHARD C. ALLEN)

Korea's Syngman Rhee

WILLIAM HENRY SEWARD

Lincoln's Right Hand

JOHN M. TAYLOR

Brassey's

Washington • London

Copyright © 1991 John M. Taylor

Taylor, John M., 1930–
    William Henry Seward: Lincoln's right hand / John M. Taylor.--
1st Brassey's Five-Star pbk. ed.
            p.   cm.

            Originally published: New York, NY:HarperCollins, ©1991.
            Includes bibliographical references and index.

        ISBN 1-57488-119-1

        1. Seward, William Henry. 1801–1872. 2. Cabinet officers– United
States–Biography. 3. Statesmen–United States–Biography. 4. United States. Dept. of
State–Biography. 5. United States–Foreign Relations--1861–1865. 6. United
States–Politics and government--1861–1865   I. Title.
[E415.9.S4T38 1996]
973.7'092–dc20
[B]   96-2816
                                                                                    CIP

For P. S. T.

CONTENTS

PREFACE

As a young man, William Henry Seward once remarked that he was an enigma, even to himself. Historians have not disputed this self-appraisal by one of the more complex figures in American political history. Privately Seward was simultaneously a devoted husband and an absentee spouse. Politically he was a reformer who worked in close alliance with one of the first political bosses of his day, Thurlow Weed. Seward longed for the Republican presidential nomination in 1860, yet spent half the year preceding the Republican convention on holiday in Europe. As Lincoln's secretary of state he pressed unsuccessfully for authority comparable to that of the president himself, but when rebuffed went on to become one of Lincoln's most loyal wartime associates.

As secretary of state, Seward helped avert the one development—foreign intervention—that might have led to a Confederate victory in the Civil War. But students of that conflict, preoccupied with what took place on the battlefield, have been inclined to slight his role. There are, at this writing, several thousand books about Abraham Lincoln; the Louis A. Warren Lincoln Library, in Fort Wayne, Indiana, lists more than ten thousand Lincoln titles (although these include pamphlets as well as books). In contrast, there are no more than a dozen about Seward, of which only two—Burton Hendrick's 1946 volume, *Lincoln's War Cabinet,* and the 1967 biography by Glyndon Van Deusen—have any place on a contemporary bookshelf.

Why has Seward been largely ignored over the years? In some quarters it was felt necessary to denigrate Seward in order to build up Lincoln. This attitude is in itself remarkable, for Lincoln's achievements require no gilding. But Lincoln's successes were not achieved in isolation, and in leading the country during the Civil War he had no abler lieutenant than the man he defeated to become his party's presidential nominee.

A complicated and occasionally devious person, Seward was one of the political giants of his generation, and he deserves recognition in his own right. As governor of New York, Seward was a pioneer in prison reform. In the U.S. Senate, he sought to contain the expansion of slavery with a view to its eventual abolition. As secretary of state during the Civil War, he fended off—through a combination of threats and cajolery—foreign intervention until the Union victory at Gettysburg made such intervention clearly inadvisable. Under Andrew Johnson, he maneuvered the French out of Mexico, set the stage for arbitration of the *Alabama* claims, and almost single-handedly brought about the purchase of Alaska from Russia.

*   *   *

The search for the real Seward begins at the Seward house in Auburn, New York. The home in which William Henry and Frances Seward lived as newlyweds, and in which Henry died, remained in the Seward family until 1951; it was subsequently opened to the public and in 1964 became a historical trust. To the visitor little appears to have changed since Seward's day. The foyer is chockablock with souvenirs of the secretary's travels to foreign lands. On the second floor the walls are covered with prints and photographs of the sovereigns and foreign envoys with whom Seward dealt as secretary of state—"my tormentors," as he called them. The gazebo in the garden is much as it was when Frances Seward, sorely afflicted, sought refuge there during the war. The carriage house contains the vehicle from which Seward was thrown in April 1865, causing him to be at home recuperating on the night Lincoln was shot, and thus an easy target for one of Booth's accomplices.

Although the literature relating to Seward is sparse, a few volumes are of special value to the biographer. One is the three-volume biography published by Seward's son Frederick in 1890. In retirement Secretary Seward had begun an autobiography, but he died before describing his years of national political prominence. Frederick completed the work, quoting extensively from his father's letters—a contribution in itself, for William Henry Seward's handwriting was as wretched as that of any prominent American of his day.

In 1900 Frederic Bancroft published a two-volume biography that was more objective than Frederick Seward's work, though not so detailed. Not until nearly seven decades later was Seward the subject of a major study by a professional historian. Van Deusen's work, mentioned earlier, is exhaustive in chronicling Seward's rise in New York politics but somewhat less satisfactory in its treatment of the Seward family and of Seward's wartime diplomacy.

* * *

A number of people have assisted in the writing of this book. Betty Lewis, curator of the Seward House, not only shared her encyclopedic knowledge of the Seward family but made available photographs and press clippings as required. Karl Kabelac of the University of Rochester Library facilitated my use of the Seward Papers there. Ruth Cook of the Louis A. Warren Lincoln Library provided photographs and several old pamphlets. Dr. John K. Lattimer, an author and a collector of assassination memorabilia, provided a photograph of the knife with which Seward was nearly killed in 1865. The staff of the Goshen, New York, Historical Society and the Schaffer Library at Union College, Schenectady, New York, photocopied Seward letters in their collections on my behalf. Susan Lemke, chief of special collections at the National Defense University, helped locate several elusive books, as did Elden ("Josh") Billings, a longtime collector of literature relating to the Civil War. An autograph collector in Manhattan who requested anonymity made available several unpublished Seward letters.

Two distinguished scholars, Robert C. L. Scott of Williams College and Terry Alford, a biographer of John Wilkes Booth, read sections of the manuscript and provided valuable criticism. My London-based daughter, Alice Taylor McVeigh, offered a number of useful comments.

This book, like others by me, has benefited greatly from repeated readings by my wife, Priscilla, a professional editor whose publications include the Phi Beta Kappa quarterly newsletter. Her comments have gone beyond style and format to include many suggestions as to the interpretation of Seward's complex character.

1

A Convention in Chicago

THROUGHOUT MUCH OF the nineteenth century, Americans were fascinated with the West. For the generation that witnessed the Civil War, the lure of the West—which many thought began at the Alleghenies—was irresistible. California enjoyed a mystique not unlike that of outer space today. In the words of one old-time orator, Caleb Cushing, the day was approaching "when the great West shall stretch forth its arm of power . . . to command the destiny of the Union."[1]

It was this desire to identify with the frontier that prompted the fledgling Republican party to select a growing western metropolis, Chicago, for its 1860 presidential convention. Not that the city was a universally popular choice, for in the Windy City the hog was king. One newspaper boasted that 32,900 hogs had arrived in the city in a single week. Allowing three linear feet for each hog, the paper concluded that Chicago had been host to a line of pork almost nineteen miles long.

This sort of distinction tended to limit the city's charm for outsiders, and there were more visible defects as well. At the junction of Madison and Dearborn streets, a perpetual mudhole drew oaths from teamsters unlucky enough to be sucked into its morass. Thousands of rats made their homes under the city's wooden sidewalks. Cattle roamed the streets. Refuse from stables was emptied into Lake Michigan, the source of the city's drinking water. Not surprisingly, Chicago, with its 110,000 residents, had the highest death rate of any American city.

None of this fazed the city's energetic boosters, however. Chicago was on its way to becoming the nation's railroad hub; on a typical day, some 150 trains stopped at its seven stations. The economy was booming, and Cyrus McCormick was shipping fifty thousand of his reapers

each year. The city's newspapers were beginning to rival in influence
those in the East, while Chicago's merchants did a growing business in
consumer goods for the carriage trade—wigs and pianos, hoop skirts
and chandeliers. To the distress of the clergy, however, the city's saloons
far outnumbered its churches.

By 1860 Chicago had developed into a convention city of sorts. It
claimed to have some fifty-seven hotels, eight of which the town fathers
classified as deluxe. In the competition for the Republican Convention,
the metropolis had committed itself to putting up a special hall for the
gathering. The result was an unsightly wooden structure designed to
hold ten thousand people or more, a building that somehow became
known as the Wigwam. Its interior resembled a theater, in which the
delegates would be seated on the stage, facing a gallery built on two
levels. There were no fire marshals to monitor the number of spectators
who would pack the hall during the four days of the convention.

The city's role as host for a national convention was a source of pride,
particularly because most Chicagoans assumed that the convention
would be choosing the next president. Although the Republican party
of 1860 was hardly the political juggernaut it would later become, the
opposition appeared hopelessly disorganized. Just days before the Republicans were scheduled to convene, the Democratic Convention,
meeting in Charleston, South Carolina, had adjourned without nominating a ticket. The *New York Times* editorialized: "The political condition of the country is as completely chaotic as the most zealous lover of
disorder could possibly desire. At no period within twenty-five years has
there been so complete a rupture of all the bonds that usually hold
parties together."[2] Assuming that the party could unite on a ticket, a
Republican victory in November seemed assured.

That meant, people said, that the sixteenth president of the United
States would be William H. Seward, the sprightly senior senator from
New York, who was the acknowledged front-runner for the Republican
presidential nomination. Just turning sixty, Seward looked more like a
professor than a politician. He was frail, slightly stooped, and had a
weak chin. His eyebrows were full and bushy, his ears tended to pro-
trude, and his ample shock of sandy-gray hair seemed perpetually in
need of attention. Seward's most prominent feature was his nose, which
gave him the aspect of a jocular bird. Henry Adams wrote of the senator's "unorderly hair and clothes; hoarse voice; offhand manner; free
talk, and perpetual cigar."[3]

Although the candidate's appearance was unprepossessing, his political credentials were sound. Seward had twice been elected governor of

his state, and in Albany he had been an early champion of penal reform and immigrant rights. In the Senate he had emerged as a key spokesman for the antislavery movement—not a flaming abolitionist, to be sure, but a thoughtful opponent of any extension of slavery into new territories. Seward was, in the words of one journalist, "the central figure of the whole [antislavery] movement, its prophet, priest, and oracle." A presidential election without Seward, he concluded, "would be the play without Hamlet."[4]

Moreover, behind the symbol there was substance. Few politicians of the day could match the clarity and logic of Seward's important papers, a fact that prompted one of the country's influential editors, Edwin L. Godkin of the *Nation*, to call him "the clearest-headed statesman" and "perhaps the greatest constitutional lawyer" in America.[5] The senator also possessed charm. He was a friendly, outgoing man who enjoyed people and loved life. He delighted as did few others in an evening passed in convivial conversation over a glass of port. He was not an inspired orator, but few men were more persuasive in a small group.

Seward was a gifted phrasemaker—perhaps too gifted. In 1850 he had spoken eloquently of a "higher law" than the Constitution. Eight years later he had called the struggle against slavery "an irrepressible conflict." Speeches like these had made Seward anathema in the South, causing even his supporters to wonder whether their man had made himself unnecessarily controversial. But the New York delegates were proud of their former governor; they called themselves the Irrepressibles and regarded the convention in Chicago as akin to a coronation.

The Seward people not only had the best-known candidate, they also had the man thought to be the best political manager of his generation. Thurlow Weed, the editor and political boss from Albany, knew all the devious tricks of politics and was totally devoted to Seward. At his headquarters at the Richmond House hotel, Weed held court for visiting delegates while his aides took their own soundings elsewhere. Although Weed was called the Dictator, his style was gracious and his manner hearty. He addressed the convention delegates by name and unfailingly complimented them for their good work for the party. Weed would then move on to the subject of his candidate. "We think we have in Mr. Seward just the qualities the country will need," he told members of the Kansas delegation. "He is known by us all as a statesman. . . . We expect to nominate him on the first ballot."[6] Thurlow Weed seemed the perfect man to strengthen the wavering or to instill confidence among delegates already pledged to Seward.

Weed's confidence appeared justified. Apart from Seward, the con-

tenders in Chicago were a lackluster bunch with little appeal beyond
their own regions. Edward Bates of Missouri was a venerable conservative who had helped to frame the Missouri Compromise forty years
earlier. Gov. Salmon P. Chase of Ohio looked like a president but had
an unctuous manner that won him few friends. Sen. Simon Cameron,
the political boss of Pennsylvania, was a power to reckon with, but few
thought him presidential timber. And, finally, there was Abraham Lincoln of Illinois. Lincoln had engaged Sen. Stephen Douglas in a series
of well-publicized debates on slavery in the territories. Otherwise he was
little known outside the West. In Auburn, New York, the Finger Lakes
village where Seward lived, his neighbors trundled a brass cannon to
the rambling brick house on South Street where the candidate waited.
Nomination of the town's most famous son would trigger a night of
fireworks and celebration.

*   *   *

Thurlow Weed was not the only astute political manager in Chicago.
Three-hundred-pound David Davis, who reminded some of a sleepy
mountain, led the Lincoln delegation. He had known Lincoln since they
had traveled the legal circuit in rural Illinois, and he was convinced that
Seward was not nearly so strong as he appeared. In Davis's view, if
Lincoln could survive the first ballot, he had a good shot at the nomination.

The Lincoln people had some arithmetic in their favor. The conventional wisdom, Democratic disarray notwithstanding, was that the
Republicans had to win at least three of the four pivotal Northern states—
Illinois, Indiana, New Jersey, and Pennsylvania. As a relatively new
organization—this was only the second presidential election in the Republicans' short history—the party had none of the confidence that stems
from past success. In most states the party was an amalgam of factions
that in some cases had long been antagonistic. It included outright abolitionists, for whom slavery was the only issue. There were Free-Soilers,
who drew the line at any expansion of the slave states. There were the
nativists, or Know-Nothings, who gave highest priority to the curbing
of immigration. Finally, the party had drawn together a variety of former Whigs and Democrats who, though unhappy with their old parties,
still nursed grievances against former rivals who had themselves also
switched allegiance to the Republicans.

In any case, the spirit of reform was on hold in Chicago, where the
platform committee had watered down the antislavery rhetoric of four
years before. The new platform denounced any reopening of the African

slave trade and characterized John Brown's raid at Harper's Ferry as "among the gravest of crimes," but it included no language comparable to that of 1856, in which the Republican platform had castigated slavery as a "relic of barbarism."[7] The *New York Times* reporter in Chicago concluded that the sentiment of the convention "is decidedly conservative, and opposed to anything like interference with Slavery in States where it exists."[8]

For all his prestige, Seward had incurred certain liabilities over three decades in politics. The nativists, who were especially strong in Pennsylvania, Indiana, and New Jersey, were bitterly opposed to Seward, a longtime champion of immigrant rights. Erstwhile Democrats had difficulty warming to the New Yorker, a former Whig. And despite the fact that the South was largely unrepresented at Chicago, the degree to which Seward had become a symbol of Northern radicalism was a source of unease. One Southern congressman had called the New Yorker a traitor, a person whom Southerners "could neither consistently support, or even obey, should the nation elect him President."[9] The governor of Virginia, in his annual message, had announced that the idea of Seward in the White House was totally unacceptable.

Finally, there was the question of Thurlow Weed. Although Weed was personally honest and had a wide circle of friends, his handling of the New York legislature over the years had overtones of brandy and cigars. So, too, did his fund-raising for Seward; many of his contributions came from corporations and promoters eager to remain in the Dictator's good graces. Some years earlier Seward and Weed had made an enemy of Horace Greeley, the irascible but influential editor of the *New York Tribune,* when they denied him appointment to state office. Now, in Chicago, the moon-faced Greeley made the rounds of doubtful delegations, warning them that the party could not win with Seward as its standard-bearer.

In the parlors of the Lincoln headquarters at the Tremont House, the candidate's managers sought to separate fact from rumor. A newspaper editor, Murat Halstead, described how "men gather in little groups with their arms about each other, and chatter and whisper as if the fate of the country depended upon their immediate delivery of the mighty political secrets with which their imaginations are big. . . . There are now at least a thousand men packed together in the halls of the Tremont House, crushing each other's ribs, trampling each other's toes, and titillating each other with the gossip of the day."[10]

The Lincoln camp was optimistic about the four crucial states. Illinois was Lincoln's own turf, firmly if not unanimously behind its favorite son. The neighboring state of Indiana was leaning toward Lincoln; Davis had cultivated the Hoosiers assiduously, and there is some evidence that he had promised a cabinet post to the leader of the Indiana delegation, Caleb Smith.* Elsewhere, his assistants had been working hard with the New Jersey delegation. As far as Davis could tell, Lincoln had far more votes than any candidate except Seward. Pennsylvania looked promising, too. Andrew Curtin, one of the leaders of the Pennsylvania delegation, was in close contact with Henry Lane of the Indiana delegation. Both men hoped to be elected to the Senate by their respective legislatures—the standard practice of that day—and both were opposed to Seward. Curtin believed that a more conservative candidate than Seward was required to carry Pennsylvania, and Lane felt the same was true of his state. They listened politely to Thurlow Weed, with his promises of financial support for their state campaigns, but in the end they joined the stop-Seward movement.

Because the New England states were to be called first in the convention voting, their votes were likely to carry considerable psychological impact. Weed had worked hard to make New England solid for Seward. Six months earlier he had contributed funds to the New Hampshire Republicans for use in local elections in the Granite State. He now counted on New Hampshire's stated commitment to Seward. But despite Weed's best efforts, New England's support for Seward was soft and in some places nonexistent. Ex-Democrat Gideon Welles, a power in the Connecticut delegation, assured Davis that Seward would receive no votes from his state or from Rhode Island. When the Lincoln managers met with the New Hampshire delegates, the assurances they had given Weed earlier were forgotten: the New Hampshire caucus went for Lincoln. By the time the voting began, the Lincoln camp had made serious inroads into Seward's supposed strength in New England.

Weed had high hopes for Pennsylvania. Of all the political bosses assembled at Chicago, Pennsylvania's ambitious Simon Cameron seemed most likely to respond to Weed's offer of financial contributions from the Seward campaign war chest. But here, too, the Lincoln people proved more effective. On May 18 David Davis had a visitor, Judge Joseph Casey, from the Pennsylvania delegation. According to Casey, Cameron wanted to make a deal. He would deliver Pennsylvania to Lincoln on condition that he be made secretary of the treasury, with complete control over appointments in his home state. The Lincoln managers, uneasy about the proposal, telegraphed the gist of it to Lin-

---

*In fact Lincoln appointed Smith secretary of the interior.

coln in Springfield. Lincoln wired back that he would authorize no bargains. On reading Lincoln's telegram Davis is supposed to have said: "Lincoln ain't here and don't know what we have to meet, so we will go ahead as if we hadn't heard from him and he must ratify it."[11] Lincoln would ultimately honor his manager's unauthorized pledge, although Cameron's portfolio would be the War Department rather than the Treasury Department.

While the Lincoln men canvassed, the Seward contingent celebrated. "Few men," Halstead wrote, "have had friends who would cleave unto them as the Sewardites to their great man."[12] There were no polls in 1860, but straw votes on incoming trains pointed to an overwhelming victory for the New Yorker. The northwestern states—Michigan, Wisconsin, and Minnesota—were pledged to Seward. So, too, were California and Massachusetts. The largest delegation at the convention, the one from New York, was of course solidly for its favorite son. Before nominations began Horace Greeley glumly wired his paper that Seward was the probable winner.

Notwithstanding Davis's confidence, the Lincoln men sounded out Thurlow Weed concerning the vice-presidential nomination for their man in the event of a Seward victory. Weed said he would be happy to have Lincoln. One of the Lincoln delegates promptly wired the candidate to ask whether he would take second place, and Lincoln replied that he would if his managers so advised. His managers chose, wisely, to keep all their options open. The air was heavy with intrigue.

For the first two days of the convention, the Wigwam seemed saturated with Seward banners. But Lincoln's managers had found a means to capitalize on the fact that the convention was on their candidate's home ground. The Seward managers had offered no objection to Chicago as the convention site, in part because the threat of a serious challenge from Lincoln seemed remote. But after the formal opening of the convention on May 16, the crowds of Lincoln supporters made their presence felt. Hour after hour, day and night, thousands of Lincoln supporters sang and shouted for their man. On May 19 one of Davis's aides, Ward Hill Lamon, called on the convention printer with a special order. By obtaining a special supply of tickets to the Wigwam, Lamon was able to pack the gallery with Lincoln supporters as the balloting began.

Because political speeches in the 1860s often ran for an hour or two, the convention organizers had specified that the nomination of candidates was not to be the occasion for extended speeches. Seward's name was placed in nomination very briefly by William M. Evarts, a prominent New York attorney. Lincoln was nominated in a single sentence by Norman Judd, an Illinois lawyer who had been a major force in bringing the Republican convention to Chicago. Although Seward's name was warmly received, the response for Lincoln was overwhelming. One reporter compared the uproar to "all the hogs ever slaughtered in Cincinnati giving their death squeals together."[13] Weed's heart must have sunk as he reflected on the crowd factor.

When the clamor subsided, balloting began. Seward's vulnerability quickly became apparent. Although New England was supposed to be in Seward's pocket, Maine gave him only 10 of its 16 votes. New Hampshire gave Lincoln 7 votes out of 10. Taken as a whole, New England cast 32 votes for Seward and 19 for Lincoln, with the rest scattered.

New York's 70 votes, solid for Seward, brought Seward a lead of 102 to Lincoln's 19, but from then on the New Yorker faced stiff resistance. New Jersey voted for its own William Dayton, and most of Pennsylvania stayed with Cameron. Virginia, widely regarded as in the Seward camp, gave Lincoln 14 votes and Seward only 8. On the first ballot Seward received 173½ votes to Lincoln's 102, with the remainder scattered. With 233 votes required for the nomination, Lincoln had done better than expected, and there were no signs of a stampede to Seward. It now dawned on the delegates that the conventional wisdom of the night before—that Seward would have things his own way—was badly off the mark. Indeed, Lincoln, not Seward, appeared to be favored among those delegations pledged to favorite sons on the first ballot.

The trend became clear on the second ballot. Seward lost votes in New England, and Pennsylvania—honoring its agreement with Davis— swung into the Lincoln camp. At the end of the second ballot Seward had 184½ votes to 181 votes for Lincoln; the front-runner had picked up a scant 11 votes, while his principal rival had gained 79. There was indeed a bandwagon in Chicago, but it was a Lincoln bandwagon.

Presiding officer George Ashmun called for a third ballot "amid excitement that tested the nerves." Four Massachusetts delegates switched from Seward to Lincoln, who also picked up three votes in New Jersey and four more in Pennsylvania. There was a big switch in Ohio, where Lincoln gained 14 votes. When the roll call ended, Seward's total had dropped to 180 and Lincoln's had reached 231½—just 1½ votes short of the necessary total. No candidate had ever come so close to victory and not gone over the top.

"A profound stillness," wrote one spectator, "fell upon the Wigwam; the men ceased to talk and the ladies to flutter their fans; one could distinctly hear the scratching of pencils and the ticking of telegraph instruments on the reporters' tables."[14] One of the Lincoln men in the hall was Joseph Medill of the *Chicago Tribune*. At this critical juncture Medill told Ohio delegate D. K. Carrter that if he could swing Ohio to Lincoln, "Chase can have anything he wants." "H-how d-d'ye know?" stammered Carrter, who had a speech impediment. Medill replied, "I know, and you know I wouldn't promise if I didn't know."[15]* The galleries grew quiet as Carrter asked for recognition from the chair. The Ohioan announced a switch of four votes in his delegation from Chase to Lincoln. There was silence, followed by a great roar from the gallery. Other delegations vied for recognition in order to jump to the winning side. An immense poster of Lincoln was brought into the hall and nailed over the rostrum. Jubilant delegates seized the various state banners and began a march up and down the crowded aisles. Sadly, Evarts rose and moved that the nomination be made unanimous.

Orville Browning, a Lincoln delegate, was recognized, and he made one of the last remarks the stenographic reporters were able to pick up before the din became overwhelming. "We struggled against the nomination of the illustrious statesman from New York, solely because we believed here that we could go into battle on the prairies of Illinois with more hope and more prospect of success under the leadership of our own noble son."[16] But the New Yorkers were inconsolable. Thurlow Weed buried his face in his hands, tears running down his cheeks. The New York delegates refused to join the celebration in the Wigwam and slowly made their way back to their hotels.

The news from Chicago reached Seward's hometown of Auburn by wire. The candidate's friends at the telegraph office quietly dispersed, ignoring the last-minute vote switches and the closing speeches. Dr. Theodore Dimon, an old friend who had been transmitting the news to Seward as it arrived, now had a thankless task. It was a fine spring day, and Seward was seated in the garden with another friend, John Austin, when Dimon was shown in. Dimon handed Seward a terse message: "Lincoln nominated third ballot." According to Dimon, there was no change in Seward's easy demeanor as he heard the news; the defeated candidate remarked briefly that Lincoln would doubtless be elected and that he had "some of the qualities to make a good president."[17] Dimon exchanged a few words with neighbors on the Seward lawn, and the town cannon was returned to its accustomed place in the park.

* * *

The defeat in Chicago brought to a close a decade-long campaign for the White House that had preoccupied Thurlow Weed as much as it

---

*Lincoln subsequently named Chase secretary of the treasury.

had Seward. The candidate refused to criticize his friend, writing to Weed on May 18: "You have my unbounded gratitude for this last, as for [your] whole life of efforts in my behalf, and I wish that I was sure that your sense of disappointment is as light as my own. It ought to be . . . for . . . I know not what has been left undone that could have been done."[18]

The candidate was overly charitable. In retrospect the Seward camp had underestimated Lincoln from the start—a fatal error. In agreeing to Chicago as the convention site, Weed had exposed the Republican delegates to a barrage of Lincoln ballyhoo that, over time, took its toll on undecided delegates. Alexander McClure, a Lincoln supporter, writing three decades later, commented, "Had the convention been held in any other place than Chicago, it is quite probable that Seward would have been successful."[19]

The Seward forces had also overestimated their own candidate's strength. Seward and Lincoln were in agreement on most policy matters. But whereas Lincoln was little known and noncontroversial, Seward carried with him the political baggage of three decades in politics. Nativists at Chicago could not forget his long record of opposition to the Know-Nothings. Former Democrats were unhappy at Seward's position in favor of suffrage for blacks. The New Yorker's long association with "Dictator" Weed was itself a liability. Even Seward's leadership in the antislavery movement was a handicap. Although Lincoln had called the United States a "house divided," much as Seward had spoken of an "irrepressible conflict," the words of a little-known Illinois politician had attracted none of the criticism that had come Seward's way. Correspondent Murat Halstead wrote perceptively:

> The fact of the convention was the defeat of Seward, rather than the nomination of Lincoln. It was the triumph of a presumption of availability over pre-eminence in intellect and unrivaled fame—a success of the ruder qualities of manhood and the more homely attributes of popularity, over the arts of a consummate politician, and the splendor of accomplished statesmanship.[20]

Thus Seward went into the convention with serious liabilities, but these might have been overcome had the Seward forces played their cards better at Chicago. The fact was, in the words of one historian, that while Weed was offering money and platitudes to visiting delegates, David Davis "established a futures market in Lincoln's cabinet and sold it off chair by chair."[21] There is a certain irony here, for whereas Seward's association with Weed offended many purists, it was the Lincoln forces who had peddled appointments for votes.

In Auburn, Seward responded philosophically to a flood of letters deploring the result at Chicago. To one supporter he wrote: "We have no warrant for supposing that we can control circumstances so as to command positions for doing good."[22] Privately, however, Seward was despondent, and several weeks passed before he indicated that he would campaign for the Republican ticket in the fall. Although friends wrote that he was certain to be offered a position in Lincoln's cabinet, Seward declined one speaking invitation with the words: "My cares increase and my hopes are at an end."[23]

Lincoln! Seward tried to recall the single-term congressman with whom he had shared a hotel room twelve years before when both had been speechifying in Worcester, Massachusetts. A pleasant enough fellow, but hardly the man to deal with the sectional crisis that already threatened civil war. Seward looked back on what he supposed to be the wreckage of his political ambitions and wondered what had gone wrong.

2

"A Sweet Little Valley"

IN SOUTHERN New York State, just sixty miles north of New York City, lies the village of Florida. Situated west of the Hudson and south of the Catskills—in an area remarkable mainly for its rolling hills and fertile farmland—Florida, a mere hamlet at the beginning of the nineteenth century, has retained its village atmosphere for nearly two centuries.

Seward's father, Samuel, of Welsh descent, was one of Florida's leading landowners. The son of a Revolutionary War officer, Samuel Seward had studied medicine at King's College—later Columbia—but had not made medicine his sole vocation. At various times he was a farmer, a land speculator, and even a politician, serving briefly in the New York legislature. In a period when many land speculators ended in debtors' prison, Samuel Seward was extraordinarily successful. The $300,000 estate he left in 1849 would have made him a multimillionaire in late-twentieth-century terms.

Samuel Seward was less successful as a father, however. A strict, sometimes harsh, disciplinarian, for many years he does not appear to have been close to any of his children. But his Irish wife, Mary Jennings, was as affectionate as her husband was strict. She seems to have been especially close to young William Henry—called Harry—the fourth of her six children, who was born May 16, 1801. Harry's health was fragile, and perhaps because of this he became a family favorite. In his own words, "My health caused me to be early set apart for a collegiate education, then regarded, by every family, as a privilege so high and so costly that not more than one son could expect it."[1]

In Harry's boyhood, Florida was a hamlet of perhaps a dozen houses.

The nearest schoolhouse was a one-room affair half a mile away. Many decades later Seward would recall sitting on a rough pine bench that had no back support and rested on two blocks of uneven height. When the boys at the high end would slide into those at the lower, the culprits were flogged. School under such conditions must not have been an uplifting experience, but Harry was a quick study. On one occasion his father raised him onto the counter of the general store and told him to recite a poem. As Seward recalled the incident, he completed his recitation "amid great applause."[2]

At the age of nine Harry was sent to the Farmer's Hall Academy, six miles up the road at Goshen, where his father had once studied. There Seward boarded with two cousins, both of whom became his friends. But school itself proved something of an ordeal; as a boy from outside town, he frequently had to defend himself in the school yard. The regimen was strict, and the master on one occasion precipitated a mutiny by scheduling classes on Christmas Day.

In time a college graduate passing through the area established a school in Florida itself, a development that pleased the Sewards. There Harry was a bright but occasionally fractious student. He would later recall his pique at being humiliated in front of his classmates in connection with a translation of Virgil. In retribution he managed to lose his Latin books on the short walk home. For once Samuel Seward appears to have mediated a crisis: Explanations led to reform, and young Harry went on to become a star student. Like the young Lincoln, Seward would spend much of his time studying and reading. Books would play an important part in his life.

Meanwhile, in fragile health or not, young Harry had a full share of work around the Seward farm. He drove cows to and from the fields each day. He chopped wood for the parlor fireplace, carried grain to the mill, and fetched lime from the kiln. In retirement Seward would look back on these years with a certain nostalgia. "How happy were the winter evenings," he wrote, "when the visit of a neighbor brought out the apples, nuts and cider, and I was indulged with a respite from study, and listened to conversation, which generally turned upon politics or religion."[3]

Much of village life centered on church, and the theology of the day relied heavily on exhortation. But thanks to Mary Seward, young Harry was spared a religious upbringing that stressed hellfire and damnation. Seward would recall his relief at hearing his mother argue, in debate with some of her orthodox neighbors, that she did not believe that there were infants in hell. Seward, who would later be accused of lacking conviction, shared his mother's tolerance of others and her lack of interest in religious or political ideology.

In Florida, as in most American villages, the Fourth of July was an occasion for pageantry and celebration. Seward recalled how, for one such holiday, the Floridians constructed a float by mounting a skiff from the millpond on a carpet-draped wagon. In the stern was Harry's brother Jennings, representing Columbus.* The centerpiece was the prettiest girl in the village, one Fanny Bailey, dressed as the Genius of America. Harry was among "the curious and anxious crowd of boys who clustered around the wagon as it moved, to the measured strains of martial music, along the road to the foot of the hill which is crowned by the village church."[4]

Was there anything else notable about Florida, with its pastoral lifestyle? Indeed there was, for Samuel Seward, though he lived far north of the Mason-Dixon line, was a slaveholder. The landowners of Orange County made significant use of slave labor on their farms, and the county at one time ranked second in the state in the number of its slaves. Not until 1827 would slavery be entirely eradicated in New York State.

Young Harry took the presence of three slaves in the Seward household for granted; on occasion he found their company more congenial than that of the adults in the parlor:

> The tenants of the kitchen . . . had a fund of knowledge about the ways and habits of the devil, of witches, of ghosts, and of men who had been hanged; and, what was more, they were vivacious and loquacious, as well as affectionate, toward me. . . . If my parents never uttered before me a word of disapproval of slavery, it is but just to them to say that they never uttered an expression that could tend to make me think that the negro was inferior to the white person.[5]

So it was that Harry Seward grew up in a family where the father's strictness was to a considerable degree mitigated by the mother's sensitivity, and where slaves were remembered as part of an extended family. At a time when religion and politics were taken very seriously in most parts of the country, the Sewards were neither religious zealots nor strong political partisans. The atmosphere of tolerance in which Harry Seward was reared would ultimately become an essential part of his character.

---

*Seward and two of his three brothers, Benjamin Jennings and Edwin Polydore, were known in the family by their middle names and are so referred to in this book.

When Harry was fifteen, his father enrolled him in Union College, an all-male institution in Schenectady, New York. Seward's journey to Schenectady in 1816 as a new sophomore—he had been accorded advanced standing—represented his first extended travel outside "the sweet little valley in which I was cradled." He went by stage to Newburgh where, for the then-exorbitant cost of eight dollars, he boarded a steamboat up the great Hudson to Albany. Young Harry was taken with the state capital, then a city of fifteen thousand, but he had little time to admire it. The last, short lap of his journey, from Albany to Schenectady, was once again by stage, along a potholed road with only the occasional roadside tavern to break the monotony.

Union College, founded in 1795, was one of a string of liberal arts colleges established in New England and upstate New York in the final years of the eighteenth century. Most enjoyed the backing of one or more religious denominations; Union derived its name from the fact that it was supported by several Protestant groups. The college reflected the personality of its president, Eliphalet Nott, a Presbyterian clergyman who would head the college for more than a half-century. The reform-minded Nott was an effective speaker for antislavery and temperance groups. He was also an innovator, having raised money for the college by means of a lottery at a time when most clergymen frowned upon gambling. In a letter to his father written in 1816, Seward characterized Nott as "a very able, smart [and] good old man . . . clever but strict."[6] Under Nott, Union College enjoyed a liberal reputation by the standards of the day.

Seward would come away from Union College with mixed feelings. He found the atmosphere pleasant, despite a schedule of classes, recitations, and prayers that most twentieth-century undergraduates would find intolerable. He developed a congenial circle of acquaintances, and President Nott became a lifelong friend. But Seward was critical of the education he received. Little was required of the students except that they deliver their recitations without error, and although such rote learning was by no means unusual, Seward felt in retrospect that he had "hurried mechanically through the miserable rudiments of an American collegiate education."[7]

Harry Seward adapted easily to life away from home. A family friend who visited him at Schenectady wrote Samuel Seward that "the confidence which [your son] has in himself and the ease of his manners render him quite pleasing."[8] But there was subtle peer pressure at work on the precocious teenager, pressure that shortly led to rebellion. The allowance provided Harry by his father appears to have been miserly even by standards of the day, and upperclassmen teased him as some form of country bumpkin. When Harry then proceeded to run up bills with the tailors of Schenectady, Samuel Seward refused to pay.

Harry had been a respectful son, who began letters to his father with the salutation, "Revered Parent." His entire demeanor as a young man suggests that he benefited from the support of a close-knit family. But if the elder Seward expected his son to beg forgiveness for the tailoring bills, he was badly mistaken. For perhaps the first time, Harry rebelled. On New Year's Day, 1819, he ran away from college in the company of a classmate who had accepted a teaching position at a small rural academy in Georgia. The two runaways traveled by stage to New York City, where Harry's first impression of the metropolis was dampened by fear that he would be apprehended and sent home. The two youths booked passage on a schooner to Savannah and arrived there after a seven days' voyage, for part of which Harry was thoroughly seasick.

Harry and his classmate, whom he never identified by name, went by stage from Savannah to Augusta, where Harry's companion found a job more promising than the one at the rural academy that had enticed him to Georgia. The seventeen-year-old Seward thereupon decided to apply for the position in Putnam County that had originally attracted his friend. Union Academy, in Eatonville, Georgia, which had not even opened its doors, shortly advertised that Mr. William H. Seward, "late from Union College, New York," would be teaching "the Latin and Greek languages, theoretical and practical Mathematics, Logic, Rhetoric, Natural and Moral Philosophy, Chemistry, Geography, English grammar, and such other branches as are usually taught in Northern Colleges."[9] His salary was to be one hundred dollars per year plus board, but because the building was not yet finished, the directors agreed to provide Harry with a horse and carriage and to board him among the directors without charge.[10]

Seward was destined to spend only eight weeks in Georgia, but he would retain fond memories of his brief stint as a teacher. At the academy he was treated like an adult. The local farmers liked him, and the school trustees appeared pleased with their instructor. Harry found the slaves, with whom he mingled freely, uniformly curious about life in the "big North." There were, however, some unpleasant experiences. On one occasion he encountered a slave woman who was in tears because she could not make a heavily laden horse cross the bridge over a swollen stream. Seward attempted to help, but in leading the balky horse he caused it to become stuck in the planks and timbers of the bridge. Harry rode to the house of the slave's master and sought to explain that the fault was his rather than hers. For his pains Seward was subjected to a tirade from the slaveowner.[11]

Eventually someone showed Samuel Seward the advertisement in which Union Academy had told of Harry's hiring. Shortly thereafter a school trustee showed Harry a letter from his father, denouncing young Seward as "a much-indulged son who, without just cause and provocation, had absconded from Union College . . . plunging his parents into profound shame and grief."[12] In the letter Samuel Seward said that he was aware of his son's whereabouts and threatened legal action against Union Academy. As the mails brought anguished letters from Harry's mother and his sister Cornelia, the young teacher decided that he should return to his family. With the blessing of the academy trustees, to whom he promised a replacement, Harry turned toward Savannah and home. Years later Seward would recall the hospitality with which he was treated in Georgia, but would add that his sojourn there had deepened his hostility toward slavery.

After studying law in Goshen for several months, Seward returned to Union, this time determined to graduate. The college had just been granted a chapter of the academic honor society, Phi Beta Kappa, and Harry was determined that he should be tapped. In Seward's words, he and his roommate "supplied ourselves with provisions for living in our own room throughout the long period of trial. We rose at three o'clock in the morning, cooked and spread our own meals, washed our own dishes, and spent the whole time which we could save from prayers and recitations, and the table, in severe study."[13]

The results were all that could have been hoped: Both Harry and his roommate made Phi Beta Kappa. In July 1820 Seward graduated with the highest honors and was one of the commencement speakers.

*   *   *

Nineteen years old at the time of his graduation, Seward was slim in appearance and shorter than average—about five feet five inches. His eyes were blue and his complexion light, but his most pronounced physical features were a prominent nose and a shock of undisciplined red hair. Self-conscious about his voice, which was slightly husky as a result of a childhood illness, Harry also tended to be careless in dress, even with the assistance of those Schenectady tailors. Although Seward almost certainly felt superior to most people with whom he came in contact, he kept his feelings to himself. People liked Harry Seward.

Although Seward felt no special enthusiasm for the law, it had long been assumed that this was to be his vocation. Following his graduation from college, Harry returned home and resumed his legal studies with Goshen lawyer John Duer. In the course of a year he worked up a dislike for both legal research and the town of Goshen. When Samuel Seward agreed to his son's request that he continue his studies in New York City, Harry's attitude improved. He found New York City fascinating. He and a fellow student, David Berdan, went to the theater and enjoyed the bright lights to the extent their limited finances permitted. Harry chased so many girls that Berdan was amazed to hear, on Seward's return to Florida, that he was thinking of becoming engaged to a girl from Skaneateles, Mary Ann Kellogg.

Seward was by temperament a conciliator, and one way or another he became reconciled with his father. Samuel Seward lent him money to travel to Utica for the bar examination, and Harry was admitted to practice in October 1822. On his way back to Florida, Harry stopped at Auburn, then a prosperous little village of two thousand, on Lake Owasco southwest of Syracuse. His main purpose was to call on Frances Miller, a young woman he had first met in Goshen, through the good offices of his sister, Cornelia, a contemporary of Frances Miller's at Miss Willard's finishing school in Troy. In Auburn, however, Harry was pleasantly surprised to find two law firms seeking junior partners. He agreed to join one of them, which just happened to be the one headed by Frances Miller's father. In December 1822 Harry moved his few belongings from Florida to Auburn, the town he would call home for the rest of his life.

*   *   *

The Finger Lakes, according to legend, resulted when an Indian spirit pronounced a benediction on his tribes. Seward was impressed with the possibility of beginning his law practice there, and moved into Mrs. Brittam's boardinghouse, which catered to unmarried professional men. Even as he began his law career, however, Harry's thoughts were on marriage. While he was still attracted to Mary Ann Kellogg, his interest was turning to Frances Miller. In the summer of 1823 he proposed to Frances and was accepted. Probably under prodding from his fiancée, Seward began attending at St. Paul's Episcopal church.

On October 20, 1824, Frances Miller and William Henry Seward were married in St. Paul's. The nineteen-year-old Fanny—attractive, intelligent, and of good family—was a prize catch for young Seward. She was a devout Christian, retaining much of her grandmother's Quaker perspective even after becoming an Episcopalian. To a greater degree than most young women of her day, she was interested in social and political issues. But she differed from her husband in important respects. Frances Seward was a very private person for whom life centered on religion and the home. Politics and public office held no allure. Equally important, notwithstanding her dark good looks, Frances was physically frail. Over the years she would suffer from a succession of ailments, and her health would be a constant concern to her husband.

For reasons that are not entirely clear, the young couple's honeymoon was a family and community affair. Following the wedding and a reception at the Miller residence, Henry and Frances were joined by a number of relatives and friends who drove with them to Rust's Hotel near Syracuse. The next day the entire party returned to Auburn, where Henry moved into Judge Miller's five-acre establishment. Everyone in Auburn knew Judge Miller's residence on South Street—a large, square house of unpainted brick, set back from the road amid poplar and apple trees. It was regarded by many as the finest house in town.

Henry's move into the Miller household was the most unusual aspect of the marriage. Elijah Miller, a widower, had exacted from his son-in-law a promise that Frances would live in the Miller house for as long as her father lived. Henry may not have been pleased with this arrangement, but he was in no position to argue. He was still in debt to his father, and Judge Miller was making an offer he could hardly refuse: a lovely bride plus a partnership in his law firm, complete with a guaranteed minimum income. Considering the neurotic attachment to the residence on South Street that Frances would manifest over the years, it was almost certainly a mistake for her and Henry to begin their married life as part of the Miller household. The newlyweds joined an extended family that comprised the fifty-two-year-old Judge Miller, his seventy-four-year-old mother, and Miller's unmarried younger sister, Clarinda. It was hardly an ideal situation for young lovers, and it may have caused Frances to remain emotionally tied to her father and his home:

> [Frances] had acquired a husband and in due course would acquire children, but the pattern of her days remained essentially unchanged. She made no sharp break in her girlhood and was not forced to accompany her husband or to adjust to new and different responsibilities. This probably set the pattern for her later problems. She came to believe that families should at all times be together and that security, for her at least, lay only in the house of her girlhood.[14]

Seward returned to his law practice with mixed feelings. He enjoyed the full confidence of Elijah Miller, who was already turning over to him all except his most difficult cases. But Henry was not wedded to the law. He conceded that "only necessity reconciled me to a toleration of the technicalities of the practice, to the uncertainty of results, and to the jealousies and contentions of the courts."[15] Nevertheless, at a time when young Abraham Lincoln was ferrying produce down the Mississippi, William Henry Seward was financially secure and increasingly attracted to politics.

* * *

It was more than coincidence that the little town of Auburn had openings for two young lawyers. The national economy was booming, and the growth of industry was providing the impetus for improved transportation. The Cumberland Road, designed to connect the eastern states with the vast land beyond the Alleghenies, had been started in 1811. Six years later New York State had begun the 350-mile Erie Canal, designed to link the Hudson River to Lake Erie and thus to open up the future states of Ohio, Illinois, and Michigan. Nineteenth-century Americans were restless, mobile, and eager for material prosperity. Politically the country was enjoying a period of relative calm. The old Federalist and Democratic parties had broken down, but in the absence of divisive issues no national parties had yet sprung up to replace them. It was a period of political gestation. Although there was competition for office, politics during Monroe's "era of good feeling" tended to be on the state and regional levels.

As a teenager Henry Seward had been critical of the Federalists for their lukewarm support of the War of 1812. Subsequently he had briefly supported the "Albany Regency," an organization led by future president Martin Van Buren, which was arguably the country's first political machine. It ran New York State for the Jacksonians and in time would serve as a model for the Whig organization that Seward himself would develop in partnership with Thurlow Weed. In 1824, however, Seward concluded that the Regency had become corrupt and declared himself a supporter of John Quincy Adams for the presidency. "I have taken a last farewell of the Albany Junto," he wrote his father, "and [will] sink or swim hereafter with the People."[16] In old age, Seward would occasionally reminisce about these formative years. "Brought up in the Jeffersonian Democratic party," he later remarked, "I learned at an early period that [the Democratic] party was shielding and defending slavery. . . . and so I became an Anti-Mason and an Adams man."[17]

In the latter half of the decade both Adams and Seward were caught up in the strange politics of Anti-Masonry. The Freemasons had been an active order for most of the nation's history, claiming among their members such Revolutionary heroes as Washington and Lafayette.

Then, in 1826, came the bizarre affair of William Morgan. Morgan, a resident of upstate New York, was a renegade Mason whose publication of certain of the order's rituals violated his oath of secrecy and infuriated other Masons. In September local Masons secured Morgan's arrest on trumped-up charges and then abducted him from jail. Morgan was never seen again, and the weight of the evidence suggests that he was murdered and his body dumped into the Niagara River.[18]

When the investigation of Morgan's disappearance appeared to be obstructed everywhere by Masonic sheriffs and judges, Anti-Masonry became a movement. There had long been a strain of hostility toward the role in a democracy of an order that was both secret and elitist; now, public-spirited citizens called for the ouster of Masons from all positions of authority. North of the Mason-Dixon line, Anti-Masonry spread like wildfire. Much of its strength derived from the fact that on the national level its only competition came from Jacksonian Democracy. For ambitious young politicians like Henry Seward, Anti-Masonry provided an organizational umbrella under which to oppose Jackson and the Regency.

Although Henry's flourishing law practice allowed him to discharge his debts to his father, there were other concerns at home. When Henry came down with a severe case of tonsillitis ("quinsy") two months after his marriage, he nearly fell victim to the primitive medicine of the day. "The physicians bled, cupped, blistered, phisicked & scarified me so severely," Henry wrote, "that I cannot yet get strength enough to enable me to attend to business."[19] Then, in January 1825, Frances had a miscarriage, and for several weeks her health was a source of anxiety. Twenty months later, however, she gave birth to their first child, a boy they named Augustus Henry.

Meanwhile Henry had problems with his own family. His sister Louisa, to whom he was especially attached, had married a man of whom Samuel Seward bitterly disapproved. Henry's three brothers, Jennings, Polydore, and George, all had business problems, and Polydore was an alcoholic. At one time or another all would turn to Henry for assistance. Henry lent his brothers money and gave his father advice when asked. But when Samuel Seward urged him to return to Orange County, Henry pointed out that his income would be sharply reduced. He made it clear that his nostalgia for the "sweet little valley" in which he had been raised was limited:

I am a subject of the stern king Necessity and must so . . . direct my course as may meet his approbation. . . . I [also] have a loathing toward . . . Goshen, a disgust that is too violent to be suppressed. A low, mean and grovelling race are most of its inhabitants. . . . It is not so here, for here I have friends who wish me well, and I have no enemies who can injure me.[20]

In February 1829 Henry attended an Anti-Masonic conference in Albany. The following year he delivered an address denouncing Masonry as a "secret government" incompatible with American liberties. In 1830 the Anti-Masons held their first national convention in Baltimore. Seward presented the report of the committee on resolutions and gave a glowing account of the progress of Anti-Masonry nationwide. His report came in for considerable praise, and Seward doted on praise. When there was other work to be done Seward was usually available to do it, and to do it well. Clearly the red-haired young lawyer from Auburn was a man to watch.

3

Anti-Masons and Whigs

In 1824, WHEN Henry and Frances had been returning from a family outing to Niagara Falls, their carriage lost a wheel while passing through Rochester. Among those who came to their assistance was a tall, strong, young printer who was in the city attempting to start a newspaper. The son of an itinerant farmer who had served time in debtors' prison, Thurlow Weed had had little schooling and had started to work at eight as an assistant to a blacksmith who payed him six cents a day. By the time he was eleven he was a printer's apprentice. In Rochester, Weed was being bankrolled in his newspaper project by prominent Anti-Masons, and he soon discovered that the lawyer with the defective carriage wheel—four years his junior—was also active in Anti-Masonic politics. With the serendipitous meeting in Rochester began a friendship that would last for Seward's lifetime.

For Seward the years 1828 and 1829 were largely devoted to seeking some degree of rapport between the National Republicans and the Anti-Masons of Cayuga County. The National Republicans were in decline but remained a factor to be reckoned with, as Seward discovered. In 1828 the Cayuga Anti-Masons nominated Seward for Congress, and Henry hoped that the National Republicans would accept him as well. But at the National Republican Convention Seward was jeered as an apostate, and he reluctantly withdrew as a candidate. Each party then ran its own nominee, and the Regency candidate won easily over the divided opposition.

Weed, meanwhile, had moved his newspaper operations to Albany, from where he kept his eye on the young man from Auburn. At age thirty-three, Weed was proprietor, editor, reporter, and occasionally

proofreader for the *Albany Evening Journal,* and in his spare time served
as a member of the New York legislature. In 1830, while Seward was
in Baltimore attending an Anti-Masonic convention, Weed engineered
his nomination for the New York state senate. That fall, the Cayuga
district sent young Seward to Albany with a majority of two thousand
over his Regency opponent. It was Henry's first brush with elective
politics. He would never look back.

In the final days of the year, Henry Seward packed his trunks and
took the stage for Albany. While Frances, in Auburn, fretted over
whether she should have accompanied her husband, he and his seven
fellow travelers rattled along the Albany road, taking two-and-a-half
days to make the 165-mile trip east. They stopped only to change horses,
to get a meal at the occasional tavern, or to snatch a few hours of sleep,
and the young legislator had ample time to reflect on what the future
might bring.

*   *   *

America was changing dramatically as Seward began his career as an
elected official. New technology was revolutionizing the national economy. The steel plow and the cotton gin were stimulating farm produc-
tion, while textile mills along the little rivers of New York and New
England were evidence of the country's industrial growth. A transportation revolution, based in large measure on the steamboat, was nowhere more evident than along the Hudson. The rise of banks and the
growth of cities were transforming the country's culture as well as its
economy.

Albany, the capital of New York State, was one of the cities undergoing rapid growth. The town had almost doubled in population, to
24,000, during the 1820s. It now boasted several banks, factories, and
a waterfront that boomed for as long as the river was open. High-gabled
houses, favored by the original Dutch settlers, gave an Old World flavor
to the better sections of town. Albany also had a large number of taverns
and coffeehouses, but their business was to some degree seasonal, de-
pending on whether the legislature was in session. Visitors generally
avoided the Pasture, a dank, low-lying slum that most people associated
with funeral corteges.

The Eagle Tavern on South Market Street and Bement's Hotel on
State Street were among the boardinghouses favored by transient legislators. It was at the Eagle, overlooking the Hudson, that Henry Seward found lodgings early in January 1831. The senator from Cayuga
was the youngest member of the thirty-two-member state senate, and
he was one of seven Anti-Masons in that body. Among his colleagues

were Millard Fillmore, a Buffalo lawyer with national ambitions, and Francis Granger, the recently defeated Anti-Masonic candidate for governor. A third collegue, Albert Tracy, was a handsome thirty-seven-year-old who had served three terms in Congress as a Democrat; Henry looked up to him, and the two became close friends. But the legislator who would have the greatest influence on Seward was the Good Samaritan from Rochester, Thurlow Weed. The chance encounter with Seward had earlier led to correspondence; now, with both men in the state senate, it ripened into friendship. Seward listened raptly to stories out of Weed's youth—how he had made maple sugar in the winter, barefoot except for old bits of carpet tied around his feet; how he had worked at an iron furnace, living on salt pork and bread; how delighted he had been when, in 1817, the old *Albany Register* had allowed him to write his first editorial paragraphs.

Weed had sought to make up in hard work what he lacked in formal education, and young Seward was impressed. He wrote to Frances that Weed was a politician "whose exciting principle is personal friendship or opposition, and not self-interest." He was "generous to a fault, kind beyond description, open-hearted, and sincere beyond most men's sincerity."[1] Time only confirmed Henry's high regard for his friend. In January 1832 he wrote to Frances:

Weed is the only man whose entire confidence I have or who has mine. He tells me all his own feelings. He is generous in act, word and thought. . . . He has spent his life building up his friends without care for himself.[2]

Weed, for his part, was equally captivated with Seward. He saw in his friend a thoughtful, outgoing exponent of his own anti-Jacksonian philosophy. Both men were ambitious, but Weed was less interested in holding office than in being a power broker. In addition to politics they shared an interest in literature and the theater. Many were the evenings when the two men would walk to the marble museum at State and Market streets, where scientific displays and even vaudeville performances were to be seen. On other occasions Weed would drop by Seward's room simply to pass the time. Years later "Dictator" Weed would write, "I saw in [Seward] . . . unmistakable evidences of stern integrity, earnest patriotism, and unswerving fidelity. I saw also in him a rare capacity for intellectual labor, with an industry which never tired and required no relaxation; to all which was added a purity and delicacy of habit and character almost feminine."[3]

Seward and Weed were political activists in search of a party. Frontiersmen and the debtor classes were rallying to the standard of Jacksonian Democracy. But what of those who mistrusted Jacksonianism? Merchants and other conservatives, behind John Quincy Adams and Henry Clay, had created the short-lived National Republican party. It in turn had been largely eclipsed by the rise of the Anti-Masons. Yet opposition to Masonry was hardly the stuff of which political careers were built.

The problem for anti-Jacksonians was especially acute in New York State, which had been so successfully organized by the Democrats under Martin Van Buren. In the previous century the Founding Fathers had disapproved of political parties because they believed them merely to reflect their leaders' selfish interests. This view was changing. Among the Jacksonians, parties were seen as democratic instruments that facilitated popular participation in government. Van Buren spoke for a new generation when he wrote: "Political parties are inseparable from free governments," and the "disposition to abuse power . . . can by no other means be more effectually checked."[4]

The glue that held the Regency together was patronage—the control of appointments to statewide office. Circuit judges propagated the gospel in their travel through the state. At a lower level, Van Buren and his lieutenants controlled hundreds of justices of the peace, county judges, and other local officials. An essential tool for any party was a newspaper for communicating with the party faithful. The Regency sponsored the *Albany Argus,* which was itself a major recipient of patronage; the Regency designated its editor as the official state printer, and stipulated that only the *Argus* could publish state laws at public expense.

In the absence of allies and a statewide organization, the seven Anti-Masonic senators in Albany represented little threat to Democratic control of the state. They were competing not only against the Democrats, but to some extent against their allies, the National Republicans. But because party lines were in flux, Seward was able to have some influence in Albany even while in the minority. During his first year he spoke in favor of a law abolishing imprisonment for debt, and the measure generated enough support to pass. A year later he took up penal reform, a topic he would make his own. His bill, which established a separate prison for women and provided for more humane treatment of all prisoners, also became law. Meanwhile, a succession of charters for new railroads and canals came before the senate. Seward supported most of them, for he was a firm advocate of the infrastructure development that in those days went under the rubric of "internal improvements."

The senate normally met at eleven, conducted two or three hours' worth of business, and then adjourned. Seward was on good terms with most of his colleagues, who tended to be older men, sent to Albany by respectful communities that wanted to reward a prominent citizen in his sunset years. Only occasionally did national issues intrude on senatorial deliberations. Seward took special notice of the Nat Turner slave rebellion in rural Virginia, which in 1831 took the lives of fifty-seven whites and perhaps twice that number of blacks. In Seward's view the rebellion demonstrated that if the federal government could not bring an end to slavery, there would be other violent uprisings.

Because political parties in the 1830s exerted little discipline over their elected representatives, Seward enjoyed a considerable degree of independence in dealing with the issues of his day. In the controversy over whether South Carolina could nullify a tariff law of which it disapproved, Seward upheld President Jackson in asserting the preeminence of federal law. Subsequently, however, Seward opposed the president on another national issue: Jackson's attempt to close down the Bank of the United States. The bank performed many of the functions of a central bank and could claim a considerable credit for the country's sound currency. Nevertheless, its president, Nicholas Biddle, had been guilty of political favoritism, and Andrew Jackson was determined that the bank's charter would not be renewed. In Albany the Democratic majority in the legislature proposed a resolution of support for the president.

In an address that took portions of two days to deliver, Seward praised the service provided by the Bank of the United States, contrasting it favorably with the various state banks. He conceded that the Biddle's institution should be subject to more regulation than in the past, but he emphasized the importance of a sound banking system if the country was to prosper. The speech was for the most part well received, to the vast relief of young Seward, who was fully aware that he had tackled a very complex subject.

                            *   *   *

In Auburn, meanwhile, Seward's law practice flourished. Judge Miller had made his own retirement official, enabling Seward to take on a younger partner, Nelson Beardsley, and increase the volume of business. Henry's marriage, however, was undergoing stress. Frances had been in fragile health ever since the miscarriage in 1825, and now her husband's work in Albany caused him to be away four months of each year in addition to his trips on legal business. Her father, in retirement, was sometimes gruff and irascible. Frances's distress became sufficiently acute that she and Henry made a short-lived bid to become independent of the Miller household. Late in 1829 Henry put down a deposit on the William Brown house across South Street from the Miller residence and moved there with Frances and three-year-old Gus. But the experiment failed, for Henry's election to the state senate kept him away so much of the time that Frances, lonesome, returned to her father's home.

If Frances was lonely in Auburn, an obvious solution was for her to accompany her husband to Albany. When Henry took her, however, as he did to two of his four legislative sessions, Frances remained unhappy. While Henry was a free spirit, Frances found the formal calls and other social obligations of a senator's wife onerous and took a dislike to most of the people she met. Frances feared that she and Henry were growing apart, and as she worried her health worsened. She complained of headaches, pains in her eyes, and an assortment of other ailments. A second son, Frederick William, had been born to the Sewards in 1830, and her children became Frances's main comfort.

Young Fred had pleasant memories of his childhood. His earliest recollections of his father were of his "clear blue eyes, red hair, quick, active movements, and merry laugh. . . . The house was always cheerful when he was in it."[5] Not that he was ever in it for long. Among Fred's early memories was a trip to Albany in the winter of 1833–34:

> My brother and I, sleeping together in the trundle bed, are suddenly awakened at night, and find the candles all lighted. My father is kindling a fire in the small box stove. Then my mother takes me up to be dressed. From the talk between her and the nurse, I learn that we are about to start on a journey, and that it is three o'clock in the morning. . . . At the gate are two bright lanterns, and horses are stamping in the snow. . . . We get inside of the dark, cold stage, groping for seats among the buffalo skins. . . . The stage starts and goes sliding and bumping over the rough road. Wrapped up in my mother's lap, I soon fall into a doze, and after a series of naps, wake up again in daylight, to be told that we have come twenty-six miles to Syracuse.[6]

More often than not Seward was without his family for the winter legislative term in Albany. It was a hardship, for Seward was devoted to his family, but he was not so devoted as to forgo a career in politics. He attempted to compensate by means of correspondence. While in Albany, Henry wrote Frances almost every day, describing his activities in minute detail. His colleague Fillmore, Henry wrote, had risen to his present position from that of a wool carder. Henry found him "popular and honest." He wrote of some legal business that had led him to call on the aged Aaron Burr. "I could not but think," wrote Henry, "as I ascended the dirty, narrow stairs to his lodgings . . . of the contrast between his present state and that [which] he enjoyed when he contended . . . with Jefferson for the presidential chair."[7]

Given the limited demands on his time while in Albany, Henry had ample opportunities for sightseeing—an activity he tackled with his customary curiosity and diligence. He chronicled his travels to Frances—a visit to Dr. Nott at Union College, a trip to a Shaker community outside Albany. "The dress of the Shakers is simple, neat and uniform," Henry wrote. "No part of the person is exposed save the hands and face."[8]

Seward had a family visitor during his first term in Albany—his father. The senior Seward was in good health, financially secure, and sufficiently impressed with his son's status to deal with him as an equal. Henry marveled at their changed relationship, and probably reflected on the fact that it was from Samuel Seward that he had inherited his energy and capacity for work. The senior Seward would still have liked his son back in Orange County, but he could not help being pleased at Henry's bright political prospects.

In the latter half of 1831 Henry was caught up in the maneuverings for the Anti-Masonic presidential ticket for the following year. South Carolinian John C. Calhoun, an outspoken opponent of Jackson, was a possible candidate. Seward was dubious about the party's prospects in the South, however, and therefore cool to any discussion of a Southern candidate. "The cold, clear, intelligent North is the field for the growth of Antimasonry," he told Weed, and in November he traveled to New England to urge the candidacy of Supreme Court Justice John McLean.[9]

Seward's trip was probably a political plus in that he gained exposure outside his home state. But the main effect of his conversations was to underscore the continued divisions between the National Republicans and the Anti-Masons. In Quincy, Massachusetts, Seward called on John Quincy Adams, whom he had supported for the presidency in 1824. He gave Frances a vivid account of his pilgrimage to the Adams homestead:

> At nine o'clock I was shown into the house, and waited in the parlor till I was announced. The house is very plain and old-fashioned. . . . Very plain ingrain carpeting covered the floor, very plain paper on the walls; modern but plain mahogany chairs, and a piano about like yours, composed the simple furniture of the room. . . .
>
> A short, rather corpulent man, of sixty and upward, came down the

stairs and approached me. He was bald, his countenance was staid, so-
ber, almost to gloom or sorrow, and hardly gave indication of his superiority over other men. His eyes were weak and inflamed. He was dressed
in an olive frock coat, a cravat carelessly tied, and old-fashioned, light-
colored vest and pantaloons.

Seward described the visit in such detail and with such relish that it
was obvious that his morning with the ex-president had been heady wine
for a small-town legislator:

> [Adams] spoke enthusiastically of [Richard] Rush. . . . He said that he
> should have more confidence in Rush than in Clay as President. . . . He
> spoke of General Jackson and the Seminole War without one word of
> reserve or bitterness or unkindness; thought his Administration ruinous,
> but still doubted not that he would be reelected. . . .
>   Our interview lasted three hours. He was all the time plain, honest
> and free in his discourse; but with hardly a ray of animation or feeling
> in the whole of it. In short, he was just exactly what I supposed he was,
> a man to be respected for his talents, admired for his learning, honored
> for his integrity and simplicity, but hardly possessing the traits of char-
> acter to inspire a stranger with affection.[10]

Clearly Seward was not captivated by the dour Adams, whose personality was so different from his own. Yet he left Quincy full of admiration for the ex-president, and his meeting with John Quincy Adams
began an association with the Adams family that would endure throughout Seward's lifetime.

*   *   *

The following year was an educational one for Henry Seward. Samuel
Seward had long wanted to travel to Europe, and early in 1833 he asked
his son to accompany him there at the close of the legislative session,
with Samuel paying all expenses. Henry was delighted at the prospect,
notwithstanding Judge Miller's warnings that Henry's law practice
would suffer. Politically the trip looked like a plus, for Seward arranged
to write a series of travel letters that Weed would publish in the *Evening
Journal*.

There were as yet no steamers crossing the Atlantic, so when the two
Sewards sailed on June 1 it was aboard a mail packet bound for Liverpool. The voyage took eighteen days—considered fast for the day—
and the occasional calm allowed the more athletic passengers, Seward
included, time for a dip in the ocean.

In England the Sewards took in the cathedral towns of southern England and all the sights of London. Henry obtained an introduction to Joseph Hume, a prominent opposition leader in Parliament, who provided him with a pass to the House of Commons. In observing the debates he was particularly impressed with the Irish nationalist, Daniel O'Connell, and with Robert Peel, who later became prime minister. Little escaped Henry's notice. He liked the physical arrangement of the Commons, writing that "dignity, decorum, as well as earnestness of attention, all are promoted by the arrangement of the chambers so as to bring the members in close proximity to each other. . . . [Never] when I visited the House of Commons have I witnessed such listnessness as generally prevails in the House of Representatives, when the subject of debate is uninteresting."[11]

The two Sewards next had a rough crossing to Ireland, where the poverty they encountered made a strong impression. Instead of the neat villages and comfortable cottages he had expected in the countryside, Seward found "poverty and wretchedness." Suddenly aware of his own Irish roots, Seward became convinced that the basis of Ireland's problems was absentee landlordism and that the solution lay in emigration. Throughout his political career Seward would prove a staunch friend to the Irish, and although his rhetoric at times would take on political overtones, his basic sympathy was apparent early in his career.

Scotland proved more pleasant than Ireland. The Sewards lingered long in Edinburgh and departed with regret. From Britain they crossed the Channel to Holland and Germany. In Switzerland Henry climbed Mont Blanc; he was almost as vigorous elsewhere, often rising early so that he could set out, walking, ahead of the stagecoach. In Paris he visited the Louvre and the Tuileries Gardens, deploring the nude statuary in the latter. He was as interested in France's Chamber of Deputies as he had been in Britain's House of Commons. One of the Sewards' letters of introduction was to the venerable Lafayette, whom Henry had greeted in Auburn during the general's triumphant tour of America in 1825. The marquis invited the Sewards to his villa, La Grange, some thirty miles outside Paris, and devoted an entire day to his American visitors. Henry's description suggests that he himself was more interested in his surroundings than in the general's rambling discourse:

La Grange . . . is surrounded by a moat, with military drawbridges. . . . The staircase was decorated with flags, tricolored and American. I was received by the general . . . in a parlor . . . [containing] busts of Washington and Franklin, and some American maps, and also portraits of all the Presidents of the United States. The library was filled with American books; the sleeping rooms had only pictures of American battle scenes, on land and sea, Mount Vernon, John Hancock's house, and Quincy.[12]

All told, it was a remarkably instructive tour for Seward; he had seen the sights but had also gained some understanding of the political dynamics of the countries of northern Europe. He continued to find Britain a puzzle, in part because only the upper class had an effective political voice and because it was not favorably disposed toward the upstart republic across the Atlantic. Henry doubted whether there could be any warmth in Anglo-American relations until increased emigration from Britain to the United States developed a rapport between the English-speaking peoples.

In October the two Sewards set sail for New York from Le Havre aboard the *Sully*. The westbound journey took thirty-two days and was far rougher than the voyage out. Henry may have been eager to see his family, but this desire did not keep him from stopping in Albany to consult with Thurlow Weed on his way home. Weed was enthusiastic about Henry's letters from Europe; he viewed them as both a political and a literary bonanza, and was preparing to run excerpts from them in the *Albany Evening Journal*.

4

⎯⎯⎯◦⧜◦⎯⎯⎯

"I Was the Criminal . . ."

WHEN HENRY SEWARD returned from his grand tour, he found the political landscape in ferment. The 1832 election had seen Jackson triumphantly reelected over an opposition that divided its vote between the Anti-Masonic and National Republican tickets. The obvious need for effective cooperation among Jackson's foes was given impetus by the president himself. Jackson's election-eve veto of a bill rechartering the Bank of the United States did him no political harm, but a subsequent move against Biddle's institution—transferring federal deposits from it to state "pet" banks—served to galvanize his opponents. Adopting the name *Whig*—which many Americans had employed during the revolt against England—the Anti-Masons, National Republicans, and Southern Democrats merged into a formidable national movement.

Jackson's course on the bank invited his enemies to unite in opposition to "executive usurpation." But there was more to Whiggery than opposition to Andrew Jackson. To a considerable extent the new movement represented the interests of the country's expanding commerce. In a period of rapid economic growth, the Whig party spoke for the middle class: merchants, industrialists, and many farmers. The Whigs were strongest in the towns and the prosperous farming areas; they tended to be weak on the frontier and among immigrant groups in the cities. Over the years the Whigs would favor the use of federal funds for development—"internal improvements"—and, once the country had become more industrialized, they would become advocates of a protective tariff. But the party included a reformist element, and over time the antislavery faction would become dominant in the Northern states. The later disintegration of the Whigs as a national party would result from differences over slavery.

So it was that the country returned, in the early 1830s, to something resembling a two-party system. On the local level Democrats and Whigs alike developed more efficient mechanisms for turning out the vote, including state and local conventions, precinct and ward committees, and a network of party newspapers. In no state was the organizational competition more keen than in New York, where Thurlow Weed was creating an organization to challenge the Regency. The key to his apparatus was the state Central Committee, composed of six or eight persons, including Weed. The committee selected candidates, made major decisions on party strategy, solicited contributions, and lobbied members of the legislature. Weed dominated the committee through his ties to the party's most important financial backers, his control of the state's most important Whig newspaper, and the force of his personality. As time went on Weed's influence would increase because of his close association with the state's most promising young politician, William Henry Seward.

Meanwhile, the state's most promising young politician was undergoing a family crisis that threatened to wreck his marriage. The immediate cause appears to have been Henry's junket to Europe with his father. It is not certain that Frances had wanted to go along; in all likelihood she wished only that her husband would spend more time at home. Nevertheless, in Henry's absence she had begun a flirtation with Albert Tracy, her husband's erstwhile colleague in the state senate. Tracy was handsome, chivalrous, and a sympathetic listener. Frances confessed to her sister on one occasion that "I love him very much."[1]

When Henry returned from Europe, Frances agreed to accompany him to his final legislative term in Albany—only the second time she had left the security of the Miller residence for the vicissitudes of boardinghouse living. At some time in 1834, however, probably back in Auburn, Frances and Henry had an emotional scene. Tormented by her correspondence with Tracy and conscious of her husband's continued devotion, Frances confessed her feelings for Tracy and the guilt they had inspired. She showed her husband Tracy's love letters—letters that Henry refused to read. Whatever passed between the couple at this time, their marriage was in serious trouble. There was no immediate resolution, and Henry continued his political activities and law practice much as before.

Seward's senate term ended in the spring of 1834. Although he was tempted by the possibility of running for governor, Frances and her father wanted him to quit politics for a time and earn some money.

Weed, for his part, thought that Seward should stand for reelection to the senate, believing as he did that the Whigs were not yet strong enough to challenge the Regency for control of the statehouse. The fact remained, however, that the Whigs needed to establish credibility as a new party, and to do so they needed a strong candidate with whom to challenge Gov. William Marcy, who was running for reelection.

The Whigs had scheduled a convention to be held in Utica in September to choose a ticket for the fall elections. Weed and Seward were both on the nominating committee, and both felt that Seward had a chance to be nominated for lieutenant governor. In their search for someone to head the ticket, the group first sounded out Congressman Francis Granger, but this veteran Anti-Mason had been twice defeated for the governorship and preferred a safe run for Congress. A second possibility, Jesse Buel, editor of the Albany-based farm journal the *Cultivator*, was dismissed when he was found to have endorsed Jackson's actions with regard to the bank. Quietly, almost imperceptibly, Seward moved into contention for the gubernatorial nomination.

Seward relates in his memoir the surprise of his neighbors—some of whom regarded him as too young for the state ticket—when the convention at Utica nominated him to run for governor, with Silas Stilwell, a New York City attorney, as his running mate. But most Whigs from the western part of the state were delighted. A gathering of young Whigs made a pilgrimage to Auburn, where the candidate was given a fifty-gun salute. Henry enjoyed the attention, and the thought crossed his mind that he might even be elected. To Weed, who had engineered the result at Utica, Seward wrote that he felt a sense of "infinite obligations."[2]

The campaign that followed was marked by the rhetorical excesses typical of the day. The Whigs portrayed their movement as a revolution against "King Andrew" as surely as their forebears had led the revolution against George III. They raised liberty poles to make the point. Van Buren and his colleagues were accused of living in regal splendor while trampling the rights of the people. The Democrats, however, were happy to wrap themselves in Jackson's mantle. In New York they attempted to capitalize on Seward's inexperience, spreading rumors that he was only twenty-two years old and calling him "a red-haired young man" without a record. But the campaign was less a vote on Seward's capability than a referendum on Andrew Jackson. The Democrats focused on Jackson's successful confrontation with the South Carolina secessionists and his defeat of the Bank of the United States. Jackson was the hero of the American workingman, and the Regency exploited his popularity to the fullest.

Henry assured a friend that he was prepared for any eventuality and might even find greater happiness in defeat than in victory.[3] Weed nonetheless warned him against undue optimism, and the results fully justified the warning. On election day the Dictator wrote from New York City that the Whig ticket had been overwhelmed by illegal voters.[4] Seward ran well in western New York but overall lost the state by some eleven thousand votes. Henry insisted to Weed that he was taking the loss in stride, and Weed pointed out that it had been a Democratic year in most of the country. Nevertheless the Whig candidate felt badly let down.

Seward returned to Auburn, but at the end of the year he traveled to Albany for a session of the state appeals court. The days were short and the nights were cold, and he had ample time to reflect on the state of his marriage. His first letters to Frances were in his normal, chatty vein; then came a confession. He had awakened, Henry wrote, "from a long and feverish and almost fatal dream." Despite her doubts, Henry wrote, he knew he loved her. His ambition had driven them apart. He had been cruel, reacting unsympathetically to her piety and her attempts to win him to religious faith. He had denied her the love that was her due, "and when the wretched T[racy] took advantage of my madness . . . and your heart was half won by his falsehoods, still I did not know and see that I was the criminal."[5] Henry went on:

> My dearest Frances, I have always loved you, as the best and chief of my affections. I have been led afar off by an ambition which has only this mitigation, that it was neither sordid nor selfish. But suppress that passion . . . and my heart turns to you, possibly with less than its original force but still with all the energy . . . left to it. . . . Heaven only knows whether I can become a Christian. That I ought, I know and feel.[6]

Frances, in reply, insisted that Henry reproached himself too severely. He had always been good and kind, and with God's grace he could become a Christian. She did not know whether he could love her as deeply as she loved him, but she should not expect a return of her "too intense affections." She had concluded, following the dalliance with Tracy, that she could never love anyone other than Henry "unless God utterly deserted me." God had not deserted her, and if her husband could only subordinate ambition to love, she believed that they might be happier "than in the earliest and brightest days of our union."[7] Thus Frances and Henry were reconciled. Henry would not turn his back on politics, but he would never again be so inattentive to his wife as he had been in 1832 and 1833.

There remained the matter of Albert Tracy. Henry did not break off a friendship capriciously, and the letter he wrote to his wife's lover was remarkably free of venom:

> I was reluctantly forced to the discovery that, whether with or without deliberate intent, you were pursuing towards the one being nearest and dearest to me a course which, but for the strength of her virtue, would have destroyed my peace . . . if not my honor. . . . I have long since forgiven you this wound, for weakness I know it was, but I cannot forget it.[8]

Seward was a man of reason, but his mild reaction to Tracy's betrayal is nevertheless noteworthy. In a situation that most husbands would regard as unambiguous, Seward appeared to go out of his way to find extenuating circumstances on Tracy's behalf. He insisted that he still regarded Tracy as a friend. Then, as though aware of his own inconsistency, he made a revealing admission, writing: "I have all my life found myself an enigma to myself."

*   *   *

Frances continued to be troubled by a variety of health problems, not all of which are readily translated into twentieth-century terminology. Doctor after doctor examined Frances and could find little wrong. In July 1834 Henry wrote his father that Frances was bothered by dyspepsia—a catchall term for digestive ailments—and by problems with her eyes, "being altogether unable to use them in the evening."[9] Three months later he wrote that "Frances has been very sick since I last wrote, and has suffered more pain than I supposed she could endure. . . . Her complaint was a tumor in the intestines."[10]

Frances believed that she suffered from some affliction of the nervous system. Her headaches and nausea suggest that she may have been a victim of migraines. She may also have suffered from a malady now called postpartum depression. Such a condition can develop after a number of normal births, or it can start with the first confinement and become progressively more severe. The most detailed study of Frances's symptoms concludes that "the saga of Frances' difficult pregnancies, slow recoveries, and increasingly lengthy depressions would suggest that her 'vapors' had their roots in motherhood."[11]

In 1835, with Frances still very weak, the Sewards, on her doctors' advice, embarked on an ambitious tour that would take them as far south as Virginia. They chose for the trip a light, two-passenger carriage, and young Fred accompanied them, occupying the front seat alongside coachman William Johnson. The tour proved a tonic for the Seward marriage. Both Henry and Frances were enthusiastic about the natural wonders of the Susquehanna Valley. In Philadelphia, Frances consulted with the renowned doctor Philip Physick, and both Sewards had portraits painted by Thomas Sully.

In Virginia the travelers found Harper's Ferry a disappointment but were much impressed with Natural Bridge. In Charlottesville, Henry pronounced the University of Virginia superior to any northern college with which he was familiar. But the most vivid memories that the Sewards would bring back from Virginia were vignettes of slavery. They talked with a black woman whose husband and six children had been sold away, and saw a group of black boys driven to a horse trough to drink before being put to bed in a shed. From Orange Courthouse, the home of James Madison, Henry wrote to his father:

> The entire country in Virginia exhibits melancholy evidence of the unprofitability of slave labor. Virginia is apparently 100 years behind the Empire State in improvement. [However,] a sudden flow of prosperity has recently come upon her. The abolition of slavery in the West Indies, and the great increase of cultivation of new land in the Southern and Southwestern states, have seen the value of Negroes [increase] . . . and trade in the blood, bone and sinew of men made in God's own image, is brisk.[12]

Frances had begun the trip with a variety of physical complaints, including headaches, chest pains, and insomnia. But when she and Henry returned in early September, her health was considerably improved. Two months later she was pregnant with the Sewards' third child, and on August 25 she gave birth to a girl, Cornelia, named after Henry's sister. Henry was often away on legal business, but he came home as often as possible, and Frances appeared happier than she had been for years. Then came tragedy. Cornelia contracted smallpox, which left her both blind and scarred. She died the following January, and Henry and his son Augustus contracted a mild form of the disease as well. The following spring, while still in mourning, Seward allowed himself to be baptized in the Episcopal church. He wrote Thurlow Weed that he did not anticipate any great change in his habits but hoped that a closer relationship with God would "gradually elevate and refine my motives for action."[13]

Henry's thoughts were never far from politics, however, and he maintained an active correspondence with Whig leaders all over the state. Prospects for the Whigs, both nationally and in New York State, appeared bleak. Seward favored William Henry Harrison as the party's presidential nominee in 1836, but he doubted whether Jackson's chosen heir, Van Buren, could be defeated under any foreseeable circumstances. The Whigs could not succeed, Seward wrote, "until there is a time of popular convulsion, when suffering shall make men feel, and because they feel, think!"[14]

*   *   *

The Sewards had hardly returned from their journey south when Henry was called to the western part of the state in connection with a large and sensitive real estate venture. Decades earlier the Holland Land Company, run by Dutch businessmen, had purchased from Revolutionary War financier Robert Morris a huge tract of New York State west of the Genesee River. Demand for the land had proved disappointing, however, and in 1835 the company had sold its entire holdings in Chautauqua County, 365,000 acres, to local bankers. Because the Holland Land Company had been a lenient landlord, often providing loans for local artisans to set up shop, the settlers viewed the sale to local interests with understandable alarm.

Grumbling changed to protest when it became known that the new owners were determined to collect interest on old debts and would raise prices for those seeking to renew their contracts. Early in 1836 squatters sacked the land office in Mayville, causing the resident land agent to flee in fear for his life. The new owners, in their headquarters at Batavia, began looking for an agent who might calm the settlers' wrath and even collect a few debts. Their choice fell on William H. Seward.

For Seward to place himself at the head of a massive collection operation hardly seemed the way for a budding politician to win the hearts of his constituents. Still, the annual salary was $5,000 plus stock and travel expenses. Seward accepted. He traveled first to the company's main office at Batavia, midway between Rochester and Niagara Falls. He found there a situation of near anarchy, with settlers holding protest meetings daily and the Holland Land Company premises protected by armed guards. Seward took one look and arranged for the transfer of the land office to Westfield, on Lake Erie.

Seward had broad authority from the Holland Land Company's new owners, and he was determined to deal fairly with the settlers. Anyone who paid 25 percent of his outstanding debt and agreed to terms on the balance received a deed to his property. Settlers were allowed as long as ten years to pay. As a result Seward estimated that out of five hundred delinquent loans, only about fifty became subject to foreclosure. Tempers cooled, and Henry Seward became a respected figure in western New York. By the end of 1836 some eighty thousand acres had been conveyed to settlers, and payments to the company were being made on schedule. Henry himself began to speculate in land.

Although Seward was discharging his legal responsibilities to considerable applause, he was away from Frances for long periods of time and appears to have felt pangs of both guilt and self-pity. Frances reproached him for his absences, and his father still pressed him to relocate in Orange County. Seward was defensive and lonely; he took young Fred with him on occasion but did not feel that the seven-year-old should be away from his mother for extended periods. Early in 1837 he wrote Frances from Westfield:

> We are again separated, my dear Frances; I have returned to you the boy you lent me; now you have both, all, in your keeping; you have our living and our dead with you, and the home with which they are associated, and I am far away and all alone. . . . I was never so reluctant to leave you; I yet regret very much that I had not insisted on your coming with me.[15]

The domestic responsibilities that came Henry's way were considerable. He was caring not only for his own family but to some extent for his siblings. Jennings, the oldest of his three brothers, needed the least help. In 1837 Henry had made him a partner in his Holland Land Company enterprise, an arrangement that allowed Henry more time for politics and family. But George, the youngest, failed in a variety of business ventures and was constantly asking for money. Polydore, the alcoholic, was a burden to the entire family. He repeatedly abandoned his wife and children, causing his distraught wife to write Samuel Seward in 1839 that "to live with Polydore and have children by him any longer, to be a burden to other people, I cannot."[16]

The panic of 1837 brought virtually all land sales to a halt and threatened much of the debt that Henry had so carefully rescheduled. Seward persuaded the company trustees not to foreclose where such action could be avoided, and in 1838 he worked out a complicated refinancing agreement whereby the Holland Company sold its interest in the Chautauqua land to a consortium that included Seward himself.

*   *   *

Seward had determined to be a more thoughtful husband, but he had by no means forsworn politics. In 1837 he declined to run for office, but he made a number of speeches for Whig candidates in Cayuga County, blaming the depression on the Democrats. He made other speeches on education and internal improvements and circulated them widely in pamphlet form. Encouraged by a seeming improvement in Frances's health, Seward prepared to make another run for the governorship.

The omens were good, for state elections in 1837 resulted in overwhelming victories for the Whigs. But the field was large and included two formidable aspirants in Francis Granger and assembly speaker Luther Bradish. Predictably it was Thurlow Weed who paved the way for his friend's nomination. He crisscrossed the state, professing a willingness to let the 1838 convention pick the best candidate, but all the time seeking to generate sentiment for Seward. To friends of Granger, Weed hinted that if Granger stood aside for Seward, Weed would support him for the Whig vice presidential nomination in 1840.

The Whig convention met in Utica on September 12. Granger was strong in the western part of the state—evidence that Seward's role in the Holland Land Company transactions was still regarded as a political liability by some voters—and at the end of the third ballot Granger led Seward by one vote. But Weed was everywhere, armed with figures to show that Seward, in his losing campaign in 1834, had run well ahead of the Whig ticket. Seward was nominated on the fourth ballot, and Granger settled for the nomination for Congress. Luther Bradish was the delegates' choice for lieutenant governor.

Thanks to Weed the Whigs were united for the fall campaign. They charged the Regency with corruption and the national Democratic party with having brought on the panic of 1837. The Democrats, in turn, alleged that Seward was inconsistent in his support for internal improvements, noting that he had earlier voted against the Chenango Canal and the Erie Railroad. They painted the Whig candidate as the lackey of the Bank of the United States and of the Holland Company shareholders.

Amid the customary ballyhoo of an election in the period before the Civil War, the issue of slavery intruded like an uninvited guest. The 1830s had seen a sharp rise in the number of reform groups in the North, especially organizations aimed at the abolition of slavery. The New York State Anti-Slavery Society, led by Gerrit Smith and William Jay, had adopted resolutions urging its members to withhold their votes from candidates who would not endorse the antislavery cause. Specifically they asked the Whig and Democratic candidates for state office where they stood on three issues: jury trial for fugitive slaves, black suffrage, and repeal of a state law that permitted the detention of slaves without cause.

Seward's running mate, Bradish, answered all three questions in the affirmative, without even consulting Seward. Henry would have liked to finesse the issue, but Bradish's action forced his hand. After consulting with Weed, Seward issued a reply in which he declared his opposition to "all human bondage." He favored a law that would provide a jury trial for fugitive slaves, so long as such legislation did not conflict with the Constitution. But he did not urge repeal of the detention law, and he did not endorse giving blacks the vote. This response was not calculated to please the antislavery forces, but then the response of Seward's opponent, William Marcy, had been similarly negative. In terms of the gubernatorial campaign, the two responses canceled each other out.

In the absence of polls by which to measure his standing, Seward was dependent on correspondents across the state, and these were his supporters. Still, even the hard-nosed Weed was optimistic, writing to Seward in late October that "the indications and signs are good."[17] Seward, however, was inclined to discount favorable omens. He wrote to one supporter: "I should be confident of a large Whig majority in this state. But . . . the bias of my mind is always to anticipate the worst—a bias I always cherish because it does not [reduce] my zeal."[18]

In the end Weed's optimism was vindicated at the polls. On election day Seward carried the state by some 10,000 votes, a margin almost identical to that by which he had lost four years earlier. The Regency, after having dominated New York State politics for two decades, had at last been overthrown. Seward studied the vote tally at the offices of the *Auburn Journal* and took special satisfaction in winning by 2,200 votes in Chautauqua County, despite charges in the campaign that he had played some sinister role in the Holland Company Land negotiations. He wrote to his mother:

> The excitement of the election has ceased, and my thoughts . . . seek you as I have no doubt your solicitude has followed me through the hazards I have passed. Heavy responsibilities will soon be heaped upon me. For your sake, for mine and my country's, give me your prayers that I may discharge them in the fear of God and with his blessing.[19]

Seward's election as governor of New York represented the most important Whig victory up to that time, and congratulations poured into Auburn from all over the country. His fellow townspeople celebrated the election results with a hundred-gun salute. In Albany, Weed's *Evening Journal* devoted its entire front page to the picture of a great eagle with outstretched wings.

But Seward's euphoria was tempered by his wife's inability to share his triumph. Frances took to her bed, insisting that she would not go to Albany. Weed, who by then was confidant to the entire Seward family, came to Auburn and suggested to Frances that she would be better after a couple of months' rest. A few days later Henry was able to write to his brother Jennings that Frances had improved and that they were beginning their preparations for the move to Albany.

5

The Governor

IN THE NINETEENTH century state governors had considerable power. The government in Washington was not then viewed as the primary source of financing for the local economy; communities looked instead to the state. A governor had at his disposal a significant number of appointive positions, many of them requiring no confirmation by the legislature, and for this reason alone was the most powerful politician in his state. Above and beyond this tangible authority, a governor was elected by the direct votes of his neighbors—in contrast to the president, who was chosen by the electoral college, and U.S. senators, who at that time were chosen by state legislatures. A governor's influence was especially formidable in a state as important as New York. His position was also one of considerable prestige, and even when Seward later served as a U.S. senator and secretary of state, he always preferred the courtesy title Governor.

Seward may not have been a hero to the antislavery forces in 1838, but his election as governor of New York was one product of a reform movement that had been gaining momentum since the early 1830s. Whereas slavery was its main focus, it also included such causes as temperance and prison reform (but not woman suffrage, which would not emerge as a movement for another decade). Abolitionism even had its martyrs. In 1837 antislavery leaders were outraged by the murder of Elijah Lovejoy, an abolitionist editor. Lovejoy's inflammatory editorials had infuriated many conservative residents of Alton, Illinois, and his presses were repeatedly destroyed. One day, when Lovejoy refused to surrender his new press to a mob, shots were fired and Lovejoy was killed.

Seward was part of the antislavery movement, but his immediate concerns were more mundane. He left for Albany on December 21— Frances was again pregnant and unwilling to travel—carrying with him a draft inaugural address that he planned to circulate for comment. Because he disliked the house just vacated by Governor Marcy, Seward's first priority was to find a suitable residence. He finally settled on the Kane mansion, situated on a wooded four-acre tract at the corner of Waterloo and Broad streets. A large hall, some fifty feet long, would accommodate receptions, while the adjoining room could comfortably seat twenty or more diners. A well behind the manor provided drinking water, and almost every room had its own fireplace. The house was in keeping with Henry's new status, but it would prove a serious financial drain. Rent and maintenance each year would consume more than twice the governor's $4,000 annual salary.

New Year's Day, 1839, was Inauguration Day in Albany, and Seward and Bradish took office in a simple ceremony. The city was filled with jubilant Whigs, and to accommodate the crowds the inauguration was moved to the lobby of the capitol building. As he left the capitol, Henry penned a brief note to Frances: "We are here. The ceremony is over. A joyous people throng the Capitol."[1] Henry's messenger was his new private secretary, nineteen-year-old Sam Blatchford. Sam owed his position to the fact that his father, Richard Blatchford, was a wealthy backer of the governor, but young Sam proved so capable that his association with Seward would be a long one.

From the capitol Henry went to his residence, where a crowd of several thousand awaited the traditional inaugural reception. The carpets had been taken up and long tables installed, each covered with turkeys, hams, cakes, and bowls overflowing with punch. The doors were opened at noon, a band played festive airs, and the mob descended. Some guests went through the formality of congratulating their new governor, but others made straight for the refreshments. Because only a portion of the crowd could fit into the mansion, trays of food were passed through the windows to the throng on the grounds. The merrymaking went on until dark, and Seward estimated that he had shaken hands with three or four thousand people.

It was a mark of the prestige of the New York State governorship that the governor's inaugural message received much of the national attention that is reserved today for a president's inaugural address. Seward's first message is of particular interest as an early expression of his political philosophy.

In 1839 Seward saw in America tremendous undeveloped resources and great social potential. He was convinced that surplus labor from Europe could help to exploit America's vast resources to the full. Rather than seek to exclude immigrants, therefore, the United States should make them welcome: "To accomplish this, we must extend to them the right of citizenship. . . . We must secure to them as largely as we ourselves enjoy, the immunities of religious worship. And we should . . . [establish] schools in which their children shall enjoy advantages of education equal to our own."[2] Although Seward was on sensitive ground here, he never faltered in his belief that the United States should be a magnet for people from all over the world and that the new immigrants should have schools in which they could be taught in their native languages.

The governor moved on to specifics. With respect to economic development, nothing was more important than the Erie Canal, the 350-mile "ditch" that connected Buffalo on Lake Erie to the Hudson River at Albany. Seward proposed widening the canal, as well as constructing three new railroads, with state money if necessary. He expected such projects to pay for themselves, estimating that increased canal revenues alone would justify the annual expenditure of $4 million dollars on internal improvements.

Elsewhere, Seward proposed the establishment of a state board of education and improvements in the curricula of public schools. Noting the high crime rate among blacks in the state, Seward saw improved education as the remedy. He also endorsed two other bills, one providing jury trials for fugitive slaves, the other extending the vote to all free blacks and not merely to property holders. In a passage that recalled his earlier interest in penal reform, the governor quoted from a report on cruelties in the state prison system:

> If our system of imprisonment . . . cannot be maintained without the infliction of such punishments as are disclosed by this report, then it was established in error, and it ought to be immediately abandoned. But such is not the case. . . . Equality and justice, kindness and gentleness, combined with a firmness of temper, would, with very few exceptions, secure the cheerful obedience of even the tenants of our state prisons.[3]

For all his eloquence, however, the new governor was not in a position to enact a comprehensive legislative program. Although the Whigs controlled the assembly, the Democrats retained control of the senate, and Seward initially found himself unable to secure confirmation of those appointments that required senate approval. The legislature provided funds for widening the Erie Canal and passed a few minor bills aimed at improving the public schools. But Seward's proposal for a state board of education fell on barren ground, and nothing came of his measures for special educational programs for blacks and the children of immigrants. In the area of prison reform, however, Seward was less dependent on the legislature. The administrators appointed by Seward dismissed incompetent supervisors at the state prisons at Auburn and Sing Sing and instituted programs for vocational training. Whipping was abolished at Auburn and restricted at Sing Sing, and prison food was improved at both institutions.

Office seekers badgered the governor incessantly. Seward had some fifteen hundred appointive jobs at his disposal, and he fully intended to use his appointments to develop a Whig organization to replace the Regency. But pitfalls abounded. For instance, dissident Democrats had contributed to Seward's election, and a prominent member of this group was U.S. Senator Nathaniel Tallmadge. Tallmadge asked for and received Seward's support in his bid for reelection, but Seward's action infuriated Whig aspirants for the post. A casualty at this time was Seward's friendship with Millard Fillmore. When Seward refused to appoint the Buffalo man to state office, Fillmore complained that he was being treated like a political enemy rather than a Whig and an ally.

The governor's political problems eased somewhat when elections in the fall of 1839 brought about Whig control of the state senate. But Seward soon found himself immersed in a land dispute potentially as serious as the Holland Land Company protests. Farms in the Helderberg Mountains, in Albany and Rensselaer counties, were subject to some of the most archaic rent laws in the United States. When the heirs of landlord Stephen Van Rensselaer sought to collect $400,000 in back rent, farmers on his $700,000 tract revolted against feudal laws that required them to pay rent to the patroon in perpetuity. With the eruption of the "Helderberg War," farmers took the law into their own hands and forcibly ejected sheriffs who attempted to serve papers on delinquent tenants.

The Helderberg War was the first crisis Seward faced as governor. His sympathies were with the tenants, but, as with the Holland Land Company, the law was on the side of the landlord. When gun-toting tenants turned back an armed posse sent from Albany, Seward mobilized the militia and called on the tenants to obey the law. He promised, however, to bring their case to the attention of the legislature. The appearance of the militia ended resistance for the time being, but it would be more than a decade before the tenants would be able to gain permanent relief.

*   *   *

Because his focus was largely on issues that related directly to New York State, such as education and prison reform, Seward did not seek a leadership position in the antislavery movement. Nevertheless, when fate handed him an issue that grew out of slavery, Seward used it to enhance his prestige among the abolitionists. In 1839 three black seamen, residents of New York, unsuccessfully attempted to smuggle a slave aboard a ship bound from Virginia to New York City. Gov. Thomas Gilmer of Virginia demanded that the three seamen be returned to Virginia for trial. Most such requests for extradition between states were routinely complied with. But in his reply to Gilmer, Seward declined to turn over the fugitives and made an issue of the crime with which the three men were charged:

> There is no law of this State which recognizes slavery, no statute which admits that one man can be the property of another, or that one man can be stolen from another. . . . The act charged in the affidavit, if it had been committed in this state, would not have contravened any statute. . . . It results from this view of the subject that the offense charged . . . is not a felony nor a crime within the meaning of the constitution.[4]

Seward's legal position was tenuous, and the controversy dragged on for years, with each side advancing legal arguments in support of its position. Public opinion predictably divided along regional lines. "The controversy has hitherto been much more ably managed by Seward than by the Virginians," John Quincy Adams wrote in his diary. "But there have been symptoms of the basest defection [from] the cause of freedom among the New York Whigs, and a disposition to sacrifice Seward to the South."[5]

One result of the publicity surrounding the Virginia affair was that the New York legislature passed legislation recommended by Seward that guaranteed a jury trial for fugitive slaves. Virginia became so incensed that it began to harass New York–based ships that called at Old Dominion ports. Antislavery leaders praised Seward for his courage; Southern newspapers denounced him. South Carolina, always in the lead in matters related to states' rights, resolved to cooperate with sister states in dealing with New York's unwillingness to respect laws that were valid in the South. Whereas Seward's campaign for penal reform had struck few sparks, his confrontation with Virginia was a different matter. It placed Seward squarely in the antislavery camp at a time when the abolitionists were gaining prominence on the national political scene.

Seward may have felt that a liberal position on slavery-related issues would work in his favor politically, but his reformist sympathies led him to support causes whose rewards were uncertain. There were few votes in prison reform, and fewer still in championing the Indians. During Seward's two terms as governor, the Oneida Indians of the Iroquois nation were forcibly resettled to the western territories under policies begun under Andrew Jackson. In some instances the Oneidas had been led to cede their land by fraud. Seward was in no position to reverse history. Still, he made a point of receiving Moses Schuyler, the gray-haired chief of the Oneidas, at the governor's mansion. To Schuyler, who had fought for the United States in the War of 1812, Seward spoke awkwardly of "how reluctantly I have consented to the sale of your lands."[6]

The governor's sympathy with the Oneidas was largely symbolic, but his efforts to improve education for the children of immigrants bore fruit. In 1840 he again urged that the state assist "foreign" children who attended religious schools. His primary target group was the Irish, although there were also significant numbers of German-speaking immigrants in the state. Seward's motives were probably mixed. He had a genuine sympathy for all immigrants; at the same time, he doubtless hoped to make some Whig converts in a voting bloc that was predominantly Democratic. Seward's special sympathy for the Irish probably grew out of the fact that he himself was half Irish, as well as from his memories of the poor conditions in Ireland at the time of his visit there in 1833.

What Seward had in mind was allowing the Catholic church to use state money in the running of parochial schools—a concept that would be raised many times in the course of the next century and a half. He found an ally in Bishop John Hughes, who became a close political supporter of Seward's over the next two decades, but the proposal raised a storm of protest. The Democrats, predictably, charged the governor with political opportunism and with attempting to break down the constitutional division between church and state. Conservative Whigs and some Protestant groups accused Seward of having sold out to the pope. The school issue made Seward a hero to the foreign born, but many other Americans came to view him as a demagogue willing to betray his heritage in pursuit of political advancement.

Ultimately, Seward settled for half a loaf. A statute drawn up by John C. Spencer, the New York secretary of state, placated conservatives by prohibiting state support to religious schools. But the law also provided for New York City schools to be administered by an elected school board, which in effect ended control of the city schools by the conservative Public School Society.

While the bulk of Seward's programs as governor appear to have been prompted by his liberal sympathies, his enemies were not always off the mark in their charges of political opportunism. The temperance movement was very much in vogue during Seward's terms as governor, and in 1842 Seward himself, to Frances's amazement, took a pledge of abstinence. Wine disappeared from the Kane mansion, to the consternation of state legislators and Whig functionaries. The exact period that governor's mansion remained dry is unclear, but it was not long. Although Seward himself rarely touched liquor, he was accustomed to wine in the evening, and quickly regretted his dalliance with the prohibitionists.

*   *   *

Nationally, the Whigs were determined to run a single presidential candidate in 1840 and thereby to avoid a repetition of 1836, when the Whigs had nearly matched the Democrats in the popular vote but had divided their vote among four contenders. New York, with its forty-two electoral votes, was the most important state in a national election, a fact that made its governor a major player on the political stage.

Henry Clay was again eager for the Whig presidential nomination, but he had a number of rivals, led by Generals Winfield Scott and William Henry Harrison. Seward and Weed, convinced that Clay could not carry New York, did what they could to promote Scott, whose military exploits along the Canadian border during the War of 1812 were still remembered in upstate New York. In August 1839 Clay made a trip through several Northern states in his pursuit of the nomination. He stopped in Auburn to pay his respects to the governor, but Seward just happened to be away when the "Harry of the West" came calling. Although Seward would later claim that his only reservations about Clay were political—relating to his ability to carry New York State—one suspects there was some bad personal chemistry as well between the popular Kentuckian and the ambitious governor of the Empire State.

New York did its best for Scott at the Whig convention, but the ticket finally chosen was headed by the venerable William Henry Harrison. In nominating Harrison the Whigs had come up with a homespun military hero who, from the Whig perspective, contrasted favorably with the urbane incumbent Van Buren. Because of the financial collapse of 1837 and the hard times that had followed, Van Buren was a beaten man.

The gubernatorial campaign was a different matter. Although Seward was easily renominated for governor by the New York Whigs, and the Seward-Bradish ticket entered the fall campaign confident of victory, the Democrats seized the initiative by nominating William Bouck, a popular and able canal commissioner whom the Whigs had previously removed from office. Seward's zeal for internal improvements, the Democrats said, had saddled the state with ruinous debt that could be met only by increased taxes. He had allied himself with feudal land-owners in the Helderberg War, employing the militia against peaceful citizens at a cost of some $3,000 per day. He had been elected in 1838 only with the connivance of illegal voters from Philadelphia. The Whigs were no more to be trusted in 1840 than earlier. The Regency's *Albany Argus* trumpeted: "We are about to be overrun with fraudulent voters."[7]

Both parties were doubtless guilty of buying votes, but whereas voting fraud made headlines, Seward's real problem was the state deficit. Expanded canals and railroads had increased the state's debt by $16 million in an era when deficit financing was frowned on. Although much of Seward's program was farsighted, it had raised interest rates and had damaged the state's credit rating. Economic development had made enemies as well as friends for the governor, arraying one county against another in the competition for state money.

The most contentious charges with which Seward had to deal related to education. Many Protestants and nativists viewed his interest in immigrant education as a shameless wooing of the Catholic vote. Henry may have encouraged this view by inviting Bishop Hughes to Albany for the nineteenth-century counterpart to a campaign photo opportunity. If Seward was guilty of opportunism, however, he chose an issue that promised few rewards. New York's Irish Catholics continued to vote Democratic, and although Seward may have won over a few votes he also triggered defections among conservative Whigs. Seward himself would admit to no political motive; he wrote in his abbreviated memoir:

> I early learned the injury the state was suffering from the failure of our public schools to educate a large portion of foreigners in our cities. . . . I have believed [that] no system of education could answer the ends of a republic but one that secures the education of all. I ventured to promise myself that one of the chief benefits I might render the state was to turn the footsteps of the children of the poor foreigners from the way that led to the House of Refuge and the state prison.[8]

On the national scene the Whigs waged their campaign on personalities, laying the depression squarely on Martin Van Buren's doorstep.

A Democratic newspaper, the *Baltimore Republican,* provided the Whigs with a propaganda bonanza when it wrote derisively that Harrison would probably be content to live out his days in a log cabin with "a pension of $2,000 and a barrel of cider." In the "log cabin and hard cider" campaign that ensued, the Whigs presented their candidate as a son of the frontier and a man of the people. Thurlow Weed helped launch a campaign newspaper called the *Log Cabin.* As editor he tapped young Horace Greeley, for whom the *Log Cabin* would lead eventually to a far more influential organ, the *New York Tribune.*

Although Harrison's popular majority that November was not overwhelming, his victory in the electoral college was decisive. In New York, Seward—who had hoped to double his ten thousand majority of 1838— ran behind the national ticket, winning by fewer than six thousand votes. In his replies to well-wishers the governor kept a stiff upper lip, maintaining that a Whig victory both nationally and in New York State was all he could have hoped for. Privately Seward's disappointment was keen, but it would have been even greater if he had realized that his name had gone before the voters for the last time.

* * *

When Abraham Lincoln chose Seward to be secretary of state in 1861, his primary objective was a politically balanced cabinet. The considerable diplomatic experience Seward had gained while governor of New York was a minor factor. Nevertheless, Seward as governor was involved in a major diplomatic imbroglio as a result of political unrest in Canada.

In the fall of 1837, portions of Canada had rebelled against British rule under circumstances that led some observers to compare the revolt with the American Revolution. Northern New York provided a convenient base for rebels, as well as a safe haven for fugitives from Canadian justice. Van Buren issued a neutrality proclamation in January 1838, but the Canadian–U.S. border continued to provide sanctuary for the insurgents.

The most serious border incident predated Seward's tenure as governor. In December 1837 a Canadian militia force had crossed into New York State near Niagara Falls and destroyed the *Caroline,* an American vessel that had ferried supplies to the insurgents, killing one American in the process. The British government largely ignored Washington's protests until, in 1840, a Canadian named Alexander McLeod was arrested in New York State and charged with murder in connection with the *Caroline* affair. The Palmerston government promptly demanded

McLeod's release, on the grounds that he could not be held responsible for acts committed under orders from Canadian authorities. Seward attempted to take a middle ground. With an eye toward popular opinion, he insisted that New York State had jurisdiction and that McLeod would be tried for murder. Privately, Seward intimated that if McLeod *were* convicted, he would be pardoned.

The spring of 1841 saw a spirited exchange of letters between Seward and Secretary of State Daniel Webster. Seward felt put upon, for the American position upholding New York State's jurisdiction had been laid down under the Van Buren administration. Now Van Buren's Whig successors—eager to consummate what would become the Webster-Ashburton Treaty with Britain—seemed determined to cut the ground out from under a governor of their own party. Part of the problem was that there was no love lost between Seward and Daniel Webster. Webster aspired to the presidency, but Seward and Weed were known to believe that Webster was so closely identified with banking interests as to be unacceptable as a Whig presidential candidate.

The ultimate resolution of the McLeod case was anticlimactic. At his trial in October 1841 McLeod established an alibi—it seems he was drunk at the time of the raid—and was acquitted. The affair resulted in strained relations between Seward and the administration of John Tyler, who had succeeded President Harrison after the latter's death in April 1841. Seward, like a good politician, had sought to identify himself with anti-British sentiment along the border. At the same time, he had cooperated with federal authorities in seeking to preserve order along the frontier and to prevent incursions into Canada by Americans sympathetic to the rebels. Seward's demonstrated skill at the diplomatic balancing act would serve him—and the nation—well twenty years later.

*   *   *

Seward was a morning person. In a letter to Frances in 1841, he noted that he normally rose at six and worked at his desk until noon. Weed customarily came over for an hour or so after lunch. Henry then returned to his desk or visited one of the departments. He closed his letter to Frances with the observation: "We are very quiet and staid here."[9]

Henry, for all his good cheer, was under considerable stress. The problem may have been partly physical, for, despite his reassuring comments to Frances, he smoked too much, often worked late hours, and complained of a malady that he described as "a rush of blood to the head." Moreover, not even Seward's sunny disposition could entirely erase the disappointment over his narrow reelection victory, the drum-fire of criticism concerning the state debt, and irritations growing out of his cool relationship with the administration in Washington. There was also the matter of Seward's own finances. Henry had been living on a scale well beyond that covered by the governor's salary, and he continued to carry a heavy load of debt from his Chautauqua real estate dealings. The possibility of bankruptcy was real.

Over the winter of 1840–41, Seward appears to have undergone a period of severe depression. His papers for this period include a prayer written in his own hand—an unusual item in a collection devoted largely to political correspondence—in which Seward repented his sins and asked God "to sustain me in this trouble." God knew "the wicked thoughts it has excited and the desperate and dangerous purposes it has brought me to contemplate." Henry asked for "meekness and humility" and prayed that "this affliction [will] work its rightful effect in my mind and upon my feelings and actions."[10]

When Seward's creditors became insistent, it was Thurlow Weed who came to the rescue. Weed lent his friend money, soothed irate creditors, and helped locate new sources of financial assistance. Richard Blatchford, Sam's father, took charge of Seward's financial affairs. Henry's morale gradually improved, although it was imperative that he return to private practice and recoup his financial fortunes.[11]

In the spring of 1841 Seward announced that he would not be a candidate for reelection. He rationalized his decision on political grounds, writing to Congressman Christopher Morgan, "My principles are too liberal, too philanthropic, if it be not vain to say so, for my party." He went on to complain to Morgan that, because he was on the liberal wing of the Whig party, his program had not fared well. But, he concluded a bit smugly, "my principles are very good and popular ones for a man out of office; they will take care of me, when out of office, as they always have done."[12]

To read Seward's letter one might think that he was leaving office in disgrace. This was hardly the case—witness the testimonial dinners in his honor and the letters that poured into the Kane mansion following Seward's announcement. His development of the state's canals and railroads was widely recognized as a factor in the improving economic outlook. He had helped to improve the New York City school system, even if the political benefits had been limited. He had contributed mightily to making the state's prison system more humane, and he had moved to the forefront among those determined to oppose and eventually to eradicate slavery. When John Quincy Adams wrote that he hoped Seward was not retiring from politics permanently, the New Yorker replied that if his services should ever again be needed, he would be ready.

The final months of any governor's administration are marked by a flurry of demands for pardons. However, Seward's interest in humane treatment for prisoners did not extend to the indiscriminate use of his pardoning authority. Whereas his predecessor had averaged a hundred pardons per year, Seward averaged about seventy. His general practice was not to issue a pardon until at least half the sentence had been served.

One politically sensitive appeal for clemency involved a prominent Whig editor, James Watson Webb. The fiery Webb was a notorious duelist, who, in 1839, had fought an inconclusive duel with a political opponent in contravention of New York's rarely enforced antidueling statute. Incarcerated in the Tombs prison in New York City, Webb could only hope that his friend Seward would not forget him. Seward did not, and Webb went on to become Seward's most faithful editorial supporter in the New York City metropolitan area.

Philip Hone was a wealthy New York City Whig who had watched his governor closely. As Seward's term drew to a close, Hone noted in his diary:

> Now that [Seward] is about retiring from office, the people of this State seem willing to give him credit for the talent which he certainly possesses in an eminent degree, and some of his own party cease to cavil at some of his public acts. . . . It has been said (and I think not without reason) that he has courted popularity a little too much, especially in some injudicious concessions to the Roman Catholics; but I believe he was always influenced in those measures by good motives, [and] by a sincere desire to serve the cause which is supported by his political friends.[13]

On New Year's Eve, 1842, Henry penned a letter to Thurlow Weed:

> The end has come at last. My successor and the New Year come together. . . . The thousand perils through which I have passed, the thousand enemies by whom I have been opposed, the hundreds by whom I have been causelessly hated, and the many whom I have unavoidably or imprudently offended, rise up before me; and yet I am safe. . . . [I feel] gratitude to God, and gratitude and affection toward my friends, and most of all to you, my first and most efficient and devoted friend.[14]

6

"Our Conflict Is with Slavery"

FOR ALL HIS lofty political pronouncements, Seward left Albany a troubled man. His debts, including mortgages, totaled about $200,000, of which $11,000 was owed to Weed and $13,000 to Richard Blatchford. Seward saw himself chained to his law practice for an indefinite period while he worked off his debts. But the picture was not altogether dark. Henry's financial fortunes were retrievable, and Frances was delighted to have him back in Auburn. Even his political timing appears to have been good, for the Whig party was undergoing a major convulsion.

John Tyler had been elected to Congress as a Democrat. He had subsequently broken with Jackson, and the Whigs had put him on the 1840 ticket with Harrison in the hope of attracting the votes of conservative Democrats. The presence of Tyler on the Whig ticket may have contributed to the first Whig victory in a presidential race, but the Whigs had not reckoned with the unexpected: President Harrison's death after only a month in office.

All was harmonious for a time. Tyler retained Harrison's cabinet and continued the late president's replacement of Democrats with Whig appointees. But the Whigs were handicapped by a surplus of ambitious leaders. Henry Clay considered himself, and not Harrison or Tyler, the real leader of the party. Daniel Webster lacked Clay's national following, but he too harbored presidential ambitions. Because Tyler was intent on assuming all the prerogatives of the presidency, he and Clay, in particular, were on a collision course.

In the Senate, Clay offered a set of resolutions that he viewed as a kind of platform for the Whig party. Among his proposals were measures for the creation of a new Bank of the United States, an increase in the tariff, and the distribution of proceeds from government land sales to the respective states. Although Tyler accepted some elements of Clay's program, he disapproved of others. Soon the party split over the bank issue.

The Whigs were committed to restoring a central bank similar to Biddle's Bank of the United States. Tyler, a states' rightist, opposed the concept of a national bank and repeatedly vetoed legislation that provided, in one guise or another, for a central banking institution. The upshot was that Tyler's entire cabinet, except for Webster, resigned. To take their places, Tyler appointed five men of his own conservative persuasion, all former Democrats. The Whigs watched in anguish as Tyler ran the country with proslavery Democrats.

The reform movement, which had helped to propel Seward to the governorship of New York, had fallen on hard times. The Underground Railroad in the Northern states still helped slaves escape from the South, but the actual number of such escapes was minuscule. In Washington a "gag resolution" passed by Congress in 1836 effectively blocked petitions on subjects relating to slavery. Membership in antislavery societies stagnated and then began to slip. For a man who needed a period to recoup his fortunes, Seward's timing could hardly have been better.

*   *   *

The outgoing governor got a warm send-off. In the words of a Whig newspaper, "William H. Seward, Esq., left this city for Auburn, his former and future residence, carrying with him the unfeigned and heartfelt wishes of thousands of our citizens for his happiness and prosperity."[1] In Auburn the welcome was equally warm.

Two days later the shingle reading "Wm. H. Seward" was hung at the Exchange Building on Genesee Street, where Seward had offices on the second floor. His junior partners were William Beach and George Underwood, each the son of an Auburn neighbor. Seward quickly attracted a coterie of young law students, who occupied the back room of the second-floor office. Years later one of them, James Cox, reminisced about his time as one of "the Governor's" clerks:

> Constantly interrupted during the day by the visits of inconsiderate friends and village politicians, [Seward's] most efficient labor was generally done at night. He would come into the office after supper, sit down in his writing-chair, and rapidly throw off [pages of manuscript] which would drop on the floor around him like the leaves of the forest. . . .
> We never knew him to be fatigued, or to claim allowance for exhaus-

tion. Yet, while thus laboring in the duties of his profession, he was all the while studying . . . the political condition of the country.[2]

As Auburn was still a town of consequence, Seward soon had all the legal business he could handle. But riches would never be his goal. Once Seward was able to pay off his debts, his interest in the law was limited to being able to meet his family's immediate needs. And although Seward was an astute bargainer on political issues, he disliked negotiating on financial matters. Fred would recall an instance when Henry decided to sell one of his horses. On examining the horse, the buyer began a pro forma recitation of the animal's shortcomings, complaining about his wind, gait, conformation, and hooves. Seward said nothing but shortly told the stable boy to take the horse away. When the horse dealer expressed surprise at this, Seward remarked that if the animal had all the faults alleged, he was not worth the dealer's buying or his selling.[3]

There was a reason why Henry had his office on Genesee Street— Frances would not allow him to have one at home. She had objected to the prospect of a home office, knowing that her house would be filled with cigar-smoking clients with muddy boots. But soon, predictably, Frances was complaining that she never saw Henry except at meals.

Frances may have been hard to please, but her lot was not an easy one. Judge Miller was an irascible paterfamilias; on one occasion he moved his bed into the living room and announced that he planned to sleep there all summer.[4] And her husband was all too free in offering hospitality. In 1843 Henry's parents, complete with maid, moved in for several months, arriving while Frances was visiting friends in Rochester. "My dear mother is comfortably bestowed in our little nursery-parlor," Henry wrote. "My father seems quite vigorous and cheerful."[5] When Henry's brother Jennings died, Jennings's son Clarence moved to Auburn and became part of Henry's family. The house was also a menagerie of sorts. Henry loved animals and birds, and the grounds of the house on South Street became a refuge for stray dogs and cats from far and near.

Frances was put to yet another test in the summer of 1843. John Quincy Adams, returning from a trip that had taken him as far as Montreal, had put Auburn on his itinerary. On his arrival there he was met by a torchlight parade that escorted him, naturally, to the Seward residence. Alas, Henry had failed to mention to Frances that Adams and his entourage would be staying at their house, so while Seward, in the garden, addressed a few words of greeting to the ex-president and his party, Frances put on a fresh dress for her guests. Henry's welcoming remarks, and Adams's reply, were drowned out by the anguished exclamations of Frances's aunt: "There goes a rose bush"—"They have broken one of the oleanders"—"The gates are down"—"The fence is falling."[6]

Henry would never be so attached to the Miller home as Frances was, but he delighted in the grounds and spent long hours improving the garden. In 1843, while Frances was visiting friends in Rochester, Henry gave her a report on his activities:

> You will scarcely recognize the place when you see it with so many of the trees cut down. . . . I took Augustus with me and two laborers into the woods, and brought home fifteen fine, thrifty elms. . . . I have engaged also fifty evergreens and a few mountain ash trees. . . . We have also set out choice gooseberries and raspberries in large quantities.[7]

Frances probably realized that although her husband was back in Auburn, his thoughts were as much of politics as they had ever been in Albany. Henry was devoted, on his own terms. Nevertheless, by the early 1840s Seward was growing closer to his children. The taciturn, seventeen-year-old Gus appeared interested in a military career. Frederick, four years younger, was much the best student of the boys. William Henry, born in 1839 and not much of a scholar, was the most outgoing of the three. The last of the Seward children, a girl, was born in 1844. Fanny Seward—so called to avoid confusing her with Frances, for whom she was named—would in time become her father's favorite. Henry had always been a faithful correspondent with his wife; now, when Holland Land Company business took him to the western part of the state, he wrote to his children as well.

In November 1844, told that his mother was dying, Seward traveled in haste to his parents' home in Florida. By the time he arrived, however, Mary Seward's condition had improved. Henry proceeded to New York City on some legal business and then returned to Auburn. But his mother had a relapse, and days after Frances gave birth to Fanny, Seward returned to Florida to assist with funeral arrangements. "My mother retained her memory, senses, and affections until the last," Henry wrote Frances. "Her last inquiry was whether there was a letter from me, and whether you had safely passed through your crisis."[8]

*   *   *

For all his family concerns, Seward never followed the political scene more closely than in 1843 and 1844. He and Weed exchanged long letters every week, Seward corresponded with Whig leaders across the state, and there were also speeches. Daniel Webster was scheduled to speak at one agricultural fair in Rochester, but at three o'clock in the afternoon the Divine Daniel was drunk. Seward, who was on hand, was asked to fill in. He described the events of the day to Weed with a certain smugness:

> [Webster] was at first disquieted, moody, and morose. . . . He author-
> ized himself to be announced to speak in the field at three o'clock. . . .
> All Western New York turned out at three to hear him. . . . The audi-
> ence sent forth their shouts for "Webster!" "Webster!" but he came
> not. The messengers went for him. He pleaded sickness, and the people
> called out for me to speak in his stead. It was kind in them, and they
> received what I said in kindness.[9]*

The appearance of the antislavery Liberty party in 1844 was a commentary on the divisions that beset the Whigs and the Democrats, and on the growing importance of the antislavery movement. Antislavery leaders several times sounded out Seward about running for president as the Liberty party candidate, but Seward refused to be tempted. He had an institutional loyalty to the Whig party that is curious, considering that party's brief existence and the diverse elements it housed. He also was adamant about not running for office in 1844 as a Whig. But Seward was deferring his ambitions, not scotching them. When Thurlow Weed, weary of Whig factionalism in New York State, threatened to retire from the *Albany Evening Journal,* Seward persuaded him to reconsider. He needed the Dictator.

Though Seward was a Clay man, he was not a committed one, for the presence of any slaveholder on the national Whig ticket threatened the party's prospects in New York State. When the Kentuckian gained the presidential nomination at an enthusiastic convention in Baltimore, Seward swallowed his misgivings and set out to demonstrate that his preference first for Scott and then for Harrison in 1840 had not reflected any personal animus toward Clay. But the Texas issue weighed heavily on Clay's candidacy, for Northern Whigs like Seward opposed annexation lest more slave states be carved out of the new territory. When,

---

*Although Seward in his letter does not charge Webster with drunkenness, others have been less charitable. Merrill D. Peterson, writing of this occasion, concludes: "If Webster was not already drunk, he became so at dinner that evening then, it was said, he fell into the arms of the mayor, who was presiding, after offering a toast." Merrill D. Peterson, *The Great Triumvirate* (New York: Oxford University Press, 1987), 394.

in April 1844, both Clay and his Democratic opponent, Van Buren, published letters opposing the immediate annexation of Texas, the net effect appeared to be a strengthening of Clay's candidacy. But the Democrats passed over Van Buren for the presidential nomination and instead chose dark horse James K. Polk, an ardent expansionist.

The election centered on Texas and on Henry Clay. As the year went on and popular sentiment for annexation increased, Clay modified his position, stating in July that, far from having any objection to the annexation of Texas, he would be glad to see it, if it could be accomplished "without dishonor, without war, [and] with the common consent of the Union."[10] Most antislavery Whigs had, like Seward, supported Clay and resisted any temptation to defect to the fledgling Liberty party and its candidate, James Birney. But Clay's waffling on the key issue of Texas began to drain away support. Seward tried to deal with this issue in a speech before an antislavery group in Syracuse:

> But you will say that Henry Clay is a slaveholder. So he is. I regret it as deeply as you do. I wish it were otherwise. But our conflict is not with one slaveholder, or with many, but with *slavery*. Henry Clay is our representative. You are opposed to the admission of Texas. . . . Will you resist it by voting for James G. Birney?

At the same time Seward, like many other thoughtful observers, saw the promised annexation of Texas as permitting the expansion of slavery. He put some distance between himself and Clay by making it clear that he was opposed to annexation:

> What will Texas cost? It will cost a war with Mexico—an unjust war—a war to extend the slave trade and the slave piracy—piracy in the judgment of Christendom. In such a war the nations of Europe and South America would decide against us, and the Almighty has no attribute which would induce him to bless our arms.[11]

In the end Clay lost the 1844 election because he lost New York. He lost the state—by some five thousand votes—because nearly sixteen thousand antislavery voters voted for Birney rather than for the Whig ticket. Seward appears to have labored valiantly for the cause, but he delivered many of his speeches for Clay out of state, apparently in the belief that New York was safe for the Whigs. Clay's defeat left his followers sullen and suspicious. In 1840 Seward had openly opposed their hero; it was hard to believe, four years later, that Seward was not somehow responsible for Clay's most galling campaign loss.

Texas was not the only cause of the Whig defeat. Anti-Catholic riots took place in several eastern cities, and German-born citizens, opposed to nativist sentiment among the Whigs, voted heavily Democratic. Denunciations of Seward by nativist Whigs prompted Henry's friend George Grier to write him a cautionary letter from Goshen. But if there was one issue on which Seward was totally committed it was immigrant rights. In his reply to Grier, Seward noted that if Grier could see "the kindness and affection bestowed upon me and hear the blessings invoked upon me in the cottages of the Exiles [that is, the Irish] . . . you would think I had purchased such affectionate regard cheaply enough."[12] Seward believed that the Whigs had lost in 1844 because of the nativists and because of Clay's equivocation on the slavery issue relative to Texas.

The year 1844 was a turning point for Seward. He had always planned a return to elective politics, but the new furor over Texas and the expansion of slavery presented him with an issue about which he felt strongly and one that promised political rewards. Even before the final election votes were tabulated, Seward wrote to a friend, Edward Stanbury: "Slavery is now, henceforth and forever among the elements of political action in the Republic. Let Mr. Clay treat it as he may, and be the results of this [election] what it may, the ground the public mind has traveled cannot be retraced."[13]

It was one thing to identify the most critical issue of the day; it was another for Seward to engineer his own return to politics. Although he might have run again for governor, such a step would not provide the national forum that Seward now sought. For the moment he wanted only to keep his options open, and he chose not to embrace the more antislavery elements. He and abolitionist Gerrit Smith maintained a friendly correspondence, and late in 1844 Seward assured him of his continuing interest "in the contest for Human Rights." But Seward's instincts were those of a mainstream politician, and he spurned Smith's overtures on behalf of the abolitionist Liberty party.[14]

When the second session of the Twenty-eighth Congress convened in December 1844, Tyler recommended that the annexation of Texas be consummated by a joint resolution of Congress. It was the first time a joint resolution had been employed to acquire territory, and it circumvented the opposition to the acquisition among Northern Whigs—opposition that would have precluded ratification by two-thirds of the Senate, as would have been required by a treaty. Slavery, in the form of the Texas question, was once again firming party lines.

Meanwhile, Seward was involved in a painful accident. He was returning by stagecoach to Auburn from Florida—the river was closed by ice—when his carriage lost a wheel, throwing Seward onto the hard-packed road. Strictly speaking, he was paying a price for his heavy smoking. Knowing that his cigars disturbed other passengers, Seward customarily rode on top of the stage with the driver, where his cigars offended no one and where the coachman was invariably willing to fill him in on local politics. When his coach lost a wheel, however, Seward was catapulted onto the road and suffered a dislocated shoulder and a severely bruised thigh. He was nursed back to health by a friendly Quaker family, but it was a week before he could be moved to Auburn and several weeks more before he could shave himself.

*   *   *

Henry and Frances were entering middle age. Henry began wearing reading glasses in his mid-forties and, after his carriage fall, took to using a cane when walking at night. Frances continued to suffer from a variety of ailments, to which were added dental problems that resulted in her acquiring an uncomfortable set of dentures. She sought relief in homeopathic medicine, despite Henry's insistence that such treatment was worthless. Convinced that Henry was away from home too much, Frances remained seldom willing to travel.

Meanwhile, Seward's law practice was as busy as ever. When Greeley's *New York Tribune* made a harsh attack on novelist James Fenimore Cooper, who was active in Democratic politics, Cooper sued for libel and Greeley enlisted Seward to lead his defense. Seward based his case on a broad construction of freedom of the press. "The conductors of the press have legitimate functions to perform," Seward told the jury, "and if they perform them honestly, fairly, and faithfully, they ought to be upheld, favored, and protected, rather than discouraged, embarrassed, and oppressed."[15]

Seward won an acquittal for his erratic editorial supporter, and Greeley was seemingly appreciative. But the initial rapport among Seward, Weed, and Greeley was already showing signs of strain. As practical politicians Seward and Weed were wary of their colleague's crusades on issues as varied as communal living and vegetarianism. Greeley, for his part, was developing an appetite for appointive office that neither Seward nor Weed was inclined to indulge. As Seward accepted congratulations for his successful pleading on Greeley's behalf, he could hardly have foreseen that Greeley's opposition would be a factor in his own failure to gain the Republican presidential nomination in 1860.

Early in 1846 Seward traveled to Washington in connection with two patent cases he was pleading before the Supreme Court. It was not his first visit to Washington. Seward was, however, sufficiently removed from national politics that his letters home have a certain wide-eyed quality. He recounted a long call on the venerable John Quincy Adams and another on General Scott, who, Seward reported, was preparing to run for the presidency. He called on President Polk but was not impressed; the president, he wrote Frances, "is a gentleman of fifty, of plain, unassuming manners and conversation, and does not at all inspire awe or respect."[16] Despite their past political rivalry, Seward was warmly received by the ex-governor of New York, William L. Marcy, now Polk's secretary of war.

The debate over possession of the Oregon Territory was in full cry during Seward's visit to the capital. Seward urged the Whigs in the New York congressional delegation to support Polk in his insistence that the joint Anglo-American occupation of the territory must end, but he stopped short of endorsing "Fifty-four Forty or Fight," the slogan of the most rabid expansionists. Later in the year, the crisis abated with the acceptance by both Washington and London of the forty-ninth parallel as the northern border of the Oregon Territory.

After taking care of his legal business, Seward made an excursion by boat to Richmond, Virginia. On his departure for Baltimore, again by water, a large group of slaves was herded on board the vessel. Seward watched them, huddled on the lower deck, with profound sympathy. Several hours downstream the blacks were transferred to another vessel for the trip to the slave markets of New Orleans. In Seward's words:

> The captain of our boat, seeing me intensely interested, turned to me and said, "Oh, sir, do not be concerned about them; they are the happiest people in the world!" I looked, and there they were—slaves, ill protected from the cold, fed capriciously on the commonest food—going from all that was dear to all that was terrible, and still they wept not. I thanked God that he had made them insensible.[17]

Although the crisis over the Northwest had eased, Texas was a different matter, and it soon appeared that the Polk administration was prepared for war in the interest of annexing Texas. Seward, ever the peaceful expansionist, was appalled, remarking in one speech that "I would not give one human life for all the continent that remains to be annexed."[18] But he urged the Whigs to be careful. If war broke out, the Whigs should not put themselves in a position of voting against measures required to support American soldiers in the field.

It was one thing to be a counselor to Whig officeholders; it was another for Seward to return to office himself. Henry set his sights on the United States Senate. If the Whigs could gain control of the New York legislature, 1849 could be his year.

7

"Hold Him to Be a Man"

AUBURN IN THE mid-1840s was still a place of consequence. With a population of about five thousand, it was larger than Rochester and about the same size as Syracuse. The town had, however, a split personality. It was an antislavery center, one of the stops on the Underground Railroad, and among its residents were a disproportionate number of prosperous professionals like Seward and his partners. But Auburn was also home to one of the state's two prisons, and the correctional facility was the town's leading employer. Moreover, for all Auburn's liberal politics, blacks were hardly better off there than elsewhere in the country. A dozen or so black families were largely confined to a section of town known as New Guinea. Black children were not permitted to go to school with whites.

Prison conditions throughout the United States were deplorable, and violence was endemic. In 1845 an inmate of the Auburn prison, Henry Wyatt, was indicted for the murder of a fellow convict. Wyatt, who was black, had no money and was unable to obtain counsel until Seward volunteered his services the day before the trial. After meeting with Wyatt, Seward became convinced that an insanity defense was warranted, despite the fact that it was extremely difficult to secure an acquittal on grounds of insanity. The judicial view of insanity reflected a widely held belief that each person, however eccentric, was responsible for his actions. This popular view coincided closely with the narrow legal definition of insanity—the so-called M'Naghten test—under which a person was considered legally sane if, at the time of his alleged crime, he knew that what he was about to do was unlawful. Insanity as a legal defense was in its infancy, and the public viewed it with skepticism.

Nevertheless Seward mustered sufficient evidence of Wyatt's diminished competence that, at his trial in February 1846, the result was a hung jury. A new trial was scheduled for June. Seward thereupon left Auburn on a long-scheduled trip as far west as the Mississippi. As a result, he was far away when Auburn experienced one of the most gruesome multiple killings the state had known.

William Freeman was a twenty-two-year-old black man who had been born and reared in "New Guinea." His father had died of "brain disease," his mother was an alcoholic, and two siblings were regarded as insane. In 1840, on testimony from another black, Freeman had been convicted—perhaps falsely—of stealing a horse. He had been sentenced to five years in the Auburn prison, where he proved a brooding, ugly prisoner. As a result he became a target for guard brutality; on one occasion he was struck with a plank and deafened in one ear.

After his release in September 1845 Freeman wandered about, talking of revenge. He misguidedly blamed his misfortunes on John Van Nest, a white farmer who lived outside Auburn and who Freeman came to believe owed him money. On the night of March 12, 1846, Freeman, armed with two knives, murdered Van Nest, his wife, and two others. With no escape plan, the assailant was apprehended the following day. He freely admitted to the killings and was returned to prison. The *Albany Argus* observed: "It was with the utmost difficulty that the people of Auburn could be prevented from executing summary justice upon the fiend in human shape."[1]

An immediate casualty of the popular reaction against Freeman was Seward's client, Henry Wyatt. Wyatt's second trial ended in conviction, and the prisoner was sentenced to hang. Popular feeling ran high against Seward, Wyatt's counsel, particularly when it became known that Freeman had attended portions of the first Wyatt trial and had listened to Seward's defense. While Seward made his way back to Auburn, his law partners were busy assuring the townspeople that he would have no part in Freeman's defense.

But Seward's colleagues overlooked the fact that there were in fact two William Henry Sewards. One was a politician—liberal in his sentiments but prudent and reluctant to get too far ahead of public opinion—while the other was an impulsive humanitarian, one who had been deeply impressed by the face of poverty in Ireland and Virginia. When Seward returned to Auburn, gossip circulated that "the Governor" was in fact prepared to defend Freeman. The mood was ugly. Seward was denounced in local bars and became the recipient of hate mail. His friends urged that he reconsider, if only on grounds that a successful defense of Freeman was impossible. But Seward stood his ground, writing to Weed:

> There is a busy war around me, to drive me from defending and securing a fair trial for the negro Freeman. People now rejoice that they did not lynch him; but they have all things prepared for . . . a mock trial. . . . He is deaf, deserted, ignorant, and his conduct is unexplainable on any principle of *sanity*. It is natural that he should turn to me to defend him. If he does, I shall do so.[2]

Judge Bowen Whiting had been ordered to Auburn to conduct the trials of Wyatt and Freeman. The Democratic administration in Albany, seeking to capitalize on the law-and-order sentiment inspired by Freeman's dark deed, sent Attorney General John Van Buren, son of the ex-president, to prosecute the case. On June 1 Whiting ordered a preliminary hearing to determine whether Freeman was competent to stand trial. The jury, under pressure from Whiting, concluded that the accused could tell right from wrong, and on July 10 Freeman went on trial for his life. Seward's request for a change of venue was denied. Because the preliminary hearing had determined that Freeman was sane for the purpose of standing trial, the trial itself centered on his competence at the time of the murders just three months before.

Seward and Van Buren each called on a succession of doctors who offered conflicting testimony concerning Freeman's mental state the previous March. On July 23 Seward began a marathon summary of the case on Freeman's behalf. Before a packed courtroom, he began with an acknowledgment of the biblical strictures against murder. If the prisoner was guilty of murder, Seward conceded that never had a murderer been more deserving of punishment. But he reminded the jury that the biblical injunction not to kill applied to jurors as well as to defendants. He asked the jury to consider the prisoner in terms of his obvious mental state. Freeman had not even understood the basic questions put to him in preparation for trial. "He is a convict, a pauper, a negro, without intellect, sense, or emotion." Seward asked the jury to put aside the matter of race:

> He is still your brother, and mine, in form and color accepted and approved by his Father, and yours, and mine, and bears equally with us the proudest inheritance of our race—the image of our Maker. Hold him to be a MAN. Exact of him all the responsibilities which should be exacted under like circumstances if he belonged to the Anglo-Saxon race.[3]

Seward evoked some technical and somewhat unconvincing legal precedents that might justify an acquittal by reason of insanity. He then attacked the traditional definition of insanity as far too narrow. Given the ills that afflicted mankind, why could a brain not be diseased, much as any other organ could be? Seward, far in advance of the medical and legal doctrine of his day, had some thoughts on this subject. "Although my definition would not perhaps be strictly accurate, I should pronounce insanity to be a derangement of the mind, character and conduct, resulting from bodily disease."

The defense dismissed the possibility that Freeman was capable of feigning insanity. Seward sought to compare the prisoner's behavior before his incarceration and brutalization with his subsequent behavior. An array of testimony from the black community testified to Freeman's having been, years earlier, a normal, good-natured teenager. Seward cited previous instances of insanity that had resulted from imprisonment and then recounted the brutality that had been visited on Freeman. He argued that the accumulated evidence demonstrated that Freeman's behavior had changed drastically during the period of his incarceration. He quoted approvingly a black witness who had testified: "They have made William Freeman what he is, a brute beast; they don't make anything else of our people but brute beasts; but when we violate their laws, then they want to punish us as if we were men."

Seward's eloquence was unavailing. The jury returned a guilty verdict after only an hour's deliberation, and the following day Judge Whiting sentenced Freeman to death. The defense immediately appealed, citing the court's prejudice against the prisoner. The state supreme court reviewed the case, concluded that the presiding judge had made serious errors, and ordered a new trial. Seward had won a partial victory, one that would prove to be a milestone in criminal law. He attempted to explain to Freeman himself what had transpired, but the prisoner's condition had deteriorated so badly that he could comprehend little of what his attorney told him. There would be no new trial for Freeman. Still in jail, he sank into a coma and died, nominally of tuberculosis.

The Freeman case was a turning point for Seward in several respects, not the least of which was domestic. Frances, as committed to Freeman's cause as her husband, assisted in the defense. Each evening during the trial Seward and his assistants met at the Miller residence, where a hurried supper was followed by conferences in the study. For once Frances had no complaints about cigar smoke and muddy boots, and as a result of her research she became something of an expert on insanity defenses. She wrote to her sister, Lazette: "I love Henry, but when I see him battle for principle and a human life and his convictions in the way he is doing here, then my adoration for him is beyond my capacity for description."[4]

Henry needed all the support he could marshal, for his participation in Freeman's defense had made him a controversial figure in Auburn. Never one to minimize his role, Henry wrote to one friend that he had been abandoned by every friend in and out of his hometown except for his family.[5] On the positive side, however, the Freeman case returned Seward to the public eye. A volume titled *Argument in Defense of William Freeman,* prepared from notes by Seward's secretary, Sam Blatchford, went through four printings. Although Seward's sympathy for Freeman was real, there was political appeal, too, in his ringing peroration at Freeman's preliminary hearing:

> In due time, gentlemen of the jury, when I shall have paid the debt of Nature, my remains will rest in your midst, with those of my kindred and neighbors. It is very possible they may be unhonored, neglected, spurned! But, perhaps, years hence, when the passion and excitement which now agitate this community shall have passed away, some wandering stranger, some lone exile, some Indian, some negro, may erect over them an humble stone; and thereon this epitaph, *"He was faithful."*[6]

*   *   *

Although his prosperous law practice was rapidly erasing the debts with which he had returned from Albany, Seward was becoming restless, for he was drawn irresistibly to politics. His views on subjects such as territorial expansion and black suffrage were well ahead of popular opinion, and this was a source of concern to Thurlow Weed. Seward, however, wrote to Weed, "I cannot, I will not change, to win the highest honor of the Republic. And you know I scorn any humbler one."[7]

Brave words, but how was Seward to reenter politics, much less achieve his lofty goals? He had no interest in another race for the governorship, which, even if successful, would have had overtones of a political plateau. He did not yet have the national stature that would permit a race for the presidency in 1848. But the Whig vice-presidential nomination was a possibility, and Seward worked at keeping a high profile. When the Irish independence leader Daniel O'Connell died in 1847, Seward delivered an eloquent eulogy and made sure that it received wide distribution. When John Quincy Adams died in 1848, Seward not only wrote a thoughtful eulogy but engaged a ghostwriter to help him expand it into a biography that was published in 1849.

Seward spent more time in Washington. He volunteered his legal services in a famous fugitive slave case involving one John Van Zandt, who lived on a farm near the Ohio River. In 1842 Van Zandt had assisted a group of escaped slaves. All but one of the fugitive slaves were eventually captured and returned to their owners, but their owner nevertheless sued Van Zandt for damages. Seward joined Ohio attorney Salmon P. Chase in appealing Van Zandt's case before the United States Supreme Court, and the spring of 1847 found Henry boarding at Coleman's Hotel in Washington. With Congress in recess, the city seemed lifeless and empty:

> I write with my window open. The beauty and fashion of the city are abroad; the pedestrians sweep the pavements which the wheels cover with dust. . . . Nothing could seem more indolent and wearisome than the life of this city population. Their occupation ends with the adjournment of Congress, and even their amusements. The capital of an empire of twenty millions sinks into a quiet country village.[8]

As Seward feared, the Supreme Court ultimately ruled against Van Zandt. Seward wrote Gerrit Smith that "a different [verdict] could hardly have been expected from a Court of which half the judges are Slaveholders."[9] Seward made a good impression on Chase, who would later be a colleague in Lincoln's cabinet. "I regard [Seward] as one of the very first public men in our country," Chase wrote. "Who but himself would have done what he did for the poor wretch Freeman?"[10]

While Seward had been defending Freeman, the country had gone to war. In January 1846 Polk had ordered Gen. Zachary Taylor to move his force into disputed territory near the Mexican border. When, in April, a Mexican force exchanged fire with Taylor's command, the Polk administration asked for a declaration of war. Although "manifest destiny" was very much in the air, the country was far from unanimous on the question of war. Although only fourteen congressmen voted against the declaration, sixty-seven Whigs voted against one of the initial war appropriations. Henry Clay spoke for many Whigs when he wrote: "A war between two neighboring Republics! Between them because the stronger one has possessed itself of territory claimed by the weaker! . . . This unhappy war would never have occurred if there had been a different [outcome to] the Presidential contest of 1844."[11]

Seward's feelings remained mixed. His support for expansionism was predicated on its being peaceful and on the acquisition of free territory, not new slave states. Although the Mexican War met neither of these criteria, there were mitigating factors. One was that the war had gone very well for Taylor's and Scott's armies. "Every military movement has been successful," Seward wrote, "and some have been brilliant; and yet the war is odious, and the Government [is] sinking under the divisions and discontents it has produced."[12]

The turmoil produced by the war was evident in Seward's own household. Since he was a boy Augustus had been interested in the army, and Winfield Scott had helped him obtain an appointment to West Point. Frances had protested, even to the point of urging Gus to resign before graduation. But Gus had paid no heed. When the Mexican War broke out after he had graduated, Frances was frantic with worry. She renewed her pleas that he resign. Ultimately Gus did spend six months in Mexico—and he simply stopped opening his mother's letters. During the war Frances's distress was such that Henry feared for her sanity. Even after the war she repeatedly pressed Henry to get their son out of the army.

The Mexican War posed a political dilemma for the Whigs. Notwithstanding their tepid support for the war, it was producing two heroes, Zachary Taylor and Winfield Scott, both of whom were thought to be Whigs. In the spring of 1846 Thurlow Weed, traveling to New York City by steamboat, had fallen into conversation with Col. Joseph Taylor, a brother of the victor of Palo Alto. Under questioning by Weed, Taylor advised that his brother had no strong political beliefs beyond a hearty loathing for Andrew Jackson. That was enough for Weed. Informing Taylor that his brother might well be the next president of the United States, Weed returned to Albany determined to make his prediction come true.[13]

Eighteen forty-seven turned into 1848. In France the commune ruled Paris. In Germany, Marx and Engels published the *Communist Manifesto*. Ireland continued to send a stream of emigrants, desperate to escape famine, to the New World. In America gold was discovered in California, and at Seneca Falls, New York, only a short distance from Auburn, a group of suffragists led by Lucretia Mott and Elizabeth Cady Stanton adopted a series of resolutions for women's rights.

In Auburn, Seward's law practice continued to grow. Although he changed partners with some frequency, two of his favorite associates were Christopher Morgan and Sam Blatchford, both of whom had read law in Seward's offices. Blatchford had been his private secretary for years, and Morgan had served two terms in Congress. By the late 1840s Seward and his partners were well established in the newly lucrative field of patent law. With his personal finances once more secure, Seward could return with confidence to his first love: politics.

*   *   *

The appearance of the Liberty party in 1840 was evidence that the two-party system in the United States was again under strain. Seward took comfort from divisions among the Democrats in New York State, but he was compelled to acknowledge that his own party was scarcely more unified. He and Weed, supportive of internal improvements and immigrant rights, and active in the fight against slavery, epitomized the party's progressive element. Arrayed against them, however, were conservatives such as Millard Fillmore and John Collier, who were opposed to immigration and who were critical of Seward and Greeley for supporting the tenants against the Hudson Valley landlords. Elsewhere, hard-core followers of Henry Clay still suspected that Seward and Weed were only lukewarm in support for their hero.

The Democrats held their national convention in May, but their meeting was unsettled by the issue raised earlier by an obscure Democratic congressman, David Wilmot of Pennsylvania. In August 1846, shortly after the outbreak of the Mexican War, Wilmot had added to an appropriations bill an amendment stating that slavery would be excluded from any territory acquired as a result of the war with Mexico. The proviso differed sharply from the position of the Polk administration, which proposed that slavery in the new lands be governed by the 38°30′ line of the Missouri Compromise. The Wilmot Proviso did not pass, but it had the effect of putting all new territory in limbo. Settlers in the American West were largely without government because Congress could not decide what to do about slavery there. Oregon was finally admitted as a free state, but no agreement was reached on California, New Mexico, or Utah.

Because of the slavery issue, the Democrats split sharply at their convention in Baltimore. Northern liberals were so outraged at the nomination of conservative Lew Cass, on a platform disavowing any interference with slavery, that they called a convention of the new Free-Soil party in protest. The new party nominated ex-president Martin Van Buren for president on a platform based on the Wilmot Proviso; it attracted Northern liberals as prominent as Charles Sumner, Charles Francis Adams, and Salmon P. Chase. The new party chose as its slogan, "Free soil, free speech, free labor, and free men."

At the Whig convention in June, the presidential contenders were Taylor, Scott, and the perennial Clay. As Seward had expected, the nomination went to Taylor on the fourth ballot, on a platform that consisted of little more than a recitation of his military successes. To appease the Clay men, disappointed yet again, the New York delegation successfully urged a Clay supporter, Millard Fillmore, for vice president. The conservative tone of the Whig convention was underscored when delegates voted down a resolution affirming the right of Congress to control slavery in the territories.

In time the Free-Soil party would include in its ranks "Conscience Whigs," who deplored their party's nomination of a slaveholder for president. But Seward would not be among them. Initially unhappy with the Taylor-Fillmore ticket, he stifled his discontent, probably because he saw a Whig victory in November as a vehicle for his own return to office. As summer turned into fall, he stumped the state for his party, warning Conscience Whigs that a vote for the Free-Soilers was "only a negative protest against the slavery party. Real friends of emancipation must not be content with protests. They must act wisely and efficiently."[14]

In September, Seward toured New England on behalf of the Whig ticket, attempting to set forth a viable policy on slavery. In Boston he was one of several Whigs who addressed a large audience at the Tremont Temple:

> On the slavery question, to this extent all Whigs agree: that slavery shall not be extended into any territory now free, and they are doubtless willing to go one step further—that it shall be abolished where it now exists under the immediate protection of the government. To these principles the Whigs are already pledged; and I trust that . . . the time will soon arrive when further demonstrations will be made against the institution of slavery.[15]

Seward was followed by Congressman Abraham Lincoln of Illinois, who delivered what Seward later called "a rambling story-telling speech, putting the audience in good humor, but avoiding any extended discussion of the slavery question."[16] This appears to have been the first meeting between the two. For all the difference in their backgrounds, their political views were quite close. Both were antislavery Whigs who nonetheless supported Zachary Taylor for president. The main issue on which they might have differed was Henry Clay; Lincoln was a great admirer of the Kentuckian, while Seward always worried about Clay's effect on Whig voters in New York.

The following night Lincoln and Seward found themselves sharing the same room in a Worcester, Massachusetts, hotel. In Seward's recollection: "We spent the greater part of the night talking, I insisting that the time had come for sharp definitions of opinion and boldness of utterance. Before we went to sleep Mr. Lincoln admitted that I was right in my anti-slavery position and principles."[17]

On election day the result in New York State once again proved decisive. The Whigs carried the state for Taylor and Fillmore over an opposition so divided that Van Buren and the Free-Soilers defeated the "regular" Democratic ticket headed by Lewis Cass. Ten percent of the vote nationally went to the Free-Soil party, evidence of the growing importance of the slavery issue. Within New York State, the Whigs elected Hamilton Fish governor and gained a majority in both houses of the legislature. Control of the legislature was important, for the Senate term of New Yorker John Dix was to end in March 1849, and the election results assured that Dix's successor would be a Whig.

Seward, with the popular recognition he had gained as a result of the Freeman trial and his speeches for Zachary Taylor, was clearly the front-runner. Millard Fillmore might have been a formidable rival, but he was now vice president–elect. The opposition to Seward coalesced instead around John Collier, whose supporters charged that Seward was far too liberal to work closely with the new Taylor administration. Weed was everywhere, however, buttonholing assemblymen and brandishing a letter from Joseph Taylor testifying to the high regard in which Seward was held by his brother Zachary. The outcome was in doubt for a time, but Collier was damaged by the appearance of a forged letter, purporting to be from Seward, which attacked several members of the legislature. Both Seward and the nominal recipient denounced it as a fake, to Seward's political benefit.

On February 6 Seward was elected over Collier by a vote of 121 to 32. For once even Frances rejoiced in her husband's political triumph; she had come to view Henry's success as a victory for humanity. Congratulations poured in, one of them from President Nott of Union College:

> It is by the defense of free principles, of the poor man's rights, that you have become what you are. Your future rise or fall must depend on your adherence to your principles, and the rise and fall of those principles. . . . You have no way but to continue [as freedom's] calm, courteous, but unflinching advocate.[18]

When Seward traveled to Washington, he discovered that, thanks to Weed's thorough preparation, he had easy access to the new president. Taylor even asked the freshman senator to review his inaugural address. Seward tried to be humble, but he was beginning to hear 'voices. Already there were those in the nation's capital who saw Seward himself as presidential material.

8

A Higher Law

THE WASHINGTON, D.C., to which the Sewards moved in 1849 was not popular with itinerant legislators. Whereas the capitals of Europe were important cultural centers, Washington was merely a patch of tropical swampland carved out of the state of Maryland. Charles Dickens, writing of his visit to the capital in 1842, told how "the hotel in which we live is a long row of small houses, fronting on the street and opening at the back upon a common yard, in which hangs a great triangle. Whenever a servant is wanted, somebody beats on this triangle from one stroke up to seven . . . and as all the servants are always being wanted, and none of them ever come, this enlivening engine is in full performance the whole day through."[1]

Dickens may have been fortunate that no farm animal responded to the bell. Many of the city's forty thousand residents owned pigs or cows, and these were allowed to roam freely during the day; normally, they sought out their owners only at feeding time. The federal government did little to improve the condition of the city's streets and sidewalks, and the municipal government was never able to raise sufficient funds, despite taxes on real estate and slaves, and license fees for dogs, theaters, carriages, and billiard tables.

The part of the city that mattered was bounded on the east by the Capitol and on the west by the White House. Antebellum Americans were less preoccupied with the presidency than their descendants would be, but for many visitors a trip to Washington nevertheless began with the President's House, as the executive mansion was known. Although the mansion was neither luxurious nor especially well maintained, it was an object of great interest to visitors, who marveled at its great

public rooms and ornate mirrors and carpets. Unfortunately, the south lawn bordered on one of the capital's main health hazards—an unsightly and malodorous sewage canal that separated Pennsylvania Avenue from the Mall. Few presidents elected to chance the dangers inherent in passing the summer in Washington.

Strolling eastward on Pennsylvania Avenue from the President's House, the visitor encountered the massive Treasury Department, which dwarfed the unpretentious Department of State on the corner of Fifteenth and F streets. The north side of Pennsylvania Avenue was marked by such hotels as the capital offered: the National, the Kirkwood, and Brown's. Their inadequacies would shortly lead two brothers, Joseph and Henry Willard, to try their hand at something better, and Willard's would ultimately become the hotel for the carriage trade. In 1849, however, the choice was very limited. On the north side, too, were the foreign legations. Connecticut Avenue made its way north of the President's House, but within blocks it disappeared into country so wild that residents could shoot rabbits in the area of today's Dupont Circle.

The south side of Pennsylvania Avenue was the "wrong" side. Ugly shops and shabby boardinghouses alternated with saloons and bordellos. Washington was a Southern town, and anyone seeking to replace a slave needed scarcely go farther than the Decatur House on Lafayette Park, behind which Gatsby's Auctions ran weekly slave sales. Southern legislators tended to be comfortable in Washington; Northern legislators were not.

A visitor continuing eastward would have passed the Patent Office and the Post Office, which occupied two of the corners at Seventh and F streets. On the Mall the red-brick Smithsonian Institution was under construction, as was the Washington Monument, for which the foundation stone had just been laid. Near the Capitol, a visitor could find shelter from the sun under elms that had been planted by Thomas Jefferson.

On Capitol Hill two new wings of the Capitol extended to the east and west. Sections of the marble columns that would eventually support the roof littered the grounds. The Capitol rotunda was still a great open space into which workmen would eventually place the dome, section by section. Also on the grounds was a statue of George Washington, sculpted in Rome by artist Horatio Greenough. When the work finally arrived, a bemused public found that Greenough had portrayed the Father of his Country as a Roman senator seated on a throne, wearing a toga and unclothed above the waist. Some people thought the yet-unfinished Capitol to be the most impressive building in Washington.

Frances Trollope, visiting the city in 1827, had commented that she had not expected to see so imposing a structure on the American side of the Atlantic.[2] Nonetheless a certain amount of imagination was still required to envisage the entire edifice, for the great marble wings were bare and unfurnished and the grounds defaced by wagons, lumber, and workmen's sheds.

Inside the building the 244-man House met in one chamber; in the other, more intimate, hall sat the 62-man Senate. The vaulted roof of the Senate chamber gave it excellent acoustics. The senators sat in rows at mahogany desks placed on semicircular platforms, each row elevated above the one in front. Although this arrangement was ideal for speechmaking, the building was deficient in other respects. Unless they were chairmen of standing committees, senators (like congressmen) had no staff. Indeed, they had no offices; except for work they might accomplish in vacant areas of the building or in the Library of Congress, senators transacted all their business at their desks on the floor. In an early letter to Frances, back in Auburn, Seward complained of favor seekers who had access to the Senate floor. "One insists on driving me, and another has offered to employ me as Counsel."[3]

As a new senator Seward had a limited choice of desk locations. He finally chose one next to Henry Clay—he was still attempting to persuade Clay's friends that he was not hostile to the Kentuckian—in the back row. There he had more privacy than most of his colleagues, yet he could still be heard in the chamber.

The Thirty-first Congress was a transitional one in antebellum politics. Although the old guard remained in command, the Thirty-first Congress would be the last to have the services of the triumvirate of Clay, Webster, and John C. Calhoun. Clay, now seventy-two years old, was still the dominant figure. His army of admirers could not yet accept the fact that he would never reach the presidency. Harriet Martineau, the English writer, was fascinated by the sight of Clay, seated on a sofa, holding forth in a soft, deliberate voice on the topics of the day.[4] Clay continued to command the personal friendship of many political rivals, but his bitterness over Taylor's nomination was such that his relations with the new administration were cool.

Dark-browed Daniel Webster still spoke for the conservative Whigs of New England. The Divine Daniel was widely regarded as the finest orator in the nation, but his personality was cold—the reverse of Clay's—and he had never been able to expand his political base beyond New England.

Calhoun, like Webster, was a sectional spokesman. The onetime nationalist, now frail and suffering from an incessant cough, was the champion of slaveholding in the new territories. It was he who had devised the scheme for admitting Texas into the Union by means of a simple joint resolution.

To these old lions were added senators of a younger generation just as eager to make their mark. Jefferson Davis of Mississippi, humorless and austere, was a rising spokesman for the South. Davis's principal rival among the Democrats was Stephen A. Douglas of Illinois. Thirty-two years old and scarcely more than five feet tall, Douglas was a florid, persuasive orator who could speak for hours at a stretch.

The Thirty-first Congress did not meet until November 1849, but the year was a busy one for Seward. Samuel Seward died in August, naming Henry and Goshen attorney George Grier co-executors. Henry inherited perhaps a third of his father's $300,000 estate. He was also named trustee for a number of his brothers, nieces, and nephews, so Henry's family responsibilities were destined to increase along with his political commitments. Under the terms of his father's will, Henry likewise became president of the Samuel S. Seward Institute in Florida, a vocational school the elder Seward founded two years before he died.

Frances could not be pried away from Auburn for any length of time, but she did help to settle Henry in Washington. In fact, for a time during the winter of 1849–50, Seward's entire family was with him— except for Gus, who had been posted to California. The Sewards rented a ten-room brick row house on F Street near Seventh for $400 per year. Considered to be in a good neighborhood and within walking distance of the Capitol, it had a backyard privy and drew its water from an adjoining well. As the core of their domestic staff, the Sewards brought two black servants from Auburn.

For a brief time Frances enjoyed being a senator's wife. She complained of Henry's entertaining but wrote her sister that ''there are evidences of refinement in the society here that I have never found elsewhere.''[5] Early in her husband's term she formed a warm friendship with the junior senator from Massachusetts, Charles Sumner. Frances found him a man of ''clear moral perceptions'' and ''so fearless a champion of human rights.''[6]

Frances was not above using Henry's position to further her own ends, and she did so in the matter of Gus's military postings. For her it was bad enough that he was in the army at all; that he was stationed in distant California was especially regrettable. Prodded by Frances, Henry called on the commanding general, Winfield Scott, early in the Taylor administration. Soon Gus was transferred to Washington. Wherever he was posted, however, Augustus Seward remained inscrutable. In contrast to dependable Fred and happy-go-lucky Will, Gus was taciturn and withdrawn and had few friends. Away from the family he rarely wrote; with them he rarely spoke. Henry attempted from time to time to draw Gus out of his shell, but his efforts were in vain.

While Henry felt close to Fred and Will, the apple of his eye was his only daughter, five-year-old Fanny. His affection was reciprocated in full; when Fanny was four, her mother wrote: "Fanny is her father's shadow—she cannot bear to have him leave the house."[7] Henry was off to Washington, but as soon as Fanny was old enough to write, the two would begin a correspondence that would last through her brief lifetime. Both parents worried about Fanny, whose health was frail from the outset. She was also shy and slow to make friends. In time, however, she came to share her parents' interest in literature.

Soon Washington began to pall for Frances, and she returned to Auburn, taking Fanny with her. The pattern of long separations that characterized the Sewards' marriage continued, even when Henry's work kept him in one place. Occasionally, gossip would link Henry with one or another femme fatale in the city, but there is no evidence that he was other than a faithful husband. And rarely can there have been two more devoted correspondents. "I am glad you like *David Copperfield,*" Frances wrote from Auburn, where she and Henry had played host to Charles Dickens eight years before. "Dickens has assuredly done much to make the world more loving and charitable."[8]

*   *   *

Seward was forty-eight years old when he arrived in Washington in 1849. The red hair of his youth had taken on a brownish tinge, but strangers still remarked on his youthful appearance. In a city where the behavior of politicians ran the gamut from unrelieved boorishness to affected dignity, the junior senator from New York was a fresh breeze— courteous, outgoing, and genial. By the standards of the day, however, he was unprepossessing in his manner and appearance. Not a fastidious dresser, Seward was usually to be found in a plain black suit that made him look like a prosperous accountant. A reporter for Greeley's *Tribune* analyzed the head shapes of Seward and Daniel Webster and found the New Yorker's wanting. Webster's "ample brow, broad forehead, and lofty bearing" reminded him, he said, of some literary giant. The same could hardly be said of Seward, who appeared "thin and studious" and had "a compact, well-made head, with nothing extraordinary about it to the casual observer."[9]

Nor did Seward fit the mold of the nineteenth-century orator. He spoke in a hoarse, flat voice that was often difficult to hear. He disdained the rhetorical flourishes of his colleagues in favor of restrained, often legalistic, expositions. The most striking aspect of a Seward speech was its close; when the New Yorker finished and sat down, he would invariably reach for his snuffbox, take a pinch, and blow his nose on an outsize yellow handkerchief.[10]

If Seward was bothered by any of these real or imagined deficiencies, he gave no sign. He sought to view his own performance with the same detachment that he brought to draft legislation. He was ambitious but he was also determined that neither success nor failure should disturb his equanimity. He saw little in Washington that he did not consider himself capable of managing. "It is very wonderful," he wrote Frances, "with how little wisdom government is carried on here."[11]

Seward had entered the Senate at a critical time. California, with President Taylor's encouragement, had applied for statehood with a new constitution prohibiting slavery. Up to that time, few Southerners had challenged a state's right to outlaw slavery. But the South had been shaken by the near passage of the Wilmot Proviso, aimed at prohibiting slavery in any territory acquired from Mexico. Now the governor and legislature of South Carolina spoke openly of a convention of Southern states as a prelude to secession. In the minds of some Southerners, containment of slavery meant the end; slavery must expand if it was to survive. The sectional animosity manifested itself in a bitter fight over the election of the Speaker of the House. Southern Whigs opposed the Whig candidate for Speaker, Robert Winthrop of Massachusetts, because the Whig caucus had refused to pledge opposition to the Wilmot Proviso. The House required three weeks and sixty-three ballots before it elected Howell Cobb of Georgia as Speaker.

As a junior member of the opposition in the Senate, Seward received no committee assignments. Nevertheless, he was in the unusual position of being perceived as the power behind a president, Taylor, who was anathema to many Northern voters. Was Seward, the liberal reformer, prepared to support the Southern slaveholder who occupied the White House? For the moment, Seward had chosen the path of party orthodoxy.

On the suggestion of Weed, who was widely credited with having brought about Taylor's nomination and election, Seward had written a letter to Whig editor James Watson Webb assuring him that he, Seward, could oppose slavery without opposing the Taylor administration. But Seward had not set himself an easy task, especially where patronage was involved. To whom was Taylor to turn for recommendations for office in New York State—his vice president, Fillmore, or the Whig senator from that state, Seward? The senator and the vice president met with Weed in Albany to see whether they could agree in advance on some formula for dividing the spoils. The meeting was amicable but inconclusive; both Seward and Fillmore were intent on building up a political following in the Empire State, and the vague assurances of goodwill agreed on in Albany would prove short lived.

Seward's first few days in Washington were unnerving, for the president, notwithstanding his obligations to Weed and Seward, had at first been inclined to leave all New York patronage to Fillmore. Seward pressed his own case with Taylor, exerting his charm and making good use of his earlier acquaintance with the president's brother, Joseph, and with Secretary of State John Clayton. Seward wrote Frances that he was trying to get along with Fillmore, but that the vice president "demands all for friends and associates and gives nothing, leaves nothing, for the great body of Whigs."[12]

Gradually Seward began to pull ahead in the patronage sweepstakes. Fillmore's supporters accused Seward of trickery in placing his nominee in the position of U.S. marshal for western New York. In response, Weed denied that he and Seward had allocated to Fillmore the post of naval officer for the Port of New York, and Seward secured the post for a wealthy supporter, Philip Hone. Finally, Seward pulled off a coup. He solicited and received a letter from Gov. Hamilton Fish, Thurlow Weed, and others of the state government advising that he, Seward, spoke for the Whigs of New York State. With this letter his ascendancy over Fillmore was complete.

Even as Seward consolidated his position with the Taylor administration, sectional bitterness in Congress was growing. Southern spokesmen asserted that either the passage of the Wilmot Proviso or the abolition of slavery in the District of Columbia would provide valid grounds for secession by the South. Abolitionists insisted that it was the North that should secede. To defuse this explosive situation Henry Clay now used his formidable powers of conciliation. On January 29, 1850, he rose in the Senate and proposed a series of resolutions on which he had been working and consulting for months. These provided for the admission of California as a free state; the organization of territorial governments in New Mexico and Utah, without mention of slavery; a new and stringent fugitive slave law; abolition of the slave trade in the District of Columbia; and assumption of the Texas debt by the federal government.

In a speech that lasted for the better part of two days, Clay appealed to the North for concessions and to the South for peace. He asked the North to forgo passing the Wilmot Proviso as such while achieving its substance, and in return to fulfill its obligation to return fugitive slaves. He reminded the South of the benefits inherent in the Union and warned against the delusion of peaceful secession. Above all Clay sought to rekindle a sense of nationality; the Constitution had been created not for any one generation "but for posterity."

Political leadership was to be looked for not in the White House but in the Capitol, and Clay's resolutions set the stage for one of those dramatic Senate debates that, in the nineteenth century, determined policy. It was a measure of Clay's adroitness that his compromise package came under attack from extremists in both the North and the South. Sen. Salmon P. Chase of Ohio saw it as "sentiment for the North, substance for the South," while Sen. Henry Foote of Mississippi— known as Hangman Foote because he had once vowed to hang Sen. John P. Hale of Maine—thought Clay's speech more odious than all the outpourings of the abolitionists. Nevertheless, in the words of one historian, Clay had "seized the initiative from the president, centered it in the Senate under his leadership, and set the legislative agenda for the country."[13]

Calhoun, haggard and emaciated, had to be helped to his seat during the weeks of debate that followed. In a speech delivered for him by James Mason of Virginia, the South Carolinian reminded his listeners that he had long feared that agitation over slavery would lead to disunion. He recited a litany of wrongs against the South: injurious tariff laws, the exclusion of slavery from new territories, violations of states' rights. In Calhoun's view, the Union could be preserved only by assuring the South that it could safely stay within it. Calhoun had no comprehensive program, only a gloomy rejection of Clay's proposals.

The next great voice to be heard was that of Daniel Webster. Before introducing his resolutions, Clay had solicited Webster's support. But the New Englander, whose constituency was a hotbed of abolitionism, had been noncommittal. Support for Clay's proposals, including as they did a fugitive slave law, would be violently assailed and might even end his political career. Nevertheless on March 7 Webster rose to deliver perhaps the most famous lines ever delivered in the U.S. Senate: "I wish to speak today not as a Massachusetts man, nor as a Northern man, but as an American. . . . I speak today for the preservation of the Union. Hear me for my cause!"[14] Viewing the situation much as Clay did, Webster supported the Kentuckian's proposals as a means of avert-

ing disunion, and in so doing brought on his own head the denunciations of the Northern literati such as Whittier and Emerson.

Seward was opposed to Clay's proposals from the first; he dismissed
them as "magnificent humbug" that would protect the slave interests.[15]
Because Zachary Taylor was known to oppose Clay—the slaveholder in
the White House was proving no friend of the South—Seward accorded
the compromise little chance, writing in February 1850 that "the storm
is blowing, [but] when it has spent, we shall admit California just as if
it had not rained at all."[16] One of Seward's first acts as a senator had
been to propose a measure that would guarantee a jury trial to fugitive
slaves; he could hardly now endorse a legislative package designed to
deny fugitive slaves all protection. But compromise was very much in
the air, and antislavery senators were a very small minority.

Seward had put much preparation into his first major speech in the
Senate. He was assured of attention, in part because he was said to be
a rising star, but primarily because his speech was part of a debate that
was riveting the nation. Henry showed his draft to a number of people
and sent a copy to Frances in Auburn. Frances Seward loathed politics,
devoutly wishing that her husband were not in Washington. But she
loathed slavery even more and thought his maiden speech splendid.

When Seward took the floor on March 11, the galleries were full. The
crowd, accustomed to the oratory of Clay and Webster, overflowed into
the lobby and the rotunda. Seward, reading from a prepared text, began
with a lengthy appeal for the admission of California as a free state, as
desired by the Taylor administration. Twirling his glasses in his left
hand while occasionally gesturing with the other, Seward spoke in such
a subdued monotone that the galleries began to empty. But the new
senator gained confidence as he went on, and soon the slight figure in
the black frock coat held the full attention of his peers. From California,
Seward moved on to the other portions of Clay's package:

> But it is insisted that the admission of California shall be attended by a
> compromise of questions which have arisen out of slavery. I am opposed
> to any such compromise in any way, and in all the forms in which it has
> been proposed. They involve the surrender of the exercise of judgment
> and conscience.[17]

In particular Seward balked at the proposed fugitive slave law; he
would not impose on others a chain that he would defy all human power
to lay on himself. Similarly it was not enough to abolish the slave *trade*
in the District of Columbia; slavery itself must be banished from the

capital. After denying, at some length, that slaveholders had a constitutional right to take slaves into the new territories, Seward made a point that would later be quoted out of context:

> The Constitution regulates our stewardship; the Constitution devotes the domain to union, to justice, to defense, to welfare, and to liberty. But there is a higher law than the Constitution, which regulates our authority over the domain, and devotes it to the same noble purposes. The territory is a part . . . of the common heritage of mankind, bestowed upon them by the Creator of the universe. We are his stewards, and must so discharge our trust as to secure, in the highest attainable degree, their happiness.

When Seward spoke of a "higher law" he did not, as his enemies would maintain, seek to disparage the law of the land. Rather, he sought to remind his audience that there was Caesar's law and there was God's law. It was from the law of God that man's law drew its sanction. This distinction did not sit well with those who had earlier heard the senator from New York argue that the Constitution gave Congress the right to legislate concerning slavery in the territories. Perhaps God had strong views on this subject that might take precedence over the Constitution?

Seward went on to refute the argument that compromise was required to preserve the Union. In his view, natural and economic factors made disunion impossible. Moreover, it was inconceivable that the Union might be sundered "to secure the institution of African slavery." It would not be the last time that Seward would underestimate the threat of secession.

Reaction to Seward's address largely followed sectional lines. Horace Greeley was extravagant in his praise. The American Anti-Slavery Society distributed ten thousand copies of the address. Dr. Nott wrote from Union College, "Your speech has made and left an impression that no other speech has."[18] In Auburn, Frances noted that a number of South Carolina clergymen had sent Henry copies of his speech together with insulting comments. She was inclined to believe that the offending clerics were Episcopalians, "as they are more opposed to progress . . . than most others."[19]

In New York City, Philip Hone found Seward's address "able," but "wild on the subject which ignites the country."[20] Sen. Willie Mangum of North Carolina warned President Taylor that if Seward spoke for the administration, he, Mangum, would go into opposition. An editorial in the Washington, D.C., *Republic* accused Seward of riding roughshod over the Constitution and attempting to legislate for God Almighty.

Seward's speech was a courageous—and in some eyes, foolhardy— act, for he had not cleared it with the White House. In effect the senator from New York was charting a course more liberal than anything espoused by the administration. The White House did not know what to make of the speech; Taylor himself was opposed to Clay's package, but he did not want to associate his administration with so extreme a position as Seward's. And Thurlow Weed was a problem. While the Albany boss conceded that the speech was eloquent, he feared it would divide the Whigs in New York State. His protégé had not sought his advice, and the thought rankled. Seward sought to appease his friend:

> Your apprehensions of evil [from the speech] have given me much pain. I have reflected upon the exigency upon which I spoke, and the question which demanded examination. . . . With the single exception of the argument in poor Freeman's case, it is the only speech I ever made that contains nothing that I could afford to strike out or qualify.[21]

But a price had to be paid. Many New York City merchants were irate over Seward's opposition to Clay's package, in part because they feared a loss of Southern trade. Businessmen called for a mass meeting in New York to encourage Congress to resolve the sectional impasse quickly. Some were so irate with Seward and Weed that they decided to fund a newspaper in Albany as a rival to Weed's *Evening Journal.*

If his "higher law" speech was a political albatross, Seward did not treat it as such. Demand for the text was overwhelming, and Seward sent out about fifty thousand copies. Horace Greeley reprinted it in full. The March 11 speech, in a single stroke, had made Seward the leading antislavery spokesman in the Senate. This was a mixed blessing, as Seward would discover. But for the moment the New Yorker felt the quiet pride of one who has said something that had to be said. He wrote to Weed, "I know that I have spoken words that will tell when I am dead, and even while I am living, for the benefit and blessing of mankind, and for myself this is consolation enough."[22]

9

The Flames of Kansas

CLAY'S COMPROMISE PACKAGE was the Senate's principal business during the spring and summer of 1850. At first, conservative Whigs and Democrats sought to pass a single "omnibus" bill that contained all the elements Clay had proposed. But the old soldier in the White House remained adamantly opposed to the package approach. So were many legislators, though many actually objected to only one or two features. Confusion on the Hill was compounded by divisions among both the Whigs and the Democrats over the slavery issue. In 1848 antislavery Democrats had deserted their candidate, Lewis Cass, for Martin Van Buren and the Free-Soil party. The nomination of a slaveholder, Taylor, by the Whigs had opened a schism between Conscience Whigs such as Charles Sumner, Salmon P. Chase, and Charles Francis Adams and more conservative Whigs, represented by Clay, Webster, and Fillmore.

As the Senate labored through the heat of a Washington summer, Henry's daily letters to Frances reflected his concerns:

> Every hour brings forth new developments, new fears, and new doubts. I am quite satisfied that the North is to be betrayed in the Senate. Mr. Cooper [Senator James Cooper of Pennsylvania] "came out" yesterday, going for the "Compromise." [Senator James] Shields has been flattered into the same course. I have no hope of [Stephen A.] Douglas and I begin to find that nobody is reliable, save those whom I know to have been sent here by the people upon a due examination of the question of freedom.[1]

Seward made a second major speech in opposition to the omnibus bill on July 2, but the balance of forces was about to be tipped not by oratory but by happenstance. On July 4 President Taylor listened under a hot sun to two hours of patriotic oratory while cooling himself with copious draughts of iced milk. When the president came down with gastroenteritis, the pestilential capital prepared to claim another victim. Taylor died on July 9 and was succeeded by Seward's rival, Millard Fillmore.

Amid the mourning for Old Rough and Ready, proponents of compromise could scarcely restrain their glee. Daniel Webster, a friend of compromise, became Fillmore's secretary of state, reportedly at Clay's behest. As for Seward, he went overnight from being one of the most influential figures in Washington to a junior senator thoroughly in eclipse. "The government is in the hands of Mr. Webster," Seward grumbled to Weed, "and Mr. Clay is its organ in Congress."[2]

Fillmore had earlier declared himself in favor of Clay's proposals, and in September the individual bills began to emerge. Stephen A. Douglas, never a believer in the omnibus strategy, separated the various elements and helped to organize a majority for each component. Many Northern Democrats joined Southern representatives in enacting a stronger fugitive slave law and in organizing New Mexico and Utah as territories without regard to slavery. Voting was for the most part along sectional rather than party lines. In the South the compromise strengthened the hands of Unionists. In the North it won acceptance from most Democrats and conservative Whigs—but Free-Soilers and Conscience Whigs denounced it in vitriolic terms.

Seward continued to oppose all aspects of the compromise except the admission of California. In much of the nation, however, the compromise held considerable appeal. A Whig administration appeared to have done what no party had accomplished earlier—settled the question of the extension of slavery. In New York State a Democratic convention applauded "the recent settlement by Congress of questions which have unhappily divided the people of these States."[3] When Congress adjourned at the end of September, Seward returned to Auburn to attend the wedding of his nephew Clarence and to mend some political fences.

Fillmore's accession ended the uneasy truce between the Fillmore and Seward-Weed factions in New York State. Relations between the principals were barely correct, and the president was being importuned for appointments by New Yorkers who had long considered themselves frozen out by Thurlow Weed. Fillmore's appointment of a new postmaster general effectively took away from the Seward-Weed organization all post office patronage. Printing contracts now went to conservative Whig newspapers.

Returning in December for the second session of Congress, Seward lay low on the issue of slavery. When Charles Sumner, in 1851, forced a Senate vote on repeal of the Fugitive Slave Act, he was supported by only three other senators, Seward not among them. Black editor Frederick Douglass, whose Rochester, New York, newspaper *The North Star,* received financial support from Seward, thought that he and other antislavery leaders had been "shorn of their moral strength."[4] Actually, Seward was only biding his time. In the interim he welcomed exiled Hungarian revolutionary Louis Kossuth to the capital, sponsoring a resolution in favor of Hungarian independence that ultimately passed both houses. In an apparent reference to the warm greeting given Kossuth, Seward wrote to his Goshen friend George Grier: "How strange that people will go mad *for* the freedom of *White* men, and mad *against* the freedom of black men. You can see in this great contradiction some excuse for me if I sometimes feel as little respect for public opinion as public opinion sometimes feels for me."[5]

Seward managed to put in a good word for the Irish whenever he could. The revolutionary agitation in France in 1848 had spilled over into Ireland, triggering an insurrection that had prompted the usual crackdown from London. Two Irish leaders, William O'Brien and Thomas Meagher, were convicted and sentenced to death, a sentence that was subsequently commuted to exile to Australia. In December 1851 Senator Foote of Mississippi introduced a motion in which he asked that the president negotiate with Britain to allow O'Brien and Meagher to settle in the United States. He was quickly joined by Seward. "The patriots of Ireland," Seward declared, "are suffering imprisonment in consequence of an effort, honestly made, to restore their native land to liberty and independence." Brushing aside any suggestion that the United States was interfering in Britain's affairs, Seward insisted that the Irish people "are affiliated to us, as we are to the people of Great Britain." Whenever a democratic revolution failed, be it in Hungary or Ireland, Seward maintained that the United States had a duty to open its doors to the unsuccessful revolutionaries.[6]

Back in Auburn, Seward tended to personal affairs. Gus was still in the army, but Fred was having doubts about the law as a profession. Henry discussed Fred's interests with Weed, and the latter, ever-accommodating, started Frederick on a career as a newspaper editor that the young man—his father's future assistant—found very congenial. Frances's father, Judge Miller, died in 1851, leaving Henry and Frances the sole proprietors of the South Street residence. At last the Sewards were financially secure. Henry's earlier investments in Chautauqua lands had entailed heavy debt, but now his holdings were yielding steady returns.

On a visit to Buffalo, Seward was detained for an extra day by bad weather. It all seemed serendipitous when he discovered that Charlotte Cushman was in town for a performance of *Romeo and Juliet.* Seward, who along with much of the country considered her the finest actress of the day, managed to obtain a ticket. Alas, the same storm that kept Seward in Buffalo had marooned the crews of several lake boats and canal barges, who were well represented in the standing-room-only crowd. The roughnecks took vocal exception to the fact that the famed Miss Cushman played the male lead, Romeo, rather than Juliet. Eventually, the audience became so disruptive that Seward returned to his hotel.[7]

*   *   *

In Washington, by the end of the year, the excitement of the spring had subsided. Times were good. Industry was booming, especially in the North, and railroads were supplanting canals as the favored form of transportation. Immigration was increasing, providing a continuing supply of labor but also fueling nativist sentiment in states like New York and New Jersey. High cotton prices made for prosperity in the South, even as they increased that region's dependence on slave labor.

In the Senate, Seward attempted to improve his delivery as a speaker. When time permitted he would write out a full draft of the address he planned. On the day he was to speak, however, he would leave the manuscript at home and speak from notes, developing his points as he went along, much as he had done as a trial lawyer. His gestures remained wooden, and even in the small Senate chamber his voice could not always be easily heard. Seward rationalized these shortcomings, telling his intimates that his speeches were meant to be read, not listened to.

On arriving in Washington Seward had announced self-righteously that he did not intend to deal in personalities. Considering the Senate's reputation for invective, this was a somewhat novel approach, but Seward made a real effort to abide by his pledge. After Mississippi's "Hangman" Foote had threatened to "currycomb" him in one exchange on the floor, Foote was astounded to receive an invitation from Seward to a dinner of terrapin, fried oysters, and roast duck. Shortly after Louisiana's Judah P. Benjamin finished excoriating Seward and his allies on the Senate floor, Seward buttonholed him in the aisle. "Benjamin," he remarked, "give me a cigar, and when your speech is printed send me a copy."[8].

When Frances was in Auburn, Henry could occasionally prevail on Fred and his wife, Anna, to come down to Washington for some social occasion. With or without Frances, Seward was a sought-after dinner guest. By the standards of the hard-drinking Senate he was a model of sobriety, but there was general agreement that his natural loquaciousness was enhanced by the flowing bowl. The vivacious Rose Greenhow, a prominent hostess whose path was destined to cross Seward's in less pleasant circumstances, once commented that while Seward was the soul of reticence during the workday, "after supper and under the influence of the generous gifts which the gods provide, [he is] the most genial and confidential of men."[9]

Off the floor Seward and the Jefferson Davises became friendly neighbors. One January, Varina Davis became critically ill after giving birth. The city was in the grip of a snowstorm, and word reached Seward that Mrs. Davis's nurse was unable to reach her through the blizzard. Although Seward had not yet met Mrs. Davis, he ordered his own carriage brought out and, after several mishaps, the nurse was conveyed to the Davis home.[10] Later, when Seward learned that his Mississippi colleague was in danger of losing an eye to an infection, he became a regular visitor to the Davis home. "There as an earnest, tender interest in his manner which was unmistakably genuine," Varina Davis wrote. "He was thoroughly sympathetic with human suffering, and would do the most unexpected kindnesses to those who would have anticipated the opposite only."[11]

There were times, however, when Seward lost patience. He himself knew that his supporters at home expected him to work on their behalf, and he labored diligently to assure that New York State received its share of government contracts. When so engaged, he did not require lectures from his colleagues on the obligations of statesmanship. On one occasion Seward asked the pompous Charles Sumner to support a subsidy for the New York–based Collins Steamship Line. When Sumner questioned the economic justification for the subsidy, Seward asked for his vote as a personal favor. Sumner loftily replied that he had not been sent to the Senate to get Seward reelected. Seward walked out, remarking: "Sumner, you're a damned fool." The two did not speak for months.[12]

* * *

The rivalry in New York between the competing Whig factions of Fillmore and Seward-Weed was hastening the party's collapse. On the local level, it was an unedifying squabble over appointments. A new postmaster general, Nathan Hall, set about replacing Seward-Weed appointees in New York State with Fillmore men. The collector for the Port of New York, Hugh Maxwell, initiated a purge of Taylor appointees who had been approved by Seward. Nor was the bloodletting confined to New York State; the editor of the *Detroit Tribune* complained that he had lost his government printing contract because of his paper's "Sewardism."[13]

Beyond the struggle for patronage, Fillmore and Seward differed on matters of substance. Fillmore saw the Whig party as a national organization that was in danger from antislavery zealots such as Seward. Preservation of the party required accommodation of its Southern wing. The new president had no strong personal feelings about slavery, other than knowing it was the one issue that could wreck his party. This perspective quite naturally had led Fillmore to support the Compromise of 1850.

Seward, too, had plans for the Whig party—he hoped it would take him to the presidency. But he insisted that the party take a stand against slavery. In September 1850 the Whig convention in Syracuse was a battleground for the contending Whig factions. The committee on resolutions, dominated by Fillmore men, endorsed the "finality" of the Compromise of 1850. But the Seward-Weed delegates promptly voted down these resolutions, substituting language that, while praising Fillmore, declared that "the thanks of the Whig party are especially due to William H. Seward" for his thoughtful expositions of Whig doctrine. When the delegates approved the substitute language, the Fillmore partisans walked out and the cleavage in the state party was deeper still.[14]

By 1852 both the Whigs and the Democrats were badly split. But whereas liberal Democrats, as a result of the Compromise of 1850, were inclined to return to the fold, the Whigs proved unable to reconcile their differences. Thurlow Weed concluded gloomily that 1852 was going to be a Democratic year and favored the nomination of a conservative Whig—either Fillmore or Webster—as a sacrificial offering. Seward was not convinced. Ever the optimist, he saw Gen. Winfield Scott as a possible reincarnation of William Henry Harrison—a military hero capable of rallying the voters.

The Democrats held their convention in Baltimore and after many ballots nominated dark horse Franklin Pierce, of New Hampshire, on a platform that pledged full support for the Compromise of 1850. The Whigs proceeded to nominate General Scott, notwithstanding rumors that the old warrior would only be Seward's pawn. But Seward did not have everything his way at the Whig convention. Much to his disgust, the party endorsed the Compromise of 1850, leaving liberal Whigs out in the cold. In November the Democrats won overwhelmingly in what proved to be the last election the Whigs would contest as a party.

The election debacle, in which the Whigs carried only four Northern states, speeded the party's process of disintegration. Southern Whigs were torn between loyalty to the Union and devotion to a way of life that depended on slavery. Most had supported the Compromise of 1850, and they remained deeply suspicious of the antislavery Northern Whigs.

Whereas Southern Democrats were comfortable under the leadership of a sympathetic Northerner like Pierce, Southern Whigs, since Calhoun's death, were expected to support a Whig party increasingly dominated by Seward and other Northern reformers.

There were other irritants. The Compromise of 1850 had not cured the nation's ills. The strengthened Fugitive Slave Act was a particular source of discord. Under it, a black claimed by his master, even after the passage of decades, was denied bail, trial by jury, and even the right to testify on his own behalf. Private individuals who, like Van Zandt, aided in a slave's escape or who refused to assist his pursuers, were subject to heavy fines or even imprisonment. In the North heartrending accounts of escaped slaves being returned to their masters assured that the issue of slavery would not be forgotten. So, too, did the publication of *Uncle Tom's Cabin*. Harriet Beecher Stowe's tale of slave life in the South, first published in 1852, hardly presented a balanced picture. But its propaganda effect has never been equaled by another American book.

In 1854 sectional issues broke open with the controversy over the Kansas-Nebraska Act. The political compromise reached in 1850 became a casualty of pressure for westward expansion. Following the additions of California and Oregon to the Union, the pressure to build more transcontinental railroads was intense. In the fashion of the day, Sen. Stephen A. Douglas had a financial interest both in western land and in several railroads. But until the land was organized as a territory, its appeal to settlers was limited, and until there were settlers there was little profit for the railroads. A Mississippi congressman complained that everyone talked about a railroad to California, but "in the name of God, how is the railroad to be made if you will never let people live on the lands through which the road passes?"[15]

Douglas, like Seward, believed that America's destiny was to expand ever westward. Unlike Seward, Douglas had little interest in whether new territories to the west were slave or free. He preferred free states to slave states, but was content to rely on physical and climatic factors to keep slavery out of Kansas and Nebraska. In contrast to colleagues like Seward and Sumner, he saw no moral dimension to the slavery issue.

In 1854 Douglas introduced a bill that would grant the vast Kansas-Nebraska area territorial status with the understanding that the issue of slavery would be resolved by its citizens in a referendum, a process that later became known as "squatter sovereignty." In his search for Southern support, Douglas framed his measure so that it included an explicit repeal of the Missouri Compromise of 1820, under which slavery was barred north of 36°30'.

Douglas's move caught Seward by surprise. The first version of the Nebraska bill, in January 1854, provided that Nebraska, when admitted as a state, could come in with or without slavery. Seward, writing to Frances, observed nonchalantly that "Mr. Douglas has introduced a bill for organizing the Nebraska Territory, going as far as the Democrats dare toward abolishing that provision of the Missouri Compromise which devoted all the new regions to freedom."[16] But the first bill did not meet the requirements of the Southerners whose votes Douglas needed, so the senator from Illinois rewrote his bill to include a specific repeal of the ban on slavery north of the Missouri line. In his pursuit of Southern votes, Douglas had opened a hornet's nest.

After his initial surprise Seward became one of the leaders of the opposition to repeal. In scores of letters he urged New Yorkers to sponsor public meetings on Kansas-Nebraska, and he sought to divide the South by pointing out to Southern Whigs the dangers in repudiating the Missouri Compromise. On February 17, Seward delivered a three-hour speech on the subject of Kansas-Nebraska. After painting a picture of the slave power in constant search for new conquests, he characterized Douglas's bill as illustrating the eternal conflict "between conservatism and progress, between truth and error, between right and wrong." He insisted that the Compromise of 1850 had not supplanted that of 1820, but suggested that compromise had only whetted the appetites of those who desired the expansion of slavery.[17]

Seward's address was warmly received by the anti-Nebraska forces. From Springfield, Illinois, attorney William Herndon wrote that Mr. Lincoln, his partner, thought it a splendid speech. Seward himself was pleased with it, having felt more at ease in its delivery than during previous efforts. Predictably, the address drew the ire of Southern fire-eaters. Sen. Andrew Pickens Butler of South Carolina insisted that Seward pretended to be in direct communication with the Divinity, but in fact was "like the condor that soars in the frozen regions of ethereal purity, yet lives on garbage and putrefaction."[18] At one point during the debate Douglas referred ambiguously to Seward's having used "that free nigger dodge." Seward is credited with the response, "Douglas, no one who spells Negro with two *g*s will ever be elected President of the United States."[19]

Considering the implications of the Kansas-Nebraska bill, it is remarkable that opposition to the measure proved so ineffectual. But with Douglas's energetic leadership in the Senate and Pierce's support in the White House, the South had powerful allies. When the Senate voted, it passed the Kansas-Nebraska bill 37 to 14. In the House, where reformist sentiment was better represented, the vote was closer, 113 to 100.

The Kansas-Nebraska Act struck the North like a thunderbolt, for in theory it opened the entire West to slavery. As Congress worked toward its close in June, antislavery men prepared to move the battle to the prairie itself. "Since there is no escaping your challenge," Seward told the victorious Kansas-Nebraska coalition, "I accept it in behalf of the cause of freedom. We will engage in competition for the virgin soil of Kansas, and God give the victory to the side which is stronger in numbers as it is in right."[20]

* * *

While Seward was dealing with issues of national import, the political partnership of Seward, Weed, and editor Horace Greeley was undergoing considerable strain. If Seward was an idealist, he was also a political realist who played politics by the rules. The peripatetic Greeley, in contrast, was attracted to every reformist experiment from communal living to temperance. By 1854, Greeley was upset with Seward and Weed as a result of their close relations with Henry Raymond, the proprietor of the recently established *New York Times*. But most of all, Greeley felt frustrated in his desire for office. He had repeatedly indicated his availability to Weed, only to be rebuffed.

In November 1854, after the Whigs had won a narrow victory in statewide elections in New York, Greeley wrote a letter to Seward in which he formally withdrew from the partnership. In a long recitation of grievances, Greeley complained of having been spurned in his ambition for public office and having been particularly pained by Weed's choice of his rival, Raymond, as the Whig candidate for lieutenant governor. Greeley professed high regard for Seward, but he indicated that the period of formal cooperation was over and that henceforth he would "take such course as seems best, without reference to the past."[21]

Seward found Greeley's letter disturbing; he complained to Weed that it was "full of sharp, pricking thorns." He asked Weed whether some state appointment might be offered to Greeley, but did not press the matter. Years later, long after Greeley had worked diligently to deny Seward the Republican presidential nomination, Seward was asked whether it might not have been better for Greeley to have been given some office. Blowing cigar smoke toward the ceiling, Seward concurred, replying, "I don't know but it would."[22]

* * *

The evidence is scant, but about this time Seward may have undergone another period of depression like the one he experienced while heavily in debt at the end of his second term as governor. He spoke openly of retirement. When Weed warned him of possible defections among those in the state legislature on whom he was counting for re-election, Seward instructed Weed vaguely to do whatever he thought best. Seward was weary of the stream of advice he received from Albany and took exception to some criticism from Weed about White House fever. For a time there was an estrangement between him and the Dictator. But the two were reconciled at the end of the year, bringing to a close what Seward described as "the most trying portion of my life."[23]

Weed applied himself with his customary energy to assuring his friend's reelection. Notwithstanding Seward's national prestige, he was strongly opposed by the nativists of his home state as well as by Democrats and conservative Whigs. To remind the legislators of Seward's antislavery record, Weed published in the *Albany Evening Journal* an intemperate article form the *Richmond Whig* blasting Seward as a threat to the nation. Hamilton Fish was among those who marveled at the partnership between Seward and Weed. "The history of their connection and intimacy is peculiar," Fish wrote to a Whig colleague, "and it exhibits many evidences of a disregard to self on the part of Weed. . . . All of this I respect and admire."[24]

Fortunately for Seward the opposition was unable to unite on any single opponent, and in the voting on February 6, 1855, the man from Auburn polled a majority in both houses. In the senate, he won 18 of the 31 votes, with the remainder scattered. In the assembly he received 69 of 126 votes cast. Seward wrote to Weed on February 7:

> I snatch a minute from the pressure of solicitations of lobby men, and congratulations of newly-made friends, to express not so much my deep and deepened gratitude to you, as my amazement at the magnitude and complexity of the dangers through which you have conducted our shattered bark; and the sagacity and skill with which you have saved us all from so imminent a wreck.[25]

The official election result noted simply: "William H. Seward was duly elected a Senator of the United States for six years, from the 4th of March, 1855."

10

"An Irrepressible Conflict"

SEWARD HAD A curious attitude about residence in Washington. Even when he had a reasonable prospect of living part of each year in the capital for the next six years, he refused to buy property there. Instead, on returning for his second Senate term, he leased a somewhat more gracious property on the corner of Twenty-first and G streets. The effect was to locate on the western edge of town more than a mile from the Capitol, but in a house that was much more spacious than its predecessor. The move from Auburn—in which Frances and the three youngest children joined him—was not an easy one. Seward complained to his clerk, Sam Blatchford, "I came here on Friday night [and] found Mrs. Seward shut up in her sick room, in a house half furnished, with a staff in the basement half organized."[1]

Gradually the house took on a lived-in look. Seward hung a portrait of Dr. Nott over the mantel, bought books for the library, and came to enjoy the spacious parlors and comfortable dining room. Soon he was once again playing the genial host. He loved an impromptu dinner—shad or venison or ham for a half dozen political friends—often followed by a game of whist. The wine flowed freely and the conversation sparkled. On more formal occasions, a dinner would last from six until ten o'clock, and might involve ten or more courses. After a second dessert of apples, nuts, and prunes, the ladies would retire, leaving the men to talk politics over brandy and cigars. Henry loved to talk and so did his guests. An evening at the Sewards' was rarely dull.

*　　*　　*

The Senate had undergone vast changes since Seward first entered it in 1849. The old lions—Clay, Webster, and Calhoun—were gone. In fact, only fourteen of the sixty men who had made up the Senate then remained. Whereas Seward in 1850 had only Chase of Ohio and John P. Hale of Maine as antislavery allies, he now found himself leading an informal coalition of a dozen Northern liberals. He was sufficiently senior to receive committee assignments, including one on the important Commerce Committee. Although Democrats still controlled the Senate, the winds of change were perceptible. "I think a mistake has been made in this Nebraska business," a New York Democrat complained. "The effect will be to consolidate the Whig party in the North & divide the Democrats."[2]

But it would not be the Whigs who benefited from the reaction to the Kansas-Nebraska controversy. In July 1854 a new party had been formed in Michigan opposed to any extension of slavery. The new party, which called itself Republican, was stronger in the Midwest than in the East and had yet to demonstrate any staying power. Liberal Whigs like Seward were not sure that any new party was called for, and Free-Soilers felt that theirs was the banner around which antislavery elements should rally. But the Republicans were the party of the future.

The timing of the new party's creation was unfortunate from Seward's perspective. He was up for reelection in 1855 and was dependent on some degree of cohesiveness among the Whigs of the New York legislature. Seward admired the Republicans' principles, but he had in mind not so much a new party as a rejuvenated Whig party, devoted to antislavery principles. Even in New York State, however, Whiggery had fallen on hard times. In August a gathering of antislavery factions at Saratoga adopted an anti-Nebraska platform, declaring that free and slave labor could not coexist. It stopped just short of embracing the Republicans, declaring that each state should act as it saw best in maintaining or discarding existing state organizations.

Seward hesitated. Supporters throughout the state wrote him pleading that he cut loose from the Whig organization. Sen. Henry Wilson of Massachusetts told Seward that, if he would abandon the Whig party, he would have Wilson's full support in a bid for the presidency. But Seward saw problems in the new group. It appeared likely to draw into it a variety of special interests, including temperance advocates, whom Seward kept at arm's length, and nativists, whom he abhorred.

In religion he was an Episcopalian, Seward was fond of proclaiming, and in politics he was a Whig. Seward had remained loyal to the Whigs for as long as an effective Whig organization existed; many felt he had been far too loyal. When asked in February 1856 to attend an organizational meeting for the new Republican party, Seward sent regrets. Part of Seward's problem was with the nativists—elements opposed to immigrants, especially Catholic immigrants. The two causes that Seward had championed throughout his political career were those of free labor and immigrant rights. In much of the East, however, there was a rising tide of resentment against immigrants. The Irish, in particular, tended to congregate in urban slums and to manifest a dangerous talent for political organization. There had long been nativist splinter groups, but in 1854 they coalesced as the American party, popularly called the Know-Nothings, and they were well represented among the Republicans as well.

Although the nativists were conservative, they could not be dismissed altogether as ethnic bigots. Much as the Anti-Masons had earlier attracted a generation of politically ambitious young men, so the Know-Nothings appealed to voters whose interests went beyond the Kansas-Nebraska Act. In New York there was enough opposition to Thurlow Weed's organization, and to Seward's "pro-Catholic" policies, to make the state a hotbed of Know-Nothing sentiment. The Know-Nothings lacked the strength to defeat their opponents without allies, as had been demonstrated by Seward's reelection; nonetheless, they were a group to be reckoned with.

Preston King, one of the founders of the new Republican party, told Seward early in 1856 that he could probably have the party's presidential nomination that year. He warned, though, that his running mate would in all likelihood be a nativist. Although noncommittal, Seward slammed no doors, and that spring he quietly allied himself with the Republicans.

The fact was that Henry had definitely been bitten by the presidential bug. As early as 1852 he had cooperated with a journalist, George Baker, who had put out a three-volume collection of Seward's speeches—a sure-fire indicator of White House ambitions. For people who might not require all three volumes Baker had produced a one-volume *Life and Works* in 1855 that was tantamount to a campaign biography. In Albany, Weed's *Evening Journal* touted Seward as the spiritual successor to John Quincy Adams. Although Greeley's *Tribune* was by then cool toward the man from Auburn, Seward was gaining the confidence of Henry Raymond, editor of the *New York Times*. The senator's office maintained a lengthy list of opinion makers, not all of them in New York, to whom Seward sent copies of his important speeches.

But what of the 1856 Republican nomination? No new party had ever gained the White House on its first try. There was also the question of party leadership to consider. In the early months of 1856 Seward saw the developing boom for explorer John Charles Frémont and fretted. Weed counseled restraint: Although the fulfillment of Seward's presidential ambitions was very much on Weed's mind, the time, in his view, was not ripe. When nativists began deserting the Know-Nothings in favor of the Republicans, Weed decided that the Republican nominee should be someone who would attract rather than repel the nativists.

June was convention month. The Democrats nominated a ticket headed by James Buchanan, a party warhorse who, as U.S. minister to Great Britain for four years, had been untainted by the Kansas-Nebraska controversy. The Republicans met subsequently in Philadelphia, where there appeared to be as much sentiment for Seward as for Frémont. When Sen. Henry Wilson, in a speech, suggested the possibility of nominating "the foremost statesman of America, William H. Seward," the convention broke into its greatest ovation yet.[3] James Watson Webb, editor of the New York *Courier and Inquirer* and a strong Seward supporter, begged Henry to accept the nomination. But Seward bowed to Weed's judgment, characteristically attempting to infuse a moral dimension into what had been a calculated political decision. He wrote Frances on June 17 that he had declined to allow his name to go before the delegates because they were not prepared to adopt his principles.[4] Ultimately the convention nominated Frémont, with William L. Dayton—regarded as acceptable to the Know-Nothings—as the vice-presidential candidate.

*   *   *

The opening of the Kansas Territory to settlement under Douglas's "popular sovereignty" formula put that concept under considerable stress. Almost by definition it triggered a race between pro- and antislavery forces to settle the territory. As a result the campaign of 1856 was waged against a backdrop unlike that of any previous election—called "Bleeding Kansas." Armed clashes between pro- and antislavery settlers led to the establishment of rival legislatures. When, in January 1856, President Pierce chose to recognize the proslavery territorial government, he in effect put the weight of his administration behind the admission of Kansas as a slave state.

By late spring the territory was in a state of civil war. The sacking of the town of Lawrence by proslavery "border ruffians," in particular, served to inflame opinion in the North. A few days later the abolitionist fanatic John Brown retaliated by leading a murderous guerrilla attack on a proslavery settlement, killing five men. In Washington the legislative debate on the future of Kansas proceeded in an atmosphere that grew increasingly strident. Seward was in his conciliatory mode, contending that talk of violence and civil war was uncalled for and that the Kansas issue could be resolved without endangering the Union. But as leader of the Senate Republicans, Seward introduced a bill calling for the immediate admission of Kansas under the Topeka antislavery constitution.

A problem with the Topeka constitution was that it had been drafted by a one-party convention called in defiance of the territorial government. Seward sought to dismiss the problem ("There can be no irregularity where there is no law prescribing what shall be regular"), but this argument carried more than a whiff of partisanship. In attempting to rally support for the Topeka constitution, however, he spoke with considerable eloquence:

Senators of the free states, you know . . . that slavery neither works mines and quarries, nor founds cities, nor builds ships, nor levies armies, nor mans navies. Why, then, will you insist on closing up this new territory of Kansas against all enriching streams of immigration, while you pour into it the turbid and poisonous waters of African slavery?[5]

For most of the summer the halls of Congress rang with the debate over Kansas, and Seward portrayed himself as a voice crying in the wilderness. A few years before, he reminded his listeners, he had been roundly castigated for opposing the Compromise of 1850, which was supposed to lay the slavery controversy to rest once and for all. Now, he maintained, the same Southern elements that had promoted the compromise were seeking to open new territory to slavery.

During the debate Charles Sumner prepared a bitter denunciation of the "slave oligarchy" for its attempt to take over Kansas. Sumner's speech included attacks on several senators, including the venerable Senator Butler of South Carolina. Before he delivered the speech, Sumner read it to Seward, who suggested that he tone it down and remove some of the personal references. Sumner paid no heed. On May 19 and 20 he delivered a tirade titled "The Crime Against Kansas." Two days later Congressman Preston Brooks, a relative of Senator Butler, accosted Sumner in the almost-deserted Senate chamber and beat him nearly to death with a cane. It is a measure of the passion of the day that, although some Southerners feared the propaganda effect of the assault on Sumner, public approval of Brooks's act was widespread in the South. The *Richmond Enquirer* called the attack "good in conception, better in execution. . . . The vulgar Abolitionists in the Senate are getting above themselves." Brooks himself remarked that "every Southern man sustains me. The fragments of the stick are begged for as *sacred relics.*"[6]

Seward deplored the assault on his colleague but felt that Sumner had provoked it—a view shared by many Northern moderates. Robert Winthrop, once a senator from Massachusetts, wrote Hamilton Fish that, however he deplored Brooks's assault, he hoped never again to read a speech in the Senate as distasteful as Sumner's. "Would that every member of the Senate, in his discussions, would take counsel of your distinguished colleague [Seward], whose speeches are not more remarkable for ability than for decorum, good temper [and] good taste."[7] Frances Seward, however, was indignant. Asked whether she thought that Brooks would hang if Sumner were to die, Frances was sure that he would not. Only slaves received such punishment in Washington, she maintained, and for them, hanging was sometimes viewed as too mild a penalty.[8]

Frances was back in Auburn, of course. Her widowed sister, Lazette Worden, had moved into the house on South Street, so that now Frances had some companionship when Henry was in Washington. Her symptoms, including depression, were worsening. Although she was convinced that her nerves were diseased—she undoubtedly suffered from some nervous disorder—her condition most likely involved an element of hypochondria as well. An evening at the home of the British minister, Francis Napier, had been marred by Frances's complaints that the gaslights made her feel as though she were in a furnace. Piano playing in the course of the evening upset her even further; she wrote to her sister that she would not go again to "so unsuitable a place." Henry took her out on carriage rides, but jouncing over rough pavement sometimes made her ill. Henry spoke to Sumner of his concern for Frances, remarking: "She is too noble a woman to think of parting from and too frail to hope to keep long."[9]

Seward, in need of both an assistant and a hostess, filled both posts from within the family. Fred, while working for Thurlow Weed in Albany, had met and married a local girl, Anna Wharton. The Fred Sewards were frequent visitors to Washington in the 1850s, and because of Frances's health problems, Anna increasingly served as her father-in-law's hostess for important functions. Over the winter of 1856–57, Seward invited Anna to assume the responsibility on a full-time basis ("Whoever does it cannot change session by session, much less week by week"), and the Frederick Sewards agreed. At the same time Fred became his father's principal legislative assistant.

* * *

The slavery issue came, over time, to nearly monopolize Seward's attention. Yet this very preoccupation grew out of a faculty rarely observed in the parochial United States Senate: a truly global perspective. Seward was not by instinct a philosopher. His recreational reading ran heavily toward Walter Scott and Charles Dickens. His speeches lacked the formidable classical references of Charles Sumner's. But he had a vision of America that stretched well into the next century—prosperous, democratic, and expanding not by conquest but by providing an example that the civilized world must inevitably emulate.

Seward the senator was as strong a supporter of economic development as he had been while governor of New York. He was the principal advocate in the Senate of a transatlantic cable, the brainchild of Cyrus W. Field. Early in 1857 Seward introduced a bill to subsidize the cable project. Debate was extensive but ultimately the bill passed. In less than two years the cable provided a tantalizing hint of its potential before parting in midocean.

The story was much the same on the transcontinental railroad. Since 1854, when he was placed on a special committee for the "Pacific railroad," Seward had lobbied for a line that would unite East and West. The political implications were considerable, for there were a number of feasible routes and every Western senator wanted a piece for his state. Year after year Seward urged his colleagues to see the project from a national perspective and to agree on a route and a subsidy. In 1859 he promoted the railroad as a means of unifying the nation in the face of regional differences over slavery. In the end, however, there would be no legislation until after the Civil War had broken out.

Although Seward tried to view international issues on their merits, domestic political considerations had a way of intruding. As a Republican and representative of a manufacturing state, he put aside a personal belief in free trade and supported a protective tariff. And while Seward believed strongly in the United States' "manifest destiny" to be the dominant power in North America, he opposed an effort by the Pierce administration to annex Cuba, on grounds that it would add more slave territory to the Union.

The senator was also a strong believer in the Monroe Doctrine. When reports reached the United States in 1856 that Britain was increasing its influence in Central America, Seward was among several senators who voiced concern. He interpreted the growing British presence in Honduras as a violation of the Clayton-Bulwer Treaty of 1850, in which Britain and the United States had agreed, among other provisions, not to colonize, or exercise dominion over, any portion of Central America.

Speaking in January 1856, Seward deplored the possibility of war with a "fraternal state" but insisted that the provisions of the Clayton-Bulwer Treaty must be upheld. He proposed notifying Britain that the United States would "interfere to prevent [Britain's] exercise of dominion in South America, if it shall not be discontinued within one year." If war came, Seward maintained, it would be fought in Canada and would probably result in the annexation of Canada. But he anticipated that, even without war, British influence in the Western Hemisphere would disappear within twenty-five to fifty years. Ultimately, British interest in Central America waned, and the United States turned a blind eye to the coaling station Britain maintained in British Honduras. But in London men like Palmerston and Gladstone took note of Seward's stand and concluded that the senator from New York was no friend of the Crown.

*   *   *

Seward was slow to involve himself in the 1856 election campaign, but in the fall he made a number of speeches. Should he speak of "the tariff, National Bank, and internal improvements, and the controversies of the Whigs and Democrats?" he asked one audience. "No," he replied, in answer to his own question. "They are past and gone. . . . Kansas . . . is the theme . . . and nothing else." The slaveholding class must be curbed, he maintained, for between slave and free labor there was "an ancient and eternal conflict."[10]

Although there was a Know-Nothing ticket, headed by Fillmore, the election in the North was between the Democrats and the Republicans. The Republicans insisted that all new territories must be free. The Democrats charged that Frémont was a Catholic and illegitimate to boot, and that the Republicans were dominated by extremists like Seward whose success would make secession inevitable.

The 1856 campaign generated more fervor than any election since 1840. Republicans marched in torchlight parades, chanting "Free soil, Free speech, Free men, Frémont." But Seward did not think that Frémont could win, and the results bore out his prediction. Buchanan carried fourteen slave states and five free states, with a total of 174 electoral votes. Frémont carried eleven free states, and Fillmore carried Maryland. Buchanan received only 45 percent of the popular vote and entered the White House with the most ephemeral of mandates. Seward might have proved a somewhat stronger candidate than Frémont, but Weed's hunch that 1856 was not to be a Republican year may well have been correct.

Buchanan took the oath of office on March 4, 1857, and two days later Chief Justice Roger B. Taney handed down his fateful decision in the celebrated Dred Scott case. A majority on the court held that the slave Scott was not a citizen of the United States and hence could not sue for his freedom in federal court. Adding insult to injury, the court also held that the Missouri Compromise was unconstitutional in that it effectively deprived slaveowners of their property without due process.

The case had been pending for years, and in 1856 abolitionist Lewis Tappan had asked Seward to associate himself with Scott's legal team. Seward had refused, perhaps because he was preoccupied with Kansas and with the incipient presidential campaign. Buchanan, in his inaugural, had predicted that the slavery issue would be "speedily and finally settled" by the Supreme Court. Buchanan spoke with some assurance, because he had been confidentially informed by two justices, Robert Grier and John Catron, that a decision was imminent and that it was inimical to Dred Scott.

In his anger over the court decision, Seward, in a speech some time later, charged that there had been active collusion between the president-elect and Southerners on the court in developing the Dred Scott decision. The day after Buchanan's inauguration, Seward alleged, "the judges, without even exchanging their silken robes for courtier's gowns, paid their salutations to the President, in the Executive palace."[11] Seward's charges caused an uproar and infuriated Chief Justice Taney, who said later that if Seward had been elected president he would have refused to administer the oath of office. "Shame, shame once more," cried Sen. Judah P. Benjamin, "upon the senator who makes charges like these without the shadow of a ground for their support."[12] Although Seward was unable to sustain his charges, there was some truth in them, for Buchanan, Grier, and Catron had all acted in contravention of accepted judicial ethics.

There seemed to be no end to the Kansas problem. Buchanan was under pressure from Southerners in his cabinet to recognize the "Lecompton constitution," which had been adopted by proslavery elements in Kansas. There was to be no popular vote on the constitution as a whole, and this perversion of his popular sovereignty doctrine so infuriated Douglas that he broke with the president. Republicans lined up to denounce Buchanan for his pro-Lecompton stance, but Seward did not join them. Notwithstanding his anger at the turn of events in Kansas, he was pleased at the prospect of a schism in the Democratic party and wanted to see it develop unhindered by the kind of Republican sniping that might bring a return of Democratic unity.

Not all Republicans were impressed with this logic. Senator Hale of Maine charged that Seward was remiss in not riding herd on Buchanan. Seward, stung, reacted in a speech of his own. Party regularity meant nothing to him, he remarked. "I know nothing, I care nothing, I never did, I never shall, for party." He sought only the nation's good, and this would be served by the admission of Kansas as a free state.[13] These remarks showed Seward at his worst—irritable and pedantic. Republican criticism led him to write a long letter to Richard Blatchford defending his stand. Seward compared the Republican party to a common scold, interested only in denouncing the wicked Democrats. His own policy, while he focused on the great issue of slavery, was to cooperate with the Democrats on lesser matters. In closing, he raised once again the threat of retirement. He had no political aspirations, Seward insisted, and would not accept reelection to the Senate.[14]*

Seward spent most of the summer of 1858 in Auburn, busy with law cases. Although he was besieged with invitations to speak on behalf of Republican candidates in the fall elections, his attention was concentrated on his own state. The Republicans had nominated a Weed protégé, Edwin D. Morgan, for governor, but the Know-Nothings, who had been denied second place on the ticket, were so incensed that they ran their own slate. When the abolitionists also fielded a separate ticket, Morgan's prospects appeared dim.

A defeat for Morgan would be a defeat for Seward and Weed at a time when the Republican national convention was only two years away. For this reason Seward made a number of speeches for the Republican ticket. The one that drew national attention came on October 25 at Rochester. Before an enthusiastic audience, Seward expounded a favorite theme: that the country rested on two radically different systems, one based on slave labor, the other on free. Improved communications, he maintained, were bringing these two systems increasingly into conflict.

---

*Seward had no intention of leaving the Senate, but when an aspiring journalist wrote to him in 1857 for career advice, Seward replied, "If I were young again & seeking where & how to lay foundations for life, I would go to Kansas. But I should expect to toil and struggle with frightful difficulties." WHS to ———, May 13, 1857, Schaffer Library, Union College.

Shall I tell you what this collision means? They who think that it is accidental, unnecessary, the work of interested or fanatical agitators, and therefore ephemeral, mistake the case altogether. It is an irrepressible conflict between opposing and enduring forces, and it means that the United States must and will, sooner or later, become either entirely a slave-holding nation or entirely a free-labor nation.

Seward then warned of how the South might succeed in extending the system of slave labor far beyond its existing limits:

By continued appliances of patronage and threats of disunion, they will keep a majority favorable to these designs in the Senate, where each state has an equal representation. Through that majority they will defeat, as they best can, the admission of free states and secure the admission of slave states. Under the protection of the judiciary, they will, on the principle of the Dred Scott case, carry slavery into all the territories of the United States, now existing and hereafter to be organized. . . . In a favorable juncture they will induce Congress to repeal the act of 1808, which prohibits the foreign slave trade, and so they will import from Africa . . . slaves enough to fill up the interior of the continent.

Seward's closing paragraph hinted at rising revolution:

I know, and you know, that a revolution has begun. . . . While the government of the United States, under the conduct of the Democratic party, has been all that time surrendering one plain and castle after another to slavery, the people of the United States have been no less steadily and perseveringly gathering together the forces with which to recover back again all the fields and castles that have been lost.[15]

Four months earlier, campaigning for the Illinois Republican nomination for the U.S. Senate, Abraham Lincoln had struck a note not unlike Seward's. "A house divided against itself cannot stand," Lincoln had pronounced. "I believe this government cannot endure permanently half *slave* and half *free*. I do not expect the Union to be dissolved—I do not expect the house to *fall*—but I do expect it will cease to be divided."[16] Lincoln's speech had prompted relatively little comment, although some of his friends thought it extreme.

Seward's Rochester speech, in contrast, inspired extensive comment. Although antislavery spokesmen praised it, Raymond's *New York Times* thought that Seward gave the impression that he sought the abolition of slavery by federal action. The Democratic press was vitriolic; the *New York Herald* called Seward an "arch agitator" more dangerous than abolitionists like Henry Ward Beecher, William Lloyd Garrison, or Theodore Parker. The different receptions accorded the speeches of Lincoln and Seward to some extent reflected their political prominence. Lincoln was a relative unknown, whereas Seward was the leader of his party. But quite apart from this fact, Lincoln's "house divided" was a philosophical look into the future, whereas Seward's "irrepressible conflict" was a call to arms.

Seward's task was an unenviable one. It was not easy to be the standard-bearer for the antislavery cause and still project the image of a leader who could be entrusted with the presidency in a deepening sectional crisis. A few days after the Rochester speech, he tried to back away from the apocalyptic implications of an "irrepressible conflict." In a speech at Rome, New York, he suggested that there might in fact be no overt conflict, because the slaveholders were now "subdued in spirit" and sustained only by the willingness of the Democratic party to act in their interest.

Whatever the long-term impact of Seward's speechmaking, the Republicans were victorious in New York State that fall, electing Morgan governor and sending a predominantly Republican delegation to Congress. For the moment Seward claimed to have no reservations about his Rochester address; he wrote to Theodore Parker that "I have great satisfaction in witnessing the contest that the slave-retainers have raised about it."[17] Some months later, however, Seward told Rose Greenhow that, if heaven would forgive him for stringing together two high-sounding words, he would never do it again.[18]

11

The Great Crusade

By 1858 the Republican party was a fixture on the political land-scape. Effectively barred from the South by its stand against slavery, it attempted to cater to the heterogeneous collection of factions that had been present at the party's creation: Northern Whigs, western Democrats angry over Kansas, abolitionists, ex-Free-Soilers, and a significant portion of former Know-Nothings.

The new party, if its platform was to be believed, posed no threat to slavery in the South. But its stand against any extension of slavery contrasted with the attempts of the Democratic party to cultivate both sides of the Mason-Dixon line. The Democrats' 1856 platform, on which James Buchanan had been elected president, endorsed the right of the people of all territories, acting through the "legally and fairly expressed will of the majority of the actual residents . . . to form a constitution with or without domestic slavery, and to be admitted into the Union."[1]

Inevitably fear and hubris were to be found on both sides. Northerners genuinely feared that the combination of a pro-Southern president and a sympathetic Supreme Court could permit the spread of slavery into most new states. Allied to this fear was a sense of outrage that slavery in America was not only surviving but flourishing. This anger manifested itself in impassioned assaults against the South and Southerners by antislavery extremists. Most Northerners were willing to leave slavery alone where it existed. But they were bitterly opposed to any expansion of the South's "peculiar institution" and deaf to tales of happy slaves and devoted masters.

Southerners' fears, which were related to their physical safety, were even more deep seated. The Nat Turner rebellion and isolated violence elsewhere had nourished fears of a slave insurrection. Only a fraction of Southern whites owned slaves, but many Southerners feared that emancipation would inevitably lead to racial integration and economic equality for blacks. As a result even nonslaveholders had an interest in sustaining the existing system. Moreover, Southerners of most political stripes resented the Northern view that slavery was cruel, immoral, and un-Christian. Were the immigrant laborers of the North any better off?

William Henry Seward was determined that 1860 would be his year, for he entered the presidential campaign with certain obvious assets. He had a national reputation, which only Chase among his convention rivals could even approach. He was widely regarded as one of the most learned men in the Senate. James Russell Lowell wrote that Seward, "more than any other man, combined in himself the moralist's [opposition] to slavery as a fact, the thinker's resentment of it as a theory, and the statist's distrust of it as a policy."[2] For one who had been in Washington for ten years, Seward had remarkably few personal enemies. And although he was in the forefront of the antislavery group in the Senate, he was not a flaming abolitionist in the mold of Charles Sumner or John P. Hale. In Thurlow Weed, moreover, he had a man who was widely regarded as the most astute political manager in the country.

At the same time Seward carried some heavy political baggage. Republicans who had formerly been Democrats tended to be suspicious of any partisan ex-Whig. Erstwhile Know-Nothings were especially antagonistic toward the New Yorker; most took the view that anyone would be preferable to Seward. And the senator's close association with Weed was itself a mixed blessing. The New York legislature was notoriously corrupt, prompting even Weed to remark on one occasion that he hoped never to see its like again. Yet the Dictator had been busily engaged in shepherding charters for various railroads through this same legislature, and it was widely believed that successful applicants were expected to contribute to the Seward campaign.

Finally there was the question of electability. Could a ticket led by Seward swing the "battleground" states of Illinois, New Jersey, and Pennsylvania? The vehemence of Southern hostility toward Seward may have intimidated some opinion makers, but rank-and-file Republicans, too, wondered whether the country would be best led by one who forecast irrepressible conflict. Northern liberals, many of whom admired Seward's erudite antislavery rhetoric, were also obliged to consider whether he was electable. In the year leading up to the Republican convention Seward had to show himself to be a man of principle, while demonstrating a capability to manage a sectional crisis if elected. It was a tall order.

The more extreme abolitionists were part of Seward's problem. For years they had predicted, and some had even sought, civil war. Kansas seemed a logical place to start, and fiery John Brown, for one, was willing to be the spark. Brown, a religious fanatic who was obsessed with the idea that slavery must be forcibly eradicated, was notorious for his 1856 raid against a proslavery community in Kansas in retaliation for the sacking of Lawrence, Kansas. By the spring of 1859 he was back east, the idol of radical reformers such as Gerrit Smith, Theodore Parker, and Thomas Wentworth Higginson. From these parlor liberals Brown raised the funds with which to finance a vaguely defined slave insurrection.

One of Brown's confidants was a British soldier of fortune living in upstate New York, Hugh Forbes. Brown and Forbes exchanged notes on military tactics, but Forbes, far from being converted to militant abolitionism, decided that Brown was a dangerous monomaniac. Forbes told Sen. Henry Wilson that Brown was planning some kind of a raid, and wrote in a similar vein to Seward. But Seward had other things on his mind; if he took any action on Forbes's warning, there is no record of it.[3]

* * *

Seward had reluctantly stayed out of the race for the Republican nomination in 1856, but the Seward-Weed team was going all out in 1860. Over the decades, despite occasional differences, Seward had become bound to Thurlow Weed by the closest of personal and political ties. Their skills and inclinations complemented one another; whereas Seward liked to focus on issues, Weed reveled in the nitty-gritty of political trading. The fact that Weed protected Seward's political base in New York was what allowed the man from Auburn to focus on critical issues in Washington. Weed's devotion to Seward was total, and now, as Seward began the final stage of his quest for the presidency, he put himself in the Dictator's hands.

The ability of any state boss to contribute to the campaigns of political allies was crucial to his success. Now, to further Seward's grand design and to compensate for his candidate's perceived weaknesses, Weed strove to make himself indispensable to Republican leaders in other states. Having ample funds, he financed their operations. He bankrolled Seward's campaign by soliciting contributions from businessmen and shaking down officeholders who were beholden to him for their positions. In

Albany lobbyists regularly importuned Weed to use his influence with the legislature on behalf of one measure or another, a service that generally required a contribution to Seward's campaign. If any of the moneys stuck to Weed's hands the record does not show it; all went to his good friend's campaign chest.

Equally zealous in his editorial role, Weed refuted in the *Albany Evening Journal* the old charges that Seward had been an extravagant governor and ridiculed rumors that he had somehow been associated with John Brown. Weed undertook to explain the "irrepressible conflict" speech, noting that if only the South would abandon its attempts to extend slavery, it would have nothing to fear from the North. But, Weed insisted, the Republicans could not allow the South's periodic threats of secession to dictate their actions. A stand against slavery must be made, and Seward was the man to make it.

Any national campaign required a string of supportive newspapers, which were the primary opinion molders of the day. Weed's *Evening Journal* was important, but less so than Raymond's *New York Times,* which, without formally endorsing Seward, was usually to be found in his corner. The "official" Seward organ in New York City was the *Courier and Enquirer,* but the combative reputation of its mercurial editor, James Watson Webb, limited its influence. The most powerful paper in the metropolis remained Greeley's *Tribune,* which, with a circulation of about two hundred thousand, was the most influential paper in the country. Weed tried assiduously to win Greeley back to the Seward cause, but the onetime junior partner in the Seward-Weed-Greeley triumvirate had other plans.

*   *   *

At this critical juncture Seward did the totally unexpected: He took an extended holiday. Making 1859 virtually a sabbatical year, he left for Europe, alone, in May, returning only in December. It was not as though he was turning his back on politics—his campaign was in good hands and it was considered poor form for a candidate to be too active on his own behalf. With many acquaintances in Europe, Seward probably felt that his political prospects would be helped by press coverage of the reception he expected to receive in the salons of England and France. But it says something about Seward that at this crucial time he was willing to leave his fate in the hands of others.

There was a poignant leave-taking in Auburn. Thirteen-year-old Fanny asked her father whether he would like to play whist on his last night, and Seward said he would. "As usual he played with me," Fanny wrote. "Dear, dear, Father."[4] The following day saw the loading of trunks into the family coach, and more farewells at the railroad depot. A week later Henry wrote Frances from New York City: "The sky is bright, and the waters are calm. The ship is strong and swift. ... . If it shall prove so you will not remain long without proof of my constant affection."[5]

Seward's departure on the *Ariel* was an important political event. Nearly three hundred invited guests, including Fred Seward and his wife, Anna, boarded the excursion boat that took Seward to the eighteen-hundred-ton paddle wheeler off Sandy Hook. As Seward transferred to the *Ariel* and was welcomed by the captain amid music and cheering, a second steamer pulled alongside to bid bon voyage to America's supposed next president. A band played "Hail to the Chief." As Fred described the scene to his mother, "And so the two steamships, side by side . . . with guns firing, bells ringing, handkerchiefs waving, flags flying, and people cheering, moved majestically out to sea."[6]

*　　*　　*

Much as Seward had predicted, the *Ariel* had a smooth crossing, reaching Southampton in twelve days. Once there Henry was the ever-observant traveler. He had planned to spend the greatest part of his time in France, but the hospitality he encountered in London led him to extend his stay in Britain to two months. Lord Palmerston entertained him at his home in Piccadilly, and Lord John Russell at his country estate, Pembroke Lodge. He attended the opening of Parliament and was made an honorary member of the Reform Club. When Queen Victoria was informed that court etiquette would prevent Seward from attending a court function because he had not been introduced at court, she arranged for a private presentation. Henry described the queen as "sturdy, small, unaffected and kind." But Seward retained mixed feelings about Britain and British society. In a letter to Frances he characterized Britain as "the wisest of the nations, though not the most learned, the strongest of nations, though not the most valorous, and the freest of nations, though not the most chivalrous."[7]

In France, Seward reflected on worldly glory at the tomb of Napoleon before traveling on by train to Rome and Naples. He deplored the anti-Semitism he found at the Vatican but concluded that Pius IX was a "good old man," perhaps because the pope expressed appreciation for Seward's attitude toward Catholics and wished him well in his hopes for "higher advancement."[8] From Naples, Seward went to Egypt and the Holy Land. Near Jerusalem he walked along the stream where David was said to have found the stones with which to arm his sling. He wrote Frances that he felt confident that the Jews would eventually triumph over the Muslims in the Holy Land.[9]

While Seward philosophized, dramatic developments were taking place in the United States. On October 16 John Brown, acting on a vague plan to establish a slave-free enclave in the Appalachians, led a band of sixteen whites and five blacks to Harpers Ferry, where he seized the federal arsenal. After two days of skirmishing Brown's little force was overrun and Brown himself captured. There could be no doubt about the outcome of the ensuing trial—Brown was quickly found guilty and sentenced to hang—but the affair at Harpers Ferry served to exacerbate hostility between North and South. Although responsible Northerners, including Abraham Lincoln, condemned the raid, there was also admiration for a brave man.

To the South, however, John Brown's raid was Seward's "irrepressible conflict" carried to its logical conclusion. Although no slave had voluntarily joined Brown at Harpers Ferry, Southerners recalled a recent, bloody slave insurrection on Haiti and shuddered. In the words of one proslavery paper, it was not Brown who was responsible for Harper's Ferry but men like Seward, Gerrit Smith, and Joshua Giddings, who "by their countenance and pecuniary aid have induced him thus to resort to arms to carry out their political schemes."[10] Sen. James Chesnut of South Carolina charged that Seward had instigated "much of the violence we have seen in the country." An advertisement in a Richmond, Virginia, newspaper offered $50,000 for the head of the "traitor" Seward.[11] Gov. James Letcher of Virginia, a relative moderate, urged the South to demand Seward's exclusion from the presidency on pain of secession. "The idea of permitting such a man to have control and direction of the army and navy of the United States, and the appointment of high judicial and executive officers . . . cannot be entertained by the South for a moment."[12]

Seward returned to New York City on December 28, 1859, having missed yet another Christmas with his family. Several hundred well-wishers braved the frigid weather to greet him, however, and Seward was doubtless warmed by the hundred-gun salute. He conferred briefly with Republican leaders at the Astor House and then headed for Auburn, where the town turned out in force. As if to challenge the winter gloom, streets were decorated, a band played, and schoolchildren received the day off. A procession of townspeople escorted Seward to South Street, where he spoke the obligatory few words. Although he had traveled four continents, Seward said, it was "not until now that I have found the place which, above all others, I admire and love the best." Auburn was the one place "where I am left free to act as an individual, and not in a representative and public character."[13]

The speech sounded positively presidential.

* * *

Congress had reconvened on December 5, just weeks before Seward's return and just three days after John Brown had been hanged. The air was filled with rancor, in part as a result of the John Brown affair and in part because, although the Democrats remained in control of the Senate, control of the House was very much in doubt. For Speaker the Republicans nominated Congressman John Sherman of Ohio, who was considered a moderate on the slavery issue. The Democrats were divided as to their own candidate but determined to deny the speakership to Sherman, who had associated himself publicly with a book critical of the South, Hinton Helper's influential *The Impending Crisis*.

Balloting went on for two months before the Republicans concluded that Sherman was unelectable. Once Sherman withdrew, the Republicans secured the election of a political nonentity, William Pennington of New Jersey, whose support for the Fugitive Slave Law made him sufficiently conservative to swing over a few crucial votes. But the election of a Speaker did not end the acrimony. In both houses members began arming themselves.

It was to this tense and cheerless atmosphere that Seward returned with the new year. His political opponents in the Senate were cool if not actively hostile. Fessenden of Maine wrote Hamilton Fish that of all the Democrats in the chamber, only Douglas had greeted Seward on his return. "Damn their impudence," Fessenden growled.[14] The candidate, however, was not looking for controversy. He spoke rarely, and when he did speak it was in a conciliatory vein. But after offering a resolution on February 21 for the admission of Kansas under its latest "Wyandot constitution," he let it be known that his speech in support of this resolution was to be a major address.

When Seward rose on the afternoon of February 29, the chamber and galleries were packed. The excitement was testimony both to the times and to Seward's reputation, for the audience could expect no Websterian declamation, only restrained argument. Seward began by addressing a favorite Southern theme: that slaves in the South were better off than the "servile" laboring class of the North. Seward said that, to avoid offense, he would characterize the North as consisting of "labor states" and the South as consisting of "capital states," because slaves in the

South were part of the economic capital of the region. This strained logic set the tone for Seward's speech, which made no mention of higher laws or irrepressible conflicts.

Seward urged the admission of Kansas under its antislavery Wyandot constitution, but he repudiated John Brown's "sedition and treason" in attempting to foment a "servile war." Reiterating that the Republicans had no intention of interfering with slavery where it existed, Seward deplored talk of disunion:

> Those who seek to awaken the terrors of disunion . . . have too hastily considered the conditions under which they are to make their attempt. Who believes that a Republican administration and Congress could practice tyranny under a Constitution which interposes so many checks as ours? Yet that tyranny must not only be practiced, but must be intolerable, and there must be no remaining hope for constitutional relief, before forcible resistance can find ground to stand on.[15]

Seward's speech represented an important shift in his position. Whereas previously he had implied that free and slave labor were incompatible, he now held out the prospect of coexistence between the sections, regardless of their different labor systems. The speech was a patent attempt by Seward to project a less radical image at the Republican convention, and Republican party organs generally applauded it. Democratic spokesmen were far less charitable. Stephen A. Douglas ridiculed Seward's labor-state/capital-state nomenclature and reminded the Senate of a speech Seward had delivered in 1848 in which he had said that slavery must be abolished, "and you and I must do it."[16]

The perceived need for Seward to modify some of his more extreme oratorical flights was damaging to his candidacy; he gave the impression of a politician trimming his sails, not a leader answering the call of a great movement. Nevertheless, as Seward positioned himself for a run for the presidency there were positive signs as well. Because there was little sentiment to renominate Frémont, the Republican nomination was wide open. None of Seward's potential rivals was so well known as the senator from New York, and Seward's moderately reformist position was probably close to that of a majority of the party rank and file. In April 1860 New York Republicans picked a delegation that was solid for Seward. The 70 votes of the New York delegation represented nearly a third of the 233 votes necessary for nomination.

Seward worried about the nativists, and it is a measure of his ambition that whereas in 1856 he had refused to consider running on the same ticket as a nativist, four years later he was ready to compromise. A few weeks before the Republican convention Seward raised with Weed the possibility of his running with Henry Winter Davis, a Maryland Know-Nothing who had turned Republican. But Weed's soundings generated opposition to any nativist on the ticket with Seward, and the Davis card went unplayed.

In Albany, Weed was hard at work. Of the doubtful states at the convention, Weed concluded that Seward had the best chance of gaining the Pennsylvania delegation, once it had cast a courtesy vote for its favorite son, Sen. Simon Cameron. Probably on Weed's suggestion, Seward paid a visit to Cameron in March. "He took me right to his house," Seward reported to Weed, "[and] told me all was right. He was for me—and Pennsylvania would be. It might happen that they would cast the first ballot for him, but he was not in, etc. He brought the whole legislature . . . to see me, feasted them gloriously, and they were in the main so generous as to embarrass me."[17]

But what of this fellow Lincoln? Like Seward, Lincoln had been slow to identify himself with the Republican party. He had nevertheless been considered as a running mate for Frémont in 1856, and he had gained a national reputation in his debates against Stephen A. Douglas in the senatorial campaign of 1858. As 1859 turned into 1860 Lincoln was most interested in another try for the Senate in 1864. But to keep his name before the public Lincoln sought to be Illinois's "favorite son" on the first ballot in Chicago. "I am not in a position where it would hurt much for me not to be nominated on the national ticket," Lincoln wrote to one of his managers, Norman Judd, "but I am where it would hurt for me not to get the Illinois delegates."[18] Judd, among others, thought Lincoln's aspirations far too modest.

In the spring of 1860 the country's attention was not yet centered on the Republicans. Rather, the focus was on Charleston, South Carolina, where the Democrats were attempting to pick a presidential candidate. Charleston was about as unhappy a convention site for Douglas as Chicago would prove to be for Seward; Southern Democrats felt duped by Douglas, whose popular-sovereignty doctrine had, over time, placed Kansas in the hands of antislavery men. Almost immediately the Democrats split over the party platform. When the platform as approved was judged too weak in guaranteeing slavery in the territories, delegations from five Southern states walked out. As a result, when balloting for the presidency began, neither Douglas nor any of his competitors could obtain a two-thirds majority. The convention adjourned, to meet on June 18 in the supposedly calmer atmosphere of Baltimore.

With the Democrats in such obvious disarray, prospects for the Republicans could hardly have been brighter. As convention time grew closer, Seward began to show signs of strain. When Joseph Medill wrote an article for the *Chicago Tribune* arguing that Lincoln was electable but that Seward was not, Seward summoned the reporter for a dressing down:

> [Seward] then proceeded to declare, with much heat of temper and expression, that if he was not nominated . . . at the ensuing convention, he would shake off the dust from his shoes, and retire from the service of an ungrateful party for the remainder of his days. He gave me to understand that he was the chief teacher of the principles of the Republican party before Lincoln was known other than as a country lawyer of Illinois. He considered himself as the logical candidate of the party for the presidency, and, if rejected for that position, he would give no more of his time and mind to its service.[19]

For the most part, however, Seward projected an impression of confidence, and there were many straws in the wind to justify his confidence. The Republican party saw to it that a half million copies of Seward's most recent, conciliatory Senate speech went out to the country. Samuel Bowles, editor of the influential *Springfield Republican,* wrote Weed that the Massachusetts delegation would be strongly for Seward. One of the New Yorker's rivals, Salmon P. Chase, concluded, "There seems to be at present a considerable set toward Seward."[20]

The candidate left Washington for Auburn on May 11. One of his last acts in the capital was to draft, with characteristic foresight, a farewell speech to be delivered in the Senate following his receipt of the presidential nomination. Like the town cannon on the Seward lawn, the speech would never be used.

12

Crisis

SEWARD PUT THE best possible face on his crushing defeat at Chicago, taking comfort in an outpouring of letters from well-wishers. His responses are interesting, for they reflect one of his more interesting traits: an ability to place developments that affected him personally in a broader perspective. To George Patterson, an old friend, he wrote that Patterson's letter was "one of some hundreds of the same kind which have made me more humble, more grateful and more content than I was before. I had not conceived all the depths . . . of the affection of my friends."[1] To another correspondent he wrote that if the result in Chicago was not the best to be hoped for, "yet how near it is to that great thing! . . . Who can certainly know that what has been done at Chicago will not prove better than what you desired to be done there."[2]

Seward considered his public service at an end, and for a time he avoided all public appearances. As time went on, however, his sense of humor reasserted itself. In one letter he commented that it was fortunate that he did not keep a diary, or there would be a record of his reaction to the news from Chicago. When Cyrus Field, the inventor of the transatlantic cable, sent him a letter of condolence, Seward replied that a wise man "might well seek rather to have his countrymen regret that he had not been President than be President."[3]

Frances was quietly pleased with the Chicago result. The prospect of life in the White House with her husband under constant scrutiny appalled her; she saw Henry's defeat for the Republican nomination as a hopeful sign—perhaps her peripatetic husband might now return to Auburn, where he belonged. There were probably words of sympathy for Henry, but Frances made her position clear: "Let those who are disposed to cavil . . . do as well as you have done. You have earned the right to a peaceful old age."[4]

Henry, though, was not yet ready for a rocking chair; indeed, for one whose outlook was normally magnanimous, he minced no words toward those who had sabotaged his candidacy in Chicago. With respect to Greeley, Seward allowed himself a small measure of revenge. He passed to Henry Raymond of the *New York Times* the letter from Greeley six years earlier in which the editor had ended the "partnership" with Seward and Weed after failing to receive a suitable appointment. So much, Raymond wrote, for Greeley's lofty professions of neutrality in opposing Seward at Chicago. The press campaign against Greeley, led by Raymond and Weed, probably prevented Greeley from being selected to fill the Senate seat vacated by Seward.

Meanwhile letters from disappointed Irrepressibles continued to pour into Auburn. Many expressed distrust of the relatively unknown Lincoln; virtually all urged Seward to remain active in politics. Whatever he decided, Seward was obliged to return to Washington for the new session of the Thirty-sixth Congress. It was an ordeal, even though old foes like Jefferson Davis and James Mason seemed genuine in their expressions of sympathy.

In due course Seward announced his support for the Republican ticket of Lincoln and Maine Senator Hannibal Hamlin, and urged his followers to work for a Republican victory. The upcoming campaign was proving to be a major political upheaval. The response of Southern Democrats to the nomination of Stephen A. Douglas had been to launch a sectional ticket led by Buchanan's vice president, John C. Breckinridge. At the same time, a group of conservative former Whigs had named a Constitutional Unionist ticket that carefully took no stand whatever on slavery. In essence, there were two separate elections: Lincoln versus Douglas in the North, and Breckinridge versus Bell in the South. Breckinridge, Bell, and especially Douglas were political veterans whose records were well known to the electorate. The unknown factor was Abraham Lincoln.

Although Douglas had been repudiated by the Buchanan administration, he was believed at the outset of the campaign to have a good chance in states that accounted for 140 of the total 303 electoral votes. If the Republicans could be denied New York's 35 electoral votes, there was even a possibility that the election might be thrown into the House of Representatives. But this was an unlikely scenario; the electoral arithmetic strongly favored the Republicans, even though they did not field their ticket in ten Southern states.

By 1860 the South was paranoid concerning its minority status. John Brown's raid had touched a raw nerve, and no assurances from Lincoln or Seward about noninterference with slavery in the states could diminish the South's anxiety. Not only did the people of the Deep South feel misunderstood, they had canonized an interpretation of the Constitution that maximized the autonomy of the states. In this view each state, when ratifying the Constitution, had authorized the federal government to administer certain collective functions but had never transferred sovereignty. Several states, most often South Carolina, had threatened secession in the past, and to Southerners such action was as constitutional in 1860 as it had been constitutional before. Throughout the summer and fall of 1860, Southern governors corresponded about the timing of secession in the event of Lincoln's election. A Georgia newspaper warned: "Let the consequences be what they may—whether the Potomac is crimsoned in human gore, and Pennsylvania Avenue is paved ten fathoms deep with mangled bodies . . . the South will never submit to such humiliation and degradation as the inauguration of Abraham Lincoln."[5]

To Republicans, however, such threats were old hat. In every election since 1852 there had been some threat of secession, and nothing had come of it. In emphasizing that he did not intend to interfere with slavery where it existed, Lincoln believed that he had said all that he could to appease the South. James Russell Lowell called the threats of secession the "old mumbo-jumbo." Seward declared that the slave power, "with feeble and muttering voice," was threatening to tear the Union asunder. "But who is afraid?" he asked. "Nobody's afraid," he replied.[6] If there was to be a crisis, Seward felt that it would be manageable.

While Lincoln stayed close to home, greeting delegations in Springfield, Seward became active in the campaign. Thurlow Weed had visited Lincoln in Springfield shortly after the Chicago convention and, after a long conference on campaign strategy, had come away impressed. Seward was in Auburn for most of June, for the marriage of his youngest son Will, but in August he made a trip through New England in support of the Republican ticket. Seward was being pressed to visit the Midwest as well, and while in Massachusetts he signed up Charles Francis Adams, Jr., the son of the Massachusetts congressman, as one of a growing entourage for a swing through the West. The heterogeneous group included George Baker, Seward's admiring biographer; Fanny Seward and a young friend; and Gen. James Nye, the president of the New York City police board, along with Nye's daughter. The schedule called for Seward to start in Michigan and to travel by rail through Wisconsin, Minnesota, Iowa, Kansas, and Illinois.

For young Adams, the trip was an eye-opener. Although Nye had the reputation of being a heavy drinker, Adams was startled at the quantity of alcohol consumed by the group as a whole. He never saw Seward in "anything approaching drunkenness," but he noted that brandy and water at times made him talkative. Both Seward and Adams were smokers and, out of consideration for their fellow travelers, the two occasionally took refuge in the baggage car. "The early morning sun shone on Seward," recalled Adams, "wrapped in a strange and indescribable Syrian cashmere coat, and my humble self, puffing our morning cigars in a baggage-car, having rendered ourselves, as he expressed it, 'independent on this tobacco question.' "[7]

Adams found Seward a delightful traveling companion but wondered how he found time to prepare "the really remarkable speeches" he delivered during the campaign swing. In fact, the majority of Seward's addresses were visionary evocations of the greatness that lay ahead for a united America. His tone was so nonpartisan that at some stops he entirely neglected to mention the Lincoln-Hamlin ticket. At Madison, Wisconsin, he suggested that the agitation over slavery would disappear as other matters assumed greater priority. If the sections could agree that slavery must never enter the territories, "that will end the irrepressible conflict."[8]

In the months leading up to the Republican convention, Seward had muted his antislavery rhetoric in the belief that a more moderate image would help his prospects for the presidential nomination. Now, with disunion a very real threat, he used language in Detroit aimed at calming Southern fears of a Republican administration in which Seward would probably be one of the principal players:

> The great fact is now fully realized that the African race here is a foreign and feeble element, . . . incapable of assimilation. . . . It is a pitiful exotic unnecessarily transplanted into our fields, and which it is unprofitable to cultivate at the cost of the desolation of the native vineyard.[9]

Not even the threat of imminent secession detracted from the quadrennial campaign hoopla. To supplement the standard fare of rallies, mass meetings, and picnics, the Republicans in 1860 created a network of "Wide-Awakes"—organized supporters who drilled and marched for the Lincoln-Hamlin ticket. Nothing quite like them had ever been seen in an American election. Wearing brightly colored caps and carrying oil torches and bright lanterns, they swung through countless towns to the crash of brass bands and the sound of cadenced cheering.

For Seward a typical whistle-stop began with music and a welcoming speech by a local dignitary, often followed by a parade of local Wide-Awakes. Then Seward himself held forth. In St. Paul, he broadened his theme, offering some prophetic remarks on the subject of Alaska's destiny:

> Standing here and looking far off into the Northwest, I see the Russian as he busily occupies himself in establishing seaports and towns and fortifications on the verge of this continent . . . and I can say, "Go on, and build up your outposts all along the coast, even up to the Arctic ocean— they will yet become the outposts of my own country."[10]

At Springfield, Illinois, Abraham Lincoln came to the depot to greet Seward and his party. Adams found the candidate "shy to a degree, and very awkward in manner." The occasion was a bit strained, as the Republican candidate briefly discussed campaign strategy with the man who had expected to be in his place. In Adams's judgment, Seward, too, appeared ill at ease.[11]

There was no telling whom you might run into with the Seward campaign party. On one stretch the train added a rudimentary sleeping car comprising tiers of bunks on each side of the aisle. One night, when the train reached Toledo, Ohio, Adams was awakened by the sound of loud cheering from a group that had just been addressed by Democratic candidate Douglas:

> I heard someone rush into the car and inquire in a loud voice, "Where's Seward?" The Governor's berth was pointed out, the inquirer stating that he was Mr. Douglas, and he at once rushed up to it, thrust the curtains aside, and exclaimed, "Come, Governor, they want to see you; come out and speak to the boys!" To this Seward replied in a drowsy voice, "How are you, Judge? No; I can't go out. I'm sleepy." "Well, what of that," said Douglas; "they get me out when I'm sleepy." Seward, however, simply said he shouldn't go out, to which Douglas replied, "Well! if you don't want to you shan't," and withdrew.[12]

Adams noted that Douglas had had a bottle of whiskey with him, and the following morning Adams was told that the Democratic candidate had been "plainly drunk."

New York State was one of a handful of states in which the Democrats ran "fusion" tickets aimed at consolidating the split tickets and denying

Lincoln a majority in the electoral college. The last flickering hope of Lincoln's opponents was that a Republican defeat in New York State might throw the election into the House of Representatives. From Auburn, Seward wrote Lincoln on October 4 that he was confident as to the result in his own state.[13] Although exhausted by his travels, Seward, at Weed's behest, delivered an address at the Palace Garden in New York City four days before the election. His remarks were unexceptional, but such was the popular frenzy near the close of the campaign that he received a thunderous ovation.

On election day Lincoln won less than 40 percent of the popular vote but carried the electoral college by a substantial majority. Thanks to the Republican victory in New York by some fifty thousand votes, the combined electoral vote of Lincoln's three opponents, 123, fell considerably short of the 180 cast for the Republicans. Significantly, the Republicans did not gain control of either house of Congress, losing nine House seats while gaining just five in the Senate. As Douglas pointed out, if the Southerners occupied their seats in Congress, the new president could end up as "an object of pity and commiseration."[14]

Amid the celebration of the Republican victory, Seward must have looked back with bitterness at the convention in Chicago that had determined that Lincoln, not he, would guide the country's destiny over the next four years. Certainly Seward's followers did. One Caleb Henry wrote to Seward just days after the election:

> While I am bound to rejoice in the triumph of the Great Cause, I do not, I never have & I never shall feel anything but chagrin & wrath at the cold calculations of the Chicago politicians, sacrificing to a low . . . notion of expediency the foremost man of the party—its Creator & rightful Leader.[15]

*   *   *

No event in American history is more remarkable than the fact that the election of Abraham Lincoln prompted thirteen Southern states to attempt to establish their own confederacy. Not only was Lincoln a minority president, but he had repeatedly emphasized that he would not interfere with slavery where it existed. Nevertheless, within days of Lincoln's election the South Carolina legislature had called for a convention aimed at taking the state out of the Union. Within six weeks, six other states of the lower South had followed suit. "Loyalty to the Union," proclaimed South Carolina's Lawrence Keitt, "will be treason to the South."[16] Within three months of Lincoln's election, commissioners from these seven states had adopted a constitution for the Confederate States of America and had elected Jefferson Davis provisional president.

Without question, many Southerners felt threatened. The *Charleston Courier* estimated that the drop in the value of slaves in the entire South as a result of Lincoln's election would amount to $430 million.[17] Moreover, even Southerners opposed to secession believed that the Constitution gave them a right to secede. "There is no incompatibility between the right of secession by a State and the right of revolution by the people," pronounced one Southern spokesman, invoking the Spirit of 1776. "The one is a civil right founded upon the Constitution; the other is a natural right resting upon the law of God."[18] Quite apart from the legalities, many secessionists expected their revolution to be a peaceful one. Robert Rhett, the rabble-rousing editor of the *Charleston Mercury,* was quoted as saying that he would eat the bodies of all men slain as a result of disunion.[19]

In North and South alike, most of the rhetoric was coming from extremists. There were, however, in the states of the upper South—Virginia, North Carolina, Kentucky, and Tennessee—influential moderates who believed in the Union and who were convinced that it was threatened by the polarization of the sections. "We have terrible times upon us," wrote Gov. William B. Campbell of Tennessee, "and if the wild notions of the South shall prevail, we will be a ruined people." Former congressman George Summers of Virginia felt much the same. "It is much easier to destroy than to reconstruct," he commented. "If disunion once begins, none can foresee where it will end."[20] Seward looked to men like these to keep the border states in the Union.

* * *

The period between the election of a president of the United States and his accession to office has often been perilous. The length of this interim has been reduced in this century, but in Lincoln's day there was a four-month period after the election when government was in the hands of the outgoing president. In 1860 all the preconditions for disaster were present. The old and the new presidents were of different parties, a crisis was at hand, and there was a need for resolute action.

Resolute action was not forthcoming. Buchanan, in his annual message, blamed the crisis on the "long continued and intemperate interference of the Northern people with the question of slavery." The government, in Buchanan's view, had no authority to "coerce" a seceding state back into the Union. Yet neither did the election of a president, whatever his views, under constitutional procedures, justify a revolution "to destroy this very Constitution." All this was a bit much for Seward. The president's argument, in Seward's paraphrase, was that "no state has a right to go out of the Union—unless it wants to," and that "it is the duty of the President to execute the laws—unless somebody opposes him."[21]

As the crisis deepened, there were signs that Seward's priorities were changing. The antislavery reformer was evolving into a man prepared to negotiate, in the tradition of Henry Clay, for the maintenance of the Union. A November 24, 1860, editorial in Weed's *Albany Evening Journal* was raising eyebrows. After deploring the state of the Union, the editorial had insisted that a solution was within grasp. It urged the restoration of the Missouri Compromise line, which had "secured to the South all the territory adapted by soil and climate to its peculiar institution."[22] It is not certain that Weed discussed this initiative with Seward—the editor had long favored a return to the old 36°30′line—but the universal assumption was that Seward was offering the South a way to open portions of the West to slavery. Any such proposal was in conflict with the Republican platform, and Seward attempted to disavow it. On December 5 the *New York Tribune* printed a paragraph that appeared to have been planted by the person most directly affected:

> Mr. Seward will make no speech immediately and will submit no proposition. . . . He is in no manner or form responsible for the various suggestions recently put forward in certain newspapers . . . and was not consulted concerning, or in any way privy to their publication. His policy is to watch the development of events and to direct them wisely at the proper time for peace and the preservation of the Union.[23]

It is well that Seward disavowed Weed's proposal, for Lincoln was in the process of forming his cabinet. In that day a president's choice of advisers was scrutinized as an indicator of his political and geographical preferences. From Weed, Seward knew enough about Lincoln's plans not to approve of them. Seward would have agreed with Lincoln's including a token Democrat, but for the cabinet to have more Democrats than Republicans—as Lincoln contemplated—seemed to him ridiculous. It would be far better to assure strong representation from the crucial border states.

To be sure, there was never any question that Seward was to be secretary of state. Or was there? *"Of course* Mr. Lincoln will offer you the chief place in his cabinet," wrote Charles Francis Adams, Sr. "I trust no consideration will deter you from accepting it."[24] But when mails brought no official word from Springfield, Seward grew edgy. The president-elect had delegated his running mate, Senator Hamlin, to sound out Seward on Lincoln's behalf, but Seward did not know this.

One December day, after the Senate had adjourned, Seward and Hamlin were walking along Pennsylvania Avenue toward their respective lodgings when Hamlin asked Seward to his room for a private chat. Seward accepted, only to talk morosely of retirement. If Hamlin had any idea of persuading him to accept a cabinet post, Seward remarked, he was wasting his time. The vice president–elect then produced two letters from Lincoln to Seward. The first was a brief, formal notification of Lincoln's intention to submit Seward's name as his nominee for secretary of state. The second letter was the one that caught Seward's eye. "In addition to the accompanying and more formal note," Lincoln wrote, "I deem it proper to address you this":

Rumors have gotten into the newspapers to the effect that the [State Department] would be tendered to you as a compliment, and with the expectation that you would decline it. I beg you to be assured that I have said nothing to justify these rumors. . . . I now offer you the place, in the hope that you will accept it, and with the belief that your position in the public eye, your integrity, ability, learning, and great experience, all combine to render it an appointment pre-eminently fit to be made.[25]

Seward was deeply moved. For all his brave talk, the prospect of exile to Auburn was the thing he most dreaded. He grasped Hamlin's hand and said something about Lincoln's letter being remarkable. He would consider the matter and give Mr. Lincoln an early reply.

Notwithstanding his relief over the appointment, Seward decided to consult with Weed before replying to Lincoln. Weed had earlier visited Springfield to discuss patronage matters with Lincoln; now he paid a second call with Seward's interests in mind. What was to be the composition of the cabinet, and what was to be Seward's role? Did Lincoln appreciate the importance of cultivating the border states?

Weed met with Lincoln on December 20, and the signals were mixed. On one hand, Weed found out that two ex-Democrats, Gideon Welles of Connecticut and Montgomery Blair of Maryland, were likely cabinet appointees, as was Chase of Ohio. None of the three was a political friend of Seward's. Quite apart from personalities, Lincoln made clear that he remained committed to a cabinet in which ex-Whigs and ex-Democrats would have approximately equal representation. He refused to commit himself to Weed's suggestion that he appoint at least two

Unionists from the upper South, in part because he did not think it prudent to appoint cabinet officers from states that might yet secede.[26]

On the other hand, Lincoln appeared to be genuinely eager to have Seward as secretary of state. In asking Weed whether Seward would be willing to champion a legislative package aimed at defusing secessionist sentiment, Lincoln seemed to acknowledge Seward's preeminence in the party. Lincoln proposed a constitutional amendment forbidding any interference with slavery in the states, combined with an amendment to the Fugitive Slave Act guaranteeing fugitives a jury trial. Weed expressed his belief that Seward would support such a bill and returned east.

Seward met Weed at Syracuse, and the two men discussed the situation on the train to Albany. Seward was doubtless disappointed at Lincoln's insistence on a bipartisan cabinet, but he probably viewed Lincoln's request that he sponsor a constitutional amendment as a positive development—confirmation that his responsibilities as secretary of state would go well beyond foreign affairs. On December 28 Seward wrote to Lincoln accepting the post of secretary of state. He told a disappointed Frances of his decision, writing: "I will try to save freedom and my country."[27]

Lincoln's proposed constitutional amendment was soon lost in a cascade of legislative proposals aimed at meeting the secession crisis. To consider them the House and Senate each created a special committee, and Seward was made a member of the Senate's Committee of Thirteen. Most of the new proposals required the Republicans to give up their stated intent to ban slavery in the territories. Northern reaction to them was unenthusiastic. "If the Union can only be maintained by new concessions to the slaveholders," thundered Frederick Douglass, "then . . . let the Union perish."[28] For others disunion was preferable to war. Greeley's *New York Tribune* was a powerful voice for allowing the "erring sisters" to "depart in peace."

Lincoln was opposed to any concessions to the South beyond underscoring his vow not to interfere with slavery where it existed. Seward was coming to regard this policy as shortsighted, but in public he continued to downplay the secession crisis. In an impromptu speech in New York City on December 22, he spoke as if his own Unionist sentiments were shared by all right-thinking Southerners. South Carolina had seceded four days before, but Seward was unimpressed. "They do not humbug me with their secession," he told the New England Society. "I do not believe they will humbug you and I do not believe that if they do not humbug you or me, they will succeed very long in humbugging themselves.'' He went on to predict that ''sixty days' more suns will give you a much brighter and more cheerful atmosphere.''[29] Seward's tone was bantering, almost playful, and he never explicitly said that the crisis would be resolved in sixty days. But as the Civil War dragged on, Seward's words to the New England Society would come back to haunt him.

Seward wrote Lincoln long letters about developments in Washington. For the most part their tone was one of watchful waiting; they certainly conveyed no sense of crisis. Near the close of a letter dated December 26, Seward returned to a familiar theme: ''Probably all the debates and conferences which we have hitherto had will sink out of the public mind within a week or two, when the Republican members have refused to surrender . . . to the State of South Carolina.'' In Seward's view, ''Sedition will grow weaker, and loyalty stronger, every day.''[30]

The most promising of the compromise proposals to emerge from Congress was a package introduced before the Committee of Thirteen by the venerable Kentucky legislator John J. Crittenden, who was seen by many as having inherited Henry Clay's role as the great compromiser. The main feature of the Crittenden proposals was to extend the Missouri Compromise line to the Pacific, protecting slavery south of 36°30'—much as Weed had urged in his editorial. In addition Crittenden's package would have prevented Congress from abolishing slavery in the District of Columbia, would have forbidden interference with interstate slave trade, and would have compensated owners who were prevented by local opposition from recovering escaped slaves. The trouble was that all such compromises tended to negate the Republican election victory, which had been won on a platform of no extension of slavery.

Implementation of Republican strategy over the winter of 1860–61 fell to Seward. There is evidence that he sympathized with the Crittenden amendment, in part because of its appeal to the border states; he told the Russian minister, Baron Edouard de Stoeckl, that if Lincoln could not carry the Republican radicals with him, he should attempt to rally conservatives of all parties in order to save the Union.[31] But although Seward was widely regarded as coleader of the Republican party, he could no longer speak for the party, and it was becoming clear that the president-elect was less disposed toward compromise than was his erstwhile rival.

On December 28, eight days after South Carolina's secession, the Committee of Thirteen voted down the Crittenden proposals by 7 to 6, with all five Republicans, including Seward, voting with the majority.

Robert Toombs of Georgia believed Seward to be intractably opposed to the Crittenden proposals. In fact the New Yorker was only conforming—reluctantly—with Lincoln's stated position. For all his show of party loyalty, Seward had by no means abandoned his belief that the secession crisis was manageable. But the means of salvation would not be the Crittenden compromise, which was voted down in the full Senate by 25 to 23.[32]

While people who observed Seward over the secession winter remarked on how he had aged, they were also impressed with his energy and his sense of optimism. Henry Adams was a dinner guest at Seward's house in December. He wrote his brother a description of the evening:

> [Seward] is the most glorious original. It delights me out of my skin to see the wiry old scarecrow insinuate advice. He talks so slowly and watches so hard under those grey eye-brows of his.
>
> After our dinner we went into the parlor and played whist. . . . [Sen. Henry B.] Anthony remarked deprecatingly: Well, things look pretty bad, Governor, don't you think so? No, growled Seward, I don't see why they look bad. . . . Poor Anthony fairly broke down and acquiesced.[33]

Notwithstanding Seward's business-as-usual facade, the political rules were changing. Until Lincoln's election the key question had been the extension of slavery. Now the issue was how to respond to the latest threat of secession from the South. Seward started with two disadvantages: He was not the leader of his party, and he underestimated the strength of the secessionist movement in the South. But at least he had a strategy, which is more than could be said for most other Unionists. Having been through earlier periods when secession had been threatened, Seward believed that sentiment for disunion was confined to a few hotheads. He was convinced that war could be averted through negotiation. Isolate the secessionists, cultivate the border states, and let time bring the sections together again.

Events generated their own momentum, however. An immediate point of friction was Fort Moultrie, South Carolina, near Charleston, where a small U.S. Army detachment occupied an indefensible position. With South Carolina's secession an accomplished fact and in the absence of orders to the contrary, the garrison commander, Maj. Robert Anderson, transferred his command to Fort Sumter, in Charleston harbor. Southerners in Washington were furious. Jefferson Davis warned the distraught President Buchanan that he was "surrounded by blood and dishonor on all sides."[34] On the same December day that Anderson transferred his force to Fort Sumter, three representatives of South Carolina arrived in Washington to request recognition of their "republic." As the president and his cabinet debated what was to be done, Seward wondered how the government would survive the remaining months of Buchanan's term. He wrote Fred Seward that "treason is entrenched in the Government; and . . . it will either be partially dislodged, or will expel what of loyalty remains."[35]

Seward was in a position to know. Buchanan's new secretary of war, Edwin Stanton, was appalled at the extent of Southern influence in Buchanan's entourage. Stanton believed that the Buchanan administration was an obstacle to any strong action against secession, and that circumstances required that key figures in Congress be kept informed of Buchanan's actions. As his two contacts Stanton chose Seward, Lincoln's representative, and Thomas Ewing, another former Whig. On December 29 Seward wrote to Lincoln:

> At length I have gotten a position in which I can see what is going on in the councils of the President. It pains me to learn that things are even worse than is understood. The President is debating day and night on the question [of] whether he shall not recall Major Anderson and surrender Fort Sumter, and go on arming the South.[36]

Stanton and Seward could not meet openly. Their intermediary was a longtime legal associate of Stanton's, Peter Watson. As December turned into January, Seward would return home in the evening and inquire about messages. Often Watson would have left word that he wished to see the senator "about a patent case." In a few instances Stanton authorized Seward to identify him to Lincoln as the source of confidential information from the Buchanan cabinet.[37]

Another of Seward's contacts was Winfield Scott. Through Scott, Seward could not help being aware that the entire U.S. military establishment consisted of some 16,000 soldiers and that its best commanders were resigning to go with their states. Scott, although decrepit, was loyal and aggressive; he appealed to Buchanan to allow him to send reinforcements to Fort Sumter, including 250 men with supplies and ordnance.

While preaching moderation, Seward prepared for all contingencies. He urged the governors of New York and Massachusetts to activate their militias so that they would be able to provide troops on short notice. When the prices on government bonds dropped precipitously, Seward proposed that Treasury bills be issued in small denominations, to enable small investors to support the government. When a delegation of New York bankers called on Seward in Washington, they were taken aback by their former senator's request that they assist the government by lending money at 7 percent, rather than the standard 12.[38]

Buchanan at last turned his attention to Scott's proposal for Fort Sumter. Backed by a cabinet that now included such staunch Unionists as Stanton and Jeremiah S. Black, Buchanan authorized the dispatch of a relief vessel, the *Star of the West*, to Fort Sumter, carrying troop reinforcements and supplies. On January 9 the ship arrived off Charleston, where shore batteries promptly opened fire. The lightly armed *Star of the West* beat a hasty retreat, and there were no casualties. But the United States flag had been fired upon, and the battle lines were drawn.

13

The Peacemaker

THE FIRING ON the *Star of the West* triggered a wave of secessions. Mississippi voted to secede on January 9. Five other states of the lower South followed: Alabama, Florida, Georgia, Louisiana, and Texas. But after Texas's withdrawal on February 1, the initial impetus ebbed, leaving the seven seceding states highly vulnerable. What would the middle South and the border states do? Five of these states—Arkansas, Missouri, North Carolina, Tennessee, and Virginia—had convened or scheduled conventions aimed at implementing some form of referendum on the secession issue.

In Washington, Seward played for time. He thought that if Lincoln could be inaugurated without bloodshed, the worst might be over. A conciliatory posture by the new administration would persuade the border states that they had nothing to fear. In a less strident atmosphere, the national government could initiate negotiations with the seceded states. Seward elaborated on this theme to the British minister, Lord Lyons. According to Lyons,

> [Seward] seems to think that in a few months the evils and hardships produced by secession will become intolerably grievous to the Southern States; that they will become completely reassured as to the intentions of the administration, and the conservative element which is now kept under the surface by the violent pressure of the secessionists will emerge with irresistible force.[1]

Meanwhile Seward was undergoing a metamorphosis. Until 1861 his career had been based on the politics of reform. It was as a leading antislavery spokesman that he had come within an ace of the presidency. Now, in the crisis that had resulted from Lincoln's election, Seward discovered that he was a Unionist first and a reformer second. His decade as a leader of the antislavery movement had rested on an assumption that there could be reform without disunion. With secession no longer a mere threat, Seward had to reconsider his priorities. Disunion, in his view, was too high a price to pay for rigid adherence to the 1860 Republican platform. At a dinner hosted by Stephen A. Douglas for the French minister, Henri Mercier, Seward offered a bold toast: "Away with all parties, all platforms of previous committals and whatever else will stand in the way of a restoration of the American Union."[2]

With Lincoln an unknown quantity, many Republicans still looked to Seward for leadership. Fully conscious of his central role, the New Yorker prepared a speech that he hoped would set the tone for the remainder of Buchanan's term. He had no shortage of advice. Frances, in Auburn, and Sumner, his senatorial colleague, were among those who implored him to avoid any suggestion of compromise. Others urged him to consider the uncommitted border states. Word that Seward was to speak drew a crowd to the Capitol on January 12. Onlookers filled the galleries and spilled into the corridors and halls. By this time four states had seceded, taking their congressional representation with them. But Jefferson Davis was present, as was Judah P. Benjamin of Louisiana, who would eventually become Seward's counterpart in the Confederate cabinet.

Seward spoke for nearly two hours, recalling the splendor of a united nation, reciting its achievements, and lauding its promise for the future. He urged a moratorium on debates on polarizing issues such as secession and slavery in the territories. He did not know what the Union would be worth, if preserved by the sword. To prevent the calamity of war, Seward would "meet prejudice with conciliation, exaction with concession that surrenders no principle, and violence with the right hand of peace."[3]

He elaborated on Lincoln's earlier proposals for the restoration of the Union, endorsing a constitutional amendment to protect slavery in the states where it already existed, to be followed by a convention to address any additional constitutional changes. As a gesture to the North he endorsed an amendment to the Fugitive Slave Law so that bystanders could not be required to aid in the search for fugitives. On the sensitive issue of slavery in the territories, he advocated the admission of the Nebraska and New Mexico territories as free states. Turning to a pet project of his own, he urged that the transcontinental railroad be expedited on both northern and southern routes. Probably anticipating that some listeners would regard his package as too conciliatory to the South, Seward included a rationale:

> I learned from Jefferson that, in political affairs, we cannot always do what seems to us absolutely best. . . . We must be content to lead when we can, and to follow when we cannot lead; and if we cannot . . . do for our country all the good that we could wish, we must be satisfied with doing for her all the good that we can.[4]

Response to the speech was mixed. The French minister, Mercier, pronounced it hazy, and Edward Everett thought it a disappointment. Frances complained of its compromising tone, saying that she feared that her Henry was "in danger of taking the path that led Daniel Webster to an unhonored grave."[5] But the poet John Greenleaf Whittier, who had written Daniel Webster's political obituary after Webster had supported the Compromise of 1850, took a more tolerant view in a poem he dedicated to Seward:

> Statesman, I thank thee!—and if yet dissent
> Mingles, reluctant, with my large content,
> I cannot censure what was nobly meant.
> But, while constrained to hold even Union less
> than Liberty and Truth and Righteousness,
> I thank thee in the sweet and holy name
> Of Peace. . . .[6]

Seward's speech pleased his principal target audience—legislators from the border states. Crittenden of Kentucky, who sat directly in front of Seward, was moved to tears during much of the presentation. But the momentum for secession could no longer be slowed by speeches. Representatives of seceding states continued to withdraw from Congress, sometimes quietly, sometimes with emotional valedictories. The departing Southerners were no more distressed than Seward himself. The day after Jefferson Davis and four other senators took their leave, Sen. Graham Fitch of Indiana moved that the president of the Senate fill all committee vacancies created by the withdrawals. In the debate that followed Seward set the line that was subsequently followed by the Lincoln administration: Secession had no legal basis, and actions arising from it were null and void. He spoke in opposition to Fitch's motion: "I am for leaving these seats here for those senators or for other senators from

the states which they represent,'' Seward declared, ''to be resumed at
their own time and their own pleasure.''[7]

In January a key border state, Virginia, sent out a call for a peace
convention. Twenty-one states responded, and on February 4 some sixty
delegates representing eleven states gathered in a converted church attached to the Willard Hotel. Three weeks of debate among the venerable
delegates generated a consensus only for something like the Crittenden
proposals, but Seward was pleased at the turn of events. Virginia, in
particular, was not likely to do anything drastic while the convention,
chaired by former president John Tyler, continued its deliberations.

Security, however, was something else. Most Northerners considered
the city of Washington a nest of traitors. Rumors were rife that Confederates would attempt to take over the capital. Seward, the recipient
of information and gossip from a variety of sources, was among those
who feared an attempt by Southern sympathizers either to prevent Lincoln from arriving in Washington or to obstruct the counting of the
electoral vote on the second Wednesday in February. On December 29
Seward warned the president-elect of a possible plot to seize the capital
and urged him to come to Washington early and without publicity.[8]

Lincoln, however, remained in Springfield until February 11, when
he began a circuitous rail journey to Washington. He was constantly
called on to speak, and the challenge of not saying anything that might
offend the border states did not bring out the best in the president-elect.
His tone was usually self-deprecatory; he called himself ''the humblest
of all individuals that have ever been elevated to the presidency.'' At
Steubenville, Ohio, Lincoln stated blandly that devotion to the Constitution was equally strong on both sides of the Ohio River. At Cincinnati
he expressed a hope that the nation's difficulties would pass away and
that ''we shall see in the streets of Cincinnati—good old Cincinnati—
for centuries to come . . . such a reception as this to the constitutionally
elected President of the whole United States.''[9]

Meanwhile, crowds were arriving in Washington, and a disproportionate number of the new arrivals appeared to be rednecks of clearly
Southern sympathies. The *Constitution,* a secessionist newspaper, urged
its readers to employ force to prevent Lincoln's inauguration. But February 13, the day the electoral vote was counted at the Capitol, passed
without incident. Seward himself would later claim that, to assure security, he had personally hired a hundred local toughs to patrol the
galleries.[10] In any case he was relieved to be able to inform Frances that
the counting of the vote had gone without incident.

In Philadelphia, where Lincoln raised a flag over Independence Hall on Washington's Birthday, the president-elect received ominous news. Detective Allan Pinkerton, who had been employed on Lincoln's behalf, claimed to have word of a plot by Southern sympathizers to murder the president-elect when he changed trains in Baltimore for the final run into Washington. Lincoln's friends pressed him to change his schedule, but Lincoln at first would hear none of it. Then Frederick Seward appeared. Admitted to Lincoln's room, Fred produced letters from his father and General Scott warning, much as Pinkerton had, of a plot to murder Lincoln in Baltimore.

On the evening of February 22, the president-elect was bundled off incognito to the train that would take him to Baltimore. At three o'clock the following morning, while most of Baltimore slept, the "invalid" in the last car was escorted through town to another depot where he boarded the train bound for Washington. Only a handful of persons knew of the president-elect's revised itinerary. There was no formal welcome when Lincoln, accompanied by two bodyguards, stepped off the train at six o'clock on a gray winter morning.

The circumstances of the president-elect's arrival hardly seemed auspicious. And why was Seward, who had helped inspire Lincoln's surreptitious entry, not at the depot to greet him? Over breakfast at the Willard ("water and gas in each room"), Seward had a sheepish explanation. He had overslept.[11] As for Lincoln, whether or not the "Baltimore plot" was real, he always regretted the mode of his arrival in Washington.

* * *

While Seward had acted for Lincoln during the short congressional session, he had done so with skill and sensitivity. He had, moreover, kept the president-elect fully informed about his own activities in Washington. His letters were detailed and comprehensive. If the information appeared sensitive, Seward would send them unsigned, relying on Lincoln to recognize his nearly indecipherable writing. Seward saw himself as having two responsibilities. One was to guide the inexperienced Lincoln in establishing the policies of his administration at a critical time. The other was to assure the South that Washington would not initiate hostilities against the newly proclaimed Confederate States of America but would pursue a policy of conciliation. Seward saw much of the Adams family in these days, and Charles Francis Adams, Jr., thought him the hope of the nation. "If Lincoln throws his whole weight in support of Seward," Adams wrote, "the party will unite and follow out a conciliatory policy which will . . . keep Virginia steady and save us

the country." Should Lincoln ally himself with the Radical Republicans, however, young Adams thought that war would break out within
a month.[12]

With Lincoln now in Washington, Seward's role suddenly diminished. Not only was the president-elect able to act as his own spokesman,
but there were signs that he did not accord so high a priority to concil-
iating the South as Seward did. Lincoln even had some ideas of his own
about the composition of his cabinet. For his first days in Washington,
however, the president-elect relied heavily on Seward to show him the
ropes. First came a call on President Buchanan, whose demeanor made
it clear that he was eagerly looking forward to inauguration day. Lincoln
then received a delegation from the Peace Convention, which was preparing to adjourn. Dinner for the Lincolns on their first night in the
capital was at the Sewards', with Fred's wife, Anna, acting as hostess.
Seward wrote Frances of his first impressions of the president-elect, with
whom he had enjoyed only the slightest prior acquaintance. "He is very
cordial and kind toward me," Henry wrote. "Simple, natural and
agreeable."[13]

Beneath the surface cordiality lurked potentially serious disagreements over the composition of Lincoln's cabinet and Seward's role
therein. Seward, as a senior party leader, had offered Lincoln some
cabinet suggestions. But the president-elect seemed determined to include the entire Northern political spectrum in his official family, and
Seward was unhappy. He wrote to Weed, "Mr. L. has undertaken his
cabinet without consulting me. For the present I shall be content to
leave the responsibility on his own broad shoulders."[14]

At the root of his complaint was Seward's uncertainty regarding his
own relationship with the president-elect. In several administrations in
the first half of the century, the president had deferred to politically
prominent members of his cabinet. John Quincy Adams, as president,
had on occasion allowed policy to be set by his prestigious secretary of
state, Henry Clay. Daniel Webster had been generally regarded as the
dominant figure in the Fillmore administration. Jefferson Davis had
enjoyed similar status in the administration of Franklin Pierce. Seward's
friends expected this situation to be repeated under the inexperienced
Lincoln, and so did many other Northerners. One letter among many
to Seward in this period advised that "the Nation looks to *you,* under
providence, for its salvation. It is feared that Mr. L. is not equal to the
emergency of the times."[15] A Union man in Edenton, North Carolina,
wrote in a similar vein. "All eyes are turned to Mr. Seward & not to
Abraham Lincoln for a peaceful settlement," he wrote. "Mr. Lincoln

is looked upon as a 3rd rate man, whilst you are called the Hector or the Atlas of not only the Cabinet but . . . of the whole North.''[16] Indeed, Seward's prestige even crossed party lines. Edwards Pierrepont, a prominent conservative Democrat from New York City, wrote William Evarts, ''There is no man of sense in the Democratic Party who does not think that Seward at the head of the Cabinet will give your party more strength, both north & south, *than any other man in the nation*. There is but one opinion upon this matter.''[17]

Whatever the new president's qualifications, he had his own ideas as to who should be in his cabinet. First, he paid off some campaign debts. Caleb Smith, who had helped swing the Indiana delegation to Lincoln at Chicago, was named secretary of the interior. He would prove to be a short-lived nonentity. The War Department went to Simon Cameron of Pennsylvania, whose timely switch in Chicago had helped assure Lincoln's nomination. But Cameron's inept administration of an important department would make his tenure brief as well.

To represent New England, Lincoln named Gideon Welles of Connecticut secretary of the navy. Welles, a former newspaper editor and a Democrat, had a flowing beard that led Lincoln to call him Father Neptune. An honest man, he was abysmally ignorant of naval matters. The attorney general, Edward Bates of Missouri, was a sixty-eight-year-old conservative whose presence in Lincoln's cabinet represented an attempt to woo the border states.

Lincoln's most controversial choices were for the posts of postmaster general and secretary of the treasury. Montgomery Blair, the postmaster general, was an outspoken Unionist from Maryland, a state Lincoln was eager to cultivate. But many liberal Republicans considered Blair's Democratic politics an encumbrance. At the opposite extreme was Secretary of the Treasury Salmon P. Chase. Chase, who had spoken so warmly of Seward at the time of the Van Zandt trial, was now an extreme abolitionist opposed to any concessions to the South. He and Seward each opposed the appointment of the other to Lincoln's cabinet.

None of Lincoln's appointees, except perhaps Smith, could be considered politically friendly to the Seward-Weed faction of the Republican party, which had worked so hard for Lincoln's election. More important, Seward had serious doubts as to whether the cabinet would work together harmoniously—doubts that would be fully justified in time. In the immediate crisis the presence of Chase as well as Seward made Lincoln's cabinet seem almost bellicose toward the South, where Seward's conciliatory posture was largely unknown and where he was still viewed as an archfiend of abolition.

To strengthen his own position in the new cabinet, and to allow the new administration to project a more moderate image to the South, Seward pressed Lincoln to dump the abolitionist Chase. On March 2, just two days before Lincoln's inauguration, Seward played his trump card: He sent the president-elect a terse note asking "leave to withdraw" his earlier acceptance of the State Department portfolio. The press was full of reports of Seward's unhappiness with the Chase appointment, and Seward probably believed that, faced with the loss of the most prominent member of his cabinet, Lincoln would pay the price and abandon Chase. Lincoln, however, called Seward's bluff. He asked his secretary of state to reconsider, and after the March 4 inauguration ceremony the two had a long, confidential conversation. There is some evidence that Lincoln offered to appoint Seward minister to Britain but urged him to remain at State instead. The next day Seward withdrew his resignation, writing Frances that he "did not dare to go home or to England and leave the country to chance."[18] Whatever Seward's rationale, the first round had gone to Lincoln.

*   *   *

Lincoln's first inaugural address came at a time of obvious crisis, and no one knew this better than the president-elect. What should he say about protecting federal installations such as Fort Sumter? He had no shortage of advice, but Seward was one to whom he looked for guidance. Lincoln had passed his draft speech to Seward on arriving in Washington, and the New Yorker had given it his immediate attention. He was distressed at Lincoln's language relating to federal property, which threatened the use of force to reclaim installations that had been taken over by the seceding states. Lincoln would not agree to Seward's suggestion that he limit himself here to innocuous generalities, but he did delete the pledge to "reclaim" federal property already in rebel hands.[19]

Seward had considerable influence on other portions of the draft as well. When he objected to references to the Republican party and the Chicago platform, commenting that they were too political, Lincoln deleted them. Seward's greatest contribution, however, concerned the close. Lincoln's draft had ended with a statement that as president he was obliged to preserve and protect the government, and that it was for the secessionists to choose between war and peace. Seward suggested he end on a more positive note, and offered some language:

I close. We are not and must not be aliens or enemies but fellow countrymen and brethren. Although passion has strained our bonds of affection too hardly, they must not, I am sure they will not, be broken. The mystic chords which proceeding from so many battle fields and so many patriot graves pass through all the hearts and all the hearths in this broad continent of ours will yet again harmonize in their ancient music when breathed upon by the guardian angel of the nation.[20]

Lincoln welcomed Seward's suggestion but thought the language might be improved upon. In the time left to him between interviews with office seekers, he revised his final paragraphs.

Inauguration day, March 4, was blustery and raw. The crowds that gathered downtown seemed curious rather than festive. General Scott congratulated himself for having posted sharpshooters along Pennsylvania Avenue to assure that no violence would mar the occasion. Late in the morning, as Seward prepared to go to the Capitol, a crowd assembled in front of his house. In response to their salutations and good wishes, Seward assured his visitors that their new president "will be just to every State, and every section, and every citizen; . . . he will defend and protect their rights and interests, their peace and prosperity, [and] he will practice the moderation that springs from virtue."[21]

Shortly after noon President Buchanan stopped at the Willard to pick up his successor. A special guard accompanied the carriage to the Capitol, where, on a temporary platform overlooking the East Front, Chief Justice Taney, who had written the Dred Scott decision, administered the oath of office. The sixteenth president then turned to the waiting crowd. Much of what Lincoln said was blown away by the wintry gusts, but the newspapers would carry his words to virtually every hamlet in the North and to much of the South as well. After speaking for thirty minutes in words that sought to convey both conciliation and resolve, Lincoln came to his peroration:

I am loth [*sic*] to close. We are not enemies, but friends. We must not be enemies. Though passion may have strained, it must not break our bonds of affection. The mystic chords of memory, stretching from every battle-field, and patriot grave, to every living heart and hearthstone, all over this broad land, will yet swell the chorus of the Union, when again touched, as surely they will be, by the better angels of our nature.[22]

From the Capitol grounds, a battery of cannons boomed a twenty-one-gun salute.

* * *

A secretary of state enjoyed a personal prestige in 1861 that belied the size of his department. No fewer than six of Seward's predecessors

had eventually been elected president, and several others had been regarded as the "prime ministers" of the administrations that they served.
But most of Seward's distinguished predecessors had brought their rep-
utations with them to the Department of State. Few Americans attached
any importance to diplomacy or to foreign affairs, and a secretary of
state who hoped to make his mark with the public was obliged to take
a broad view of his responsibilities.

The State Department of Seward's day occupied an undistinguished
two-story brick building on the corner of Fifteenth Street and Pennsylvania Avenue. Its thirty-odd rooms housed the diplomatic, consular,
and home bureaus—the latter being a security service, of which more
will be heard later. There were offices to handle miscellaneous responsibilities, too, for the State Department had long been a repository for
government functions that somehow seemed to cross departmental lines.
The department of Seward's day included a custodian for the United
States Seal, an archivist, and a commissioner of patents. At no time
during Seward's tenure would his department comprise more than a
hundred persons.

The two rooms occupied by the secretary were on the northeast corner
of the second floor, looking down Pennsylvania Avenue. They were
comfortable if not grand, the walls lined with bookshelves. Across a hall
were offices for the assistant secretary and the chief clerk. Scattered
elsewhere in the building were twenty-three other clerks, two messengers, and four watchmen. Crises came and went, but the State Department rarely gave the impression of being other than a somnolent
backwater.

Seward had considerable say in staffing the department. Disregarding
any charges of nepotism, he chose thirty-year-old Fred Seward as his
assistant secretary, remarking, "I have placed him where he must meet
the whole array of friends seeking offices—a hundred taking tickets
where only one can draw a prize."[23] He retained Chief Clerk William
Hunter—an elderly bureaucrat who had served in the department since
the days of John Quincy Adams—but he also found positions for friends,
including his biographer, George Baker. Seward's immediate challenge
was to ensure the loyalty of the remaining department staff. Buchanan's
acting secretary of state, William Prescott, had thrown in his lot with
the Confederacy, and the State Department was known to be heavily
staffed with Southern sympathizers. The result was a purge of departmental clerks, who in those days had substantive responsibilities. There
was no such thing as a civil service in the 1860s, and people known to
harbor Confederate sympathies—most were open about their feelings—

were summarily dismissed. Because loyalty was an issue and because the Republicans were taking office for the first time, the turnover was considerable.

Seward had a major voice, though not the final say, in the choice of envoys to serve abroad. The most important diplomatic post was that of minister to Britain. Charles Sumner, among others, had sought the London assignment, but Lincoln was first inclined to give it to William L. Dayton, the party's vice presidential nominee in 1856. Seward, who had favored Charles Francis Adams as secretary of the treasury, now recommended his appointment as minister to Britain. Lincoln bowed to Seward's wishes, and the dour Adams, responding to a telegram from Seward, took the train to Washington. There he was admitted to the president's office, where Lincoln and Seward were discussing appointments. Adams spoke a few pro forma words of appreciation, to which Lincoln replied rather brusquely: "Very kind of you to say so, Mr. Adams, but you are not my choice. You are Seward's man." Then, turning to the secretary, Lincoln remarked, "Well, Seward, I have settled the Chicago Post Office."[24]

The new diplomatic appointees were the standard mix of men of ability and political hacks. Adams, in London, would be outstanding. Dayton would serve competently in Paris, thanks in considerable measure to the assistance rendered by John Bigelow, the U.S. consul in Paris. Dayton, who spoke no French, requested an experienced journalist for the consular post, and Seward found Bigelow, who had just sold his interest in the *New York Evening Post* after more than a decade as its publisher. Bigelow spoke French and had good contacts in liberal circles in Paris; Seward would rely on him increasingly in the sensitive area of Franco-American relations. John L. Motley, a respected historian, was named minister to Austria. Anson Burlingame of Massachusetts, a friend of Seward's, would prove an exceptionally successful envoy to China.

Although the more important posts were filled with able men, many a political debt was paid off in the State Department. William Russell of the London *Times* told of having been kept awake on a train by a big man, bespangled with rings, chains, and pins, who was "going to Washington to get a foreign mission from Bill Seward." He didn't care for Paris, but he might take Japan if it were pressed on him.[25] The fate of Russell's traveling companion is unknown, but Seward may have winced at the appointment of David Carrter, the Ohio politician who had put Lincoln over the top at Chicago, as minister to Bolivia. Cassius Clay of Kentucky, a bellicose antislavery orator and early Lincoln supporter, became minister to Russia. Carl Schurz, an early Seward backer who had subsequently campaigned for Lincoln among German Americans, was named minister to Spain. Author William Dean Howells, who had written a campaign biography of Lincoln, was rewarded with a posting as U.S. consul in Venice.

And what of the secretary of state himself? The acerbic Russell was an early visitor to Seward's office. The Englishman had heard a great deal about the new secretary, much of it unfavorable, and he was curious about the man who would be handling U.S. foreign relations. Russell found Seward "a slight, middle-sized man, of feeble build, with the stoop contracted from sedentary habits and application to the desk. A well-formed and large head . . . projects over the chest in an argumentative kind of way, as if the keen eyes were seeking an adversary; the mouth is remarkably flexible . . . the eyes secret but penetrating, and lively with humour." Russell concluded that he was dealing with "a subtle, quick man, rejoicing in power . . . fond of badinage, bursting with the importance of state mysteries."[26]

Russell's somewhat caustic appraisal ignored some important assets that Seward brought to his new post. Seward was recognized as one of the premier intellects in politics. He had an alert and facile mind, skilled both in assessing people and in analyzing political developments. He had a deep knowledge of history and was well versed in the writings of America's statesmen, especially Jefferson. The ex-senator was remarkably well traveled: His two extended trips to Europe and the Middle East were two more than most men—Lincoln included—had made in his day.

What was even more important, Seward was the one member of Lincoln's cabinet who had a geopolitical perspective. More than anyone else in the North, for instance, he recognized that the continuing demand for American cotton in Britain and France would be a driving force in the attitudes of those countries toward an American civil war. He thought in terms of decades, believing that his country's dynamic economy and the energy of its people assured America's preeminence in the Western Hemisphere, if not the world.

On a personal level, Seward possessed a prime attribute for any diplomat: the ability to deal amiably with people with whom he disagreed. Congressman James G. Blaine—a skilled cloakroom politician—marveled at Seward's persuasiveness in one-on-one discussions. In addition, Seward enjoyed Lincoln's confidence, and the president had made it clear that he planned to leave the conduct of foreign affairs to his secretary of state.

At the same time Seward also had some serious liabilities as a diplomat. In a profession that esteems prudence above all other virtues, Seward was something of a maverick. He liked to talk and was not always discreet in conversation. He occasionally let his temper get out of hand. He did not always draw on the skills of others; the disillusioned Greeley once complained: "I cannot remember that Governor Seward ever in his life said to me, 'What do you think of the present aspect of affairs? What is our true course in this emergency?' "[27] For all Seward's kindliness in his personal relations, there was a hint of intellectual arrogance as well. Now he sought to sustain the Lincoln administration, but he wanted to do so on his own terms. Accustomed to being his own man as lawyer, governor, and party leader, he would not find the role of subordinate an easy one.

Seward also had a credibility problem, growing out of his perceived need to project a confident image. As a prominent member of the new administration he felt obliged to put the best face on a deteriorating situation. Although he recognized that his country was in crisis, Seward persisted in telling people who knew better that all was well—that he, Seward, had matters in hand. He informed U.S. missions abroad that the insurgency in the United States was likely to be of short duration and that an amicable resolution was in the interests of their host governments. But as the crisis deepened, it would prove increasingly difficult to distinguish between Seward's real views and those he put forth as the administration line.

In the early weeks of Lincoln's administration, however, Seward was far more of a pacifist than was his chief. The two disagreed about how to deal with the Sumter crisis. They attached different values to the importance of keeping the border states in the Union. Seward acknowledged that conciliation might erode morale in the North, but he was unwilling to abandon a course that held some hope of preserving the Union as he knew it. So it was that the administration that sought to deal with the threat of secession began its term badly divided.

14

War

FOR ALL THE effort that had been lavished on Lincoln's inaugural address, its beauty was largely in the eye of the beholder. No assurances from a "Black Republican" were sufficient to mollify the South, whereas the absence of any call to arms left some Northerners vaguely dissatisfied. Nevertheless, the new president, safely inaugurated, could now turn his attention to the imminent questions arising from the secession of seven Southern states. The news concerning Sumter was mixed. On the one hand, Jefferson Davis, the recently inaugurated Confederate president, had sent a new commander, Gen. P. G. T. Beauregard, to take command at Charleston and thereby keep the Sumter issue out of the hands of the volatile South Carolinians. On the other hand, Major Anderson had advised General Scott in late February that his provisions were almost gone and that he could hold out only for a month or so.

Although Sumter was the key, it was not the only federal installation facing an uncertain fate. Most military posts from Charleston to the Rio Grande had fallen into rebel hands, but federal authorities still occupied a few enclaves in addition to Sumter. One of these was Fort Pickens, at the entrance to Pensacola harbor on Florida's Gulf Coast. Like Sumter, Pickens was strategically important in that it controlled the entrance to a port. Unlike Sumter, which lay in the shadow of Beauregard's guns, Fort Pickens, if reinforced and supplied by sea, was capable of putting up a very stiff fight.

Related to the question of the forts were some rather delicate negotiations in Washington. On February 27 Jefferson Davis had sent three emissaries—John Forsyth, Martin Crawford, and Andre Roman—to

Washington to attempt to gain recognition for the Confederacy. On March 12 the three men, characterizing the Confederacy as an independent nation, asked Seward to make an appointment for them to present their credentials to President Lincoln. Seward naturally refused to make such an appointment or even to meet with the commissioners himself, but he advised them through an intermediary that his position implied no disrespect and that he would deal with them indirectly. For the next four weeks Seward communicated with the three Southerners through intermediaries, principally John A. Campbell of Alabama, a justice of the U.S. Supreme Court.

In the game of cat and mouse that followed, each side was confident that it was using the other. The Confederate commissioners had been instructed to play a waiting game while the South completed its preparations for war. One of the three, Crawford, advised Confederate Secretary of State Robert Toombs that delay "will build up and cement our confederacy and put us beyond the reach either of [Seward's] arms or his diplomacy."[1] Seward, meanwhile, embraced delay for his own reasons: The new administration likewise needed time to develop a strategy, and "doves," including Seward, hoped that delay would allow Unionist sentiment in the border states to make itself felt.

One of Seward's stable of contacts and informants in this critical period was a rotund man-about-town named Sam Ward, who would acquire, in later years, the dubious nickname King of the Lobby. Ward, with sources of his own, warned Seward that any rebuff of the Confederate commissioners would probably provoke an attack on the federal forts. One of Ward's contacts, in turn, was ex-senator William Gwin of California, a proslavery Democrat who was in communication with Jefferson Davis. In March, Gwin drafted a message to Davis concluding that, given Chase's prominence in the new administration, war was likely. Gwin asked Ward to show his message to Seward, who changed the text to read, "Notwithstanding Mr. Chase's appointment, the policy of the Administration will be for peace and the amicable settlement of all questions between sections."[2]

Clearly Seward was trying to overcome any suspicion that a cabinet including both Chase and himself was automatically a threat to the South. A master of news management, Seward was almost certainly behind some of the pacifist sentiment that found its way into print in the first weeks after Lincoln's inauguration. In Washington, the *National Intelligencer* ran an earnest editorial calling for the evacuation of Fort Sumter. On March 13 the *New York Herald*'s Washington Correspondent wrote: "I am able to state positively that the abandonment of

Fort Sumter has been determined upon by the President and his Cabinet.''[3]

Because Lincoln had not yet decided what to do about Sumter, Seward stalled the commissioners with excuses—official appointments and problems attendant to his new duties at the State Department. On March 15 Lincoln held the second of two cabinet meetings devoted largely to the Sumter question. Seward again opposed any attempt at relief. He cited General Scott's and Major Anderson's reports that any relief expedition would be costly in terms of casualties without assuring success. The North, moreover, should not make the first offensive move. When Lincoln polled his cabinet, the only clear vote in favor of reinforcing Sumter came from Montgomery Blair. Convinced that Lincoln would not override his cabinet on so important a matter, Seward was acting in good faith when he told Campbell, also on March 15, that Sumter would be evacuated within a few days. Even as he gave these promises to Campbell for transmission to the Confederate commissioners, he was informing Virginia Unionist George W. Summers that the fort would soon be evacuated. Summers wrote back that this news had greatly strengthened the position of the Virginia Unionists.[4]

Whatever Seward may have thought, Lincoln remained undecided about Sumter. He had promised in his inaugural address to defend federal property, and the evacuation of Fort Sumter hardly seemed an auspicious way to start. The president sent several personal envoys to South Carolina. Not even their generally dire assessments of the militancy they found there brought Lincoln to the point of ordering an evacuation of Fort Sumter. Part of his problem was political. Rumors of a withdrawal drew fire from important elements of Lincoln's own party. Newspapers editorialized: HAVE WE A GOVERNMENT? and WANTED—A POLICY. Carl Schurz, a spokesman for German Americans in the North, reported to Lincoln that there was widespread dissatisfaction over the Sumter stalemate, but that ''as soon as one vigorous blow is struck, as soon, for instance, as Fort Sumter is reinforced, public opinion in the Free States will rally to your support.''[5]

Seward's border-state correspondents told a very different story. John A. Gilmer urged him not to attempt to hold either Sumter or Pickens, because to do so would give the more bellicose secessionists an excuse for precipitating hostilities. Gilmer thought Southern extremists more and more inclined toward violence to maintain the momentum of their revolution. Their only hope, Gilmer believed, was for shooting to break out, and this contingency above all was to be avoided.[6]

Whereas Lincoln favored doing something about Sumter, Seward was increasingly convinced of the folly of any attempt at reinforcement. Administration policy on the issue had not yet been set, so honorable men might differ. Seward, unfortunately, muddied the waters by expressing his views openly, often in a manner that led his listeners to assume that he spoke for the administration. One source on the frenzied politics of the secession winter is an anonymous observer whose *Diary of a Public Man,* published in 1879, has tantalized historians ever since. The "public man," who may have been lobbyist Sam Ward, knew Seward, and his entry for March 7 affords an interesting view of the loquacious secretary of state:

> I found Mr. Seward in a lively, almost in a boistrous mood. . . . [He assured] me in the most positive and earnest terms that he had no doubt whatever that Fort Sumter would be evacuated at a very early day, that there were no military reasons whatever for keeping it. . . . He spoke very severely of what he called Major Anderson's folly in going into Fort Sumter at all. . . . He gave me to understand that negotiations were, in fact, at this moment going on, which . . . would very soon relieve the Government of all anxiety on the score of Charleston Harbor and its forts.[7]

Meanwhile the clock was running. On March 21, six days after Seward had given Justice Campbell his assurances that Sumter would be evacuated, Campbell called again. He accepted for transmission to the Confederate commissioners Seward's reiteration that his assurances of March 15 still held, although "a few days" had already passed. But Seward had a problem, because sentiment in the cabinet was changing. Chase was now foursquare for reinforcing Sumter, and old Edward Bates was hedging.

As Seward's hopes for peace faded, he felt the strain. He had received no explicit authorization from Lincoln to tell the Confederate commissioners what he had told them. His uncertainty regarding administration policy led him to contradict himself. One day he was assuring William Russell that Lincoln's inaugural speech had accurately stated administration policy, and that the government fully intended to defend its military posts. The next day he was telling Campbell that his Southern friends need not concern themselves over Sumter. On yet a third day he told the Russian minister, Edouard de Stoeckl, that the government intended to leave the seceded states at peace until they returned to the Union. A few days later, at the home of the British minister, Lord Lyons, he spoke so belligerently of blockades and other coercive measures against the South that Lyons became apprehensive for his country's cotton supply.[8]

*   *   *

Seward continued to find much that he liked in President Lincoln. He remarked to Charles Francis Adams, Jr., early in March that "the president has a curious vein of sentiment running through his thought, which is his most valuable mental attribute." But, in Seward's view, Lincoln had "no system, no relative ideas, no conception of his situation."[9] The secretary of state had assumed that his chief would arrive in Washington with a plan for meeting the crisis. He had not. Now the new president was besieged by office seekers, and when he consulted Seward it was often in connection with some minor appointment. Actually, Lincoln was gradually coming to the conclusion that he had to assert federal authority or lose the confidence of Unionists, North *and* South. But the impression he projected during his first weeks in office was one of indecision.

Seward, in contrast, had a program. It was based on isolating the states that had seceded by cultivating the border states that had not. If another course was more promising, let Lincoln pursue it. That the president, in a time of crisis, should be devoting his energies to the selection of assistant postmasters seemed inexcusable.

It was while he was in this state of mind that Seward composed a notorious paper, "Some Thoughts for the President's Consideration," in which he gave full vent to his frustration. The memorandum was guaranteed to get Lincoln's attention, for it began with the assertion that the administration, after a month in office, was "without a policy, either domestic or foreign." There were extenuating circumstances, Seward conceded, but he thought the president was spending too much time on minor matters.

Seward then turned to domestic policy. In his view the principal issue between North and South should be changed from the future of slavery to the question of union—from an issue widely perceived as partisan to one of patriotism and national unity. Because the continued occupation of Fort Sumter was seen in some quarters as a partisan matter, Seward would withdraw Anderson's garrison. At the same time he would reinforce the more defensible forts in the Gulf of Mexico and recall the navy from distant postings.

The most controversial portions of the memorandum were those dealing with foreign relations. Both France and Spain had shortly before embarked on ventures in the Caribbean that smacked of defiance of the Monroe Doctrine. Spanish forces had just annexed San Domingo, and

France was moving to occupy neighboring Haiti. With these developments as background, Seward desired that the administration immediately demand explanations from Spain and France. If satisfactory assurances were not forthcoming, Seward would "convene Congress and declare war against them." But whatever policy was adopted, "there must be an energetic prosecution of it." Either the president must take the lead or some member of his cabinet should. Seward closed with the memorable line, a landmark in disingenuousness: "I seek neither to evade nor assume responsibility."[10]

If Seward intended to get the president's attention, he was entirely successful. Meeting with his secretary of state on the same day he received Seward's "Thoughts," Lincoln cited his own inaugural address as guidance on administration policy. He zeroed in on Seward's ambiguous attitude regarding Fort Sumter, asking why its reinforcement was somehow a partisan matter while the defense of Fort Pickens was a "national and patriotic" issue. Finally Lincoln underscored that whatever must be done, "I must do it."

Seward's memorandum to Lincoln and the president's response remained a secret between the two men until the publication of the multivolume Lincoln biography by his two secretaries, Nicolay and Hay, in 1890. By then the deification of Lincoln was well under way, and nothing that Seward wrote before or after would bring down on his head such widespread condemnation as did "Some Thoughts for the President's Consideration." In subsequent decades Lincoln's reply to Seward was cited as an example of the charitable Lincoln, tolerating his upstart secretary of state while putting him firmly in his place. In Carl Sandburg's view, Seward was saying that Lincoln was a failure as president but that he, Seward, "knew how to be one." A popular college text speaks of Seward's "April Fool's Day paper" and his "mad policy."[11] Another writer on the Civil War period, William C. Davis, concludes that "thanks to Lincoln's enduring patience, and his ability to see through his associates' petty personality faults,"[12] Seward was not summarily dismissed.

In fact no record exists of what passed between Lincoln and Seward on April 1; such knowledge as we have of Lincoln's response comes from a reply that he drafted but appears never to have sent.[13] If the episode had any effect on relations between the two principals it went unnoticed at the time. Writing in 1902, Frederick Seward minimized the exchange, insisting that after April 1, business between Lincoln and Seward went on "just as it had before."[14]

It is worth recalling that when Seward made his recommendations, the incoming president had shown few signs of competence, much less

of greatness. Seward's first charge—that the administration lacked co-
herent policies—was but the judgment of the newspapers of Lincoln's
own party. The harsh criticism that has come Seward's way for volun-
teering to assume greater responsibilities overlooks the almost universal
belief in 1861 that Lincoln himself was not up to the job.

As for the specifics in Seward's memo, there can be little doubt that
Lincoln was spending excessive time on minor matters, especially appointments. The broader question—that of shifting the sectional issue
from slavery to disunion—was one on which Lincoln and Seward were
in general agreement; Lincoln would not even deal with this in his reply.
Seward is least persuasive on the subject of Fort Sumter, because to
argue that all forts *except* Sumter should be defended is curious logic
indeed. What could be better calculated to fire up national spirit than
the defense of a beleaguered fort? It is hard to avoid the feeling here
that Seward was embarrassed over his commitments to the Confederate
commissioners and wished that the Sumter issue would somehow go
away.

Seward's memorandum is most vulnerable in its recommendations
regarding foreign policy. As has been noted, the secretary was slow to
recognize either the extent or the intensity of disunionist sentiment in
the South. If there was ever a time when a foreign policy crisis might
have reunited the nation, that time had long since passed. Still, it is
possible that Seward saw opportunities in the Caribbean that others did
not. Historian Allan Nevins, no admirer of the secretary, believes that
Seward sought to play on Southern anxiety concerning the islands of
the Caribbean:

> The moment Washington opened war on Spain, Seward believed, the
> cotton states would tremble lest Cuba become free soil—either as an
> independent republic or a State of the Union. . . . To avert such a ca-
> lamity, he hoped that Southerners would join the attack. If the Confed-
> eracy did not forgo its independence to share in the new conquest, then
> the United States would at least gain a great island base for operating
> against the Confederates, and for closing the Gulf.[15]

Actually, Seward did not expect a shooting war with any European
power. According to his memorandum, war was to be considered only
in the absence of "satisfactory explanations" by France and Spain. Seward obviously did not anticipate hostilities, for he began his next sentence with the words, "But whatever policy we adopt. . . ." What he
sought was a foreign affairs crisis to divert attention from secession. Yet

for him to believe that such an episode would somehow exorcise the "irrepressible conflict" was itself a serious error in judgment.

Any analysis of the specifics of Seward's memorandum overlooks its overriding purpose, which was to jar the president into making some decisions that Seward felt to be overdue, and to give Seward himself a greater role in formulating those decisions. In addition, his "Thoughts" included a number of practical suggestions, many of which were implemented with Lincoln's approval in the next few weeks. The gulf forts were reinforced, the fleet was recalled, and secret agents were sent to Canada to ascertain sentiment there.

With Lincoln's approval, Seward protested Spain's seizure of San Domingo in a note that stated that Spanish moves to reestablish itself in the Western Hemisphere would be met with "prompt, persistent and, if possible, effective resistance." But given the insurgency within its own borders, the United States was in no position to police the Caribbean. Spain declared its occupation of San Domingo to be a fait accompli, and France began to formulate its own plans for Mexico.[16]

Because both protagonists kept their exchange confidential, we can only speculate on whether Seward ever saw Lincoln's written response to his "Thoughts." Quite possibly Lincoln's own memorandum represented a way of organizing his thoughts, and Seward never saw it. But one way or another the president made it clear that he would control his own administration, and he appears to have made this point without offending his secretary of state. Seward continued, with Lincoln's blessing, to regard himself as the "premier" of the administration. But as the debate over Fort Sumter would demonstrate, the president would reserve to himself the final decision on all matters of importance.

*　　*　　*

On March 29 Lincoln called the cabinet into emergency session to consider a memorandum from General Scott. That old warrior had long opposed any attempt to relieve Sumter; now he argued on political grounds that both Sumter and Pickens should be abandoned. "The evacuation of both the forts," Scott wrote, "would instantly soothe and give confidence to the eight remaining slave-holding States, and render their cordial adherence to this Union perpetual."[17] With regard to Sumter, Scott's position was hardly different from that of most of Lincoln's cabinet two weeks before. But since then sentiment had stiffened. Now, at a time when Lincoln had almost convinced himself that an attempt must be made to resupply Major Anderson, the commanding general was taking a line suspiciously like that of the secretary of state. Once again Lincoln polled his cabinet on provisioning the two forts. The result was dramatically different from that of March 15. This time only Caleb Smith stood with Seward; Blair, Chase, and Welles were in favor of holding on, while Bates equivocated and Cameron's view went unrecorded. In a significant step Lincoln directed Fox to organize an expedition to reprovision Fort Sumter.

Seward remained the cabinet dove on Sumter, but he continued to make a distinction between Fort Sumter and Fort Pickens. He was prepared for the government to take a stand that might bring war, but he insisted that Pickens rather than Sumter was the place to take such a stand. "The dispatch of an expedition to supply or re-inforce Sumter," he wrote the president, "would provoke an attack and so involve a war at that point. . . . I do not think it wise to provoke a civil war . . . in rescue of an untenable position." Fort Pickens was at least defensible. "I would at once and at every cost prepare for a war at Pensacola . . . to be taken however only as a consequence of maintaining the . . . authority of the United States."[18]

This position represented a considerable change for Seward, who probably made the shift to avoid becoming completely isolated within Lincoln's cabinet. There is no evidence that Seward was less committed to a policy of reconciliation, and his mail, especially from the South, tended to support this approach. One of Seward's more perceptive contacts was John A. Gilmer, who remained in touch with Seward even after he declined Lincoln's offer of a cabinet post. Gilmer believed that both federal forts must be given up if the upper South were to be kept in the Union. So did most of Seward's other border-state contacts. Frederick Roberts, another North Carolinian, warned: "Once this unfortunate Controversy produces a clash of arms, it will unite the whole South. There will be no Unionists or dis-unionists, but one solid column of Southern bretheren."[19] Virginian Joseph Churchill wrote from Richmond that any action "leading to hostilities with the Secessionists will drive this state out of the Union."[20] A letter signed merely "A Southerner" pleaded: "May I in God's name, in the name of Humanity, in the name of Posterity, beg for God's sake to save us from Civil War!"[21] Nevertheless, Seward's policy of conciliation had been rejected; Lincoln was bowing to Northern pressure for a hard line.

But the secretary was not yet done. As Bruce Catton put it, the ordinary human eye could not quite follow all that Seward was attempting in the weeks following Lincoln's inauguration.[22] The cabinet meeting of March 29 triggered a flurry of activity on his part on at least three tracks. One track was represented by Seward's April 1 memo to Lincoln, which failed in its immediate objective of persuading the president to abandon Fort Sumter. A second track concerned the Confederate commissioners. A third was to see that Fort Pickens was not ignored in the furor over Sumter.

The Confederate commissioners would not be put off, for the "few" days at the end of which Sumter would be evacuated had come and gone. On March 30 Campbell had met again with Seward, leaving with him a telegram from Gov. Francis Pickens of South Carolina, inquiring about the delay. Seward told Campbell that he would have to consult the president. On April 1, knowing that Lincoln was outfitting an expedition for the relief of Fort Sumter, Seward met again with Campbell. There was no plan to reinforce Sumter, he assured the justice, probably seeking to blur the line between an expedition to reinforce Anderson's garrison and one designed to resupply it with provisions. Campbell, however, recognized the signs of a policy in transition. When he showed Seward a telegram in which one of Lincoln's emissaries, Ward Hill Lamon, was quoted as promising that Sumter would be evacuated, Seward told him that Lamon was not authorized to speak for the president. Campbell emphasized the importance of reassuring Governor Pickens about Lincoln's intentions, at which point Seward reached for pen and paper. His assurance to Campbell and the Confederate commissioners read: "I am satisfied the government will not undertake to supply Fort Sumter without giving notice to Governor Pickens."[23]

Seward's promise to Campbell was breathtaking in its audacity. From a position of assuring the Confederate commissioners that Fort Sumter would be evacuated he had moved to providing assurances that *when* the fort was resupplied, South Carolina would be given courtesy notification! Paradoxically there was little danger that the talks would break down. The Confederate commissioners had been directed by Jefferson Davis to spin out the negotiations so that the Confederacy might improve its war readiness; as a result, they did not consider breaking off the negotiations because of Seward's about-face. There was considerable confusion about attitudes, as well as about who was using whom. Mary Chesnut, the perceptive Dixie diarist, commented regarding developments in Washington: "That serpent Seward is in the ascendancy just now." She then added, with some bewilderment: "He is thought to be a friend of peace."[24]

On April 4 Lincoln decided to go ahead with a Sumter relief expedition and assured Anderson that help was on the way. Because a full-scale attempt to reinforce the fort would be certain to provoke shooting and because such a development would probably drive the upper South into the Confederacy, Lincoln sought to separate the resupply effort from any military reinforcement. He would attempt to send in supplies, but the navy's warships and transports would go into action only if the supply vessels were fired upon. Fox traveled to New York City and began chartering supply vessels.

Thanks to Seward, a Pickens expedition was also in the works, and it was all that Lincoln's inexperienced cabinet could do to keep two such expeditions on track. On March 29 Seward had taken an army engineer, Capt. Montgomery Meigs, to meet the president. Seward had known Meigs for years and had high regard for his role in constructing an aqueduct for the District of Columbia. Meigs knew Fort Pickens, considered it defensible, and made enough of an impression on the president that Lincoln put him in charge of an expedition to reinforce it. Seward told Meigs on March 29, after the two of them had met with Lincoln, that all men of sense could see that war was coming. But he, Seward, was willing to give up Sumter and hold Pickens instead as part of a campaign to detach Texas from the Confederacy.[25]

By April 5 relief expeditions were under way for both Sumter and Pickens. The one for Sumter was quite properly a navy affair, but Seward, who had little respect for Gideon Welles, appears to have persuaded Lincoln that he, Seward, should supervise Meigs and navy Lieut. David D. Porter in directing the expedition to Fort Pickens. Moreover, because of the presence of suspected secessionists in the Navy Department, the expedition was to be kept secret—even from Welles. The harassed Lincoln had earlier authorized Porter to take command of a powerful paddle wheeler, the *Powhatan,* but a few days later had approved papers for Welles making the *Powhatan* part of the Sumter relief force. The result was that, in New York City, two naval officers had conflicting orders relating to the *Powhatan.*

On the evening of April 5 Seward made an awkward call on Secretary Welles in his rooms at the Willard, where Welles heard for the first time of the Pickens expedition. When the secretary of the navy discovered that ships were being moved about without his knowledge, he was furious. At Welles's insistence the discussion moved to the White House, where Lincoln told Seward to turn the *Powhatan* over to the Sumter expedition.* In conversation with Welles, Seward attempted to pour oil

---

*The matter should have ended here, but it did not. In directing Porter to turn over the *Powhatan,* Seward put his own name on the telegram. Porter, on receiving it, insisted that his previous orders from the president took precedence. The *Powhatan* went to Pickens, and Welles was convinced that Seward had intentionally arranged it all.

on troubled waters, remarking that "old as he was, he had learned a lesson from this affair," namely, that he "had better attend to his own business and confine his labors to his own Department." To this Welles had "cordially assented."[26]

It was at this time that Seward's dealings with the Confederate commissioners came to a climax. The press was treating every rumor as fact; in the Northern journals, Sumter was to be supplied on one day, only to be abandoned on the next. By April 6 the Confederate commissioners were convinced that Pickens was to be reinforced, and perhaps Sumter as well. On Sunday, April 7, Campbell sent a note to Seward, stating that the conflicting reports were causing his friends anxiety, notwithstanding the fact that he had passed them Seward's earlier assurance of prior notice concerning any change in the status of Forts Sumter and Pickens. Seward, ignoring Campbell's suggestion that a commitment had been made with regard to Fort Pickens, gave Campbell a note that read: "Faith as to Sumter fully kept; wait & see."[27]

The secretary was in a position to know. On the previous day Lincoln had sent a State Department clerk, Robert Chew, to Charleston with a message for Governor Pickens. The message advised that an attempt would be made to reprovision Sumter, but that in the absence of armed resistance no attempt would be made to send in military supplies or reinforcements without further notice. Chew delivered his message on April 8, while Seward, in Washington, assured the Confederate commissioners that federal moves were entirely defensive.

Gustavus Fox had been delayed in his preparations for the Sumter expedition but his three vessels set out from New York City on the morning of April 9. Foul weather delayed their arrival off Charleston until April 12. By then Jefferson Davis and his advisers had determined on war. There was no military logic to an attack on Sumter—the fort in federal hands was no threat to South Carolina—but in the eyes of Davis and his hard-line advisers its mere existence had become an affront to Southern "independence." Within the Confederate cabinet, only Secretary of State Robert Toombs saw the implications of the South's firing the first shot. "You will wantonly strike a hornet's nest," he warned Jefferson Davis. "Legions, now quiet, will swarm out and sting us to death. It is unnecessary; it puts us in the wrong; it is fatal."[28]

On April 10 Davis instructed General Beauregard that if he was satisfied as to the bona fides of Lincoln's messenger, "you will at once demand [Fort Sumter's] evacuation, and if this is refused proceed . . .

to reduce it."[29] War came on April 12, when rebel batteries fired on the fort, forcing its surrender the following day.* Momentous events followed in quick succession. On April 15 Lincoln issued his call for volunteers, effectively ending most support for the Union in the border states. Two days later the Virginia State Convention voted 88 to 55 in favor of secession, aligning the Old Dominion with the Confederacy. Arkansas, North Carolina, and Tennessee followed suit within the next two months, and the status of Maryland, Kentucky, and Missouri was exceedingly doubtful.

*   *   *

The dilemma that Lincoln and Seward faced in the final weeks of the secession crisis has been studied in depth by scores of historians. Twentieth-century scholars have not been charitable toward those who, like Seward, went the extra mile for peace. Kenneth Stampp judged Seward to be guilty of "incredible blindness" in acting as though the Union could be peacefully reunited.[30] Allan Nevins dismissed Seward's policy as "appeasement" and called it evidence of "a profound moral defect."[31]

The closest Seward came to explaining his course in the secession crisis may have been a letter written on February 23, 1861, to the editor of a small newspaper, the *New York Independent.* In it he wrote:

> The American people in our day have two great interests. One, the ascendency of freedom over slavery; the other, the integrity of the Union! The slavery interest has derived its whole political power from bringing the latter object into antagonism with the former.
>
> Twelve years ago freedom was in danger and the Union was not. I spake then so singly for freedom that short-sighted men inferred that I was disloyal to the Union. I endured the reproach without complaining, and now I have my vindication. Today, practically, freedom is not in danger, and Union is. With the loss of Union all would be lost.
>
> Now, therefore, I speak singly for the Union. . . . For this singleness of speech I am now suspected of infidelity to freedom. In this case, as in the other, I refer myself not to the men of my time, but to the judgment of history.[32]

---

*On April 12, on the Gulf Coast, the government succeeded in reinforcing Fort Pickens. Because the Union navy dominated coastal waters, Union forces were able to retain control of Fort Pickens during the war that followed. Federal control of the enclave, however, had little political or military significance.

In courting the border states, Seward was neither blind nor guilty of a character defect. He was, however, relying heavily on improvisation. Had Fort Sumter been evacuated, secession would probably have been averted in Virginia, North Carolina, and other border states. But at what cost? The seven states of the lower South showed no signs of rescinding their acts of secession, whereas the government in Washington, had it retreated from Sumter, would have raised serious questions as to its conviction in dealing with the crisis. Lincoln could have bought some time by following Seward's recommendations, but he would have paid a heavy price in terms of Northern unity.

One lapse on Seward's part was his apparent belief that if peace were preserved over the short term, the seven states of the lower South would see the error of their ways and somehow drift back. Conceivably they might have, over a period of decades, as passions cooled and trade and cultural ties made political separation seem pointless. But for the short and middle term, there were few signs of reconciliation. Sectional feeling was strong in the South, and newly independent entities, flush with the privileges of sovereignty, do not often seek to rejoin the mother country. A second error was Seward's underestimation of the North's willingness to fight. Although himself a Northerner, Seward did not fully realize that most Northerners, whatever their views on slavery, were prepared to fight for the Union.

Related to these misjudgments was Seward's overvaluation of Unionist sentiment in the border states. Many of Seward's nominal allies proved, in the end, to be weak reeds. Lincoln was not fooled; he remarked to one visitor: "Yes! your Virginia people are good Unionists, but it is always with an *if!*"[33] What Unionist sentiment existed in the South vanished in the wake of Fort Sumter and Lincoln's subsequent call for troops, prompting Unionists such as John Gilmer and George Summers reluctantly to cast their lot with the Confederacy.

Lincoln was clearly prepared to risk war to carry out his inaugural pledge to hold on to federal property in the South. But this is not to say that he deliberately provoked war. Rather he set out to accomplish what he sought—the reprovisioning of Fort Sumter—under circumstances in which any "first shot" would come from the South. In the words of Lincoln scholar James G. Randall: "To say that Lincoln meant that the first shot would be fired by the other side *if a first shot was fired,* is not to say that he maneuvered to have the shot fired."[34]

For the period comprising December 1860 and the first two months of 1861, Seward was the most powerful person in Washington. Because Lincoln lingered in Springfield, and because it was known that Seward was his secretary of state–designate, the New Yorker was widely regarded as a leader of the new administration on a par with Lincoln himself. In retrospect, Lincoln may have wished that he had come to Washington in January, as Seward had urged. But for the most part Seward proved a worthy surrogate. If he pointed the new administration toward a more conciliatory policy than the one that Lincoln followed, it was better to err in the direction of peace than toward war. When he found himself out on a limb with his commitments to the Confederate commissioners concerning Sumter, Seward extricated himself as gracefully as circumstances permitted.

Did Seward's dealings with the Confederate commissioners have any bearing on the outcome? His repeated assurances regarding the early evacuation of Fort Sumter were clearly misleading and inaccurate, but Seward probably believed them at the time they were given. The stakes were sufficiently high, in any case, to justify Seward's telling the commissioners anything that was useful to the Union cause. The Confederate commissioners did not come to the negotiations as wide-eyed innocents. From the start they recognized Seward as a shrewd, dangerous antagonist. In any case the administration ultimately did give notice of the proposed reprovisioning of Fort Sumter as Seward had promised.

Before leaving Washington on April 11 the three commissioners sent Seward a blistering letter in which they reiterated the right of secession and accused the Lincoln administration of blindness and perfidy. The United States, they said, was responsible for any war that would ensue because of its failure to bargain in good faith. They had no fear of the result, for the Confederacy would fight "while a freeman survives in the Confederate States to wield a weapon."[35]

The crash of the Confederate batteries that fired on Fort Sumter on April 12 signaled the collapse—at least for the time being—of the American republican experiment. "If political democracy be defined as government by the consent of the governed," one historian has written, "the shells over Sumter made clear that a large minority among the American people had withdrawn their consent from the existing federal institutions."[36] Although Seward acknowledged no regrets about his dealings with the commissioners, the outbreak of war was shattering. He could not conceive that a cabal of Southern hotheads would destroy the Union in the face of the assurances provided by the new administration. The outbreak of war was also a political blow to Seward. He had staked his reputation on the certainty that the initial wave of secessions by the cotton states could be "managed," and both peace and Union be preserved. But Lincoln had rejected his counsel regarding Fort

Sumter. Had Seward been the unprincipled politician he was sometimes accused of being, he would have joined the clamor for firm action with respect to Sumter. Instead, in his search for peace, he had made himself vulnerable to the charge of being "soft" on the prosecution of the war.

For a year little had gone Seward's way. He was secretary of state, not president. Lincoln had emphasized that policy would be set by him, not Seward. Now negotiation had given way to war. But Seward was nothing if not resilient. He had come back from the shattering disappointment of Lincoln's nomination; now, following Fort Sumter, he turned to his diplomatic responsibilities. Both North and South began the war with a militant conviction that God was on their side, and eventual victory therefore only a matter of time. But both sides recognized that there was a wild card—foreign intervention—that could upset all calculations. Seward took on the responsibility of assuring that there would be no such intervention on behalf of the Confederacy.

15

Mr. Seward's Little Bell

IN THE WAKE of the attack on Fort Sumter, Lincoln was ready to make war. On April 14, when word of Major Anderson's surrender reached Washington, Lincoln met with the cabinet and prepared a call to arms. Citing the existence in seven states of "combinations too powerful to be suppressed" by ordinary means, he asked the states to provide 75,000 militia with which to suppress the insurrection. He called a special session of Congress to meet on the Fourth of July.

The fervor for secession that had flashed through the South was now matched by patriotic demonstrations in most of the North. Speeches were delivered, funds raised, and mass meetings held to pledge devotion to the Union. Young Fanny wrote to her father from Auburn: "All is excitement here. . . . The merchants have hung their windows with tricolors—flags are flying from public and private houses—every day there is a presentation of a bible or a sword or revolver to the captain or someone of the companies."[1] The atmosphere was not conducive to dissent. A Chicago newspaper editorialized: "From this hour let no Northern man or woman tolerate in his or her presence the utterance of a word of treason." In New York City, where the *Herald* was suspected of secessionist sympathies, an angry crowd shouted jeers and threats until the management displayed an American flag.[2]

In Washington, by contrast, the atmosphere was subdued. General Scott still had only a few hundred men with which to defend the city, and residents of the capital could clearly see the Confederate flags flying over Alexandria, across the Potomac. The city was alive with rumors. A secessionist mob was said to be en route from Baltimore to burn the capital. Rebel vessels were headed up the river from Norfolk to bombard it. If there was a blessing for the new administration, it was that most office seekers chose this time to leave town.

Seward accommodated himself to the new realities. "Treason is a painful fact," he wrote to Frances, "and at last we have the stern necessity of meeting and treating it as such."[3] Indeed, Seward had favored the mobilization of 100,000 troops rather than the 75,000 called for by Lincoln, and was constantly telegraphing his associates in New York State to expedite forces to Washington. Only a few additional troops had reached Washington before secessionist rioters in Baltimore, on April 19, halted rail travel, effectively isolating the capital. Not until the Seventh New York regiment arrived a week later was there any significant force to protect the seat of government. Seward sought to set an example in calmness. In retrospect, however, he would regard this as one of the most unnerving periods in the war. In 1864, while artist Francis Carpenter was painting his famous rendition of Lincoln and his cabinet debating the Emancipation Proclamation, Seward told him that his theme was not sufficiently heroic. Carpenter should portray instead something like the firing on Fort Sumter or the grave deliberations in Washington following the Baltimore riots.[4]

Whereas Fort Sumter had awakened the North, its repercussions in the border states were every bit as negative as Seward had feared. In Virginia people rallied to the Confederate cause. North Carolina and Kentucky declined to provide troops in response to Lincoln's call; the allegiance of these and other border states was very much in doubt. Ultimately, Virginia, North Carolina, Tennessee, and Arkansas would side with the Confederacy; Kentucky, Missouri, and Maryland would stand by the Union. The sagacious but inexperienced Lincoln faced the unenviable task of preparing to restore the Union by force, even while seeking to forestall additional defections. He used his cabinet secretaries, especially Seward, Blair, and Chase, as advisers on a broad range of issues. Lincoln would pay a price for his politically diverse cabinet—there was constant friction—but he assured himself of a broad range of counsel.

At the State Department Seward drafted long letters of instructions to U.S. envoys overseas. In some cases identical messages went to all posts, but in most instances Seward tailored his instructions to a particular envoy, demonstrating his extensive knowledge of the internal political situation in the host country. On May 4 he issued a dispatch spelling out the grounds on which the Civil War would be fought:

> The insurgents have instituted revolution with open, flagrant, deadly war to compel the United States to acquiesce in the dismemberment of the

Union. The United States have accepted this civil war as an inevitable necessity. The constitutional remedies for all the complaints of the insurgents are still open to them, and will remain so. But. . . . there is not now, nor has there been, nor will there be any . . . idea existing in this government of suffering a dissolution of this Union to take place in any way whatever.[5]

Seward was speaking here for the Lincoln administration rather than himself, and the wording is considerably tougher than anything he voiced during the pre-Sumter period of "masterful inactivity."

*   *   *

Early in May, Seward moved into the three-story, red-brick town house on Lafayette Park, diagonally across Pennsylvania Avenue from both the White House and the State Department, that would be his residence for his eight years as secretary of state. The house had known several identities. Built by Commodore John Rodgers in 1830, it had been converted into a boardinghouse and then had become the home of the Washington Club. In 1859 the "Old Clubhouse," as it was known, achieved its greatest notoriety. On a spring day Philip Barton Key, son of the lyricist of "The Star Spangled Banner" and reputed to be the handsomest man in Washington, was crossing Lafayette Park to the club when he was accosted and shot by Congressman Daniel Sickles of New York, whose wife Key had seduced. Friends carried the handsomest man in Washington into the clubhouse, where he died in what would become the Sewards' parlor.* Key's murder would not be the last violence associated with the Old Clubhouse.

The outbreak of the war found the Seward family geographically divided. Frances and Fanny were in Auburn, for Frances no longer made any pretense of maintaining a home in Washington. Young Fanny enjoyed life in the capital, but as her mother's main comfort she spent most of her time in the home on South Street. Will was also in Auburn, learning the banking business but eager to serve in the army. Knowing his mother's deep opposition to war, Will at first sought to be an assistant to his father. When Henry pointed out that diplomacy was not his forte, Will returned to the military. After what must have been a heart-wrenching decision, Frances said she would not stand in his way. Soon Will was drilling a company of soldiers in the fields outside Auburn.

---

*Acquitted in a sensational trial, Sickles was to become a highly controversial corps commander in the Civil War.

In Washington the Seward establishment most often consisted of Henry, Gus, Fred, and Fred's wife, Anna. Over time Henry would become as dependent on Anna at home as he was on Fred at the State Department. Fred delighted in his work as his father's assistant and in a short time made himself indispensable.

Gus continued to be a puzzle to his family as well as to strangers. Seward had wanted a field appointment for his West Point–trained eldest son and had indicated as much to Secretary of War Cameron. Frances, meanwhile, had asked Fred to use his good offices to get his brother a safe desk job in Washington. Given the choice of a major's appointment in the field or a paymaster's billet at the same grade, the taciturn Gus chose the paymaster post.[6]

Noah Brooks, a reporter who was a close friend of Lincoln, described one of the first receptions at the new Seward residence:

> The Secretary of State does not keep great state at his residence, although his upstairs parlors were quite tastefully furnished—marble busts, engravings, flowers, and paintings being the most noticeable objects in the room, unless it was the prodigious nose of Seward. He advanced from the rear of the parlors as a batch of names was called, shaking hands with all his matchless *suavitir in modo* as each caller was presented. With a few kind words the visitor was passed over to Fred W. Seward, Assistant Secretary of State, a nice young man with black hair and whiskers.[7]

Seward had urged, even before Sumter, that naval vessels in foreign waters be recalled for use in a possible blockade of Southern ports. Now, with the nation at war, a blockade was a favorite topic for discussion in the Northern press. The issue was not simple, for a blockade was most often associated with war against a sovereign power. If there was one thing the Lincoln administration did not want, it was to accord the Confederacy the status of a sovereign power. Even more important was the question of enforcement. When Sumter fell, the entire U.S. Navy consisted of only forty-two ships—hardly a fleet with which to blockade three thousand miles of "enemy" coast. The navy now recalled its ships from foreign stations and began leasing others. Both Lincoln and Seward believed that, given Europe's appetite for Southern cotton, any move to close Southern ports must be more than a "paper" blockade.

Over the opposition of Charles Sumner, chairman of the Senate Foreign Relations Committee, Lincoln proclaimed a blockade of Confederate ports on April 19. To finesse the question of Confederate sovereignty, the proclamation was justified on grounds that the existing insurgency was preventing the collection of revenues. Although the federal government's initial inability to enforce a blockade prompted ridicule in the South, no pronouncement issued during the war had a greater long-term effect on the strategic balance. As early as May, Federal blockade ships were billowing smoke off Confederate ports such as Wilmington, Savannah, Mobile, and New Orleans. While the Union blockade would never be airtight, its mere existence was a deterrent to all except the most daring captains.

Confederate privateers were another maritime issue that required Seward's attention. On April 17 Jefferson Davis issued a proclamation offering Confederate sponsorship for privateers. The response of the Lincoln administration was immediate: Any vessels acting under such illegal authorization would be treated by federal authorities as pirates. Seward instructed American envoys abroad to be alert to evidence of the outfitting of privateers. He undertook legal action as well. In 1856 the principal maritime powers had agreed, in the Declaration of Paris, to the abolition of privateering as a mode of warfare. In addition they had defined the categories of goods that might be seized during wartime from neutral vessels. Although the United States had never gotten around to ratifying the Declaration of Paris, Seward on April 24 directed American envoys to advise their host governments that the United States was a party to the declaration.

Seward obviously hoped to make things difficult for Confederate privateers, but the European powers were uncooperative. Preliminary talks failed even to produce agreement on a venue for substantive negotiations. Late in the summer of 1861 the British delivered a coup de grace to Seward's initiative by disclaiming any action that might bear ''on the internal differences now prevailing in the United States.''[8] It is easy to imagine the secretary's profane reaction to London's position, one that appeared so sympathetic to the rebels.

Seward, meanwhile, was active on many fronts. He ordered James D. Bulloch, the Confederate naval agent in Britain, placed under surveillance by the U.S. consulate. He chose ciphers to be used in diplomatic correspondence. He took note of a report by Gen. William Wool, who commanded U.S. forces at Fortress Monroe, Virginia, that the British consul at Charleston was very sympathetic to the Confederate cause.

When the North was short of potassium nitrate—saltpeter—an essential ingredient of gunpowder, Seward took it upon himself to monitor the stocks and to keep Lincoln informed. He was also willing to take bureaucratic shortcuts. One morning Seward was called on by an old navy friend, John F. Winslow, who brought with him a representative of the Swedish-American inventor John Ericsson. The two visitors advised Seward that Ericsson was eager to build a Union counterpart to the ironclad warship believed to be under construction in the South, but that the Navy Board was withholding funds. Seward introduced his friends to Lincoln and the following day accompanied them to the Navy Department. The navy was persuaded to underwrite Ericsson's vessel, and the result was the famous *Monitor*.[9] Seward was constantly in touch with his political friends in New York State as to how New York might contribute to the war effort. He visited military units around Washington whenever the occasion permitted. The scope of Seward's interests did not sit well with his political enemies, however, and wags around Washington asked whether the secretary of state was head of the army or merely general manager for the administration.[10]

Nevertheless, much of Seward's time was occupied by routine diplomatic correspondence. When the regents of San Marino, a republic of some twenty-four square miles on the Italian peninsula, made Lincoln an honorary citizen, it fell to Seward to acknowledge the honor for Lincoln's signature:

> You have kindly averted to the trial through which this Republic is now passing. It is one of deep import. It involves the question of whether a Representative republic, extended and aggrandized so much as to be safe against foreign enemies, can save itself from the dangers of domestic faction. I have faith in a good result.[11]

As he had with Seward's input to his inaugural address, Lincoln would take this language and turn it into something more eloquent at a place called Gettysburg.

There were also offers of foreign assistance. The king of Siam offered war elephants for use in the military emergency, but Seward declined, expressing regrets. America's expanse did not include the tropical areas favored by elephants, Seward explained, and steam had been the country's "most efficient agent of transportation in internal commerce."[12]

*   *   *

One remarkable episode in 1861 involved an attempt to recruit to the Union cause one of Europe's most respected patriots, Giuseppe Garibaldi. Although he had not yet completed the unification of Italy, the Italian soldier had already overthrown the reactionary Kingdom of the Two Sicilies. Now, lacking the allies necessary for a march on Rome,

Garibaldi lived in semiretirement on an island off Sardinia, awaiting the Call.

When it came, it was from an unexpected direction. A junior American diplomat, Consul James Quiggle at Antwerp, read press reports of Garibaldi's interest in the Northern cause and invited him to become the new Lafayette. Acting totally without instructions, Quiggle assured Garibaldi that the destruction of slavery was the main object of the war, and that President Lincòln would be honored to bestow on him "the highest Army Commission which it is in the power of the President to confer."[13]

Although Seward was doubtless annoyed at the commitments Quiggle had seen fit to make, the man who had sponsored Louis Kossuth in America was himself tantalized by the possibility of obtaining Garibaldi's services—especially after the disastrous Union defeat at Bull Run. He discussed the matter with Lincoln and developed a new approach to Garibaldi, one that bypassed Quiggle and operated through a far more experienced diplomat, Henry Sanford, the minister to Belgium. Seward instructed Sanford to contact "the distinguished Soldier of Freedom" and to promise him a major general's commission "with the hearty welcome of the American People."[14]

Sanford did as he was told, with disappointing results. Garibaldi was willing to go, but only as commander in chief of the Union forces—a position then held by Abraham Lincoln. (In fairness to Garibaldi he probably had in mind the position of commanding general.) Sanford explained that he was authorized only to offer the rank of major general, an offer the Italian politely refused.

*   *   *

One controversial program Seward undertook with Lincoln's blessing was the arrest and detention of persons suspected of disloyalty. The problem was immediate and largely unprecedented. Major East Coast cities like New York, Baltimore, and Washington were hotbeds of Confederate sympathizers. In an era in which all journalism was strident, two of the leading newspapers in New York City openly espoused the rebel cause. Proslavery sentiment was widespread in the border states and could be found even in states like Indiana and Ohio.

The basis for Seward's brief reign as the administration's enforcer was Lincoln's suspension of the writ of habeas corpus on April 27, 1861. The Constitution provided that the writ might be suspended in cases of rebellion or in the event of a need to protect the public safety, and by late April Seward was urging Lincoln to take such action. After the war

Seward recalled that he had gone to the White House alone one day to urge that habeas corpus be suspended, but that the president had at first demurred. When Seward persisted, insisting that "perdition was the sure penalty for further hesitation," the president had changed his mind.[15]

The writ was not suspended everywhere at once, but in increments. By July 1861, the areas in which the president had suspended the writ included most of the East Coast as far north as New York City. Under Lincoln's relaxed executive style, responsibility for the arrest of dissidents was shared by the State and War departments. But Simon Cameron never took his counterintelligence responsibilities so seriously as did the secretary of state. Seward set up a special bureau in his department for internal security, hired detectives, and set about analyzing reports of dissident activity. Many cases were clear cut, especially those in which an accused person was known to have recruited for the Confederate army or peddled Confederate securities. Much less clear, and more threatening to civil liberties, were cases in which a person was charged only with speaking out in support of the rebellion.

The number of persons detained at any given time was never large; it peaked at around two hundred in the fall of 1861. No one died in detention, not even in the dank casemates of Fort Lafayette in New York Harbor or Fort Warren in Boston. But his role as Lincoln's security chief represented quite a switch for Seward, who a few years before had been denouncing British tyranny against Ireland. He is said to have remarked to the British minister, Lord Lyons, "I can touch a bell on my right hand and order the imprisonment of a citizen of Ohio; I can touch the bell again and order the imprisonment of a citizen of New York; and no power on earth, except that of the President, can release them. Can the Queen of England do so much?"[16]

Of 111 prisoners incarcerated in Fort Lafayette in October 1861, 64 were there by Seward's order.[17] Elsewhere, the most impressive catch among those arrested was an undoubted Confederate spy, Rose O'Neal Greenhow. Mrs. Greenhow, a comely widow of forty-four, had been a woman of considerable influence during the Buchanan administration, when statesmen and diplomats—Seward included—dined at her elegant house on Lafayette Park next to St. John's Church. Mrs. Greenhow had a network of acquaintances throughout the capital, and there is evidence to suggest that she was the secret mistress of Sen. Henry Wilson of Massachusetts. She and Seward had known each other for many years, well enough for Rose, in April 1861, to request of Seward that a certain army officer ("a strong Union man") be transferred from the West Coast to Washington.[18]

In July 1861, before the ill-trained Federal army of Gen. Irwin Mc-Dowell sallied forth to meet the Confederates at Bull Run, Mrs. Green-how provided a stream of reports to the Confederate high command concerning McDowell's line of march. A few weeks after the battle, detective Allan Pinkerton put Mrs. Greenhow under surveillance, sat-isfied himself that she was a spy, and had her arrested.

Rose Greenhow went on to become the most celebrated prisoner in the North. First placed under house arrest, she was so blatant in con-tinuing her communication with Confederate couriers that she was transferred to Washington's Old Capitol prison. There she made no attempt to conceal her rebel sympathies and continued to provide copy for the Washington newspapers. On one occasion she appealed to Sew-ard for permission to visit a sick friend, but Seward refused. In Novem-ber 1861 she addressed a dramatic letter to Seward, challenging him to "imprison her soul, if he dared," and blasting the Lincoln administra-tion for trampling on her rights.[19] There was just enough substance in Greenhow's complaints to make the administration uneasy. When in June 1862 the Rebel Rose was repatriated to the Confederacy, Seward, for one, doubtless breathed a sigh of relief.

Mrs. Greenhow's long acquaintance with Seward did her no good, but in some instances friendship did play a role. William Gwin, a pro-slavery former senator from California, had long been a friend of Sew-ard's; in 1858, the New Yorker had successfully averted a threatened duel between Gwin and Senator Wilson of Massachusetts, and in March 1861 Gwin had served briefly as one of Seward's intermediaries with the Confederate commissioners. Gwin returned to California in the spring of 1861, where rumor associated him with attempts to ally his state with the Confederacy. When Gwin traveled to New York City in October 1861, he and two colleagues were promptly arrested on Sew-ard's order. Their attorney had no difficulty in meeting with Seward on the case, however, and all three were shortly released. This may have been a mistake, for Gwin promptly traveled south, where he sponsored a scheme to ally Mexico with the Confederacy.[20]

Wartime Washington was filled with "agents"—rumormongers and influence peddlers of all descriptions; men able to obtain military dis-charges, furloughs, transfers, and pardons; men claiming to have infor-mation vital to the survival of the Republic. Seward took a properly skeptical view of information from such sources. On occasion, however, he acted on insufficient or unreliable evidence. In New Hampshire ex-president Franklin Pierce was bitterly hostile to the Lincoln administra-tion and sympathetic to the South's right of secession. In December

1861 Seward sent a letter to Pierce asking him to respond to an anonymous letter charging him with having traveled to Michigan and Kentucky on behalf of a subversive organization, the Knights of the Golden Circle. Pierce indignantly denied the charge, and Seward had no choice but to apologize. An investigation revealed that the letter containing the charges against Pierce was a fabrication intended to embarrass the administration. Seward had fallen for it.[21]

The targets of the administration's detention campaign were rarely "little people"; rather, they were men of means and influence. Several of Buchanan's diplomatic appointees who were believed to harbor Southern sympathies were routinely detained on their return from abroad. Four secessionist newspapers in New York City were effectively closed by denying them access to the mails. For a time the State Department attempted to censor the mails and the telegraph.

Not even legislative groups were exempt from preemptive strikes. In early September the administration received information that the Maryland legislature, which was to meet in Frederick on September 7, planned to withdraw Maryland from the Union. On September 12, Lincoln, Seward, and Fred Seward went by carriage to the Rockville, Maryland, headquarters of Gen. Nathaniel P. Banks, a Massachusetts officer of uncertain military talents but unquestioned loyalty. More than twenty state legislators were arrested over the next few days by Banks's order, and Maryland stayed in the Union.[22]

In the view of both Lincoln and Seward, the danger to the country was serious enough to justify the suspension of the most basic rights. As Lincoln put it, with characteristic succinctness: "Are all the laws, *but one,* to go unexecuted, and the government itself go to pieces, lest that one be violated?"[23] But justice was frequently tempered with mercy. Because the detainees were politically prominent, pressure was soon brought to bear for their release. Seward probably viewed the process as a deterrent to sedition rather than a punishment; in July 1861 he instructed an officer of the New York Police Commission, Seth Hawley, to reexamine the cases of all the prisoners in Forts Lafayette and Warren, and as a result some seventy prisoners were released. Others became beneficiaries of a general amnesty in February 1862. On February 14, 1862, a presidential order turned over responsibility for political prisoners to the War Department, and Seward's security responsibilities ended.[24]

A student of civil rights under Lincoln has noted that "the hand of Abraham Lincoln can be seen but dimly in the policy of repression. Always, it was the cabinet members, the generals, the United States marshals and district attorneys who ordered and carried out the arrests.''[25] In the South, where Seward was given no credit for his exhaustive efforts to avert war, he came to be hated for his role in the wartime suspension of civil rights. The anecdote of Seward and his bell crossed the Mason-Dixon line. Southern diarist Mary Chesnut, whose husband had served with Seward in the U.S. Senate, wrote of life in the North: ''Seward's little bell reigns supreme.''[26] As for the secretary of state, he would repeatedly deny having boasted about his authority. But he never doubted that the abridgments of civil liberties under the Lincoln administration were necessary given the temper of the times.

*   *   *

Lincoln, in responding to Seward's April 1 ''Thoughts,'' had cited his own paramount role in policy-making. But he did nothing to discourage his energetic secretary of state from undertaking a variety of assignments only marginally related to foreign affairs. Neither the North nor the South began the war with an intelligence network worthy of the name. On each side politicians and generals were besieged with letters from well-meaning compatriots, conveying a variety of military and political information. In the North a motley collection of ''detectives'' supplemented the information so freely provided. One of Seward's recruits was Lafayette Baker, a native of Michigan who had moved on to the California goldfields. In November 1861 Seward sent Baker, with a cavalry escort, to check on political sentiment in eastern Maryland. Writing from Port Tobacco, Baker reported that he could find no more than four or five Union men, and that even the postmaster of the town was a Confederate sympathizer.[27]

Generally, however, Seward preferred to deal with informants and correspondents of whom he had some personal knowledge. With the cabinet's approval, he sent an old friend of Lincoln's, George Ashmun, to Canada, to check on the political climate and to ascertain whether Canada might be outfitting ships for the Confederacy.[28] One of his most astute sources in 1861 was the ubiquitous Sam Ward, who managed to accompany William Russell when the British reporter visited the Confederacy. Using the pseudonym Charles Lopez and writing to Seward's aide George Baker rather than to the secretary himself, Ward smuggled a series of revealing accounts to Seward under the cover of Russell's dispatches. Seward might well have paid more attention to Ward's reports than he did, for the lobbyist and stock speculator had no illusions about latent Unionist sentiment in the South. Following the attack on Fort Sumter, he wrote from Charleston: ''While you are planning, these people are acting. . . . I feel convinced that the people *here* will *never* come back."[29]

Before the war biweekly cabinet meetings had been the rule in Washington. Most often the senior member of the cabinet, the secretary of state, handled procedural matters relating to the cabinet, including the scheduling of meetings. Seward found cabinet meetings unproductive. He doubtless made his point to Lincoln, for the president ceased for a time to hold them on any regular schedule, much less the traditional two times a week. When the cabinet did meet, Seward often dominated. It was somehow in character for Seward to ignore the sensitivities of his "junior" colleagues in a time of national emergency, and his interest in everybody's business gained him few allies.

The friends he did have were fond of referring to him as the "premier" of the Lincoln administration, and his rivals sometimes did so in a sarcastic tone. The fact remains, however, that Lincoln rarely made an important decision without consulting his secretary of state. Navy Secretary Welles, complaining of Seward's absence from several cabinet meetings, acknowledged that there was "a reluctance to discuss and bring to a decision any great decision without him."[30] Secretary of the Interior John P. Usher stated after the war that "The head of Mr. Lincoln's cabinet was Mr. Seward."[31]

16

Aggressive Diplomacy

On July 21, 1861, the first Federal offensive into Virginia resulted in a shattering defeat at Manassas. The next day Seward watched the demoralized crowds in the street from his office window. The military debacle was not of Seward's making. He felt an indirect responsibility, however, for when Lincoln had polled his advisers, asking which of them opposed General McDowell's planned advance, Seward had been silent. In any case the aftermath of defeat was an embarrassment for the secretary of state, in that a setback of the magnitude of first Manassas contradicted the administration position that the Southern insurgency was a passing phenomenon. Not for the last time, Seward sent a dispatch to U.S. missions abroad, seeking to minimize he impact of a military defeat:

> You will receive the account of a deplorable reverse of our arms at Manassas. For a week or two that event will elate the friends of the insurgents in Europe as it confounded and bewildered the friends of the Union here for two or three days. The shock, however, has passed away, producing no other results than a resolution stronger and deeper than ever. . . . The heart of the country is sound.[1]

Seward found himself not only in charge of foreign affairs but responsible for articulating Union war aims to the powers of the world. In most countries Seward's prestige made him uniquely qualified for this role. Britain, however, was an important exception. There the secretary was widely regarded as an Anglophobe, and an irresponsible one at that. Years of support for the Irish "patriots" had left a paper trail that now came back to haunt Seward. In 1850, in a debate on the Clayton-Bulwer Treaty, he had characterized Britain as grasping and rapacious.[2] As recently as November 1860, at a dinner for the visiting Prince of Wales, he had made a flippant remark to the Duke of Newcastle to the effect that as secretary of state it would be his responsibility to insult Britain.[3] The duke took the remark with total seriousness, and the reaction of the London press was so critical that Thurlow Weed, then in Britain, felt obliged to write a letter to the *Times* in Seward's defense.

Long before the secretary of state sent his controversial "Thoughts" to President Lincoln, the British foreign secretary, Lord John Russell, had speculated that Seward might attempt to manufacture a quarrel with Britain as a means of diverting attention from internal U.S. problems.[4] Future prime minister William E. Gladstone, with the condescension he employed with ex-colonials, dismissed the American secretary of state as "a vaporing, blustering, ignorant man."[5] Nor were Russell and Gladstone the only Britons who doubted Seward's capacity and goodwill; Queen Victoria thought him "often reckless and imprudent."[6] The loquacious New Yorker, with his sea-to-shining-sea vision of America, was known to believe that the peaceful absorption of Canada by the United States was only a matter of time. Anxiety in Britain over the underpopulated, weakly defended Canadian provinces was heightened by the attitude of the *New York Times,* which was widely regarded as reflecting Seward's views. Early in 1861 the paper's Washington correspondent observed that any permanent dissolution of the old Union would lead inevitably to the acquisition of Canada by the North.[7] The article, probably planted by Seward, was a warning to London that a Confederate victory might not be in Britain's interest. Lord Lyons, the British minister in Washington, advised the Foreign Office in January 1861 that Seward would be a dangerous secretary of state, "one who would play the old game of seeking popularity at home by displaying violence toward us."[8]

Seward's critics missed a key point. Although the New Yorker was a committed expansionist, he was a peaceful one. If Seward was a tiger in his public statements about Britain, in private he was a tabby cat. As a member of the Senate Foreign Relations Committee, Seward had been a moving force behind the visit to the United States by the Prince of Wales in 1860. One of his closest friends was Lyons's predecessor, Lord Napier, for whom Seward had hosted a lavish farewell in 1859. From his new post in St. Petersburg, Napier wrote a diplomatic colleague that he had received many marks of kindness from Seward, "a kindness he extends to every Englishman.'"[9] Where did the truth lie? Seward seemed genuinely ambiguous in his attitude; he respected Britain as the mother country but viewed it as a commercial rival of the United States and as a force for repression in some parts of the world, especially Ireland.

The negative comments about the American secretary of state made their way from London to Washington, where Seward, smarting, determined to put his apparent liabilities to good use. If the British regarded him as a loose cannon, he would do nothing to dispel this impression. In conversation with Russell of the *Times,* he warned Britain against providing grounds for a quarrel with the United States, adding dryly that a foreign war was the remedy "very generally prescribed" for the Union's difficulties.

*　　*　　*

When the Lincoln administration took office, it inherited no critical problems in foreign relations. U.S. foreign policy consisted largely of relations with Britain, France, and, to a lesser extent, Mexico. Britain and France, which were enjoying a period of unusually amicable relations, were not only the two most powerful nations in the world but were the primary consumers of Southern cotton. Mexico was a special case. Political instability made America's southern neighbor a tempting prize to the imperial powers of Europe; in the short term, moreover, Mexico represented a channel through which supplies might be shipped to the Confederacy to circumvent the Federal blockade.

Because it was the world's greatest maritime power and because its Canadian provinces bordered the United States to the north, Britain was inevitably the most important power with which the United States had to deal. Although most Britons were opposed to slavery, the ruling class was distrustful of democracy and wary of republican influences on British society and politics. A collapse of the brash republic to the west would be welcomed by some members of the English aristocracy, particularly because Lincoln's war was not overtly aimed at putting an end to slavery. Lord John Russell, the British foreign secretary, dismissed the American Civil War as similar to many European conflicts in which two states contended, "the one for empire and the other for power."[10]

To this faintly disparaging attitude toward the American republic Britain added an economic motive. Washington's enactment, in March 1861, of its first protective tariff in decades stirred considerable resentment in British trade circles. But the tariff was a minor irritant compared with the threatened cutoff of American cotton as a result of the blockade. John Bright, a Liberal member of Parliament, wrote to

Charles Sumner: "With our upper-class hostility to your country and government, with the wonderful folly of your tariff telling against you here, and with the damage arising from the blockade of the Southern ports, you will understand that the feeling here is not so thorough and cordial as I could wish it to be."[11]

Fortunately, both Britain and the United States were represented in the other's capital by men of sound judgment and common sense. Charles Francis Adams, fifty-four, was the third member of his family to serve as American minister to Britain. As a member of the House of Representatives he had worked closely with Seward in the years leading up to the war and, like Seward, had attempted to placate the border states in the period prior to Fort Sumter. In patience and imperturbability Adams would prove more than a match for his British hosts.

Adams's counterpart in Washington, Richard Pemell, Lord Lyons, was a ruddy, humorless bachelor of forty-four. He had served nearly twenty years in the foreign ministry, but his record was so undistinguished that President Buchanan had complained of his indifferent credentials. Lyons considered America an acquired taste; he found Washington especially dreary, lacking as it did clubs, good restaurants, or any resident theater companies. But the British envoy was diligent and observant. He was also opposed to slavery and felt none of the elation that some Britons did at the disruption of the Union.

Seward's first instructions to American representatives abroad had directed them to emphasize three points. The first and most important was that the Civil War was an insurrection within the United States; the Confederacy, therefore, had no status in international law. Related to this first point was the second—that the United States would regard any move to recognize the Confederacy as an unfriendly act. Finally the envoys were to emphasize, as evidence of Washington's peaceful intent, that the United States was not attempting to eradicate slavery where it already existed. This last point, while it underscored the fact that secession had been a precipitous act, was perhaps unfortunate, for it denied the Federal cause any moral dimension.

In his instruction to Charles Francis Adams, Seward provided some talking points in the event of particularly strained relations with Britain. Portions of them could only be regarded as threatening:

The British empire itself is an aggregation of diverse communities which cover a large portion of the earth, and embrace one fifth of its entire population. Some, at least, of these communities are held to their places in that system by bonds as fragile as the obligations of our own Federal

Union. . . . Would it be wise for her Majesty's government, on this occasion, to set a dangerous precedent, or provoke retaliation? If Scotland and Ireland are at last reduced to quiet contentment, has Great Britain no dependency, island, or province left exposed along the whole circle of her empire?[12]

Whether Adams ever had occasion to cite this heavy-handed threat to Canada is unclear; quite possibly not, for London was all too aware of the exposed position of its Canadian provinces. With Canada's vulnerability in mind, the Royal Navy was under instructions to behave with strict neutrality. In June the Palmerston government decided to send three additional regiments to Canada, rather than the one previously committed.[13]

The Confederacy, meanwhile, had diplomatic objectives of its own, the most important of which concerned the Federal blockade. The Confederate government, in the process of locating in Richmond, Virginia, had a vital interest in obtaining British intervention against the blockade because it was dependent on munitions from abroad and on the export of its own cotton. Related to the blockade was the issue of diplomatic recognition. Recognition of Confederate independence would not stop Yankee bullets, but it would hearten the peace movement in the North and perhaps provide access to European financial markets.

Even before Fort Sumter, Jefferson Davis had sent three emissaries to Europe in search of diplomatic recognition and commercial concessions. Head of the Confederate delegation was William L. Yancey, called the Prince of Fire-Eaters, a leader of the extremists at the 1860 Democratic convention. Neither he nor his associates were particularly astute diplomats, but their initial reception in London raised fears in Washington that they might succeed in their mission. On May 11, to Seward's distress, Lord John Russell held the first of two meetings with the rebel commissioners. Because the American envoy, Adams, had not yet arrived at his post to represent the North, Russell's action seemed to be an especially gratuitous slap. "God damn them," Seward growled to Charles Sumner, "I'll give them hell."[14]

Injury was soon added to insult. On May 13 the British government issued a proclamation of neutrality that had the effect of recognizing the Confederacy as a belligerent. Under international law, such status gave the Confederacy the right, among others, to purchase arms from neutral nations and to commission cruisers. It is difficult to see how Britain's action could have aroused the ire that it did in the North, for the North's blockade—Seward's artful language notwithstanding—was itself an acknowledgment of Southern belligerency. But for the seceded states to be accorded the status of a belligerent publicly contradicted Washington's insistence that "the insurgents"—Seward's deprecatory term—were little more than a small group of malcontents, a passing phenomenon.

Although Seward consciously exploited his reputation as an Anglophobe, he was as angry as any of his countrymen over Britain's supportive attitude toward the Confederacy. Could Britain conceivably be considering intervention? On May 21 Seward drafted a message to Adams that became known as Dispatch No. 10. As drafted, it constituted a vigorous protest against the Palmerston government's welcome to the Confederate commissioners. So long as contact with the commissioners continued, Seward warned, Adams should have no dealings with the British government. The United States would maintain its blockade of Southern ports and expected Britain to respect it. Recognition of the Confederacy would make the United States an enemy of Britain, with all that this implied. Seward deprecated the possibility of hostilities but said that if war came it would have been provoked by Britain. Lest there be any mistake, Adams was to pass a copy of the dispatch to Lord John Russell.[15]

It was a blistering communication, and Seward had no way of knowing that the Palmerston government had independently concluded that the Confederate commissioners should be kept at arm's length in the future. Although Lincoln rarely altered the language of Seward's diplomatic correspondence, in the case of Dispatch No. 10 he made changes. Where Seward had spoken of Washington's being "surprised and grieved" by British contacts with the Confederate commissioners, Lincoln spoke of "regrets." He deleted the section in which Seward warned explicitly that should Britain intervene in the American war, "we, from that hour, shall cease to be friends and be forced to become enemies of Great Britain." In other places as well Lincoln softened a phrase or two, and he closed by directing that Adams was to communicate only those portions that he thought proper and was not to provide Russell with a copy of the actual dispatch.[16]

Even with Lincoln's changes Adams was shocked by the tone of his instructions. Seward, he decided, was serving notice against any intervention in the Civil War, but it sounded as if the United States was prepared to declare war against all of Europe. In reading the dispatch to Russell, Adams softened the language still further. It was one thing to keep London in doubt as to Seward's temperament and intentions; it was another to provoke the British unnecessarily. Nevertheless, he would later credit Seward with shocking the Palmerston government into a more cautious policy.[17]

Seward's truculence was also troubling to President Lincoln. Because the president had neither the time nor the inclination to be his own secretary of state, his solution was to tap a new source of diplomatic expertise—Charles Sumner, the senior senator from Massachusetts. Sumner had long been a favorite of upper-class English liberals, and he regarded himself as the preeminent expert on Anglo-American relations. During the presidential campaign of 1860 he had assiduously cultivated Seward, praising his campaign speeches in terms that Seward himself probably found effusive. Months later, passed over for secretary of state, Sumner could find nothing in Seward's policies with which to agree. He quarreled over appointments, deplored the secretary's preoccupation with diplomacy as opposed to slavery, and criticized the administration decision to blockade Confederate ports.[18]

That Seward might have sound reasons for an anti-British line never seems to have occurred to the stolid Sumner, who joined Lyons and the French minister, Henri Mercier, in regretting Seward's hawkish rhetoric. Had Sumner been on better terms with Charles Francis Adams he might have seen the light, for Seward had made clear to Adams that his tough line with Lyons was deliberate. "You could do no greater harm," Seward wrote in July, "than by inducing an opinion that I am less decided in my intercourse with the British Minister than I am reputed to be, or less determined to maintain the pride and dignity of our government."[19] But Adams and Sumner were political antagonists, and Sumner's correspondents in Britain did not include the American minister.

Seward never doubted the eventual success of Union arms, and in part because of this confidence he refused to consider offers of mediation from Britain or France. He sought to discourage joint initiatives by the two countries: In June 1861 he politely declined to meet with Lyons and Mercier together, insisting on dealing with them separately. Relations between the two European powers were amicable during the American Civil War, but what was good for the peace of Europe was not necessarily good for the United States.

By June, although he no longer feared for the safety of Washington, Seward had enough problems to handle in his own department that he was less prone to meddle in the affairs of others, as he had done at the time of Fort Sumter. His relations with Lincoln were cordial and becoming more so, but there was no element of hero worship on Seward's part; in June 1861 he wrote to Frances:

> The war is ostensibly prosecuted with vigor. But you have no idea how incessant my labors are to keep the conduct of it up to the line of necessity

and public expectation. Executive skill and vigor are rare qualities. The President is the best of us, but he needs constant and assiduous cooperation.[20]

One area in which Seward was able to assist the president was in the selection of a new secretary of war. Lincoln's first choice, Simon Cameron, had proved clearly inadequate to the requirements of a major department in wartime; of all the members of Lincoln's first cabinet, he was probably the poorest administrator. Lincoln was reluctant to dismiss the Pennsylvanian, Cameron, but when his minister to Russia, Cassius Clay, indicated that he wanted to return to the United States, Lincoln informed Cameron that he would be Clay's replacement. Seward strongly urged the appointment of Edwin M. Stanton, who had provided him with much useful information on the deliberations of Buchanan's cabinet, as Cameron's successor. Although the energetic Stanton had lined up considerable support on his own behalf, Welles and Blair later acknowledged Seward's primary role in securing Stanton's appointment.

* * *

The cordial welcome accorded the first Confederate envoys to Britain was proving to be a false promise. When the three commissioners were never again allowed even an informal meeting with the foreign minister, Richmond decided that it would be necessary to upgrade the quality of its diplomatic representation in Europe. In August 1861 President Davis designated James Mason of Virginia and John Slidell of Louisiana as Confederate envoys to Britain and France. The pompous Mason was a vociferous defender of slavery and an old antagonist of Seward's in the U.S. Senate. Diarist Mary Chesnut thought him a preposterous choice as a diplomat: "The English can't stand chewing [tobacco]. [Yet] they say at the lordliest table, Mr. Mason will turn round halfway in his chair and spit in the fire!"[21] But if Mason was something of a caricature, Slidell was not. Charles Francis Adams viewed him as an adroit operator who would be very much at home in the intrigue-ridden court of Napoleon III.[22]

The new Confederate commissioners seemed in no hurry to depart, but by mid-October they were in Charleston. Slidell was accompanied by his wife and three children; Mason traveled with only a secretary. In Charleston they chartered a fast, shallow-draft steamer in which to dodge Federal blockaders outside Charleston harbor. On the night of October 12, their ship made it through the blockade, first to Nassau and then to Havana. There the emissaries discovered that they had missed the British mail packet and would have to wait three weeks for another.

The location of the Confederate commissioners was no secret, and an American naval officer made plans to do something about them. Capt. Charles Wilkes of the *San Jacinto* was a veteran of the Old Navy; after more than four decades of service his reputation was that of an "insubordinate, impulsive, overzealous, and yet fairly efficient" officer.[23] On the afternoon of November 8, in the Bahama Channel, the *San Jacinto* fired a warning shot across the bow of the British packet *Trent*. When the British vessel hove to, Wilkes sent a boarding party to remove the commissioners and their entourage.

The commissioners went cheerfully, and even today some speculation remains that the highly public sailing was intended to provoke a response that would embroil the United States with Britain. If so, initial signs were favorable. Welles congratulated Wilkes on his initiative, and Congress voted him a gold medal. Eastern cities hosted testimonial dinners in his honor. The fact that Britain—so long the bully of the high seas—was at last getting a taste of its own medicine touched a vein of Anglophobia in the Northern populace. In Richmond, meanwhile, Jefferson Davis told the Confederate Congress that Mason and Slidell, while aboard the *Trent*, "were as much under the jurisdiction of the British Government" as if they had been walking the streets of London.[24]

Word of the *Trent* affair reached London on November 27. "You may stand for this, but damned if I will!" Palmerston exclaimed, when he heard of the incident during a cabinet meeting.[25] The press promised speedy retribution for a gross insult to the British flag. The *Times* of London admitted that the British themselves had committed similar acts during the Napoleonic Wars, but nevertheless treated the *Trent* incident as totally unacceptable. Some blamed the mess on Seward personally; a Dublin paper observed that "Mr Seward's want of common sense, reliance, and principle, have long been notorious to Americans. . . . Unhappily, until yesterday, we had not been able fully to appreciate the extent and depth of his moral and mental unworthiness."[26] Thurlow Weed, who was in London on a public relations mission, wrote to Secretary of War Cameron that in Britain everyone expected war.

On the official level, however, the Palmerston government moved with deliberation. On November 30 Russell sent a dispatch to Lyons demanding the release of Mason and Slidell—who were by then in Fort Warren—and an apology by the United States. In an accompanying letter, Lyons was told that he should allow just seven days from the time he delivered the message for the U.S. response, and if no satisfactory response was received by that time he should request his passport and return to Britain. At the same time, Russell instructed Lyons to call on Seward informally, advise him of London's position, and ask him to discuss the matter with the president and the cabinet before presenting the note.[27] The effect of this additional instruction was to extend the time available for consultation within the Lincoln administration. The seven-day "clock" would not begin to run until Lyons's note was formally presented. For the most part, however, the British still viewed Seward as an obstacle. Russell wrote to Lyons on December 1 that "the best thing would be if Seward could be turned out, and a rational man put in his place."[28]

In fact, no one was more interested in resolving the *Trent* affair than Seward. As early as November 27, he had assured Adams that Wilkes had acted on his own. When Lyons, on December 19, advised him of the contents of his government's note, Seward expressed appreciation for London's forbearance, adding that he would consult with the president and give Lyons his response within forty-eight hours. Seward was already searching for a graceful exit from the predicament in which the administration found itself. When Lincoln at first indicated that he was unwilling to hand over the envoys, Seward warned him that his choices were to surrender Mason and Slidell or face a real possibility of war with Britain, "and war means the instant defense of New York, Boston and Philadelphia."[29]

Forty-eight hours, however, were not enough. Lincoln was moving toward a middle ground, that of submitting the issue to arbitration, and he was not inclined to rush his decision. Sumner, too, favored arbitration. Seward was faced with the daunting task of convincing Lincoln and, if possible, a portion of his cabinet that Mason and Slidell must be given up. But Seward knew his international law. He remarked to Fred, "We are asked [by London] to do to the British nation just what we have always insisted all nations ought to do to us."[30]

On Christmas Day a four-hour cabinet session that began at ten o'clock was devoted entirely to discussion of Seward's reply to Lyons. Sumner, chairman of the Senate Foreign Relations Committee, was also present, but as the meeting opened Seward had only one ally in advocating release of the prisoners, the acerbic postmaster general, Montgomery Blair. Although no transcript of the meeting exists, it appears to have been dominated by Seward, who argued that the release of Mason and Slidell would in fact be an affirmation of the traditional U.S.

position concerning the rights of neutrals, and that as such it could be made palatable to the Northern public.

Nevertheless this first session did not produce agreement. As the meeting broke up, Lincoln told Seward that he was inclined to draft a paper of his own, a brief for why the prisoners should not be returned. The next day the cabinet met again and in a much shorter session adopted Seward's draft, without enthusiasm but without audible dissent. After the meeting Seward commented to Lincoln that he had not produced a competing draft. The president smiled and shook his head, remarking that he had found he could not produce a convincing counterargument. [31]

Seward's note to Lyons was a long, highly political document. The secretary addressed the questions of whether Wilkes was justified in stopping and searching the *Trent;* whether the Confederate emissaries might properly be regarded as contraband; and whether Wilkes had carried out his search in a proper manner. All such questions Seward answered in the affirmative. Then he raised a question of procedure and concluded that the captives were wrongly held because the *Trent* had not been taken to a U.S. court and properly condemned! It was a virtuoso performance, one that freed the Confederate emissaries on a technicality.

As a cold dawn broke over Provincetown, Massachusetts, on New Year's Day, 1862, the residents were treated to the sight of a British sloop, the *Rinaldo,* at anchor in the harbor. Word quickly spread that the vessel was somehow related to the *Trent* affair. Late that afternoon, a tug from Boston brought the two Confederate emissaries from their imprisonment at Fort Warren. Mason, portly and bald, and Slidell, slim and taciturn, were transferred with their luggage to the *Rinaldo.* The *Trent* affair was over, and with its settlement went the best prospect for British intervention on behalf of the South.

*   *   *

In part because the press commentary was so extreme on both sides of the Atlantic, the *Trent* affair has sometimes been treated as a greater threat to Anglo-American relations than it really was. Neither Britain nor the United States had any incentive to go to war with the other. The Palmerston government, notwithstanding its distaste for the United States in general and Seward in particular, handled the problem with great skill, giving the Lincoln administration ample time to develop the position Seward so skillfully formulated. And Seward, when faced with a crisis, put aside his anti-British rhetoric and dealt with the matter as professionally as Lyons did. Paradoxically, resolution of the problem was probably assisted by the slow communications of the day, which allowed tempers to cool in both London and Washington and tended to minimize the impact of all except the first wave of inflammatory press comment.

Seward demonstrated considerable courage in taking the principal responsibility for the unpopular step of releasing Mason and Slidell, a point that Lyons, for one, was quick to recognize. So did Lyons's predecessor, Lord Napier, who wrote Seward from Russia to congratulate him "most heartily on the preservation of peace."[32] Frances felt that Henry had sacrificed himself for the nation's good, "nobody else having sufficient magnanimity to do so."[33] An unidentified source assured Russell of the *Times* that he should never be deceived by strong talk from Seward: "When Seward talks that way, he means to break down. He is most dangerous and obstinate when he pretends to agree with you."[34]

At first glance the political damage to Seward from the *Trent* affair appeared to be minimal. Even in the North, the predominant sentiment was one of relief that the issue had been peacefully resolved. A positive result for Seward was that Lincoln was less inclined to seek foreign policy advice from sources other than his secretary of state. But the outcome made Seward no friends in the cabinet, where Chase and Welles had opposed release of the prisoners. And in Congress, where there was some reluctance to attack the president in time of war, Seward enjoyed no such immunity. Sen. John Hale of New Hampshire announced on December 26 that *he* would never have submitted to "the absolute demand of Great Britain to surrender these men and humble our flag," even to avoid war.[35]

Two years later, when British recognition of the Confederacy was a dead issue, Seward's counterpart in Richmond, Judah P. Benjamin, paid tribute to his rival's diplomacy. The most surprising development of the war, he wrote to Slidell in Paris, was "the thorough conviction entertained by the British ministry that the United States are ready to declare war against England. . . . It is impossible not to admire the sagacity with which Mr. Seward penetrated into the secret feelings of the British cabinet, and the success of his policy of intimidation."[36]

17

"The Scenes Are Unwritten"

BY THE FALL of 1861 dissatisfaction over the progress of the war was growing in the North. The defeat at Manassas had been followed by stalemate in the West. The Union commander in Missouri, erstwhile presidential candidate John C. Frémont, had been relieved after issuing on his own authority an order for the emancipation of slaves. Federal military campaigns were badly coordinated, if coordinated at all. Only at sea, where the Federal navy was tightening the blockade of Southern ports, did the war appear to be going well. Even Seward had difficulty maintaining his customary good cheer, writing Frances on one occasion, "I do not yield to despondency. But I hardly dare maintain cheerfulness, lest it seem to be indulgence in mockery."[1]

In the East, McClellan was a victim both of his own inaction and of hostility from congressional radicals who sought to make abolition the North's principal war aim. Seward had initially held high hopes for McClellan, but by March 1862 he marveled at Lincoln's patience in keeping him in command. To Sam Ward, Seward expressed doubt that there were as many Confederate troops in northern Virginia as there were soldiers from New York—an estimate closer to the truth than McClellan's inflated figures.[2]

In this gloomy time the growing personal friendship between Lincoln and Seward was proving to be a solace for both men. In the first part of the year, Seward's attitude had been ambivalent. Lincoln, who liked to say that he had never knowingly planted a thorn in any man's bosom, had planted one in Seward's by denying him the presidency. But Seward liked Lincoln and was coming to respect him as well. For his part, Lincoln appears to have taken a liking to the sometimes bumptious New

Yorker, appreciating both his political acumen and his willingness to accept an uncomfortable subordinate relationship. More and more odd jobs came Seward's way: Lincoln did not believe that the responsibility belonged to the secretary of state, but would Seward examine a proposed treaty with the Delaware Indians? He would.

James Scovel, a New Jersey–born newspaper reporter who enjoyed Lincoln's confidence, had excellent access to the White House; on occasion he was even admitted on Sunday mornings, a period normally reserved for Seward and the presidential barber. Scovel could not forget the sight of Lincoln discussing recent developments with his secretary of state. "Mr. Seward in conversation was slow and methodical till warmed up, when he was one of the most eloquent of talkers," Scovel recalled. But he thought the two made an odd couple. "The impression following an hour with Seward and Lincoln was surprise that two men seemingly so unlike in habit of thought and manner of speech could act in such . . . perfect accord."[3] Even in the early months of his administration Lincoln had deferred to his secretary of state in a way that irritated men like Chase and Welles. Now, with Seward's adroit handling of the *Trent* affair, Lincoln believed that his original judgment had been fully vindicated.

Not only did Seward have free run of the White House, but the president was a frequent visitor to the Seward residence as well. The protocol was unusual, but Lincoln liked to drop in on people, and the horde of office seekers that inundated the White House made it imperative for him to have some sanctuary.

There was another problem as well, for Mary Lincoln could not abide William Henry Seward. Why the president's wife took such a dislike to the secretary of state is unclear. Part of it was political; Mrs. Lincoln was a Southerner, and to her Seward was that "dirty abolition sneak."[4] Quite apart from Seward's political views, however, his very prominence appeared threatening to Mary Lincoln. When Lincoln was still in Springfield, a political supporter of Seward's called on Lincoln and in Mary Lincoln's presence urged Seward's appointment as secretary of state. Mrs. Lincoln allegedly jumped into the conversation, crying, "Never! Never! If things should go on all right, the credit would go to *Seward*—if they went wrong, the blame would fall upon my husband. Seward in the cabinet! *Never!*"[5]

Although Seward kept his distance from Mary Lincoln, the first lady could not always be ignored. Following a state visit in 1861 by Prince Napoleon—a cousin of the emperor and second in line for the French throne—Seward was approached rather uneasily by Secretary of the

Interior Caleb Smith. Smith had received, out of the blue, a bill from Mrs. Lincoln for $900 for the dinner she had hosted for Prince Napoleon. The White House had its own entertainment budget, but Mary Lincoln did not believe in budgets and was attempting to foist some entertainment costs on the Interior Department. Seward advised Smith not to pay the bill, noting that he himself had hosted a comparable dinner for the prince for only $300.[6] Ultimately Mary Lincoln worked up so violent an antipathy for Seward that she ordered her coachman to avoid passing the Seward residence.[7]

It was a one-sided vendetta, for Seward was devoid of malice toward the Lincolns. He was especially fond of the Lincoln boys, Tad and Willie, and had earlier presented them with two cats from the Seward menagerie. Nor were others of the Seward family in any way hostile toward the man who had defeated the paterfamilias for the Republican presidential nomination. Frances was respectful, and Fred, who ran many errands between the State Department and the White House, had become devoted to the president.

When Frances Seward visited Washington in September 1861, protocol required a call on the first lady. The Sewards, probably with some trepidation, scheduled a visit. Fanny described in her diary what happened:

> After dinner, according to our previous plans, we went to call on Mrs. Lincoln. . . . We were shown by [a doorman] into the blue and gold room and all seated. . . . Father told him to tell the boys he wanted to see the cats. . . . Well there we sat . . . after a lapse of some time the usher came in and said Mrs. Lincoln begged to be excused, she was *very* much engaged.[8]

In the Seward parlor, away from Mary Lincoln and the office seekers, Lincoln and Seward could stretch out in front of a fire and discuss anything that came to mind. Both men were lawyers, and for Lincoln these visits may have been reminiscent of relaxed hours on the circuit in Illinois. Both men were keen judges of character and doubtless spent many hours discussing prospective appointments. The two men even had their little bets. Once, when navy ships were attempting to corner a Confederate blockade runner, the *Nashville,* a friend of Lincoln's telegraphed from New York City: "You have won the quart of hazelnuts from the Secretary of State. The *Nashville* is not destroyed, but is actively at work."[9]

Both Lincoln and Seward were accomplished storytellers and each

had a well-developed sense of humor. Whereas some of Lincoln's associates considered the president's jokes and stories undignified for one in
his position, Seward enjoyed them thoroughly. Tastes in humor change,
and both men's stories seem heavy and dated today, often employing
as their butts preachers, blacks, and Irishmen. One of Seward's stories
concerned a clergyman who delivered a particularly eloquent sermon
while a thunderstorm raged outside the church. Asked by members of
the congregation if they could print his excellent sermon, the minister
replied that they were welcome to print it "if you will print the *thunder*
and *lightning* too."[10]

As Lincoln and Seward became more comfortable in their relationship, the latter became a target of the president's wit. According to Fred
Seward, his father, searching for the president in the White House, once
found him polishing his boots. When Seward remonstrated, telling Lincoln sternly that in Washington "we do not blacken our own boots,"
the president was equal to the occasion, remarking good-humoredly,
"Indeed, then whose boots *do* you blacken, Mr. Secretary?"[11]

A well-known Lincoln anecdote grew out of Seward's propensity for
profanity. One day, according to the story, Lincoln, Seward, and an
unidentified staff officer used a mule-drawn ambulance in order to attend a military review on the Virginia side of the Potomac. When the
presidential party reached the Virginia side, the road deteriorated and
the driver had difficulty controlling his team. He began to swear, and
as the road became still more heavily rutted, his profanity increased.
The president asked him pleasantly, "My friend, are you an Episcopalian?" Surprised, the teamster replied that he wasn't much of anything, but when he went to services it was at the Methodist church.
"Oh, excuse me," remarked Lincoln, with a twinkle. "I thought you
must be an Episcopalian, for you swear just like Mr. Seward, and he is
a church warden."[12]

*   *   *

Lincoln and Seward still viewed the war as one to restore the Union,
but others saw it differently. Abolitionists had represented a significant
faction in the Republican party that had carried Lincoln to victory, and
as the Union military campaigns floundered, radical Republicans urged
that the war be changed into one for emancipation. Nothing more clearly
mirrored the split within the ruling party than the state of Seward's
relations with Charles Sumner. Once allies in the fight against slavery,
they were now barely speaking. The first disagreement had come over
Seward's attempts to conciliate the South prior to Fort Sumter. Their

relations were further strained by foreign policy differences, particularly Sumner's criticism of the blockade of Confederate ports. By 1862 they were at odds over war aims. Sumner thought that Seward, being merely a politician, "did not see the elemental forces" involved in the Civil War and "failed to see this war in its true character" as a struggle for human freedom everywhere.[13]

In fact Seward was fully aware that the war was also a revolution. Or was it a counterrevolution? He wrote to his minister in Brussels, Henry Sanford, that they were participants in a great drama. "The scenes are unwritten, the parts unstudied, the actors come on without notice, and often pass off in ways unexpected."[14] Seward fully expected a Union victory that would end slavery, but he was wary of the growing sentiment for emancipation. He feared its effect in those border states still loyal to the Union, writing to Charles Francis Adams early in 1862 that "every demonstration against slavery puts our assured position in Maryland, Kentucky, Missouri and [West] Virginia at hazard."[15] He was as fearful as any Southerner of the long-term effects of a slave uprising in the Confederacy, believing that such a revolutionary development would make the restoration of the Union even more difficult and might even lead Britain or France to intervene to protect its cotton supply. Moreover, premature emancipation might cause slaves in the seceded states to starve.

Among those unconvinced by this line of reasoning was Frances. She weighed in on the side of emancipation, writing to Henry in March 1862 that it would be as well "to let [the slaves] take their chance for starvation as to leave them exposed to such horrible cruelty as is sometimes their fate."[16] Later in the year she complained that Lincoln "gives the impression that the mere keeping together [of] a number of states is more important than human freedom."[17] Although Frances's nominal target was the president, the criticism was equally applicable to her Henry.

The emancipation issue inevitably led to questions about assimilation. Lincoln, who had grave doubts about assimilation, was attracted to the idea of colonization. He told a group of black leaders in 1862 that slavery was a great wrong but that blacks had little prospect of achieving equality in the United States. "There is an unwillingness on the part of our people, harsh as it may be, for you free colored people to remain among us. . . . It is a fact with which we have to deal."[18] As a result it fell to Seward to look into the possibility of exporting newly freed slaves to islands in the Caribbean. Seward had no faith in the project, for he did not believe that American blacks would consent to being shipped to foreign lands. Moreover, he professed optimism with regard to assimilation, commenting grandly on one occasion: "I am always for bringing men and states *into* the Union, never for taking any *out.*"[19]

When Seward inquired into the possibility of colonization, he met a cool reception. The European nations wanted no part of it. The U.S. minister to Nicaragua reported that the people there were strongly opposed to the scheme, and his counterpart in Costa Rica commented on "the excitement prevailing [in] Nicaragua and Honduras on account of a dreaded deluge" of American blacks.[20] But there were some positive responses as well. The government of New Granada (present-day Colombia) was receptive, as was Brazil. The minister to Brazil, Seward's erstwhile newspaper ally James Watson Webb, believed that Brazil's vast land resources made colonization feasible there. He suggested that the United States should ship freed blacks to Brazil at its own expense, and that Brazil should provide land grants and assurance of eventual citizenship. Seward, however, weighed Webb's response against the negative attitudes of other South American governments and his own misgivings, and took no action. Late in 1862, Congress provided $600,000 for the settlement of freedmen in New Granada, but by then Lincoln himself had had second thoughts, and colonization schemes disappeared into the gray limbo of bureaucratic inaction.[21]

Where he could attack slavery circumspectly, Seward did so. He supported and implemented an edict that ended the slave trade in Washington, D.C. He advocated the use of blacks in the Union armies. And in April 1862 he concluded a treaty with Britain that provided for Anglo-American cooperation in the suppression of the slave trade. Under the treaty, certain vessels of the British and U.S. navies were allowed to stop and search ships of the other nation that might be trading in slaves. The importance of this treaty in reducing the commerce in slaves is debatable, but Seward commented: "If I have done nothing else worthy of self-congratulation, I deem this treaty sufficient to have lived for."[22]

Seward's zeal for the nation's blacks had limits, however. When a group of black soldiers complained that their wage scale was lower than that of white soldiers, Seward replied somewhat testily: "The duty of the colored man to defend his country . . . is the same [as] that of the white man. It does not depend on . . . what the country pays us or what position she assigns us; but depends on her need alone."[23]

Seward was remiss in failing to appreciate the propaganda potential of a stronger stand on slavery in dealings with foreign governments. As noted earlier he could have added a moral dimension to the Union cause merely by suggesting in his diplomatic circulars that the United States hoped that the war might hasten the end of slavery. Instead, throughout 1861 and much of the following year, U.S. diplomats were under instructions not even to discuss the emancipation issue with their host governments. John Bigelow, the American consul in Paris, was one of those who protested. Publicity was Bigelow's specialty, and he complained in October that Confederate agents in Europe were insisting that blacks were no better off under Lincoln than under Jefferson Davis. Seward, in response, took refuge in platitudes, writing on one occasion that "foreign sympathy . . . never did and never can create or maintain any state."[24] To Thurlow Weed, Seward wrote cryptically in April 1862 that it was either too early or too late for an emancipation proclamation.[25]

Seward's foot-dragging on the emancipation issue was unusual, for he and Lincoln saw eye to eye on most such matters. This coincidence of views was just as well, for Seward was in the process of losing such independent political strength as he retained. Lincoln early fell into the habit of convening the cabinet only when he had something to discuss. Written notification came from Seward, who usually employed Fred as his messenger. Welles and Chase were among those who complained that whereas Seward was always at hand when the problems of their departments were discussed, they were never around when foreign policy was under discussion. Blair protested that Seward had too great a say about appointments in the Post Office Department. Caleb Smith, informed by Seward at the White House that a scheduled cabinet session had been postponed, grumbled that it might be just as well to cancel them altogether. Welles complained in his diary that Seward was a manipulator; he "delighted in oblique and indirect movement . . . [and] had a craving desire that the world should consider him the great and controlling mind of his party, of the Administration, and of the country."[26]

Welles is hard on Seward, but one way or another the secretary of state had made himself unpopular with virtually the entire cabinet. He thought of himself as the president's "premier," and despite his growing appreciation of Lincoln, he remained convinced that the president required firm guidance. With regard to cabinet meetings, Chase and Welles eventually had their way, as Lincoln promised to try to meet with the cabinet on Tuesdays and Thursdays.

Nor was Seward, even with Weed's backing, the power that he had once been in the Republican party. Seward described himself, in a letter to Weed, as "a man who has faith in everybody, and enjoys the confidence of nobody."[27] To be sure, Lincoln accorded him a dominant voice in patronage matters as they affected New York State. But Seward's conservatism on the question of emancipation damaged him at home, as did his renunciation of any intent to run again for elective office. Early in 1862, a group of Seward's admirers formed a Seward Club to support the New Yorker in another try for the presidency. Seward replied a bit sanctimoniously that he had been tempted to retire from government in 1860 but had chosen instead to serve where he could:

> I renounced all ambition, and came into the Executive Government to aid in saving the Constitution and integrity of my country. . . . [I renounced] all expectation of future political advantage, in order that the counsels I might give to the President . . . should . . . be recognized as being disinterested, loyal, and patriotic. . . .
> So I neither look for, nor should it be offered to me, would I ever hereafter accept, any reward.[28]

Seward was serving at the pleasure of the president, and he was serving loyally. But at times he looked back to the Republican Convention at Chicago and reflected on what might have been. When a Republican congressman called to complain that failure to give Carl Schurz a certain post would disappoint many people, Seward shot back: "Disappointment! You speak to me of disappointment. To me, who was justly entitled to the Republican nomination for the presidency, and who had to stand aside and see it given to a little Illinois lawyer! You speak to me of disappointment!"[29]

*   *   *

If foreign relations during 1861 were dominated by issues between the United States and Britain, for the remainder of the war and certainly for the period of his service in the cabinet of Andrew Johnson, Seward would be concerned with Franco-American relations as much as with his country's slowly improving relations with Britain. Napoleon III was a ruler of doubtful legitimacy, having seized power by a coup in 1851. As emperor he held all important powers, censored the press, and turned the legislature into a rubber stamp for his policies. For all his pomp, Napoleon III was personally unprepossessing. He was short and stout and, according to John Hay, walked sideways rather like a "gouty crab."[30] The emperor professed to desire a more liberal parliamentary regime as soon as his people were "ready." Meanwhile his political base was the peasantry, and continued peasant support required continued economic prosperity.

Franco-American relations bore none of the scars of an earlier separation that conditioned attitudes toward the United States in Britain. Although some Frenchmen felt a romantic attachment to the Southern "cavaliers," to most the American Civil War and the issues attendant on it seemed remote. French attitudes toward America were strongly conditioned by France's need for American cotton and by France's imperial designs in the Western Hemisphere. As early as 1862 Napoleon III was considering how best to turn Mexico into a French dependency. Whatever means might be employed, his prospects would be far better if the Civil War succeeded in dividing the United States.

Reports from the U.S. envoys in Paris, Dayton and Bigelow, in the autumn of 1861, indicated that France was leaning toward intervention on the side of the Confederacy. Some offer of mediation was in the wind—one that would probably give the Confederacy the autonomy it sought. Both the French foreign minister, Edouard Thouvenel, and his envoy in Washington, Mercier, were sympathetic to the Confederacy. French industrialists were becoming alarmed by the possibility of a cotton shortage. Late in 1861 France began pressing Britain to take joint steps to guarantee access to Southern cotton. From Washington, Mercier proposed to the foreign ministry that Britain and France both recognize the Confederacy and refuse to recognize the Federal blockade. Thouvenel was more cautious, limiting himself to expressions of hope that the blockade might be relaxed so as to allow cotton to get through.[31]

Long before Fort Sumter Southern orators had been fond of references to "King Cotton" and "King Cotton diplomacy." According to them, Europe's requirement for Southern cotton was the key to the successful establishment of an independent nation in the South. Europe would recognize the Confederacy as a means of assuring access to its primary source of raw cotton.

"King Cotton diplomacy" with respect to Britain was handicapped by the fact that for most of 1861 and 1862 the mills in Britain had a surplus of cotton on hand. As for France, which did not have a cotton surplus, Seward turned the Southern argument on its head. Union forces had already seized the ports of Mobile and New Orleans, he pointed out, and Washington would do all that it could to meet France's cotton requirements through these ports and others shortly to be occupied. Soft-pedaling the fact that Southern planters might not rush to trade through Yankee-held ports, Seward held out the prospect of at least a limited restoration of trade in cotton. As for a full restoration of the cotton trade, France could best bring it about by doing nothing to encourage the insurgents.

In cotton diplomacy, as elsewhere, Seward's mind was never at rest. He corresponded with Gen. Nathaniel Banks about the possibility of growing cotton in southern Illinois as an alternative to Southern cotton. Regarding Napoleon III as weak, he encouraged the visit to the United States by the emperor's cousin, Prince Napoleon, in the summer of 1861. The prince was warmly received, and the visit confirmed his Northern sympathies. On his return he spoke favorably of the Union cause. Seward wrote: "By becoming a defender of Democracy in its first and greatest trial on this Continent, you have established already a claim on the gratitude of mankind."[32]

In Washington, most of the diplomatic envoys represented European monarchies, and, as a result, Seward's democratic philosophy was not universally popular. Nevertheless, the secretary of state was nothing if not accessible; any request by a foreign envoy for an appointment was promptly granted. Once ushered into Seward's third-floor office, the visitor made himself as comfortable as he could in one of the heavy leather-covered chairs of the day. A conversation often began with small talk concerning activities of the diplomatic corps, but for a caller who then reflected skepticism as to Federal prospects, Seward was a formidable advocate. The "insurgents"—Seward's normal term—were but a militant minority within their own section, where the war was increasingly unpopular. The North was suffering heavy casualties, to be sure, but it was prepared to see the war to the finish. To hints that the United States was too large an area for one nation, Seward snorted that it was too small for two.

As the Army of the Potomac grew in numbers and potential, Seward wondered whether Confederate leaders might consider terms to end the fighting. In April 1862 the French minister, Mercier, requested permission to visit Richmond, ostensibly to check on the status of French nationals there. Although Seward was probably aware of the Frenchman's sympathies, he approved the trip and allowed Mercier to use the army telegraph to request that a French frigate, then at Norfolk, call at Washington to provide transport. Knowing that Mercier would be seeing Davis, Benjamin, and other Confederate leaders, Seward—probably after consulting Lincoln—made what would be his final effort to avert further bloodshed. He told Mercier:

> You may . . . tell them that they have no spirit of vengeance to apprehend from me personally, and that they would be cordially welcomed back to their seats in the Senate, and to their due share of political influence. I have not said so to any other person, but I'll tell you that I am

willing to risk my own political station and reputation in pursuing a conciliatory course toward the South, and I am ready to make this my policy and to stand or fall by it.[33]

When Mercier met with Benjamin, he carried a warning of his own. The North was assembling an immense war machine, Mercier said, and the South could expect no help from Europe. The coastal cities of the Confederacy must inevitably fall to the Federal navy. Should not the South respond to Seward's olive branch, which might become "serious guarantees?" Benjamin was totally unresponsive, telling Mercier that the time for such "patching-up" had passed. "We are two distinct peoples," he told the Frenchman, "and each should have its separate existence." If the coastal cities fell, Southerners would fight the Yankees in the interior.[34]

Seward may have erred in approving Mercier's trip south. When the Frenchman returned to Washington, he shared his impressions with Lyons—impressions that were quite different from the optimistic line being promoted by the State Department. Lyons quoted Mercier as being impressed by the South's devotion to its cause. Southerners, the Frenchman said, "will endure any privations and sufferings rather than be again united to the North."[35] Seward, too, heard Mercier's story and had him repeat it to Lincoln. The president listened without comment. The war would continue.

* * *

In the spring of 1862 France was reluctant to take unilateral action toward recognizing the Confederacy or to be more active in urging mediation. Despite setbacks in the East, Union successes in fighting along the Mississippi and in opening Southern ports to cotton exports dictated caution in dismissing Union prospects. In this changing situation, Seward's threats of dire consequences in the event of European interference could not be taken lightly.

But although the North had powerful friends in Britain like reformers John Bright and Richard Cobden, it had few influential friends in France. John Bigelow, in Paris, reported in August that the emperor had lost "pretty much all of the little faith he had in our ability to reduce the South . . . and he is now hovering over us, like the carrion crow over the body of the sinking traveler." At the same time, Bigelow also felt that the French public was sufficiently hostile toward slavery that it would not approve any policy helpful to the South.[36]

Into this delicate balance lurched the Russian bear. Few nations had less in common than the United States and imperial Russia. Not only did their peoples have different backgrounds, speak different languages, and represent disparate cultures, but few Americans had anything but distaste for the repressive despotism of czarist Russia.

Nevertheless, common interests brought the two countries together in the 1860s. Lincoln and Seward saw Russia as the one European power that might be of assistance in the event of trouble with Britain or France. Russia saw the United States as the primary counter to British maritime dominance. Thus a common antagonism toward Britain was perceived in St. Petersburg as the basis for an entente cordiale with Washington.

Following Gen. George McClellan's defeat before Richmond in May 1862, Napoleon III decided that the time for intervention had arrived. He informed Russell that France was prepared to recognize the Confederacy if Britain would go along, and he was also available for any attempt at mediation. The Palmerston government was sympathetic but inclined to procrastinate. September brought the great battle at Antietam, followed by Lee's withdrawal to Virginia. Palmerston reminded Russell that any successful attempt at mediation required a major Southern victory, one that would put the North in the right frame of mind.

Gladstone made a speech in October in which he remarked that the Confederates had created an army and a navy, "and they have made what is more than either—they have made a nation."[37] Because Gladstone was a prominent member of the Palmerston government, his speech inevitably triggered speculation that Britain was about to recognize the Confederacy. But Charles Francis Adams soon informed Seward that Gladstone had spoken unofficially and that many of his countrymen thought his remarks ill advised. Not until October 23 did the British cabinet formally consider France's proposal for bilateral intervention. By then Russia's position was cause for anxiety.

The Russian minister in Washington, Edouard de Stoeckl, had served in the Russian legation in various capacities since 1841. He had made many friends in the United States, and his long residence in Washington had given him an entrée to the powerful and the prominent. Stoeckl, like his colleagues Lyons and Mercier, had doubts about the viability of the Union. But he did not think that his government should rush into action that might damage Northern prospects and thereby serve British interests. He made it clear to his superiors that although a few Northerners like Horace Greeley favored mediation, neither Lincoln nor the congressional radicals supported such action. He wrote in one dispatch that he himself was keeping in the background: "To people who have spoken of mediation, I have replied that the intentions of goodwill on the part of the imperial government are . . . well known."[38] In short, Russia wanted no part of mediation so long as the United States did not desire it.

In Britain, meanwhile, opposition to intervention was reinforced by new information from America. The government was advised by a "special agent" that even if the war ended immediately, there would probably be a long delay before appreciable amounts of cotton reached Britain. In addition, it was said, the Northern states, particularly those in the West, strongly supported the war. When the cabinet finally met to consider the French initiative, opinion was divided. Russell favored a joint demarche, but others were indifferent or hostile. The preliminary Emancipation Proclamation had improved the Union image throughout Europe. In November, Lord John Russell informed France that Britain was not prepared to intervene.[39]

*　　*　　*　　**

France's interest in mediation represented neither capricious meddling on the part of Napoleon III nor undue concern over bloodshed in North America. In addition to his concern about guaranteeing a supply of cotton for the mills of France, Napoleon sought a sphere of influence in the Western Hemisphere, to which the United States represented a serious obstacle.

Mexico in 1861 was just emerging from a three-year civil war in which liberal elements led by Benito Juárez had defeated a conservative oligarchy supported by most of the European monarchies, including Britain, France, and Spain. As in many a Third World country today, an immediate problem faced by the Juárez administration was its foreign creditors. In July 1861 the Mexican parliament had passed a law suspending payments on the country's $80 million foreign debt for a period of two years. The result was that the three European powers agreed to collect what was owed them by force. In early 1862, when the United States was in no position to protest, Britain, France, and Spain occupied the principal Mexican ports with a view to seizing customs duties equal to what was owed them.

Britain and Spain were relatively easily satisfied; after coming to agreements with the Juárez government, they withdrew their forces. France was a different matter. Napoleon III proceeded to submit spurious claims for $27 million, an amount far beyond Mexico's capacity to repay. It was clear in Washington that France had long-term designs on Mexico, but it was also clear that the United States in 1862 was in no position to fight a foreign war. Seward noted to Minister Dayton in March that the United States was fully aware of the "extraordinary proceedings" taking place in Mexico. "We shall be just to ourselves," he wrote, "and at the same time shall practice the prudence that will avert any new complication in our affairs."[40]

18

"Remove Him!"

THE SUMMER OF 1862 brought more gloom to the Union cause. Stonewall Jackson's heroics in the Shenandoah Valley were followed by McClellan's withdrawal from his lines before Richmond. When most of McClellan's troops were turned over to a new commander, John Pope, the result was yet another Federal disaster at Manassas. Suspicions that McClellan had somehow contributed to Pope's debacle were rife in Washington, and when Lincoln reinstated McClellan in the wake of Second Manassas, many congressional Republicans were furious.

Seward claimed no competence in military matters, but the North's setbacks in the field weighed heavily on the secretary of state. At the end of his day he would often call for his carriage and ride out to visit some army unit. One day he took John Hay, the president's secretary, with him to Tenleytown, on the northern edge of the city. There the two men, one grizzled and silver haired, the other still in his twenties, watched columns of dusty troops marching into the city. Occasionally an officer would recognize the secretary of state and offer a salute, or a company of soldiers would raise a ragged cheer. Seward could do little to assist Lincoln in his search for competent commanders, and he was frustrated. "What is the use of growing old?" he grumbled to Hay. "You learn something of men and things but never until too late to use it." A few days before, Seward had watched the Army of the Potomac embark at Alexandria; he had considered it united and unbeatable. Later it had been divided and McClellan's successor, General Pope, roundly defeated. Sadly Seward told Hay, "I have just now found out what military jealousy is."[1]

Although Seward construed his responsibilities as secretary of state broadly, he rarely meddled in strictly military matters. He had earlier helped Gen. Nathaniel Banks locate qualified officers and occasionally had noted to Lincoln officers said to be competent. But with respect to the war effort, he saw his main responsibility as one of helping mobilize the manpower resources that he confidently expected would bring victory.

In June 1862, following the collapse of McClellan's Peninsular Campaign, Lincoln had sent Seward to New York to stimulate recruiting. The secretary carried with him a confidential letter from Lincoln, explaining the danger and noting that the capital itself was once again under threat from the rebels. Seward, in New York City, contemplated issuing a new call from the president for volunteers. On reflection, however, he concluded that for Lincoln to initiate the call would have overtones of panic. Instead he prevailed on most of the Northern governors to *request* that Lincoln issue a new call for volunteers. The upshot was that Lincoln, seemingly in response to appeals from the Northern governors, was able to issue a proclamation calling for an additional three hundred thousand men.[2]

Seward continued his proselytizing on his return to Washington. He persuaded Secretary of War Stanton to offer new recruits an immediate bounty of twenty-five dollars when their regiments were mustered into service. He urged various congressmen to return to their districts before the end of the congressional session in order to assist with recruiting.

Congress had just enacted the Homestead Act, providing that any citizen or alien could acquire title to 160 acres of public land by residing on and cultivating the land for a period of five years. This was just the sort of stimulus to immigration that Seward would have favored under any conditions, but now it included a vital military dimension as well. He sent copies of the legislation to U.S. envoys with a covering memorandum calling the Homestead Act "one of the most important steps ever taken by any government toward a practical recognition of the universal brotherhood of nations." The resulting publicity assured a continuing flow of military manpower to the North from Ireland and northern Europe. John Bigelow, the U.S. consul in Paris, would write that Seward's circular was important for "the light it throws on the mysterious repletion of our army during the four years of war, while it was . . . being so fearfully depleted by firearms, disease and desertion."[3]

*   *   *

In addition to his military problems, Lincoln had to deal with the touchy question of war aims. Publicly he continued to argue against general emancipation, telling Horace Greeley in his famous letter of August 1862 that if he could save the Union without freeing a single slave he would do it. Indeed, Lincoln had no authority to confiscate "property" in the North, and no ability to enforce any Federal edict in territory controlled by the Confederacy. But even as he appeared outwardly intransigent, the president was weighing a proclamation that would permit partial emancipation as a war measure. Lincoln first raised the subject with Seward and Welles on July 13, 1862. As commander in chief, Lincoln argued, he could surely seize slaves belonging to the enemy just as he could capture their railroads. Seward said that he wanted time to think about it, but he and Welles both agreed that such action would be justifiable and might be necessary.[4]

On July 22 Lincoln raised the subject of emancipation with his entire cabinet. Except for Seward and Welles, they heard the news in blank astonishment. Nothing Lincoln had hinted at previously had been so sweeping. The president indicated that he was not prepared to debate the advisability of a proclamation but would consider suggestions regarding his draft. Chase thought Lincoln's proposal, which would apply only to slaves in the Confederate states, too limited, but considered it better than nothing. Blair complained that it might still damage the Union cause in the border states. Then Seward, as Lincoln told the story, put forth an argument that the president found compelling. Seward questioned the timing. Issuance of the proclamation following a string of defeats on the battlefield, he said, would hint of desperation— "the Government stretching forth its hands to Ethiopia, instead of Ethiopia stretching forth her hands to the Government."[5] Although Seward based his argument on timing, he had doubts in regard to substance as well. He feared a slave uprising that would turn a war for the Union into a class war; he was also concerned that emancipation would destroy the South's economy, raising the specter of intervention by Britain or France to protect its supply of raw cotton.[6]

The question of timing was one Lincoln had not considered before, and he was prepared to put his proclamation aside until the North had won a victory. But the president and his secretary of state clearly differed over the desirability of any proclamation. Lincoln was convinced that limited emancipation would be legal and moral and would assist the Northern war effort. Seward was ambivalent, and because promulgation of the Emancipation Proclamation had been delayed, the subject was not closed. In August, as if to reflect his troubled state of mind, Seward sent the president two letters he had received, one supporting a proclamation, the other opposing it. Proclamations without military strength behind them, he wrote Frances, were meaningless. He clung to the hope that Congress might yet adopt an earlier administration proposal for compensated emancipation.

In 1864, when visiting artist Francis Carpenter was painting his famous rendition of Lincoln and his cabinet considering the Emancipation Proclamation, Seward cornered the artist at a reception. Carpenter's painting was based on a false premise, Seward said—that the Emancipation Proclamation had freed the slaves. The death knell of slavery had effectively been tolled when Lincoln had been elected president, in Seward's view but the life of the American republic could be assured only by a military victory.[7] When Sen. Orville Browning praised the proclamation in Seward's presence, Seward said that he was reminded of a man who, after the American Revolution, could not rest until a liberty pole was erected in his village. When his neighbors asked if he did not already feel free, the man replied, "What is liberty without a pole?" Seward felt that he was being swept along by an overwhelming sentiment for some form of grand gesture.[8]

When Lincoln read the text of the final proclamation to his cabinet at year's end, Seward expressed concern that emancipation could lead to a complete breakdown of order in the South. He recommended that Lincoln include language urging the freedmen "to abstain from all violence unless in necessary self-defense," a change that Lincoln incorporated into the text. Not all Seward's changes, however, were aimed at limiting the scope of the proclamation. Where Lincoln's text had directed that federal authorities *recognize* emancipated slaves as free persons, the president, on Seward's recommendation, directed federal authorities to "recognize and maintain the freedom of such persons."

Reaction to the proclamation, even in the North, was mixed. Most Radicals thought it a step in the right direction, but Greeley attacked the president for exempting areas under Federal control. Others made it clear that they were not fighting a war for the Negro. Ohio Congressman S. S. "Sunset" Cox warned that Ohio's soldiers would not fight for the Union "if the result shall be the flight and movement of the black race by millions northward." Seward's friend Archbishop John Hughes admonished that "we Catholics, and a vast majority of our brave troops in the field, have not the slightest idea of carrying on a war . . . just to gratify a clique of Abolitionists."[9] Thurlow Weed, in the *Albany Evening Journal,* criticized the Emancipation Proclamation as turning the war into an abolitionist crusade and flayed the Radicals "by whom the administration is beleaguered, importuned and persecuted."[10]

Even in Europe, where Lincoln doubtless hoped to buttress sentiment for the North, the initial reaction was unpromising. In London the *Spectator* seized on the inconsistency of the proclamation, noting that "the principle asserted is not that a human being cannot own another, but that he cannot own him unless he is loyal to the United States." Gladstone suggested that even with emancipation a Confederate victory was likely. Over the longer term, however, the North's first, tentative step toward universal emancipation would help rally world opinion to the Northern cause.

*　　*　　*

Power, like nature, abhors a vacuum. With the Lincoln administration waging war primarily to preserve the Union, it was inevitable that politicians and editors who espoused loftier goals would make their weight felt. In the Republican—or was it Unionist?—party, the Radical element was the most vocal. Radicals had displayed their muscle when, in December 1861, Congress had created a Joint Committee on the Conduct of the War. Sen. William Fessenden of Maine had explained that the committee would "keep an anxious watchful eye over all the executive agents who are carrying on the war at the direction of the people. . . . We are not under the command of the military of this country. They are under ours as a Congress."[11]

Perhaps the committee would have been established even without George McClellan. But the inability of the "Young Napoleon" to produce victories in the field, even as he exhibited a certain sympathy toward slaveholders, encouraged skepticism about the administration's intentions. The Committee on the Conduct of the War, under its chairman, Sen. Benjamin Wade of Ohio, would have liked to have taken over responsibility for selecting the Union's generals. Because this was clearly an executive responsibility, the Radicals contented themselves with second-guessing Lincoln's generals and harassing those of Lincoln's advisers whose zeal for the war was considered suspect.

As the Radicals learned of Seward's doubts concerning the Emancipation Proclamation, their hostility toward the secretary of state increased. Thaddeus Stevens of Pennsylvania, who had known Seward since the days of the Anti-Masonic movement, denounced him as an apostate to the antislavery cause. "I have accused the prime minister to his face for having gone back on the faith he taught us," Stevens said, "and instead of arming every man, black or white, who would fight for this Union, [preventing] a well-meaning President from doing so."[12] Sumner dismissed Seward as a mere politician, incapable of understanding the issues at stake in America's struggle. "Remove him!" began the December 6, 1862, editorial in the *Boston Commonwealth,* regarded as Sumner's organ. "William H. Seward stands before the American people today as the enemy of the public," the editorial continued. "We have had enough of his paralizing [*sic*] influence on the army and the President; let the Watchword for the Hour be, *Remove Seward from the Cabinet!*"[13] Joseph Medill, writing in the *Chicago Tribune,* agreed: "Seward must be got out of the Cabinet. . . . He has been the President *de facto,* and has kept a sponge saturated with chloroform to Uncle Abe's nose."[14]

Seward was human, and he had a human craving for praise. Although he tried to shrug off the criticism, this was easier said than done. His situation was not without a certain irony. At a time when he was working loyally for the president and had renounced all political ambitions, the Radicals and their followers were holding him responsible for the administration's every perceived shortcoming. It is unlikely that Seward, with his easy tolerance, would ever have been at ease with zealots like Sumner and Wade. But the secretary of state may have exacerbated his problems by a thinly disguised disdain for his congressional critics. For instance, he had included in the published State Department correspondence for 1861 a letter to Minister Dayton in France in which he had disparaged the more-extreme abolitionists. In one sentence Seward had equated Republican extremists with Jefferson Davis and his rebels, writing that it was almost as if "extreme advocates of African slavery and its most vehement opponents were acting in concert" to precipitate a servile war.[15] Thus it was hardly surprising that Seward became a lightning rod for antiadministration sentiment on Capitol Hill.

If this were not enough, the Civil War was prompting yet another contest for power between the White House and Congress. Setbacks on the battlefield encouraged armchair warriors on Capitol Hill to interfere with traditional executive branch prerogatives, including military appointments. The Joint Committee on the Conduct of the War had been created to keep an eye on Lincoln and his cabinet. It was politically dangerous to attack the president himself in time of war, but no such immunity attached to his advisers. If it was mistaken to argue that Mr. Lincoln was too weak and his secretary of state too strong, it was safe. Not all Seward's critics were hypocrites seeking to damage the president by undermining confidence in his associates. Whereas something about Lincoln inspired confidence, Seward's tendency to appear all-wise had earned him a reputation for arrogance. Years in politics had given him a reputation for deviousness as well; even his skillful handling of the *Trent* affair did little for his personal popularity.

The motives of the Radicals themselves were varied. Some, such as Zachary Chandler, Ben Wade, and John P. Hale of New Hampshire, appeared most interested in gaining power for Congress and for themselves. The articulate Fessenden, one of the ablest of the Radicals, asserted that the Senate "should no longer be content with its constitutional duties" but should play a greater role in making policy for the administration. Others, like Sumner, Joshua Giddings, and Stevens, had a history of devotion to abolitionism that lent a certain probity to their attacks on a conservative administration. What virtually all the Radicals lacked was a willingness to acknowledge that reasonable men might differ as to the ends for which the war was being prosecuted. There were such men in Congress, but in the turbulent months of 1862 their voices were muted.

The bloody stalemate at Antietam in September had provided Lincoln with his opportunity to issue the preliminary Emancipation Proclamation. Northern voters, however, were not impressed. Some deplored Lincoln's failure to prosecute the war more vigorously; others had doubts about the administration's repressive measures at home; many, like Seward, had doubts about turning the war into a crusade against slavery. Whatever the reasons, the November 1862 elections were a disaster for the administration. Although the Republicans, in an attempt to appeal to War Democrats, campaigned as the Union party in most states, the Democrats increased their representation in the House from 44 to 75, reducing the Republican margin there to 18. Even in states the Republicans carried, their margins were much smaller than in 1860.

The situation in New York was particularly unfortunate. Seward and Weed had hoped for a Union ticket there—one that was conservative on the issue of emancipation—with the capable Gen. John A. Dix as candidate for governor. But Seward and Weed, who under Lincoln had been obliged to divide patronage in New York with the Greeley faction, were no longer the final arbiters of politics in the Empire State. Greeley, with support from Chase and Stanton, engineered the nomination of an abolitionist, James S. Wadsworth, for governor. Wadsworth went down to an overwhelming defeat at the hands of Democrat Horatio Seymour, and the largest state in the North fell to the opposition.

Meanwhile, McClellan, after the great battle at Antietam, had idled away the campaign months of the autumn, obliging Lincoln to remove him a second time in order to provide more aggressive leadership for the Army of the Potomac. Alas, the president's choice as McClellan's successor was the ineffectual Ambrose E. Burnside, who was bloodily repulsed at Fredericksburg on December 13. Fredericksburg, coming on the heels of the twelve thousand casualties at Antietam, was a new blow to Northern confidence. The aftermath was even worse, as soldiers died by the score each day in filthy hospitals and unsanitary camps. Desertions increased, at one point averaging two hundred a day. The peace movement in the North grew in strength.

Although Seward no longer expected an early peace and although he had favored the sacking of McClellan well before the president acted, he remained a target for congressional critics of the administration. Lincoln defended his secretary as best he could. After meeting with a delegation of New Yorkers associated with Greeley, who denounced Seward at great length, the president lost patience and ended the meeting with the assertion that they were prepared to destroy the government in order to "hang" Seward.[16]

On Capitol Hill, however, the Radicals were not to be put off. On December 16, three days after Fredericksburg, Republican senators met in caucus to force Lincoln to reorganize his cabinet. One of their number, Orville Browning of Illinois, later wrote that Chase's supporters had sought "to drive all the cabinet out—then force . . . the recall of Mr. Chase as Premier, and form a cabinet of ultra men around him."[17] Chase had been a key informant for the Senate Radicals, complaining to Fessenden and others of Seward's "backstairs influence." Fessenden, who wanted Seward's job, said that the immediate task facing the senators was to oust the secretary of state. Wade insisted that the Senate should go to Lincoln in a body and demand Seward's dismissal. The caucus considered a suggestion that the Senate pass a resolution of no confidence in Seward, but a motion denouncing the secretary of state by name could hardly fail to antagonize the president who had appointed him. The meeting adjourned without agreement.

On the following day, the senators passed a resolution calling for a partial reconstruction of the president's cabinet. Although the measure was clearly aimed at Seward, the language was more general. That they demanded only a "partial reconstruction" was significant, for a limited reorganization of the administration would permit the retention of Chase as well as the ouster of Seward. Thirty-one of the thirty-two senators approved the resolution, voting to send a delegation to present it to the president.

The one senator not voting was portly Preston King of New York, who had served with Seward in the Senate and was a friend of the Seward family. King left the caucus room before his name was called and headed for the Old Clubhouse on Lafayette Park. There King found the secretary of state in front of his fire, enjoying an after-dinner cigar. He quickly filled Seward in on the proceedings, adding that although some of his colleagues had sought to keep the proceedings secret, he had refused to be bound by them.

Seward, who appears to have had no warning of what was afoot, took paper in hand. "They may do as they please about me," he snapped, "but they shall not put the President in a false position on my account." He penned a one-sentence letter of resignation and told Fred to do the same. King took the two notes to the White House, while Seward returned to his reading and his cigar. Later that evening Lincoln walked across the street to the Seward residence. There was a slightly awkward exchange. Seward kept a stiff upper lip, insisting that it would be a relief to be free of his official cares. "Ah, yes, Governor," Lincoln replied, "that will do very well for you, but I . . . can't get out."[18]

When the chairman of the Republican caucus, Sen. Jacob Collamer of Vermont, asked Lincoln for an appointment on behalf of his committee, Lincoln invited the group to the White House on the evening of December 18 for what the president later characterized as an "animated" conversation. His nine visitors presented a litany of grievances, including the infrequency with which Lincoln held cabinet meetings and the general conduct of the war. But their main target was Seward, whom they charged with a lack of commitment to the war and with "too great ascendancy and control of the President."[19] They made clear that their objective was Seward's dismissal.

Lincoln met with his cabinet, minus Seward, the following morning. He told them of Seward's resignation and of his own meeting with the Republican senators. Lincoln said that he had defended his cabinet and did not want to go on without his friends. He proposed that the cabinet join him that evening for a second meeting with the senators.

That night, from seven-thirty until nearly midnight, Lincoln chaired a meeting in which he defended his administration, his right to choose his own cabinet, and the conduct of his secretary of state. He, as president, had made the critical decisions, but the cabinet had acquiesced in all the important ones. Lincoln asked his ministers if this was not so. All eyes fell on the secretary of the treasury, for those present knew that it was he who had been most critical of Lincoln's use of his cabinet. Chase squirmed in his chair, hesitant to repeat his criticism of the president or to acknowledge that he and his cabinet colleagues had been in substantial agreement on administration policy. In the end Chase waffled. He said that the cabinet had been consulted on key matters and had generally concurred in the president's course. But, according to Chase, discussion had been less thorough than he would have liked.

The meeting then focused on Seward, who was roundly condemned by Sumner, Grimes, and Trumbull. Sumner complained about Seward's handling of foreign affairs, especially the letter to Dayton in which Seward had equated abolitionists with the rebels. Trumbull took Seward to task for his "little bell." Grimes insisted that he had "no confidence whatever" in the secretary of state. But when Lincoln asked bluntly whether all present wanted Seward out of the cabinet, only Pomeroy of Kansas joined the trio of Sumner, Grimes, and Trumbull. New York's Ira Harris said that Seward's influence in New York was such that his departure from the cabinet would injure the party, while the others were noncommittal.[20]

The fact that the visiting senators ended the evening divided on the subject of Seward constituted a victory of sorts for the president. The real loser was Chase, for Fessenden and Trumbull in particular were furious over the Ohioan's duplicity and spinelessness. There were subcurrents as well; the idea that Congress should dictate to Lincoln as to the composition of his cabinet so angered Seward's colleagues that several rallied to his defense. Blair stopped by, found Seward packing, and expressed the hope that he would not leave.

At the White House, Welles volunteered to urge Seward to withdraw his resignation, and the president accepted his offer. When Welles crossed the street to the Old Clubhouse, he found Stanton and Seward in conversation. Stanton had better take care, Seward warned, or he might find himself the Radicals' next target. When the secretary of war had left, Welles made his appeal. Later he concluded that although Seward attempted to hide his feelings, the secretary of state had been deeply hurt by the senators' attack. In Welles's account of their talk— the only one available—Seward launched into a recitation of his long political experience, his "sagacity and . . . great services." He then assured the secretary of the navy that he was prepared to stay on at the president's pleasure.[21]

Welles hurried back to the White House, where he found that the president had sent for Chase. Chase told the president that he had been deeply embarrassed by the proceedings the previous evening and had written out his resignation. On hearing this, Lincoln's eyes lit up. When Chase said he had brought it with him, the president asked to have it. With a laugh, Lincoln remarked that he could now dispose of his cabinet problem. He told Chase to return to his office, that his resignation was not required.[22]

Lincoln sent identical letters to Chase and Seward that day, request-ing that they stay at their posts. Seward responded immediately, saying that he cheerfully resumed his duties. Chase, with protestations of re-luctance, stated that he, too, would persevere. Lincoln had foiled the attempt by the congressional wing of his party to dictate the composition of his cabinet, and by having in his possession resignation letters from both Seward and Chase he had secured a hold over his devious secretary of the treasury. Lincoln observed cheerfully to Senator Ira Harris, "I can ride now—I've got a pumpkin in each end of my bag."[23]

In a letter to Weed earlier in the year, Seward had characterized the president as "wise and practical."[24] So he had proved to be. The most serious cabinet crisis of Lincoln's administration ended in clear victory for the president. The end of the year found Seward more secure than ever in Lincoln's confidence, and very grateful to the president who had refused to deliver him to his enemies. Ironically it fell to Seward to draft the stiff press release that put an end to the crisis:

> The president on Saturday acknowledged the reception of the resigna-tions of the Secretary of State and the Treasury and informed them that after due deliberation he had come to the conclusion that an acceptance of them would be incompatible with the public welfare, and thereupon requested them to resume their respective functions. The two Secretaries have accordingly resumed their places as Heads of their Departments.[25]

Did Seward reflect on his own responsibility in bringing on the crisis? There is no evidence that he did, but for a man who prided himself on his political sagacity, Seward had demonstrated some curious blind spots. In casual conversation he had doubtless encouraged a belief that he was the driving force behind administration policies that were increasingly unpopular on Capitol Hill. Worse still, by gratuitously including re-marks critical of the abolitionists in his published diplomatic correspon-dence, he had played into the hands of his enemies. Remarkably, the campaign for his ouster appears to have taken Seward by surprise. Con-vinced of his own rectitude, he had underestimated the sentiment against him. It was a sobering thought that the onetime leader of the Republi-can party was almost without friends on Capitol Hill. His only admirer seemed to be Abraham Lincoln.

The Radical senators, for their part, continued to underestimate the president. They could not credit Lincoln with having concluded on his own that the nation's first priority was to restore the Union; such men-dacity had to have been the work of Seward! The secretary of state's close personal relations with Lincoln, and his very visible role in the *Trent* affair, contributed to an impression of influence that went well beyond the facts.

While it was clearly in Lincoln's interest to stand up to the Radicals, it was also in his interest to retain Seward's services. The secretary of state was not only the premier intellect of the cabinet but had proved himself totally loyal to the president as well. Had Seward departed, who might have succeeded him as "premier"? Would Lincoln have been comfortable with the ambitious, contemptuous Chase or the mercurial Stanton? Others of Lincoln's mediocre cabinet—the self-righteous Welles, the slow-witted Bates, the homesick Smith, and the nervous, ill-tempered Blair—can be dismissed out of hand. The fact was that Lincoln needed Seward almost as much as Seward needed Lincoln.

During his confrontation with the Radicals, Seward had enjoyed passive support from an unlikely source: the British legation. Lord Lyons had watched with concern the turmoil surrounding the president's cabinet; by the end of 1862 he had no desire to see Seward forced from office. He warned Russell in December that were the Radicals to gain ascendancy, "We are much more likely to have a man less disposed [than Seward] to keep the peace than a man more disposed to do so."[26]

Seward's relations with the Radical senators would continue to be cool, especially with Sumner, who during the crisis had declined a dinner invitation rather than sit at the same table with the secretary of state. Sumner transacted his State Department business where possible with Chief Clerk Hunter; he and Seward did not meet socially for three months.[27] Chase was a different matter. Seward's longtime friend William M. Evarts thought that Seward should take the initiative and attempt to force Chase out of the cabinet. This Seward declined to do; even to have attempted it would have been to undermine Lincoln's carefully wrought compromise. Instead, he invited the treasury secretary to dinner on Christmas Eve. Chase regretted.[28]

The crisis was over, leaving the quarrel to the press surrogates of the contending parties. Greeley, who considered himself the target of Seward's controversial letter to Dayton, charged indignantly that the secretary of state was sending diplomatic dispatches without the president's approval. This was technically correct in the case of routine communications, but Seward was scrupulous in clearing anything of substance with the president. Raymond replied in the *New York Times,* on the authority of both Lincoln and Seward, that not a single substantive communication had been sent to a foreign government without the president's approval. In an editorial Raymond put Seward's role in clear perspective:

> Mr. Seward is supposed to have been the leading man in the Administration—to have suggested policies and caused their adoption—to have held back the President from measures which he desired to adopt, and to have forced on him actions he did not wish to perform. We believe that all this is without the slightest foundation in fact. Mr. Seward has, unless we are greatly mistaken, followed the President's lead in every movement of his Administration. . . . He did not oppose the issuance of the Emancipation Proclamation [*sic*]. He did not resist the removal of McClellan. . . . He has attended exclusively to the affairs of his own department, and has sustained, with cheerful and hearty loyalty, whatever measures the President has deemed essential to the public good.[29]

The *Times* sounded as though its information came from excellent authority—perhaps even from William H. Seward.

*   *   *

Meanwhile, the war continued. The scarred Army of the Potomac attempted to recuperate in its camps around Fredericksburg. Along the Mississippi, Sherman's men picked their way through swamps and bayous in the first phase of the campaign for Vicksburg.

The young Seward, probably as governor of New York. (*Author's collection*)

Frances Seward in the garden of her house at Auburn *(Seward House, Auburn, N.Y.)*

From the left: Fred, Will, Frances and Gus *(Seward House, Auburn, N.Y.)*

Thurlow Weed in about 1860.
(Author's Collection)

Seward House, Auburn, N.Y.. *(Photograph by the author)*

Seward with Will and Fannie, about 1855. *(Seward House, Auburn, N.Y.)*

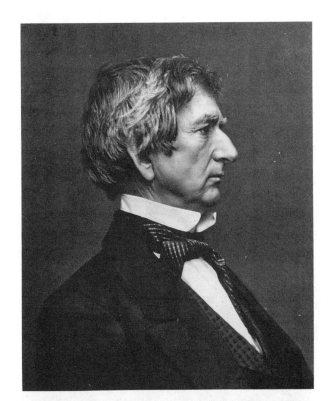

William Russell of the *London Times* saw in Seward "a subtle, quick man, rejoicing in power, fond of badinage." *(The Lincoln Museum, Fort Wayne, Ind., a part of Lincoln National Corp.)*

Richard Pemell, Lord Lyons, Britain's able envoy in Washington. *(Author's collection)*

Secretary Seward with Fred in Seward's Washinton office, about 1863. *(Seward House, Auburn, N.Y.)*

Gus, Anna, Fred and an unidentified young woman relax with Seward in Washington. *(Seward House, Auburn, N.Y.)*

The garden at Old Clubhouse. Seward leans against the column facing Gus; Fanny is to the right of the column. *(Seward House, Auburn, N.Y.)*

Seward, whom Henry Adams likened to "a wise macaw," as secretary of state. *(Library of Congress)*

"THE LITTLE BELL," 1861-65.

"My Lord, I can touch a bell on my right hand, and order the arrest of a citizen of Ohio; I can touch a bell again, and order the imprisonment of a citizen of New York; and no power on earth, except that of the President, can release them. Can the Queen of England do so much?"

Secretary Seward to Lord Lyons, see page 13.

This devastating cartoon was the frontispiece of John A. Marshall's book *American Bastille*, first published in 1869. *(The Lincoln Museum, Fort Wayne, Ind., a part of Lincoln National Corp.)*

In this first version of Francis Carpenter's rendition of the reading of the Emmancipation Proclamation, Lincoln and Seward are equally prominent. *(Library of Congress)*

By the time Carpenter's painting was hung in the Capitol, Lincoln had been made the central figure. *(Library of Congress)*

Seward, in this response to Alexander Boteler Eyre, recounts his family heritage: "The family from which I am derived was in New Jersey during the war of independence. . . ." *(Author's collection)*

Lewis Powell, alias Lewis Paine, the ex-Confederate soldier who attempted to assassinate Seward. *(The Lincoln Museum, Fort Wayne, Ind., a part of Lincoln National Corp.)*

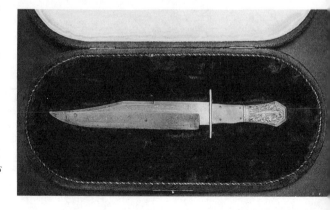

The bowie knife with which Powell attacked Seward. *(Courtesy of John K. Lattimer, College of Physicians and Surgeons)*

George Robinson, the soldier who saved Seward's life. *(Seward House, Auburn, N.Y.)*

A *Harper's Weekly* cartoon following the 1866 New Orleans race riots, which caused extensive black casualties. *(Library of Congress)*

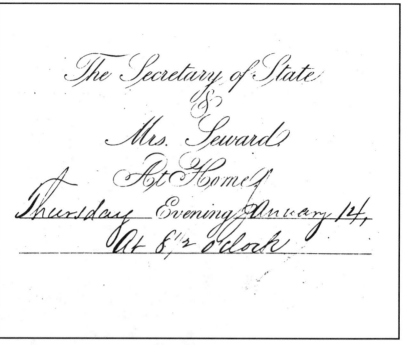

An invitation to one of Seward's popular receptions. *(Author's collection)*

A print of Sitka, Alaska, in the *Illustrated London News* following the U. S. purchase of Alaska *(Author's collection)*

Olive Risley (*left*), with her sister Harriet.
(Seward House, Auburn, N.Y.)

Seward in about 1870, showing the scars from his
encounter with Paine. *(Seward House, Auburn, N.Y.)*

Entrance hall of the Seward House, with souvenirs of the governor's travels. *(Seward House, Auburn, N.Y.)*

Seward's funeral cortege in Auburn, October 13, 1872. *(Seward House)*

19

High Tide and Rebel Raiders

WHILE IN THE Senate, Seward had been remarkably successful in maintaining civil relations with most of his colleagues. He was less successful as a cabinet member during the political and social upheaval of wartime Washington. By 1863, there was little that Seward could do to mend relations with congressional Radicals, but he would have liked to have contributed to a better atmosphere within Lincoln's cabinet. Unfortunately, the cabinet reflected political divisions found throughout the North. The energetic Stanton, when not fully engaged with running the war, was cultivating the very Radicals who sought Seward's ouster. Blair was a War Democrat who regarded Seward as insufficiently militant. Attorney General Bates, a respectable old gentleman, was, like his colleagues, inclined to resent Seward's supposed influence over the president. The secretary of the interior, Caleb Smith, was about to resign his post in favor of a judgeship in his home state of Indiana. Chase was barely civil.

It is difficult not to sympathize with Seward, who was said by many to "control" the president but who in fact had little of the power imputed to him. The New Yorker also had the unenviable task of having to get along with Gideon Welles.

As a newspaper editor in Connecticut, the Democratic secretary of the navy had worked up an intense dislike for his editorial rival, Thurlow Weed, and from Weed the antipathy extended to Seward. Although Welles brought few qualifications to his cabinet post, he was intensely jealous of his prerogatives and never forgave Seward for his meddling in the Navy Department at the time of the Fort Pickens relief expedition. However, developments at sea almost inevitably had foreign policy implications, and relations between the United States and the European powers often had implications for Welles's service. Hence the two men accepted the need for a degree of cooperation, though Welles, in his dealings with Seward, was defensive and insecure.

When Seward accepted his cabinet post, he had at first planned to keep a diary. His determination lasted one day; he remarked to Fred that, on reflection, he did not think that a diary would be appropriate.[1] Welles, in contrast, had long been a diarist and would keep a journal throughout his eight years in Washington under Lincoln and Andrew Johnson. In it he would have little to say about the Confederate enemy—but a great deal to say about Seward. Welles distrusted his colleague's intelligence and discounted his goodwill. In Welles's view Seward had "no convictions, no fixed principles . . . but is governed and moved by impulse, fancied expediency, and temporary circumstances."[2] Welles was also petulantly jealous of Seward's close and privileged relationship with the president. He wrote in September 1862: "Seward . . . spends more or less of each day with the President, absorbs his attention and I fear to an extent influences his action not always wisely."[3] On occasion, however, the caustic Welles was capable of shrewd insight. In the wake of the December 1862 cabinet crisis, Welles summarized Lincoln's retention of both Chase and Seward with the comment: "Seward comforts him; Chase he deems a necessity."[4]

Seward, for his part, had little respect for Welles, although he probably felt guilty of a tactical error in having dealt so cavalierly with the navy secretary in the first weeks of their association. As with his other colleagues, Seward sought to maintain amicable relations with the navy man. Welles had problems with one of his sons, Tom, who rebelled first against his father and subsequently against the regimen of a private school in Connecticut. Seward, who was always interested in young people, had a private talk with Tom, suggesting a navy career but asking him not to mention their conversation to his father. A few days later Welles received an instruction from the president "directing" him to appoint Tom a midshipman.[5]*

Whatever Welles may have thought of Seward as a family counselor, his official dealings with the secretary of state provided ample opportunities for friction. Both men were concerned with Confederate commerce destroyers—Seward with preventing their construction, Welles with apprehending those that got to sea. Since the transfer to the Con-

---

*Tom attended the naval academy at Newport, Rhode Island, but later resigned in order to serve in the army.

federacy of the British-built *Alabama* in July 1862, the Federal merchant marine had been at the mercy of rebel predators and Welles's navy had become a laughingstock. The Palmerston government was ostensibly neutral, but in the vital area of naval construction it was reluctant to take business from British shipyards. Foreign Secretary Russell took refuge in existing statutes, which required clear evidence that a vessel was slated for a belligerent power before it could be detained. The chief Confederate naval agent, James Bulloch, had demonstrated in the case of the *Alabama* his skill at creating a paper trail that would allow British officials to profess insufficient knowledge of a given vessel to prevent her departure. Apart from the question of commerce raiders, there remained the problem of contraband carried by British-owned vessels through the blockade to the South. The British government did nothing to discourage British blockade runners, even though their activities were incompatible with London's professed neutrality.

While Britain seemed determined to make things as difficult as possible for the Northern cause, Seward was no longer sending strident warnings to Whitehall. In April 1862 he had written Adams of the need for patience in dealing with Britain. He deplored the "sordid class of persons" who gave aid and comfort to the rebels, but there was no hint of the old bellicosity that had prompted dispatches such as the one Lincoln had modified the previous May. "Let it be our endeavor," Seward wrote Adams, "to extirpate the seeds of animosity and cultivate relations of friendship with a nation that . . . can really have no interest or ambition permanently conflicting with our own."[6]

Nevertheless, the existence of a "sordid class of persons" eager to trade with the Confederacy obliged Seward to threaten drastic action, specifically the issuance of letters of marque to American privateers. Because there was no Confederate merchant marine worth mentioning, the main targets of U.S. privateers were blockade runners of British and other European registry. Seward needed some threat to hold over British shipbuilding interests, but he got no assistance from either Sumner or Welles. Sumner viewed the proposal as one more example of Seward's virulent Anglophobia. Welles, ever suspicious, was sure that Seward, Weed, and their Whig friends intended to capture valuable prizes that would otherwise fall to the U.S. Navy.[7]

Seward did some heavy lobbying, however, and found allies on Capitol Hill. In March 1863, to Welles's dismay, Congress passed a bill that authorized the president to employ privateers at sea. Seward warned Lyons that the departure of any more vessels like the *Alabama* was "to be deprecated above all things," and that if Britain did not take ade-

quate steps he feared for the peace.[8] Lyons had no problem in understanding the secretary, but Sumner, who sought to appease Britain at
every turn, was frantic. When he failed to block passage of the privateering bill, he sent a memorandum to Lincoln denouncing it. Lincoln
invited the senator to make his case before the cabinet, but Sumner
declined.[9] In the end Lincoln—possibly with Seward's concurrence—
declined for the time being to commission any privateers. London, however, had been made aware of the depth of Washington's anger over
British construction for the Confederacy, and of the fact that Washington was prepared to retaliate if necessary.

In attempting to dispel his reputation as an unrelenting Anglophobe,
Seward sought in particular to minimize friction with Britain in the
Caribbean, where British ships carried on a flourishing trade with the
Confederacy through the Mexican port of Matamoros. Officially Washington maintained that goods so shipped were subject to seizure under
the doctrine of "continuous voyage"—that is, that their ultimate des-
tination was the Confederacy. In practice Seward sought to accommodate the British on matters of procedure, and he promised Lyons that
mail found on captured vessels would not be tampered with.

Unfortunately, Seward's conciliatory policy ran afoul of Gideon
Welles. In February 1863 a U.S. Navy ship seized the *Peterhoff* off St.
Thomas in the West Indies. The ship was taken to New York, where
Seward directed, in accordance with his commitment to Lyons, that the
mail was to remain unopened. Welles was furious, insisting to Lincoln
that the *Peterhoff* mails were under the jurisdiction of the courts. He
grumbled to his diary that Seward sought "to set aside law, usage,
principle, established and always recognized rights," in order to appease
Britain.[10] To Welles's discomfiture, Lincoln, who understood the importance of maintaining correct relations with Britain, upheld his secretary of state. (At about this time, however, Seward filled a page of
paper with miscellaneous jottings during a cabinet meeting. In one line
he reminded himself: "Mind your own business."[11])

The principal issue before Seward and Charles Francis Adams in
1863 remained that of ship construction for the Confederates. In conversation with Russell, Adams cited the privateering bill as evidence of
action that his government might take if Britain continued to outfit ships
for the Confederacy. In Washington, Seward emphasized to Lyons that
there would be no need for Northern privateers if Britain were to prevent the sale of future *Alabama*s. Perhaps embarrassed by that vessel's
depredations—the energetic U.S. consul at Liverpool, Thomas Dudley,
had produced affidavits to the effect that 90 percent of the *Alabama*'s

crew was British—the Palmerston government decided one case for the North. On April 5 it ordered the seizure of the *Alexandria* on the ground that it was a warship being constructed for the Confederacy in violation of the Foreign Enlistment Act.[12]

Although the Palmerston government disliked blocking a sale by a British builder, it had long since given up any intention of becoming directly involved in the American war. In May 1863 a Confederate partisan wrote from London: "The policy of the British Cabinet, I am sorry to say . . . would seem to be more than ever opposed to the formal recognition of [Confederate independence]."[13] However, the continuing desire of British shipyards to sell ships to whoever could pay for them, and the imprecise wording of the statutes that permitted the seizure of ships destined for belligerent powers, continued to disturb Anglo-American relations.

Meanwhile, the same Liverpool shipyard that had built the *Alabama* had begun construction on two ironclads, called Laird rams, that appeared destined for the Confederacy. The detained *Alexandria* was of little consequence compared with the Laird rams. With their armored prows, a feature that made them potentially lethal against wooden-hulled warships, these vessels were even more threatening than the *Alabama*. Seward—overlooking the immense problems of keeping these primitive steamers on station off a hostile coast—saw them as a threat to the Union blockade and even to such coastal cities as New York and Boston.[14]

The rams were scheduled to be launched in August 1863. Faced with this deadline, Seward and Adams pressed the Palmerston government to act, while Bulloch sought to maintain a facade to justify inaction on the part of the British government such as that which had permitted the escape of the *Alabama*. Although Bulloch had grave doubts as to whether even the Palmerston government could be hoodwinked again, he arranged for a French purchaser to act as a front for the Confederacy.

In Washington, Seward took a hard line. On July 11 he informed Adams that if the Palmerston government continued to permit the sale of warships to the Confederacy, the United States "will be without any guarantee whatever against the . . . building, arming, equipping, and sending forth ships of war from British ports to make war against the United States." He again raised the possibility of employing privateers in whatever manner the administration saw fit. As evidence of how seriously the United States regarded Britain's behavior, Adams was authorized to inform Russell that President Lincoln would regard any further destruction of the U.S. merchant marine as "a naval war waged by a portion at least of the British nation'' against the United States. He warned that if, ''through the necessary employment of all our means of national defense, such a partial war shall become a general one between the two nations, the President thinks that the responsibility for that painful result will not fall upon the United States.''[15]

Adams exercised the discretion accorded him and did not pass this dispatch to Russell. But on September 3 he complained to the foreign secretary about the government's failure to take action to detain the rams. The following day Adams received a note, dated September 1, advising that the government lacked sufficient evidence on which to act. The American minister replied in the sense of Seward's dispatch, telling Russell in language that would echo down the years: ''It would be superfluous in me to point out to your lordship that this is war.''[16]

On September 1 Consul Dudley had reported that the first of the rams had her masts up, machinery functioning, and turrets in place. ''I see nothing to prevent her going out whenever she chooses,'' he wrote Seward.[17] In fact, the rams were going nowhere. Russell had decided to act even before he received Adams's now-famous note, having recommended to Palmerston on September 3 that the rams be seized. Russell himself was inclined to credit the cover story of French ownership, but he recommended that the rams not be allowed to depart. They were seized by government authorities on October 9.

During the Civil War, there were two occasions when Anglo-American tensions led to talk of war. The first was the *Trent* affair; the second was the threatened departure of the Laird rams. The two cases are interesting both for their similarities and differences. In each case the ostensible bone of contention was of questionable importance. Mason and Slidell, as Confederate envoys, were of little consequence. The same could not be said of the rams, but, given the primitive state of the art of constructing ironclad warships, the two vessels might never have crossed the Atlantic. Had they reached North America, the rams would have had great difficulty finding bases.

In the *Trent* affair Seward, while avoiding a formal apology, had successfully argued that the Confederate envoys be allowed to proceed. In the matter of the rams, where international law was on the side of the United States, he was much more aggressive. In the judgment of one historian: ''Of all Seward's threats, his masterpiece was delivered in 1863'' in connection with the rams.[18] The stakes were fairly high. Although neither the *Trent* affair nor the affair of the rams would have brought on war by itself, in each case the injured party was capable of an act of retaliation that might have made the threat of war real. Worsened Anglo-American relations could have led to European intervention in the Civil War, the one development that might have saved the embattled Confederacy. Seward's actions in both 1861 and 1863—conciliatory in the case of the *Trent*, more threatening in the exchange over the rams—show him to have had a clear understanding of his country's interests.

* * *

For the remainder of the war France, not Britain, would pose the most serious problem to the United States. Long after sentiment for intervention in the American Civil War had ebbed in Britain, Napoleon III sought to influence events in North America so as to assure France a supply of Southern cotton and to reduce the likelihood of American interference with French operations in Mexico.

Franco-American relations did not manifest the peaks and valleys so characteristic of Anglo-American relations. If the emperor and his courtiers favored the South, they did so without the overt contemptuousness of a Palmerston or a Russell. Yet whereas a remedy was at hand for strained relations between Washington and London—primarily, a more stringent enforcement of Britain's professed neutrality—France was just as willing to sell contraband to the Confederacy as Britain was, and, in Mexico, France was embarked on a venture that could put it on a collision course with the United States. In terms of the Monroe Doctrine, France represented a far more serious threat to American interests than did Britain.

In June 1863 Napoleon III discussed with several pro-Southern members of the British Parliament yet another joint movement to recognize the Confederacy. Fortunately for the United States, the person chosen to present a motion in Parliament was one John Roebuck, whom Henry Adams—serving as his father's secretary—described as "rather more than three-quarters mad." In a speech on the floor, Roebuck unwisely disclosed the substance of his private talks with Napoleon III, creating a backlash in Parliament at the prospect of the British lion's tamely following policies set in Paris. Roebuck's indiscretion, followed by the Union victories at Gettysburg and Vicksburg, ended the last, tentative threat of European intervention.[19]

In August 1863 Seward sent a long instruction to Dayton in Paris, complaining yet again of France's apparent conviction that the Union was beyond salvaging. He called attention to recent developments, including the victories at Gettysburg and Vicksburg, the loyalty to the Union of key border states, the North's superiority in resources, and the growing effectiveness of the Federal blockade. For the time being, however, rebel cruisers continued to reequip in French ports and French yards worked on ironclads destined for the Confederacy. Like the Laird rams, these vessels were considered capable both of destroying Federal blockaders and attacking coastal cities. Largely without Dayton's knowledge, the astute James Bulloch had transferred his purchasing operations from Britain to France.

In France, there were senior government officials who wanted their country to observe strict neutrality in the American war. When Dayton called on the new foreign minister, Drouyn de Lhuys, in September 1863, with evidence that French yards in Bordeaux and Nantes were building warships for the Confederacy, Drouyn promised an investigation. Thomas Dudley's counterpart in France was John Bigelow. The consul in Paris had a string of informants and received many reports of ships being built in France for the Confederacy. He tended to discount these until September, when a Frenchman named Tremont, referred to him by Minister Dayton, demonstrated detailed knowledge of vessels being built for the Confederates in Bordeaux and Nantes. Equally important, Tremont had copies of documents that indicated that the builders had obtained the necessary government approvals by false representations.[20]

For a nominal fee Tremont delivered to Bigelow documents proving without question that two clippers allegedly being built for the China trade and two ironclads ostensibly destined for the pasha of Egypt had in fact been ordered by the Confederacy. Dayton passed copies of the documents to Foreign Minister Drouyn, who promised a full investigation. Seward told Dayton to warn Drouyn that the United States would hold France strictly accountable for any ships that were allowed to escape. The clear-eyed James Bulloch, however, took the airing of his secrets in stride. "The construction of the ships will not be interfered with," he predicted, "but whether they will be allowed to leave France or not will depend upon the position of affairs in America at the time of their completion."[21] Bulloch was right. His ships would never fly the Confederate flag, a result that would owe less to the efforts of Seward, Dayton, or Bigelow than to the battles won by blue-clad soldiers on the road to Richmond.

* * *

Seward took only one holiday during the first two years of the war, a visit to Auburn in the fall of 1862. Such austerity was the exception rather than the rule, for war or no war, most Washington residents who could afford to do so left the city during the sweltering summer months of July and August. The diplomatic corps customarily departed en masse, many to spas in Saratoga and Newport. Seward, in 1863, had an idea. Not even the Federal successes in July had convinced all foreign observers—as he thought they should have—of the inevitability of a Northern victory. One reason for their skepticism, in Seward's view, was that they had no concept of the vast resources of the North. To change their perspective, he invited all heads of mission to be his guests on a grand tour of New York State.

One might think that the diplomats would have been weary of one another's company, but many accepted, including Lyons, Mercier, and Stoeckl. The War Department provided a special railroad car, and Seward undertook the role of tour guide. The group, which gained and lost members at various stops, traveled up the Hudson to Albany and Schenectady in July and then turned west to Syracuse, Utica, and of course Auburn. There were boat excursions on the Finger Lakes and visits to Buffalo and Niagara Falls. The visitors could hardly overlook the fact that throughout New York State the economy was booming, with factories and mills seemingly operating at full capacity. There hardly seemed to be a war on. Could the same be said of any part of the South?

Seward had enjoyed generally good personal relations with the diplomatic corps, despite the fact that most were sympathetic toward the South. Now, diplomats like Mercier and Lyons, who had locked horns with the secretary in their official roles, saw a charming, ebullient Seward. Even Lyons was impressed. "He has . . . so much more vanity, personal and national, than tact, that he seldom makes a favorable impression at first," the Englishman wrote in a dispatch. "When one comes really to know him one is surprised to find much to esteem and even to like in him."[22]

Officially, however, the United States' most visible friend remained Russia. On September 24, just days after the bloody Federal defeat at Chickamauga, six vessels of the imperial navy sailed into New York Harbor on a friendly visit. "God bless the Russians," wrote Gideon Welles, who, like Seward, hoped that such a visible gesture of support would not be lost on Britain and France. As winter approached, the Russian ships moved down to Washington, where groups of bearded sailors wandered through the capital's well-stocked shops. Admiral Lisovski and his officers met the president and his cabinet, while the Russians in turn entertained lavishly aboard their ships. *Harper's Weekly* was impressed with the sight of the Russian fleet at anchor. "England and France have recognized the belligerent rights of the rebels," the magazine editorialized, "Russia has not. . . . If an English pirate, like the *Florida* or *Alabama,* should appear off the bay, the English and French ships would treat her as a commissioned vessel of war, [whereas] the Russian ships would treat her as a pirate."[23]

* * *

Seward could assist in keeping the European powers from adding to Lincoln's problems, but ultimately the American Civil War would be decided on the battlefield. In the early months of 1863, the Army of the Potomac had taken the offensive under a new commander, Joseph Hooker. Lincoln's inability to come up with a general to match Robert E. Lee was discouraging, but Federal shortcomings in the East tended to obscure the severe problems the Confederacy faced along the Mississippi. New Orleans was in Federal hands, and the fortress town of Vicksburg would shortly be assaulted from two directions.

By May the Army of the Potomac was on the move and in a position to strike between Lee's army and Richmond. Once again, however, Lee's military genius turned aside a great Yankee offensive. The Army of Northern Virginia crushed Hooker's army at Chancellorsville, inflicting more than seventeen thousand casualties in a two-week campaign and bringing Seward close to despair. In a telegram to Governor Morgan in Albany, he deplored the fact that only three corps of Hooker's army had been seriously engaged, adding, "You need not be told that this is less than half of his command."[24] Seward told a friend that if he himself should fall in a defense of Washington he wanted his dust to remain there. "Let it be buried under the pavements of the Avenue, and let the chariot wheels of those who have destroyed the liberties of my country rattle over my bones until a more heroic and worthy generation shall recall that country to life, liberty and independence."[25]

When Lee turned his army north for a second time, marching into Pennsylvania in late June, the Army of the Potomac had yet another commander, George G. Meade. Seward maintained business as usual while Lee moved north; actress Charlotte Cushman and her niece were his houseguests in Washington. But Will—now Col. William H. Seward II and a regimental commander—was part of the force defending Washington. Frances, in Auburn, was frantic. Henry no longer had time to write her every day but he did the best he could. "We do not yet know where [Lee] is," he wrote on June 19. "We are, I do not doubt, stronger than he, and better able to defeat him than he to subjugate us."[26] Not until several days after the Battle of Gettysburg was Seward confident that the battle had been a Union victory, but in a letter to Frances he demonstrated a clear understanding of its implications:

> The steamers of the 4th and 8th have carried to Europe intelligence of the defeat of General Lee. . . . The defeated army, however, was not destroyed nor captured.
>
> The fall of Vicksburg, on the 4th of July, undoubtedly to be followed soon by the fall of Port Hudson, must completely revolutionize the contest on the Mississippi. . . .
>
> Indications already appear that the work of dissolution is begun in the Confederacy. . . . Its capacity to raise new levies, and new armies, if not exhausted, is greatly diminished.[27]

Shortly after the Battle of Gettysburg, the governors of the Northern states arranged for the reinterment of the dead in a proper setting. The main speaker at the dedication of the new cemetery was to be Edward Everett of Massachusetts; President Lincoln was to make brief remarks. David Wills, chairman of the cemetery board, sent invitations to the cabinet, members of Congress, and the diplomatic corps. Some cabinet members were surprised that Lincoln planned to attend; Stanton agreed to provide a special railroad car but asked to be excused, as did Chase and Welles. The presidential party ultimately included Lincoln, Seward, Blair, and the new secretary of the interior, John P. Usher.

The president and his entourage left Washington at noon on October 18 on a four-car train bedecked in red-white-and-blue bunting. In addition to the three cabinet officers, Lincoln had with him two of his secretaries, Nicolay and Hay, the French and Italian ministers, a number of reporters, and a military guard. The train made frequent stops, at which Lincoln occasionally appeared briefly but declined to speak. On one occasion he turned to his secretary of state with a quip: "Seward, you go out and repeat some of your 'poetry' to the people."[28]

The train pulled into Gettysburg at sundown. Lincoln went to the Wills residence, Seward to a private home next door. The evening was mild and the air festive; when Lincoln again declined to address a group of serenaders, they trooped to the house next door, where Seward was more accommodating:

> I am now sixty years old and upwards; I have been in public life, practically, forty years of that time, and yet this is the first time that any community so near the border of Maryland was found willing to listen to my voice.

Seward spoke so weakly that John Hay could not hear him clearly. The older man must have been tired, for he was uncharacteristically brief:

> I thank my God that this strife is going to end in the removal of [slavery], which ought to have been removed by deliberate councils and peaceful means. I thank my God for the hope that this is the last fratricidal war which will fall upon the country which is vouchsafed to us by Heaven— the richest, the broadest, the most beautiful . . . that has ever been given to any part of the human race.[29]

That same evening Lincoln asked to see Seward and was informed that he was next door. Lincoln's host offered to go get the secretary but the president declined the offer. Instead, he gathered up his speech text and went next door, where he spent a half hour with Seward. There is no evidence from the text or from other surviving manuscripts that the weary secretary had any suggestions. The next day, one of those who had just heard Lincoln asked Seward if he had had any hand in the president's speech. Seward replied that no one but Abraham Lincoln could have made that address.[30]

Seward was feeling thankful for the turn in Federal military fortunes, and just before the ceremonies at Gettysburg he went to the president with a recommendation. The country had observed an autumnal Thanksgiving Day since the time of President Washington, but the choice of a date had been left to the states. Seward proposed to Lincoln that he proclaim a day of *national* thanksgiving—and he just happened to have with him a draft proclamation that he had cleared with several members of the cabinet. Even Welles had liked it. Lincoln made a few changes, then signed off on Seward's text. In so doing he formalized the observance of Thanksgiving as we know it today.

20

"Beyond the Pale of Human Envy"

As 1863 TURNED into 1864, the city of Washington manifested all the aspects of a boomtown. The population, exclusive of soldiers, had risen from 75,000 in 1860 to about 350,000. Telegraph wires were everywhere, connecting the War Department with the Capitol, the Navy Yard, and outlying encampments. Every hotel and every boardinghouse was filled—with contractors, clerks, embalmers, petty thieves, and just plain cranks. The streets rang with the clatter of army wagons and the oaths of the teamsters. Years before, Seward had observed that "the improvability of our race is without limit."[1] Wartime Washington seemed determined to vindicate him as a prophet.

There was an overriding sense of disorder. Soldiers were everywhere; so were dead horses. The city seemed as badly maintained as ever; the *National Intelligencer* called attention to the intersection of F and Eleventh streets, where the coach of an unnamed diplomat had come a cropper:

> This coach settled into the mud to the axle, and after vainly crying for planks to be brought, . . . one of the distinguished occupants was rescued by a huge negro who, wading leg-deep to the coach, brought the foreign officer in full diplomatic regalia . . . upon his back to terra firma.[2]

By 1864, prostitution was vying with government service as the town's leading industry. Anyone venturing onto Pennsylvania Avenue was treated to the sight of gaudy courtesans parading with officers or sharing their carriages. The *Washington Star* claimed to have studied the problem from a statistical perspective, and concluded that the figure of fifteen thousand prostitutes in Washington was much too high. The total probably did not exceed five thousand, according to the *Star,* up from 350 before the war.[3]

At the other end of the social scale, Washington society had never resolved to everyone's satisfaction the question of appropriate wartime decorum. By January 1864, however, there were few concessions to austerity. While life in Richmond grew increasingly threadbare, Washington saw a seemingly endless succession of levees, "at homes," dinners, and balls. Fred Seward reflected on this situation in a letter to his mother:

> Gayety has become an epidemic in Washington this winter as gloom was last winter. There is a lull in political discipline and people are inclined to eat, drink and be merry. . . . A year ago the Secretary of State was heartless or unpatriotic because he gave dinners; now the only complaint is that he don't [*sic*] have dancing.[4]

New Year's Day, 1864, saw the traditional morning reception at the White House. Reporter Ben Perley Poore noted that "Mr. Lincoln was in excellent spirits, giving each passer-by a cordial greeting and a warm shake of the hand." Secretary Seward he assessed as "sphinx-like and impassible." At noon, according to Poore, "the portals were thrown open, and in poured the people in a continuous stream. For two hours did they pass steadily along, a living tide . . . of humanity, uniforms, black coats, gay female attire, and citizens generally."[5]

Seward, assisted by Anna, entertained regularly but without ostentation. Even so, his expenses were heavy. The secretary was a wine connoisseur, and when the French minister, Mercier, was reassigned in 1864, Seward made him promise to provide a case of good Burgundy. Food and drink were the secretary's main indulgences; at a time when anyone who had connections could make huge profits from his knowledge of military contracts, Seward ignored possibilities for personal gain. It is well that his personal finances were secure, for Seward remarked on one occasion that he was spending $16,000 per year in Washington, twice the amount of his State Department salary.[6]

Apart from whist and afternoon carriage rides, Seward's main recreation was the theater. Leonard Glover, who managed one of the city's two theaters, was an old friend, and Charlotte Cushman invariably stayed at the Old Clubhouse when in Washington for an engagement. Early in 1864, Seward joined President and Mrs. Lincoln for a performance of *Richard III* at Glover's. The house was packed, for the part of Richard was played by Edwin Booth, the dean of the country's most prestigious theatrical family.[7]

The secretary of state was a catch for any Washington hostess. In a city renowned for its stuffed shirts, Seward had a deserved reputation as an iconoclast. He would often arrive late, his hair uncombed, his dress disheveled. But with the cares of the day behind him, Seward, with his "head like a wise macaw," was a peerless raconteur. He would hold forth at length in his husky voice, occasionally dominating but never dull. His humor was often self-deprecating. What is fame? he would ask rhetorically, and tell of how, in the tense days just before the Republican Convention of 1860, he caught one of the horsedrawn street cars in New York City. There he heard one of the other passengers ask his neighbor, "Who is this Governor Seward? Is he of New York?"[8]

For all his enjoyment of alcohol, Seward appears to have been careful in his conversation. To a lady who inquired about military movements he remarked pointedly, "Madam, if I did not know, I would tell you."[9]

Nevertheless, Seward was not a teetotaler, and at times he paid a price. When a group of clergymen wrote him a letter admonishing him to be more temperate, Seward wrote a letter in rebuttal but decided not to send it right away. The next day he took his letter and threw it in the fire, telling a friend that he believed he had character enough to withstand the gossipmongers, and that he would not apologize for his personal habits.[10]

Seward's relations with Lincoln were as close as ever. Fred Seward, who was sometimes present at their meetings, would recall,

> As they sat together by the fireside, or in the carriage, the conversation between them . . . always drifted back to the same channel—the progress of the great national struggle. Both loved humor, and however trite the theme, Lincoln always found some quaint illustration from his western life, and Seward some case in point in his long public career, that gave it new light.[11]

Fred Seward, a fairly reliable reporter, tells of a remarkable exchange between Lincoln and Seward during one of their evening talks in either 1863 or 1864. According to Fred, Lincoln expressed the hope that Seward would succeed him as president and that the secretary's friends, so disappointed at Chicago in 1860, would find things "all made right at last." Seward reportedly had demurred, insisting that his political ambitions were a thing of the past and that Lincoln must be his own successor. Whether Lincoln was referring to 1864 or 1868 is unclear from Fred's narrative.[12] It is an odd exchange, for Seward was sufficiently unpopular with Radical Republicans that his prospects for the nomination were only slightly better than those of Jefferson Davis. Lincoln, too, must have realized this. But Seward spoke truthfully when he said that he had put the presidency out of mind.

Perhaps prodded by Frances, to whom he had sent a homeless black man for settlement in the Auburn area, Seward periodically visited the camps where the army housed "contrabands" who had come through the lines. "I think we have kept . . . about two thousand slaves from starving in this campaign," he wrote Frances in June 1864, "but they are seemingly all old persons, women and children. It is a pleasing sight to see the light-hearted activity & tenderness of these poor creatures who find in exile & in tents an agreeable improvement in their condition."[13]

The fact that the war had turned sharply in favor of the North was not always apparent in Washington, which awaited with some skepticism the outcome of yet another campaign against Richmond under yet another commander, Ulysses S. Grant. The questions of reconstruction, however, were already intruding. In December 1863, Lincoln had issued a proclamation that outlined for the first time his plan for reconstituting the Union. He promised a full pardon to all in rebellion, except for a few leaders, once they had taken an oath of allegiance and had promised to obey all laws, including those respecting slavery. Whenever the number of voters in a state taking the oath reached 10 percent of the 1860 total, this presumably loyal core would be allowed to reestablish a state government. Because the Emancipation Proclamation had been based on the president's war powers and because its scope was limited, many Northerners, Seward included, favored a constitutional amendment that would put an end to slavery everywhere. But in 1864 there was still enough opposition to an antislavery amendment among Democrats in the House of Representatives to block the proposed legislation.

In 1861 Seward had believed many Southerners to be reluctant secessionists. With the war now approaching a successful close, he continued to view most of the "insurgents" as prodigals who should be returned to the Union fold as painlessly as possible. Given this view, he was firmly in accord with Lincoln's Ten-Percent Plan for reconstruction. Moreover, his repeated clashes with Republican radicals had strengthened his inclination to regard reconstruction as the constitutional responsibility of the president rather than of Congress.

Meanwhile, even with the settlement of the Laird rams affair, Seward had plenty with which to occupy himself in his own department, especially in the matter of France and Mexico. In June 1863 French troops had overthrown a republican government headed by Benito Juárez and had occupied Mexico City. A puppet assembly in Mexico had voted to establish a monarchy under French protection. The U.S. minister to Austria, historian John L. Motley, wrote Seward about the Austrian whom Napoleon III proposed to place on the throne of Mexico:

> The Archduke Maximilian is . . . about thirty years of age. He has been a kind of Lord High Admiral, an office which, in the present condition of the Imperial Navy, may be supposed to be not a very onerous occupation. He . . . is considered a somewhat restless and ambitious youth. . . .
>
> [The Mexican venture] is exceedingly unpopular in Austria. That a Prince of the House of Hapsburg should become the satrap of the Bonaparte dynasty, and should sit on an American throne which could not exist a moment but for French bayonets and French ships is most galling to all classes of Austrians.[14]

Nevertheless, in April 1864 Maximilian and his wife, Charlotte, left Trieste on what would prove to be the last attempt to transplant a monarchy to the New World. Under the terms of a secret convention, Maximilian agreed on behalf of his ''government'' to pay France's claims against Mexico; France, in turn, guaranteed Maximilian military protection. All this was viewed approvingly by Confederate authorities in Richmond. To facilitate trade in war goods the Confederacy had already entered into local agreements with anti-Juárez chieftains. As a result they felt no commitment to the Mexican republic. Subsequently, Confederate leaders had sought an agreement with France whereby Richmond would recognize a French-controlled regime in Mexico in return for French recognition of the Confederacy.[15] France was tempted.

At the time of the French occupation of Mexico, Washington had expressed concern but had stopped short of a formal protest. Seward continued to believe that the United States had enough on its hands without seeking a dispute on a matter largely unrelated to the rebellion. Ironically, Congress was more prepared to make an issue of the situation in Mexico than was the Lincoln administration. In January 1864 Sen. James McDougal of California had introduced a series of resolutions calling on France to withdraw its armed forces from Mexico and reiterating U.S. opposition to any European interference in Mexican affairs. The McDougal resolutions died in committee. In April, however, the House of Representatives declared unanimously that the United States was opposed to the imposition of a European monarchy on any republican government in America.[16]

Seward refused to be stampeded. He warned Dayton that the views expressed on Capitol Hill were "not in harmony" with administration policy. When Bigelow suggested that Washington's policy toward Mexico might be too conciliatory, Seward responded in a confidential letter:

> If our armies succeed as we hope, we shall have no conflict with France or with any foreign power. So long as our success in suppressing the slavery faction at home is doubted abroad, we shall be in danger of war. . . . With our land and naval forces in Louisiana retreating before the rebels instead of marching towards Mexico, this is not the most suitable time we could choose for offering idle menaces to the Emperor of France.[17]

Relations with Canada took on a greater priority in the fall of 1864. On October 19 a band of twenty-five Confederates based in Canada raided the town of St. Albans, Vermont, about fifteen miles from the Canadian border. The Confederate partisans robbed three banks and killed one resident before retreating to Canada, where about half of them were arrested by Canadian authorities. It was not the first Confederate harassing action from Canada, and when a Canadian judge ordered the release of the raiders on a technicality, Northerners were outraged.

Gen. John A. Dix, commanding the Eastern Military District, ordered that any future Canada-based raiders should be pursued across the border and, if captured, returned to the United States rather than surrendered to Canadian authorities. Dix's order clearly posed a threat of clashes between U.S. and Canadian forces, but Seward made no move to revoke it, hoping that the implied threat might lead to the extradition of the raiders or, at minimum, a more vigorous effort by Canadian authorities to police the border. Seward even instructed Adams to notify Whitehall that the United States intended to abrogate the 1817 agreement that limited armaments along the U.S.-Canadian border. By December, however, the Lincoln administration was sufficiently convinced of Canada's good faith that it rescinded Dix's edict.[18]

Seward's attitude toward Britain had changed considerably since Palmerston's precipitous recognition of Confederate belligerency. Far from behaving as an Anglophobe, he had demonstrated considerable patience in matters such as the Laird rams and British trade with the Confederacy. By the spring of 1864, the thought that Palmerston might be turned out of office was positively distressing. But Seward did not hesitate to take action that might endanger Anglo-American relations if it was important to the war effort. Throughout 1864, on Seward's recommendation, recruiters for the U.S. Army traveled across Ireland seeking to enlist Irishmen for the Northern armies. Such action was hardly in accordance with Britain's neutrality, but Seward paid no attention and the British took no notice.

* * *

In retrospect it seems remarkable that there could have been any doubt that Lincoln would be reelected in 1864. For most of that year, however, his political position was far from secure. No incumbent president had been reelected since 1832, and a number had failed to gain renomination. Many people—even in his own party—viewed Lincoln as a weak president. Yet his greatest liability was the absence of clear progress in the war. Grant's campaign against Lee, begun with high hopes in April, was by fall mired along the approaches to Richmond. Union casualties were among the highest of any time in the war.

The president's first hurdle was to assure renomination by his own party. Salmon P. Chase had used the extensive appointive power of a treasury secretary to build up support for his own nomination. "I think a man of different qualities from those of the President will be needed for the next four years," he had noted modestly at the end of 1863. When Chase's trial balloon—the so-called Pomeroy Circular—fizzled badly, Lincoln was assured at least of renomination. But enthusiasm was notably lacking. One of Lincoln's friends, Sen. Lyman Trumbull, commented in May: "The feeling for Mr. Lincoln's re-election *seems* to be very general, but much of it I discover is only on the surface. You would be surprised, in talking with public men we meet here, to find how few . . . are for Mr. Lincoln's reelection."[19]

One of those who supported Lincoln, if only tepidly, was Thurlow Weed. The Albany boss, who had given up the editor's chair of the *Albany Evening Journal* but who still headed the Republican state committee, was cool to emancipation and irritated by his limited share of federal patronage. It was Seward who, behind the scenes, reminded his old friend that there was no alternative to Lincoln, and Weed ultimately conceded as much. When the Republican state committee convened in late May, Weed rammed through an endorsement of Lincoln's renomination.[20]

At the national convention in Baltimore, there was less of a threat to Lincoln than to Seward. A large segment of the party favored the replacement of Hannibal Hamlin as vice president—not because of any aversion to Hamlin but because of a general belief that the Union ticket could count on New England, and that Lincoln's running mate should be someone with appeal outside traditional Republican states. Anti-Weed elements in the New York delegation were urging a conservative Democrat, Daniel Wilkinson, for vice president. Weed recognized that the support for Wilkinson was essentially a move against himself and Seward, because not even New York would be allowed to monopolize two positions as prestigious as those of vice president and secretary of state. "Dickinson in, Seward out" was the avowed purpose of the anti-Weed delegates.

The upshot was that Weed, working closely with Henry Raymond of the *New York Times,* rallied behind the vice-presidential candidacy of a border-state Unionist whose main qualification was that he was not from New York. The delegates at Baltimore concurred, and Andrew Johnson was chosen as Lincoln's running mate.[21] Lincoln himself appears to have played little part in the bargaining that resulted in Johnson's nomination.

The Baltimore convention succeeded in papering over the party's more visible schisms. Delegations from the "Ten-Percent" reconstructed states—Louisiana and Tennessee—were admitted, while Radicals were placated by the seating of an anti-Blair delegation from Missouri. In part because Raymond chaired the platform committee, the platform endorsed Seward's policy toward Mexico and gave its blessing to two other pet projects of Seward's—the encouragement of immigration and the completion of the transcontinental railroad.[22]

None of the Baltimore resolutions would have any real substance unless ratified by Union arms. Horace Greeley announced in August that if the election were held then, the Republicans would lose New York and Pennsylvania by a total of one hundred thousand votes.[23] Sherman's army advanced deeper into Georgia, but Grant's war of attrition in Virginia was accompanied by such appalling casualties that it was a major political liability for the administration. An ugly war became uglier with the Confederate capture of Fort Pillow on the Mississippi, where scores of black troops attempting to surrender were shot down by Gen. Bedford Forrest's Confederates. In deploring the savagery at Fort Pillow, Seward wrote to Frances with the detachment that drove his critics wild:

> The Fort Pillow massacre is shocking and horrible. While it is now clear that in any case the slaveholders would have made this war one of barbarity to the negroes and so have provoked retaliation, I nevertheless can't sufficiently regret and deplore every rash and violent utterance on our side. . . . A war of ideas is always a fearful war.[24]

In the summer of 1864 the war took on an immediacy for the Seward family with the advance on Washington by the 18,000-man Confederate force led by Gen. Jubal A. Early. Young Will Seward, who had been commended for gallantry at the Battle of Cold Harbor, now commanded an artillery regiment in the VI Corps. To meet the threat from Early, a makeshift force that included Will's regiment was hurried to Frederick, Maryland; there, at the Battle of Monocacy, Gen. Lew Wallace threw his small force, including Will's regiment, against the advancing Confederates. Early's veterans routed the defenders, but only after a brisk battle that allowed the Federals another day to bring up reinforcements. Will was slightly wounded at Monocacy, and injured again when his horse fell on top of him.

At the State Department, Seward and Fred waited uneasily as badly garbled reports of Early's advance trickled into the capital. At midnight on July 9, Seward returned home to find Stanton waiting with word that Will had been taken prisoner. In a hasty conference it was decided that Gus would go to Baltimore to make inquiries. By three o'clock on the following day, Gus informed his father that Will, though wounded, was not a prisoner. That evening Seward and Fred took a carriage out on the Tenleytown road until they encountered soldiers from Will's regiment, who praised his conduct and assured the secretary of state that his son's wound was not serious.[25]

* * *

The latter half of 1864 witnessed the remarkable spectacle of a country whose very existence was in question conducting an election to determine that country's leader. In August the Democrats nominated a presidential ticket headed by General McClellan, on a platform that declared the war a failure. With Grant struggling before Richmond, the "peace" platform had considerable appeal. Seward returned to New York in August to assist in the state campaign, where he found both Weed and Raymond in low spirits. Then Adm. David G. Farragut's ships entered Mobile Bay and Sherman's advance units reached Atlanta. All was changed! Seward, in a campaign speech in Auburn, sought to underscore the favorable military developments and to defend the actions of the Lincoln administration during the war. "Misguided but not intentionally perverse" people had complained of the suspension of habeas corpus, "as if the government could justify itself for waiting without preventive measures, for more states to be invaded or to be carried off in secession." He went on to defend the draft:

They complain that when we call for volunteers, we present the alternative of a draft, as if when the ship has been scuttled, the captain ought to leave the sleeping passengers to go to the bottom without calling for them to take their turn at the pump.[26]

Election Day, November 8, found Seward back in Washington, a cold rain and wintry gusts keeping most people indoors. That evening he joined Lincoln and John Hay in the War Department telegraph office, where returns were beginning to come in. A dispatch from the critical state of Indiana, a center of pacifist sentiment, showed the Lincoln-Johnson ticket safely ahead. Ultimately, the Union ticket would win by a national plurality of more than 400,000 votes out of 4 million cast, and by 212 to 21 in the electoral college.

Seward's relief was immense. No one sought peace more than he, but for the electorate to have repudiated the policies of the Lincoln administration was unthinkable. On the Thursday evening following the election a crowd assembled in front of Seward's house in the hope of a speech. They were not disappointed; the secretary of state recounted some of the administration's domestic accomplishments and predicted that once victory was won "you will have to look mighty sharp to find a man who was a secessionist, or an aider of rebellion." When he spoke of Lincoln, Seward was almost tender:

> The election has placed our President beyond the pale of human envy or human harm, as he is above the pale of ambition. Henceforth all men will come to see him as you and I have seen him—a true, loyal, patient, patriotic, and benevolent man. . . . Abraham Lincoln will take his place with Washington and Franklin and Jefferson and Adams and Jackson, among the benefactors of the country and of the human race.[27]

In a cabinet meeting two days after his reelection, Lincoln brought out a sealed paper, which he had asked his cabinet to sign without reading the previous August. The paper was a brief memorandum in which Lincoln had noted that his reelection appeared unlikely, and that in the event of defeat it would be his responsibility to meet with Mc-Clellan and to cooperate in attempting to bring the war to a conclusion in the final months of the Lincoln administration. McClellan should raise as many troops as he could, and Lincoln would devote all his energies to bringing the war to a close.

Seward snorted. McClellan, he said, would have answered "Yes, yes," and done nothing. "And the next day, when you saw him again and pressed those views upon him, he would say, '*Yes, yes*'; and so on forever, and would have done nothing at all." "At least," remarked Lincoln, "I should have done my duty, and should have stood clear before my own conscience."[28]

Lincoln's reelection did nothing to improve the popularity of his secretary of state on Capitol Hill. In July the president had killed with a pocket veto the Wade-Davis bill, which required that the Confederate states abolish slavery as a condition for their return to the Union and was designed as a challenge to Lincoln's less stringent Ten-Percent Plan. Although it is unclear whether Seward influenced Lincoln's thinking on this first stage of reconstruction, the Radicals assumed that the secretary of state was still pulling the strings. It was widely rumored that Congressman Henry Winter Davis, a longtime Seward foe, would attack Seward for his "soft" views on reconstruction when Congress reconvened in December 1864.

The Radicals seethed with anger and suspicion, and their numbers in the party had increased since the cabinet crisis of 1862. But to attack a president during wartime was politically dangerous; it was far safer to snipe at his advisers. On December 15 Henry Winter Davis introduced a resolution stating that Congress, as well as the State Department, was responsible for foreign affairs. It focused on Franco-U.S. relations, charging that Seward had virtually apologized to Napoleon III for congressional criticism of France's course in Mexico. Thad Stevens and other Radicals supported Davis, but the House voted 69 to 63 against his resolution.[29]

* * *

Those who knew Jeff Davis best insisted that the Confederate president would never surrender. Nevertheless, when veteran statesman Francis P. Blair sought permission to visit Davis in Richmond, Lincoln concurred. Blair's meeting with Davis brought a promise from the Mississippian that if Lincoln was prepared to receive peace commissioners, Davis would appoint emissaries "with a view to secure peace to the two countries." Lincoln replied that he would be pleased to receive overtures "with the view of securing peace to the people of our one common country."[30] The Confederate delegation consisted of three prewar moderates, Confederate Vice President Alexander H. Stephens, a onetime friend of Lincoln's; Sen. Robert M. T. Hunter; and Seward's erstwhile intermediary in his 1861 negotiations with the Confederate commissioners, John A. Campbell.

Lincoln and Seward traveled to Hampton Roads to meet with Davis's emissaries. "Our odd president is doing that odd thing," wrote Congressman James A. Garfield, "gone to Fortress Monroe to meet Stephens, Hunter and Campbell, whom both armies cheered as they came through."[31] A four-hour meeting aboard the Union steamer *River Queen* was friendly but fruitless. Lincoln made it clear at the outset that there could be no armistice, that only surrender could bring a close to the war. Stephens raised the possibility of a joint military expedition to eject the French from Mexico. But the Confederates had no bargaining position, and Lincoln was giving nothing away.

Lincoln and Seward told the Confederates that the Thirteenth Amendment, abolishing slavery, was about to be sent to the states for ratification. The administration, including Seward, had lobbied strongly for the amendment, on the ground that the South must understand that there was to be no compromise on the slavery issue. Now, aboard the *River Queen,* Seward sought to entice the Southerners. If the Southern states were to return to the Union, they would be in a position to block ratification of the Thirteenth Amendment and thereby to delay the end of slavery. If Stephens's account of the conference is credited, Seward held out to the defeated Confederates not only the prospect of delaying the abolition of slavery but of regaining the South's political clout in a restored union. Seward had come a long way since his reformist phase as a U.S. senator.

Lincoln, in Stephens's account, appears to have been noncommittal on Seward's proposal, but he offered a variant of his own. The governor of Stephens's state of Georgia, Lincoln said, should convene the legislature and recall all Georgia troops from the war. He should then ratify the Thirteenth Amendment prospectively, so as to take effect in five years or so. Thus slavery could be abolished in stages.[32]

Although the meeting on the *River Queen* was cordial, it was fruitless, for the Confederate emissaries had no authority to negotiate reunion. There were friendly handshakes as the conference broke up. Lincoln promised Stephens to return his nephew, a prisoner on Johnson's Island. The Confederate emissaries had returned to their steamer when they spied a rowboat with a black oarsman heading for them from the *River Queen.* When he reached the Confederate vessel, the oarsman passed up a basket of champagne with a note that it came with Mr. Seward's compliments. Then the three emissaries spotted Seward himself, calling to them through a boatswain's trumpet. His words were, "Keep the champagne, but return the Negro."[33]

*   *   *

March 4, 1865, was a carbon copy of the blustery inauguration day four years earlier. The inaugural procession made its way through the mud of Pennsylvania Avenue to the Capitol, where the bronze statue of Freedom at long last crowned the Capitol dome.

Inside, a packed Senate chamber awaited the administering of the vice-presidential oath to Andrew Johnson. Precisely at noon the vice president–elect entered with Hannibal Hamlin and took his seat on the dais. After some brief remarks by Hamlin, Johnson took the floor. He had been feeling unwell, and sought to brace himself with several glasses of whiskey. Now, at one of the most important moments in his career, he was drunk. In some rambling remarks Johnson gloried in the fact that he had risen from the masses, and he reminded all members of the cabinet, though he could not remember the name of the secretary of the navy, that they derived their power from the people. To Noah Brooks of the *Sacramento Union,* Stanton appeared petrified and the new postmaster general, William Dennison, was red and white by turns. Only Seward remained inscrutable.[34]

Then the ceremony moved outside to the portico, where Lincoln delivered a very different speech, the one that he considered his best:

> With malice toward none; with charity for all; with firmness in the right, as God gives us to see the right, let us strive on to finish the work we are in; to bind up the nation's wounds; to care for him who shall have borne the battle, and for his widow and his orphan—to do all which may achieve and cherish a just and lasting peace, among ourselves, and with all nations.[35]

Salmon P. Chase, whom Lincoln had just named chief justice, administered the oath of office. To Seward the inauguration was the most majestic and enthusiastic he had ever seen. And after all, Andrew Johnson was only the vice president.

21

The Man in the Light Overcoat

SEWARD HAD A habit, when things were going well, of softly rubbing the palms of his hands together. With Lincoln reelected and the war nearly won, Seward was rubbing his palms together a great deal. Except for the continuing French presence in Mexico, the country's foreign affairs were more amicable than at any time since 1861. Seward began preparing the paperwork for claims against Britain for the damage inflicted by the *Alabama*. "Our foreign affairs are closing up finely," he wrote Frances on his return from the Hampton Roads conference. During the war years Seward had become friendly with Lincoln's young secretary, John Hay. Recognizing that Hay was growing restless in Washington, Seward startled him by offering to appoint him secretary to the American legation in Paris. Hay, delighted, accepted.[1]

Seward had consistently underestimated the resiliency of the Confederacy, but by February 1865 the signs were unmistakable. Seward regarded slave prices in the South as a reliable indicator of how Southerners viewed Confederate prospects. He wrote to Frances:

I have noticed that $150 or $200 [in] United States currency is the highest price which the most marketable slave commands, either in Virginia or in Georgia. . . . I need not say that this is a confession that slaves, as property, are absolutely worthless. . . . Capital, of course, now avoids investment in slaves.[2]

Relations within Lincoln's cabinet were smoother on the eve of victory than in the anxious months of 1861 and 1862. Seward and Welles were now the only two holdovers from among Lincoln's initial appointees. Although Seward's relations with the acerbic Welles would never be warm, both men had made an effort to reduce friction. The secretary of war, Edwin Stanton, no longer felt beholden to Seward in any way, and his political views were closer to those of the Radicals in Congress than to Lincoln's and Seward's. But their personal relations were amicable; Seward referred to his colleague as the organizer of victory.

The best news for Seward had come in July 1864, when the secretary of the treasury, Salmon P. Chase, had submitted his resignation one time too many. Lincoln accepted it, appointing Fessenden of Maine in Chase's place. There was a turnover in the lesser portfolios as well. As a favor to Radical Republicans who had sought the ouster, Lincoln asked Montgomery Blair to resign as postmaster general. He was succeeded by William Dennison of Ohio. Old Edward Bates resigned as attorney general; his replacement was James Speed of Kentucky.

The spring of 1865 found Seward surrounded as usual with family and friends. Frances was not there, of course; after a visit to Washington in December she had retreated to Auburn and the security of the house on South Street. But Clarence Seward, Jennings's son, was a frequent visitor, as was Thurlow Weed. Gus was a full-time resident of the Old Clubhouse, with Fred and Anna.

Young Fanny had spent most of the war in Auburn. In October 1864, however, over her mother's objections, she had moved to Washington to be with her father. Her health remained fragile, and she was subject to colds. But she had made her debut in Washington and enjoyed life in the wartime capital. It appeared for a time that one of the president's secretaries, John Nicolay, was interested in Fanny, but romance never bloomed. Fanny continued to attend her father's dinners, shy and silent, waiting to record her impressions in her ubiquitous diary.

Richmond fell on April 3. Lincoln went there to sit in Jefferson Davis's chair in the Confederate White House, while Stanton ordered an eight-hundred-gun salute in Washington. In Lincoln's absence revelers gathered at the State Department, where they found Seward in an equally festive mood. What should he tell the emperor of China in his next dispatch? Seward asked the crowd rhetorically. "I shall thank him in your name for never having permitted a piratical flag to enter the harbors of the empire." Similarly, he would thank the sultan of Turkey for always having surrendered rebels who took refuge in that kingdom. He would tell Lord John Russell that British merchants would now find cotton legally exported from America cheaper than that smuggled through the blockade. His remarks greeted by applause and cheers, Seward even joked about his reputation for optimism:

> I do not doubt, fellow citizens, but that . . . you accede to the theory by which I have governed myself during the war—namely, that the rebellion was to end in ninety days. [Laughter and cheers] I have thought this the true theory, because I never knew a physician able to restore the patient to health unless he thought he could work a cure . . . in ninety days. [Renewed laughter][3]

The last thing that worried Seward in this time of celebration was the danger of assassination. He had been, of course, the target of many crackpot threats. But he had been out of the public eye since the cabinet crisis of December 1862, and his department affected few Americans directly. Beyond that, Seward simply did not believe assassination to be a real threat. When, in 1862, John Bigelow had written from Paris of an alleged plot against Lincoln and members of his cabinet, Seward was unimpressed. "Assassination is not an American practice or habit," he wrote in reply. It is "one so vicious and desperate" that it could never become part of the American political system. He noted how the president, in warm weather, rode two or three miles from the White House to the Soldiers' Home unguarded. So did he. "I go there unattended at all hours, by daylight and by moonlight, by starlight and without any light."[4]

On the warm spring afternoon of April 5, Seward left the State Department for a carriage ride with Fred, Fanny, and a friend of Fanny's named Mary Titus. Some distance out Vermont Avenue, the carriage proved to have a balky door that would not stay closed, and the coachman, Henry Key, stopped to make repairs. As he did so the horses bolted and turned for home. Fred, outside the coach, tried to control the team but fell. As the carriage picked up speed, the sixty-four-year-old Seward, over Fanny's protests, attempted to gather the reins. He fell heavily from the coach, which careened back toward Lafayette Park until the exhausted horses found refuge in an alley.

When help reached Seward, he was unconscious. The secretary was moved carefully back to his house, where he was first treated by an army surgeon, Maj. Basil Norris, and then by the family physician, Dr. Tullio Verdi. Seward's injuries were serious. His face was bruised and swollen and he appeared to have suffered a concussion. His right shoulder was dislocated and his right arm broken. His jaw was fractured on both sides. When Seward regained consciousness that evening he was in severe pain.

The.family informed Frances by telegraph. She came to Washington the following day. "I find Henry worse than I had anticipated," she wrote her sister. "It makes my heart ache to look at him."[5] The doctors expected a full recovery, but the setting of the patient's jaw and shoulder was an ordeal. At times Seward was delirious. To assist the family and house staff, Stanton provided a convalescent soldier, George Robinson, to act as a nurse. The assignment would turn Robinson into a celebrity.

There were many callers at the Old Clubhouse, but few were admitted to the sickroom. Among the most frequent visitors was the normally gruff Stanton. Another caller was Abraham Lincoln. The president had been in City Point, Virginia, when he heard of Seward's accident. Then came the long-awaited news of Lee's surrender. Amid the bells and salutes and rejoicing, Lincoln decided that he would return to Washington. Frederick Seward has described the president's call on his father:

> "You are back from Richmond?" whispered Seward, who was hardly able to articulate.
> "Yes," said Lincoln, "and I think we are near the end, at last."
> Then leaning his tall form across the bed, and resting on his elbow, so as to bring his face near that of the wounded man, he gave him an account of his experiences "at the front." . . . They were left together for half an hour or more. Then the door opened softly, and Mr. Lincoln came out gently, intimating by a silent look and gesture that Seward had fallen into a feverish slumber. . . . It was their last meeting.[6]

*   *   *

John Wilkes Booth was a promising twenty-six-year-old actor who, although strongly sympathetic to the South, had never quite gotten around to serving in the Confederate army. Seeking some dramatic means of giving expression to his sympathies, Booth, in about September 1864, formulated a plan to kidnap President Lincoln on some occasion when the president was riding to or from the Soldiers' Home.

In November, Booth took up residence at the National Hotel and began implementing his scheme. His first recruits were two high school chums, Samuel Arnold and Michael O'Laughlin. Washington still had more than its share of disgruntled secessionists, and Booth soon added three other kindred spirits—John Surratt, David Herold, and George Atzerodt—to his band. Booth's headquarters was Mrs. Surratt's boardinghouse on H Street. His prize recruit was one Lewis Thornton Powell, who would later be known by the alias Lewis Paine. The son of a Baptist clergyman, Powell was helping run his father's farm in Florida when the Civil War erupted. With his strapping physique, "unflinching dark gray eyes," and a "stolid, remorseless expression," Powell was a natural for the Confederate army. Assigned to a Florida regiment, he fought at Antietam and Chancellorsville, but was wounded at Gettysburg and taken prisoner. While serving as a nurse in a Baltimore hospital he escaped and joined the Confederate rangers of Col. John S. Mosby, then operating in northern Virginia. Brutalized by the war but despairing of the Confederate cause, Powell surrendered in January 1865, giving his name as Paine, presumably to cover the fact of his earlier escape.[7]

"Paine" returned to Baltimore, where he boarded with the family of a nurse-acquaintance, Maggie Branson. While there, he was reported to military authorities for having assaulted a black maid who had been impudent to him. According to testimony at the trial of the conspirators, she "called him some names, and then he struck her; he threw her on the ground and stamped on her body, struck her on the forehead, and said he would kill her."[8] But on the trial date several witnesses failed to appear. The provost marshal released Paine after administering an oath of allegiance and ordering him to remain north of Philadelphia for the duration of the war.

Paine would later testify that he had first seen John Wilkes Booth in Richmond, where Booth was appearing in a play. Paine had subsequently sought out the actor, and the two were soon on friendly terms. There is some question as to whether Booth performed in Richmond at the time indicated, but he does appear to have known Paine and to have encountered him in Baltimore in March 1865. Paine, unemployed, was an easy recruit for "Captain Booth," as Paine called him. Booth put him up at the Herndon House at Ninth and H streets, close to Mrs. Surratt's.

By then time had run out on Booth's kidnapping scheme. The Confederacy was in its last throes, and Lincoln was not yet visiting his cottage at the Soldiers' Home. Arnold and O'Laughlin had backed out of the kidnapping scheme. Booth, who by then was drinking heavily, apparently decided at this time to kill Lincoln and prominent members of his administration. While he may have hoped that the resulting turmoil would revive the Confederacy, his primary motive appears to have been vengeance. Booth made his new plans on April 14, assigning to Atzerodt the task of murdering Vice President Andrew Johnson and to Paine the killing of Seward.

Almost immediately Booth's hasty plans went awry. Atzerodt decided that kidnapping was one thing, murder another; after reflecting in a hotel bar, he determined to make no move against Johnson. But Paine, the good soldier, proceeded to carry out Booth's command. At about ten o'clock on the evening of April 14, Seward had fallen into an uneasy sleep in his third-floor bedroom when the front doorbell rang. One of the servants, nineteen-year-old William Bell, opened the door. A man in a light overcoat said that he had some medicine from Dr. Verdi to deliver to Secretary Seward in person. Bell responded that no one was allowed upstairs, but the stranger insisted. Bell led Paine to the third landing, where they encountered Fred Seward.

Paine repeated his story to Fred, who was initially unsuspecting. His father might be sleeping, he said, but he would see. Fred went to the front of the house, to the last door on the left. In a moment he was back. His father was indeed asleep, he said, asking Paine for the package. The stranger demurred; he *had* to deliver the medicine to the secretary personally. Frederick Seward began to lose patience. He would take responsibility for the "medicine"; Dr. Verdi would not blame the deliveryman if the family refused him admittance.[9]

Paine hesitated, mumbled something, and turned as if to start back down the stairs. He then reached into his coat, pulled out a big navy revolver, and attempted to fire at Fred. There was only a click. The pistol had misfired.

With two giant strides, Paine was on top of Fred, smashing him twice on the head with the pistol. Although Fred does not appear to have cried out, the noise of the scuffle carried into the sickroom, where Fanny had been reading to her father. She was preparing to turn the bedside watch over to Robinson, the soldier-nurse, and one of them opened the door to check on the commotion. Paine struck at Robinson with his backup weapon—a large Bowie knife—inflicting only a glancing blow but clearing him out of the doorway. He then made for the bed immediately to his right.

Paine had played his role to perfection thus far, locating his victim and refusing to be deterred by either Fred Seward or Robinson. Now, in the dim light of the sickroom, his luck ran out. Seward was on the side of the bed away from the door, reclining against a frame designed to provide maximum freedom for his injured shoulder and broken arm. Unable to use his revolver, Paine slashed repeatedly at Seward's head but, in the dim light, he did not always find his victim. Robinson would recall:

I saw him strike Mr. Seward with the same knife with which he cut my forehead. It was a large knife, and he held it with the blade down below his hand. I saw him cut Mr. Seward twice that I am sure of; the first time he struck him on the right cheek, and then he seemed to be cutting around his neck.[10]

By then the courageous Robinson was on him. The soldier suffered a second wound in the shoulder but succeeded in wrestling the assassin off the bed. Gus, aroused by the noise, joined Robinson in attempting to subdue the intruder. According to Gus, Paine shouted, "I'm mad! I'm mad!"[11]

Through the pandemonium, Fanny screamed for help. William Bell, on seeing Paine strike Fred, had gone to the army headquarters next door in search of help. Frances, hearing the noise, emerged from her room at the back of the house but could not comprehend what was happening. Finally Paine tore himself away from Robinson, struck Gus in the forehead, and bolted down the stairs. Near the front door he encountered a State Department messenger, Emerick Hansell, just mounting the stairs. Paine stabbed Hansell and rushed on to the hitching post where he had left his horse, dropping his knife as he ran.

The assaults on Lincoln and Seward occurred within minutes of one another, and many people heard first of the attack on Seward. Stanton was at home undressing, having spoken briefly to some serenaders, when his wife called from downstairs, "Mr. Seward is murdered!" "Humbug," Stanton replied, "I left him only an hour ago." But the secretary of war pulled on his clothes again, questioned his wife's informant, and hurried over to the Old Clubhouse.[12] The story was much the same with Gideon Welles. The navy secretary was asleep when a messenger arrived with word of the assaults on both Lincoln and Seward. "Damn the rebels, this is their work," Welles remarked, hurrying off to Lafayette Park. There was a dense crowd at Seward's house—soldiers, onlookers, and diplomats in formal dress from a nearby party. Welles pushed his way through the crowd until he spotted Stanton. The two cabinet officers were allowed up the blood-splattered staircase, where they were told that Seward and Fred were both seriously injured. Stanton ordered a guard put in front of the house; he and Welles then went to Ford's Theatre, where a still greater tragedy awaited.[13]

*   *   *

Once Paine had fled, the occupants of the house turned their attention to the injured. Poor Fanny would long remember the blood: "My dress was stained with it—Mother's was dabbled with it—it was on everything."[14] No American assassin had injured so many people in a single attack as had Paine. In the course of about three minutes, he had inflicted serious wounds on Secretary Seward and Fred; had given Hansell, the messenger, a deep wound in the side; and had inflicted less-serious injuries on Robinson and Gus. Robinson had ministered immediately to Secretary Seward, who was lying by the side of his bed, wrapped in bloody sheets like some latter-day Julius Caesar. At first Robinson feared the worst. Then he detected a pulse. Seward opened his eyes and whispered that Robinson should send for a surgeon and the police, then lock up the house. Later Seward would say that Paine's blade felt cold, and that he had felt what seemed like rain streaming down his neck. Whether he was thrown off the bed by the impetus of Paine's blows or whether he rolled off in an instinctive reaction is unclear.

The first physician to arrive was Dr. Verdi, who found the secretary back on his bed where Robinson had laid him, bleeding profusely. He feared initially that Seward's jugular vein had been severed. When this proved not to be the case, he checked the bleeding with ice water. Verdi assured the family that the secretary's wounds were not fatal, "upon which Mr. Seward stretched out his hands and received his family."[15] Soon Dr. Norris, who had treated Seward's earlier injuries, arrived, followed by the surgeon general, Dr. Joseph Barnes. Norris sutured Seward's slashed cheeks without benefit of anesthetic, but the patient later maintained that the process had not been especially painful.

Seward's narrow escape appears to have resulted from several factors: the failure of Paine's revolver, a development that forced him to resort to the uncertainties of assassination by knife; the dim light in the sickroom, which may have disoriented the intruder; and Robinson's courageous intervention. Contemporary accounts refer to Seward's having worn a cervical collar that deflected the assassin's knife, but recent scholarship has raised doubt as to whether Seward was wearing any such device. None of the witnesses at Paine's trial mentioned any cervical collar.[16]

The most seriously injured of those in the Old Clubhouse was Fred. The blows from Paine's defective revolver had fractured his skull, exposing the brain in two places. Within an hour after the attack he was unable to speak; helped to bed, he became comatose and remained so for several days. It was a month before he was judged to be out of danger.

Early the next morning, after a sleepless night, Frances told her husband of the events at Ford's Theatre. She said simply, "Henry, the president is gone."[17] Seward seemed to understand.* By then, though the bloodletting at the Old Clubhouse was overshadowed by the grief for Lincoln, there was no shortage of visitors at the Seward residence. Stanton, in particular, called repeatedly.

Seward began a slow recovery. For weeks he suffered from double vision. Because of his broken jaw and lacerated cheeks he could not speak without pain and communicated by writing on a slate. When social reformer Dorothea Dix sent him an exotic dish involving eggs and wine, Fanny asked him whether he liked it. "I like it because I like Miss Dix," Seward scrawled.[18] On April 19 the patient was able to sit up and watch Lincoln's funeral cortege as it left the White House. By then the family's greatest concern was Fred, who remained comatose. George Baker, the secretary's biographer and friend, wrote on April 24 that Fred, until recently, had been unconscious "as a sleeping man." Frances was sure that he would die. "Is it not . . . a terrible tragedy," Baker lamented. "Our good President killed, the generous, noble-hearted secretary butchered like an ox, and the amiable assistant sent to the very gates of death!"[19]

Nevertheless both Henry and Fred continued in their recovery. President Johnson and his cabinet called at the Old Clubhouse on May 9, and Henry was able to receive them in the parlor, although his jaw was secured by an iron frame that made it virtually impossible to converse. By late May, Seward was going to his office for brief periods, and on June 3 he dictated his first official letter since Paine's attack. Needing all the assistance he could obtain, Seward brought his nephew Clarence from New York City to act as assistant secretary.

As long as Fred was in danger, Frances sat by his bedside. "His pale, patient face," she wrote her sister, "is never out of my mind."[20] But as the Seward men improved, Frances herself went into a decline. As always, the cause was obscure. By late May she was bedridden, with symptoms that included nausea and an intermittent fever. To poor Fanny her mother seemed to be wasting away, becoming thinner and

---

*The fact that Seward was promptly told of Lincoln's death discredits a story that enjoyed a considerable vogue at that time. In this version, word of Lincoln's death was initially withheld from the secretary lest he be further upset. But within days of Paine's attack, he asked to be moved in order to view the spring foliage from his window. On noting flags on government buildings at half-staff, Seward stated flatly that the president was dead. To an attendant's faltering denial Seward allegedly responded, "If he had been alive, he would have been the first to call on me, but he has not been here . . . and there is the flag at half mast." Carpenter, *Six Months at the White House,* 291–92.

weaker with each day, but Fanny noted in her diary that "Father [is] very sure she [is] improving."[21]

Frances died on June 21, nine weeks after Paine's assault. Thurlow Weed, in an obituary in the *New York Times,* attributed her death directly to the anxiety resulting from the assassination attempt. Horace Greeley put aside his enmity toward Henry to characterize Frances as one "who had filled for thirty years an exalted position, without once exciting an enmity or alienating a friend."[22] Other tributes poured in, and the funeral in Auburn drew one of the largest assemblages of mourners ever seen outside New York City. Henry, who attempted to put all events into a philosophical context, had no rationale for Frances's passing, even though he had long feared for her health. He sent Fanny a tribute composed by editor George William Curtis, together with a note: "He says just what I feel." Curtis wrote of Frances Seward,

> The tenderest of mothers, the truest and wisest of counselors, the most retiring, faithful and patient of women, her influence will be forever felt in the tranquil wisdom and fidelity of her husband's service to humanity and his country. Her religious faith, her intelligent political confidence, [and] her gentle and pervasive sympathy cheered her long hours of seclusion and illness, and strengthened the heart and hope of those even who seldom saw her.[23]

The relationship between Henry and Frances was unusually complex. No one who reads the letters between the two, exchanged almost daily during their repeated separations and filled with the outwardly inconsequential details of daily life, can question their basic devotion. But Henry, for all his affection, had declined Frances's dearest wish—that he give his family priority over politics. She, in turn, by going into virtual seclusion during the 1850s, may have exacted a measure of revenge. Nonetheless, Frances's ailments—ailments that today would probably be treatable—eroded her will and reinforced her desire for privacy.

For all her domesticity, Frances was not a simpering Victorian invalid. She was vitally interested in the political and social issues of her day, and in the first two decades of her marriage had some influence on her husband's positions and writings. But her distaste for politics denied her even the pleasure that some other wives in her day derived from their spouses' political triumphs.

*   *   *

Paine's period of freedom after his assault on Seward was brief. Booth had provided no escape plan for the ex-soldier, and two days after the carnage of April 14 Paine showed up at the Surratt boardinghouse professing to be a laborer in search of work. Mrs. Surratt denied knowing him, but he was arrested on suspicion. Once he was identified as Seward's assailant, Paine was placed in irons; ten men later divided a $5,000 reward for his capture.

Booth was tracked to the Garrett farm in northern Virginia where he was killed by Federal troops on April 26 after refusing to surrender. Five days later President Johnson ordered that the remaining conspirators be tried by a military commission—a decision that, because civil courts were open and available, was of dubious constitutionality. Gen. William E. Doster, who defended Paine before the nine-man military commission convened at Washington Barracks, attempted an insanity defense, but the death of Frances Seward in the wake of the assault on her family made a successful defense of Paine on any grounds a formidable task. Reporter Noah Brooks observed Paine at the trial, commenting that "he sits bolt upright against the wall, looming up like a young giant above the others." Brooks thought he detected a "gleam of intelligence" in the assassin's eyes when the prosecution introduced the knife with which he had carried out his assault, "a heavy, horn-handled affair with a double edge at the point and a blade about ten inches long."[24]

Paine denied nothing at his trial and appeared indifferent to his fate. One of the judges was heard to remark that "Paine seems to want to be hung, so I guess we might as well hang him."[25] On June 30 he was sentenced to death, along with Atzerodt, Herold, and Mrs. Surratt. Paine was uncommunicative almost to the end but ultimately told Doster that he regretted the injury he had done to Fred Seward.[26] The four convicted conspirators died on the gallows at Washington Barracks on July 7.

Over the years scholars and assassination buffs have occasionally asked the question, "Why Seward?"* That Andrew Johnson was on Booth's list was understandable—he was both vice president and a "renegade" Southerner—but had Seward done more to bring down the Confederacy

---

*For all Seward's prominence, he did not figure in the presidential succession. Under the relevant statute (twice ammended since then), "In the case of death of both the President and Vice President, the President of the Senate pro tempore shall act as President until a President shall be elected." The vice president, of course, was unhurt. In April 1865 the president pro tem of the Senate was a relatively obscure member, Sen. Lafayette S. Foster of Connecticut.

than, say, Stanton or Grant? None of the conspirators brought to trial shed any light on this question. Paine did tell Doster that Booth had not briefed him regarding his plans for Lincoln, Johnson, and Seward until about eight o'clock on the evening of the assassinations.

One school of thought holds that Booth's objective was to produce such chaos in Washington as to permit the Confederacy somehow to fight on. If this had been the case, Seward was a logical target, for he was the best-known member of Lincoln's cabinet. But the bulk of the evidence suggests that Booth was motivated principally by a desire for revenge. In the rambling journal that he penned during his escape, Booth wrote of Lincoln: "Our country owed all her trouble to him." A Union sustained by force "is not what I have loved." He compared himself to Brutus but insisted that he, Booth, was striking down "a greater tyrant" than the Romans ever knew.[27]

If Lincoln was, to Booth, a great tyrant, Seward was presumably a lesser tyrant, but a tyrant still. The secretary may have owed his notoriety in part to "Mr. Seward's little bell," but to a Negrophobe like Booth, it was probably Seward's early antislavery rhetoric that made him a marked man. Another vulnerability was the fact that, as a result of his carriage accident, the secretary of state was easily accessible to anyone Booth sent to do him harm. Everyone in Washington knew that Mr. Seward was confined to his bed in the Old Clubhouse. Considering all that Seward had attempted in order to conciliate the South in 1861, his martyrdom is particularly ironic. In all likelihood, it was only the brave Robinson who kept Seward from sharing Lincoln's fate.*

---

*Robinson was not reticent about capitalizing on his celebrity status. He was discharged with the rank of private in May 1865 and was almost immediately appointed a clerk in the Treasury Department. He resigned in November 1866 after some wealthy New Yorkers bought him a farm and collected a fund of $1,600. He was appointed a clerk in the War Department in 1869, and two years later, in response to a request from the Maine legislature, Congress awarded him $5,000 and a gold medal. He died in 1907. Thomas R. Turner, *Beware the People Weeping* (Baton Rouge: Louisiana University Press, 1982), 196–97.

22

President Johnson

ON APRIL 24 reporter Noah Brooks turned his attention from the Lincoln rites to the Seward family. "All of the wounded in the Seward mansion are slowly recovering—even Fred Seward, who was at first thought to be mortally wounded. . . . The vitality of the elder Seward, who is now quite old, is amazing."[1]

Amazing indeed. Seward had almost no use of his mending right arm. His face was swollen, and a high collar only partially concealed the scars left by Paine's knife. The iron brace that held his broken jaw in place made speech difficult. Assistant Secretary of War Charles A. Dana described the secretary of state as "one of the most horrible spectacles that the human eye ever beheld."[2] Nevertheless, by July, Seward was spending five hours a day at the office, employing a secretary for all his correspondence. When the weather permitted, he resumed his afternoon carriage rides.

Seward found that he stood higher in public esteem now than at any time during the war. A New York City newspaper editorialized that Seward's politics were forgotten—he was one of the heroes of the war and would be judged on his great services to his country. Charles Sumner wrote of his gratification at Seward's recovery. Only Gideon Welles noted Seward's return to cabinet councils without comment. Seward appreciated all that had been done for him. The daughter of a State Department messenger who had been especially helpful during Seward's "late troubles" was enrolled at the Seward Institute with all bills paid by the secretary.[3]

Seward wrote to James Watson Webb in Brazil: "I am a *bruised* reed and the marvel is that I am not broken in pieces."[4] But Johnson asked him to continue as secretary of state, and there is no evidence that Seward seriously contemplated retirement. With Frances gone he needed his work at the State Department more than ever. For the record, Seward anticipated "a speedy and healthful restoration of the country." Privately, however, he was less sure.[5] And if the old prod of ambition was gone, vanity remained. If Lincoln had needed him, Seward thought, Johnson needed him even more.

The new president, whom Seward and Weed had helped place on the ticket with Lincoln, was a relatively unknown quantity. Orphaned at four, Johnson had been apprenticed to a tailor and in due course had set up his own shop in Tennessee. Eventually the hardworking journeyman married a shoemaker's daughter who taught him to read and write. He had worked his way into politics through conscientious study and a flair for populist oratory. Elected to the Tennessee legislature in 1835, Johnson had subsequently served a term in the U.S. House of Representatives and then a four-year term as governor of Tennessee. In 1857 he had been elected to the U.S. Senate, where he was a spokesman for the artisans and small farmers of the eastern part of his state. At Lincoln's request Johnson had left the Senate to serve as the appointed military governor of Tennessee. His courage was unquestioned, for he had defied the secessionists in his home state at a time when few Tennesseans would speak out for the Union. But was he qualified to be president? In the manner of kingmakers before and since, Seward and Weed appear never to have considered that the blunt Johnson might actually succeed to the presidency.

While Seward was still convalescent, the Radicals were urging Johnson to reorganize his cabinet. Sumner aspired to the State Department post, but the favorite of the Radicals appears to have been that inept soldier, Gen. Benjamin Butler. Another aspirant was Montgomery Blair, Lincoln's erstwhile postmaster general. Johnson and his secretary of state were so obviously different in temperament that rumors of a change persisted. On April 24, however, the *New York Times* announced that there would be no cabinet reorganization. As for Seward, the *Times* declared, the president "regards the preservation of the Secretary's life as second to that of no man in the nation, and impatiently awaits the time when he will have the benefit of Mr. Seward's counsel."[6] Johnson determined to keep Seward on seemingly less out of admiration for his capability than from annoyance with his detractors.

In the months following Good Friday, 1865, Johnson needed to prove himself a worthy successor to Lincoln. The demands on Seward were more modest. The most important business in the area of foreign affairs

remained France and Mexico. One of Seward's first actions on returning to his department was to inform France that Lincoln's opposition to
its designs on Mexico "has undergone no change by the change of
administration." This was bad news for Napoleon III, for in 1865 the
United States had the largest and most battle-tested army in the world.
Nor was Seward alone in his resentment of France's actions at a time
when the United States was preoccupied with civil war. General Grant
had keenly resented France's meddling, and in April with little or no
consultation in Washington, he had sent Sheridan's corps to the Rio
Grande as a show of force.

France was having second thoughts about its Mexican venture. During the four years of the American Civil War, Seward had reiterated
Washington's opposition to the imposition of a European monarch on
Mexico; at the same time, he had acknowledged that there was little to
be done until the war was over. Now, the situation in Mexico had the
secretary's full attention. When reports reached Washington that France
was recruiting ex-Confederates to serve in Mexico, Seward demanded
an explanation. When the State Department heard that Mexicans fighting for Juárez were being denied medical treatment as prisoners of war,
Seward sent a protest to Paris.

Napoleon III, who had gambled on a Confederate victory, now found
himself in a very exposed position. Seward was not without allies. And
the Northern press was not so preoccupied with the end of hostilities
that it overlooked developments south of the border. Some journals were
so bellicose that the emperor began to fear war against the combat-tested
U.S. Army on a battlefield six thousand miles from France.

Far from rattling his saber, however, Seward maintained a conciliatory approach that annoyed the hawks on Capitol Hill. He assured Louis
de Geoffroy, Mercier's successor as French minister, that the United
States bore France no ill will. As for sending a U.S. force to Mexico,
any such action "would increase our debt immeasurably without leading
to any clearly defined gain." Only in a case that threatened the country's honor would the United States resort to military action.[7] Whereas
Seward had adopted a menacing tone in his dispatches to London following Britain's recognition of Confederate belligerency, he fairly cooed
in discussing the unfortunate situation in Mexico. Geoffroy, grateful,
could only hope that Seward's health would permit him to remain in
government.

On January 31, 1866, Napoleon III advised his military commander
in Mexico that "circumstances stronger than my will" were obliging
him to withdraw French forces from Mexico, but that there would be a

period of twelve to eighteen months in which Maximilian would be able to consolidate his position. To John Bigelow, who had been made U.S. minister to France following the death of William Dayton, Napoleon III committed himself to a three-stage withdrawal of French troops beginning in November 1866.[8] An end to France's ill-fated Mexican venture was in sight.

In the area of Anglo-American relations some complex issues carried over from Lincoln's administration to that of his successor. Never having acknowledged the propriety of Britain's 1861 recognition of Confederate belligerency, Seward was annoyed at London's slowness in withdrawing belligerent status after Appomattox. More important was London's refusal even to discuss its responsibility for damages inflicted by the *Alabama* and other Confederate vessels purchased in Britain. Fortunately, both sides wanted to improve relations. Britain wished especially to see the issue of Confederate cruisers removed as an irritant in Anglo-American diplomacy. John Russell wrote Seward that although Her Majesty's Government declined to pay reparations, they were "ready to consent to the appointment of a commission" to discuss the matter. The stage was set for the protracted arbitration of the *Alabama* claims.

*   *   *

With the coming of peace came the issues of reconstruction. Economically the erstwhile Confederacy presented a desolate picture. Its farms were in weeds, its railroads destroyed; in parts of cities like Richmond and Columbia only brick chimneys had survived the Union armies. The collapse of the Confederacy had left some areas without effective political authority.

But if the South was subjugated, it was not prepared to admit error. Might had made right, in defiance of the Constitution. In many places hatred of the North was as prevalent as during hostilities. After the war, as before, many Southerners regarded themselves as the injured party. If the North offered conciliatory terms for the reconstitution of the Union, it was no more than the South deserved.

Attitudes in the North were sharply divided, with few precedents to provide guidance. The Lincoln administration had adopted Seward's view that the seceded states had never effectively left the Union; Lincoln's Ten-Percent Plan had been designed to facilitate each state's return to a prewar legal relationship. But the assassination itself had drastically changed attitudes in the North. Grant's generous terms for Lee's defeated army were soon followed by cries for the punishment of assassins and traitors. Johnson himself told a group of legislators "Robbery is a crime; rape is a crime; treason is a crime; . . . Treason must be made odious and traitors punished."[9] But as spring turned into summer, there was less talk of traitors and punishment. Jefferson Davis and some other top Confederates were in jail, but all would eventually be released without being brought to trial. Word of widespread destitution in the South appealed to a sense of magnanimity in the North; had Lincoln himself not regarded the rebels as his countrymen?

If the war had been fought solely for the Union, it was over. But if it had also involved the future of the black man, there remained serious differences in the North and the South. Although everyone in the South knew that slavery was dead, the prospect of universal black suffrage was anathema. In the North, just as there had been a widespread reluctance to turn the war into one for emancipation, so there was limited interest in the black problem as it affected the South.

Seward was one of those who balked at black suffrage. In 1846 he had said that he would give the ballot "to every man, learned or unlearned, bond or free."[10] That was almost two decades earlier, however. In 1865 only six Northern states permitted blacks to vote, and one of these—New York—had a $250 property qualification. In May 1865 Johnson and his cabinet debated black suffrage in the context of North Carolina's return to the Union. Under a plan proposed by Stanton, North Carolinians would elect delegates to a convention that would draw up a revised constitution under which the state would return to the Union.

Stanton proposed that all "loyal citizens," including blacks, vote for delegates to the state convention. When Stanton proposed that the cabinet be polled on the issue, Welles complained that the mechanism for a state's return to the Union had already been provided in the Ten-Percent Plan endorsed by Lincoln in 1863. The president nevertheless put Stanton's proposal to a vote. With Seward absent, recovering from the attack, the cabinet divided evenly. Stanton, Attorney General James Speed, and Postmaster General William Dennison voted in favor of black suffrage. Welles, Secretary of the Interior John P. Usher, and Secretary of the Treasury Hugh McCulloch opposed it. On returning to cabinet sessions after his brush with death, Seward cast his vote against black suffrage.[11]

The country confronted the sensitive issues of reconstruction in a period of political flux. The party structure was fragile compared with that of the early 1850s, when two virile national parties, the Whigs and the Democrats, had vied for power. In 1865 the Democrats were discredited in many portions of the North as having been the party of Jefferson Davis and his fellow secessionists. In control of the administration was a largely Republican "Union" party. The new president entered office with considerable popular goodwill but, given his background as a Southern Democrat, a very narrow political base.

In a situation without precedent, a key question concerned which branch of government had principal responsibility for reconstruction. With Congress in recess until December 1865, Johnson had considerable room for maneuver. But the grace period would mean little unless skillfully used. Some Republicans in Congress were prepared to follow the president's lead, while others saw reconstruction as a congressional perquisite. Some wished to cooperate with Johnson; others sought to distance themselves from any Democrat. Many wished to assist the freedmen; others balked at giving them the ballot.

It was a period when Johnson could have made good use of his politically astute secretary of state. Alas, Seward felt little of the easy rapport with Andrew Johnson that he had enjoyed with Lincoln. The president's health also was a problem. In July and August, when Seward was getting his strength back, Johnson himself was sick. Seward wrote in August that "the novelty of the new President's administration" and Johnson's "frequent and long illnesses" had delayed consideration of many matters and had made for poor communication between his department and the White House.[12] In Lincoln's day, Seward would have found means of making himself indispensable to the White House. But the war was over, Frances was gone, and Seward was less interested in public affairs.

Still, Johnson and Seward viewed the issues of reconstruction in much the same way. Seward doubtless concurred with Johnson's proclamation of May 29, 1865, which offered amnesty and restitution of property, except for slaves, to all former Confederates except for senior officers and officials. Not even his own near-assassination had altered Seward's commitment to a benign reconstruction. Although he approved the trial of Paine and Booth's other accomplices by military tribunal, he backed away from the idea of putting Jefferson Davis on trial. In the summer of 1865 he was instrumental in securing the parole of Davis's erstwhile vice president, Alexander H. Stephens.[13]

Because it was the State Department that processed most of the pardons for former Confederate officers and government functionaries, Seward was soon dealing again with prominent Southerners whom he had not seen since 1861. One day he encountered Robert Hunter, who had been a colleague in the prewar U.S. Senate and with whom Seward had dealt at the Hampton Roads conference. Seward invited him to dinner that evening, and when Hunter sat down to dinner he found under his plate a pardon, duly signed and executed.[14] On another occasion, Seward hosted a party exclusively for Southerners, writing to Fanny in Auburn that when she was next in Washington "you will find our house the chief resort of the recently rebels."[15]

New York had state and local elections in the fall of 1865, and Seward spent much of October in Auburn. Rumors soon circulated that he and Johnson had had a falling-out, and Seward attempted to set some of them to rest with a speech. It was his first attempt at public speaking since the brace had been removed from his jaw, and he spoke with some difficulty. Seward reflected on the war just ended. "We have lost the great and good Abraham Lincoln," he told his neighbors, speaking from the doorway of the house on South Street. Lincoln was now enshrined with Washington, but what of his successor? Seward then extolled Johnson as a "capable, inflexible and devoted patriot" who had surrounded himself with capable advisers. Seward made his own appeal to the South, saying, "Once we were friends. We have since been enemies. We are friends again. But whether in friendship, or in enmity, in peace, or in war, we are, and can be nothing else . . . than brethren."[16]

The speech, though a bit fulsome, was vintage Seward. It was part of his nature to assume the best in others. He had relied heavily on the goodwill of border Unionists in 1865 and had been disappointed. He now relied on the good faith of the South in returning to the Union under terms fair to the ex-slaves. The Radicals in Congress—as willing to blame Seward for Johnson's policies as they had been to hold him responsible for Lincoln's—were quick to attack. Sumner denounced Seward specifically, charging him with responsibility for Johnson's reconstruction policy: "the greatest and most criminal error ever committed by any government."[17]

Nevertheless, Seward sought a middle path through the thickets of reconstruction. Concerned that the Democrats sought to commit the president to recognizing the states of the old Confederacy without conditions, Seward attempted to convince Johnson of the need to cultivate moderate Republicans in Congress. When, in September 1865, the provisional governor of Florida called for the election of delegates to a state convention in order to choose a delegation to Congress, Seward, indicating that he spoke for the president, warned: "It must . . . be distinctly understood that the restoration to which your proclamation refers will be subject to the decision of Congress." But the issue was a sensitive one, both with the president and with some members of his cabinet.

Two weeks later, Seward drafted a letter to another of the provisional governors, informing him that the administration would continue to recognize the provisional governments until Congress decided otherwise. Welles objected to the language, however, and Johnson told Seward to omit any reference to Congress.[18]

Seward probably believed that differences between the president and Congress were susceptible to negotiation. He hoped that approval of the Thirteenth Amendment, abolishing slavery, would take some of the venom out of the Radicals. By December 18 twenty-seven states, including eight of the old Confederacy, had ratified the amendment, and it fell to Seward to announce that the amendment was in effect. But Congress, convening on December 4, had provided a taste of what was to come when it prohibited the clerk from even reading the names of the members-elect from the former Confederate states. A joint committee of both houses, called the Committee of Thirteen, was appointed and given authority to look into the credentials of the Southern legislators. The committee was controlled by the Radicals, and its guiding spirit was the vitriolic Thaddeus Stevens.

During this time Johnson could have taken full advantage of Seward's conciliatory talents, had he been so inclined, but the president confided little in his secretary of state. In any case, Seward's convalescence was not complete, and he was increasingly worried about Fanny's continuing respiratory problems. In January 1866 he took Fanny, Fred, Anna, and Anna's sister on a month's vacation in the Caribbean. Gideon Welles was not fooled by the talk about convalescence, however. Seward, he wrote in his diary, "wishes to be absent until the issues [of reconstruction] are fully made up and the way is clear for him [as to] what course to take. . . . The talk about his health is ridiculous."[19]

* * *

Seward returned to Washington in time to see a further erosion in relations between President Johnson and Congress. On February 19 the president vetoed a bill extending and expanding the Freedmen's Bureau, in part because the states affected were not yet represented in Congress. In effect the president was saying that any legislation passed by Congress in the absence of Southern representation was unconstitutional.

Before vetoing the bill the president had consulted with Seward, Welles, and others. Seward, probably at Johnson's request, prepared a revealing veto message of his own, recommending a veto, but "not without reluctance." He praised the work of the Freedmen's Bureau and acknowledged that the ex-slaves were entitled to protection. But, he asked, was such protection required? The Thirteenth Amendment had ended slavery, and the courts were available to blacks as well as to whites.[20] Little of this conciliatory language made its way into Johnson's tough veto message.

Seward's mail in these days included a number of appeals for sympathy from Southern whites. One man wrote from Alabama:

> Has [sic] all of our people turned against the white and in favor of the black race. Is there not a Statesman in Congress who will raise his voice in favor of the White man. . . .
> The result of [reconstruction legislation] will of corse [sic] drive all the best men out of the Country . . . but the poor whites and negros will be left in this once glorious and beautiful land.[21]

A letter from one of Seward's old pupils at Union Academy, Georgia, insisted that the South would deal with the freedmen in good faith: "Give us the writ of Habeas Corpus, remove the negro soldiers from our Midst & all will be peace and good order & in sixty days. Again I thank you for the generous & liberal policy you have manifested to the poor, ruined South."[22] Not all of Seward's mail was from the South, however, and not all of it was complimentary. A correspondent in up-state New York wrote regarding the Freedmen's Bureau veto: "I believe not more than one quarter of the Union men in the [Binghamton] district approve of the President's veto."[23]

There were enough moderate Republicans in the Thirty-ninth Congress to uphold Johnson's veto of the Freedmen's Bureau bill. But the president, far from attempting to cultivate influential moderates like Lyman Trumbull, William Pitt Fessenden, and John Sherman, did nothing of the kind. In several raucous speeches, which at times recalled his drunkenness on inauguration day, Johnson denounced his opponents by name and made reconciliation virtually impossible.

The next confrontation was over a civil rights bill that passed Congress with near-unanimous Republican support on March 19. Designed to nullify the Dred Scott decision and to counter the recently enacted "Black Codes," by which some Southern states were restricting the rights of ex-slaves, the bill avoided the sensitive area of voting rights and limited itself to guaranteeing blacks the protection of existing laws. Seward favored the bill, but with some reservations; he told the president in cabinet that whereas it might be well to pass a law declaring ex-slaves to be citizens, he regarded the bill as unconstitutional on technical grounds.[24] The cabinet, except for Welles, favored the bill. Johnson, however, remained convinced that no measure directed against the South should be enacted until the states of the former Confederacy were represented in Congress. He vetoed the Civil Rights Bill, only to see it and a revised bill providing for an extension of the Freedmen's Bureau passed over his veto in April. A Republican leader in Ohio reported that "those who formerly defended [the president] are now readiest in his condemnation."[25]

Always a pragmatist, Seward did not share Johnson's belief that reconstruction was the sole responsibility of the president. Indeed, Seward had contributed to Lincoln's last message to Congress a section in which Lincoln acknowledged that with the coming of peace the president's power to deal with the rebellious states would be shared with Congress. Under Lincoln's successor, the situation was ready-made for Seward's conciliatory skills. Although the secretary of state was unpopular with Republican radicals, he retained the respect of Republican moderates, who held the balance of power. In the secession crisis of 1861, Seward had been active on Capitol Hill, opposing precipitous action against the South. But much had changed in four years. Johnson was not Lincoln, and Seward was tired. At a time when Seward's powers of persuasion might have compensated for Johnson's obtuseness, the secretary of state ran afoul of Johnson's rigidly states' rights views.

In May 1866 Seward delivered a speech in Auburn on the subject of reconstruction. He maintained that what the country required was not reconstruction but reconciliation, and that this would come once Congress had admitted loyal, qualified representatives from the seceded states. He attempted to minimize the impasse between the president and Congress. Their disagreements over the Freedmen's Bureau and the Civil Rights Bill were "purely extraneous incidents" of passing importance. Regarding voting rights, Seward was reduced to platitudes, saying: "There is no soundness at all in our political system, if the personal or civil rights of each member of the state, white or black . . . are not more secure under the administration of a state government, than they could be under the administration of the national government."[26]

The speech was poor in both timing and content. Just three weeks earlier, a fight between black and white teamsters in Memphis, Tennessee, had triggered a riot in which city police and poor whites raided the black quarter of the city, killing and burning as they went. Most states of the Old Confederacy were in the process of rejecting the Fourteenth Amendment. Two months after Seward's speech, black marchers in New Orleans would be attacked by hundreds of angry whites, resulting in the deaths of thirty-seven blacks.

During the war Seward had been a frequent visitor to freedmen's camps around Washington. Danforth Nichols, one of the founders of

Howard University, testified that "no public officer did more or showed more interest in the condition of the Freedmen than did the Secretary of State."[27] Similarly, in August 1865, when the provisional governor of South Carolina complained of the stationing of black U.S. Army units around the town of Anderson, Seward replied that the government would permit no discrimination based on color.[28] According to Republican Congressman James G. Blaine, Seward acknowledged to friends his disappointment that the South was responding to Johnson's moderate policies in a spirit of defiance.[29]

But Seward viewed the Black Codes as an issue of secondary importance. He was now concerned more with reconciliation between the white majorities, North and South, than he was with the fate of the blacks, for whom the war had already brought freedom. In April 1866 he gave an interview to Charles Eliot Norton and Edwin Godkin, publishers of the influential magazine *Nation*. The fact that Godkin was a critic of Johnson's policies may account for some of the testiness of Seward's remarks, but the secretary's statements, as set down by Norton, are revealing. According to Seward, there should be no question about readmitting the South to full representation in Congress; it had as much a right to representation as did the North. He then responded to a question about the blacks:

> The North has nothing to do with the negroes. I have no more concern for them than I have for the Hottentots. They are God's poor; they always have been and always will be so everywhere. . . . The laws of political economy will determine their position and the relations of the two races.

As always Seward's main concern was for reunion and harmony between the sections:

> The South longs to come home now, sir. Those who refuse to take them into the family again are in my opinion guilty of a great crime. . . . If I could not forgive the enemies of my country as I forgive my own enemies, I could not have the hope that I might enter kingdom come. There is a want of charity in this refusal to forgive which is worse than the sins against which it is manifested.[30]

*   *   *

Lincoln had called Seward a man "without gall," and this quality was certainly evident in Seward's hands-off view of reconstruction. But he was an interested party in the unanswered question of whether Confederate leaders had been involved in Lincoln's assassination, and he was not completely convinced by the protests of noninvolvement by prominent ex-Confederates. Some people believed that John Surratt, the Confederate courier who was Booth's close associate, had the answer. Surratt, though, was the one member of Booth's band who escaped. He had made his way to Canada and then to England, and from there to the Papal States, where, remarkably, he joined the Papal Zouaves. He was recognized by a fellow soldier, Henry Ste. Marie, who reported his presence to the American minister to the Papal States, Rufus King.

In a cabinet meeting on October 16, 1866, Seward quoted from King's dispatches. According to Ste. Marie, Surratt had "admitted his connection with the assassination of the President" and had implicated Jefferson Davis, Judah P. Benjamin, and others of the Confederate hierarchy in the conspiracy. According to Secretary of the Interior Orville Browning, "Mr. Seward expressed his belief that Booth and Surratt had conferred with Benjamin upon the subject, and that Benjamin had encouraged and subsidized them; but he did not believe that the matter had ever been under discussion before the Richmond Cabinet or received the countenance of other members of the Cabinet than Benjamin."[31] In effect Seward was prepared to exonerate the Confederate leadership except for Benjamin, with whom he had exchanged words on numerous occasions in the prewar U.S. Senate. It was a reasonable hypothesis, in part because Benjamin had been in charge of funding the Confederate operations in Canada with which Surratt, among others, had been involved.

Surratt was arrested by papal authorities and ultimately repatriated to the United States, where he went on trial for murder in June 1867. After a two-month-long trial, he was freed when the judge discharged a hung jury, which was inclined toward acquittal. Surratt subsequently acknowledged his role in the abduction plot but implied that the eleventh-hour decision to attempt the assassination of Lincoln, Seward, and Johnson was Booth's alone. To this date there is no convincing evidence of high-level Confederate involvement in the assassination. Seward's view notwithstanding, it is highly unlikely that Benjamin would have taken the initiative in this sensitive and controversial matter without full consultation with Jefferson Davis.

23

"*He Wanders Around Like a Ghost*"

HAD SEWARD WISHED to play a major role in the early part of reconstruction, the best time would have been on his return from the Caribbean in the spring of 1866. The Radical-controlled Committee of
Thirteen in Congress, led by Pennsylvania's Thaddeus Stevens, had by
then drafted another constitutional amendment—one designed as a test
for any former Confederate state seeking readmission to Congress. The
proposed Fourteenth Amendment declared that all persons born or nat-
uralized in the United States were citizens and that no state could deny
them certain basic rights. The ostensible objective was to protect the
freedmen against the Black Codes; to cultivate public opinion in the
North, the bill barred from office anyone who had taken an oath to
support the U.S. Constitution and subsequently had joined the Confederacy. An unavowed objective was to assert the role of Congress in
reconstruction. The logic of the amendment was suspect, for the Radicals were saying that the Southern states could not qualify as members
of the Union until they had performed a function that only members
could perform—ratify a constitutional amendment.[1]

Moderate Republicans in Congress, including longtime Seward allies
like Henry Raymond and Edwin Morgan, recommended that the administration support the amendment. But Johnson saw it as one more
intrusion on presidential prerogatives and vowed to defeat it. Seward's
attitude was equivocal. In cabinet he agreed with the president that
Congress had exceeded its authority. At the same time, he met with
Stevens and attempted to negotiate a compromise. Seward left un-
touched the heart of the Fourteenth Amendment—the first and second
sections of which guaranteed the rights of citizenship and due process—

but persuaded Stevens to soften some of the bill's punitive features. Ultimately the modified amendment was approved by the necessary two-thirds of both houses, and Seward, in one of his statutory functions as secretary of state, forwarded the bill to the states for ratification. Johnson refused to accept the validity of the congressional action, and appeared annoyed at Seward's prompt action in transmitting the bill for ratification.[2]

The president had been looking forward to the readmission of his own state, Tennessee, but rather than accept the terms of the Fourteenth Amendment he sought unsuccessfully to prevent its ratification by the Tennessee legislature. Seward's attitude was very different. When the Tennessee congressional delegation arrived in Washington, Seward took them to dinner as a group, writing Fanny: "I had a calf served up in many ways, and they accepted it as 'returned prodigals.' "[3]

Johnson saw himself as a Jacksonian Democrat but felt some lingering loyalty to the wartime political coalition that had put him in the White House. By the spring of 1866 this residual loyalty was on the wane, and Johnson was exploring the possibility of a political realignment. Seward, too, was intrigued by the possibility of a new party; he ruminated in one letter that "some of our Union friends [are] preparing a bridge upon which they may expect to see the southern states and their old Democratic allies come together once more into political ascendency."[4]

Weed was wholeheartedly behind the new party movement, which, if successful, would assure his political preeminence in New York State for as long as Johnson held office. Seward, however, had reservations about a new conservative grouping in which Southern Democrats must inevitably play a prominent role. Moreover, just as he had been slow to desert the old Whig party, he now was reluctant to turn his back on the Republicans. The initiative, however, lay with the president. On June 11, Johnson met with a committee of conservative Democrats led by Sen. James R. Doolittle of Wisconsin, and approved a recommendation that a convention be convened with a view to the formation of a new proadministration party. The call for a National Union Convention, issued on June 25, invited participation by all who "sustain the Administration in maintaining unbroken the Union of the States under the Constitution." The language hinted at strong Democratic participation, leading Henry Raymond to complain to Seward that the meeting was likely to be controlled by ex-rebels and their Copperhead associates.

Although some political observers saw the hands of Seward and Weed behind the move for a new party, in fact matters were beyond their control. Seward attempted for a time to assure that there be no condemnation of the Fourteenth Amendment at the convention, but he could obtain no assurances from the managers. Seward cooled toward the entire operation. He told Raymond that with regard to the Philadelphia convention, he and his friends "could go into it if it was a success and go out of it if it should prove a failure."[5] In the end, Seward spent the week of the convention in Auburn, ostensibly supervising additions to his house.

The National Union Convention, which met on August 14 in a hall bedecked with patriotic bunting, opened to the sight of delegates from Massachusetts and South Carolina marching into the hall, arm in arm. The appearance of two prominent peace Democrats from the war years, Clement Vallandigham and Fernando Wood, put an immediate damper on the gathering. Radical Republicans derided the "Arm-in-Arm Convention," comparing it to Noah's Ark, where the animals entered "two and two, of clean beasts, and of beasts that are not clean."[6] Fallout from the bloody race riots in New Orleans further tainted the conservative agenda. The convention adopted resolutions endorsing Johnson's programs and then adjourned.

The immediate effect of the new party movement was to split Johnson's cabinet; Secretary of the Interior Harlan, Attorney General Speed, and Postmaster General Dennison resigned in protest. But the convention also served to tie Johnson to the Democrats and to confirm that the party of Lincoln was now irreparably split. There were serious implications for Seward. The inability of political moderates to forge a new conservative party left him without a political base. He was serving in the cabinet of a president who was estranged from the party that had nurtured him.

*   *   *

With the collapse of the wartime political coalition, the 1866 congressional elections loomed larger than ever. Johnson determined to take his case to the people with a speaking tour that was unprecedented for an incumbent president. The ostensible purpose for the trip was the dedication of a monument to Stephen A. Douglas in Chicago. Traveling with the president was a veritable who's who of official Washington. General Grant and Admiral Farragut headed the military contingent, which included eight generals in all. Seward and Welles provided cabinet representation. Many wives chose to come along, as did a large contingent of newspaper reporters. Several of the president's friends had misgivings about his "swing around the circle." Knowing Johnson's penchant for stump oratory, cabinet secretaries Orville Browning and Hugh Mc-Culloch warned Johnson to beware of extemporaneous speeches. He brushed these warnings aside, and Seward professed confidence that all would go well.

The presidential party left Washington on August 28. At first it met a warm reception; in New York City and in the cities of upstate New York, crowds were large and responsive. From the outset, however, Johnson's message was confrontational: the wickedness of the Radicals, their hostility to popular government, their flouting of the Constitution. In time hecklers appeared, and their insults invariably brought some response from the president. Johnson's defense of his reconstruction policy soon degenerated into exchanges of insults with provocateurs in the audience. The Radical press, which had initially sought to ignore the presidential junket, soon realized that the president was playing into their hands, while Seward's normally keen political instincts appear to have been on hold during this sensitive period. He found little to criticize in the president's conduct and did nothing to support Welles, who thought that Johnson should vary his standard speech, which was being parodied in the Radical press.[7] When Seward remarked that Andy Johnson was the best stump speaker in the country, Welles replied tartly that the president of the United States should not be a stump speaker at all.[8]

Misfortunes began to dog the presidential party. At Auburn, where they spent one night, Grant's carriage ran over a boy, injuring him so severely that his leg had to be amputated. At Niles, Ohio, the speakers' platform collapsed, spilling Seward, Grant, and Farragut to the ground. Press reports of drunkenness implicated both Johnson and Seward, but the real culprit appears to have been Grant, who overindulged in Cleveland, embarrassed himself in conversation with Mrs. Farragut, and then left the tour.[9] In Chicago, on September 6, the president spoke briefly at the dedication of the Douglas monument, but anti-Johnson placards were much in evidence and both the governor and the lieutenant governor of Illinois boycotted the ceremony. Reporters watched the thin, careworn secretary of state for any clue as to his thoughts. Seward smoked his cigars, saying little; his occasional, rather banal public remarks were supportive of the president.

Shortly after leaving Louisville on the return journey to Washington, Seward fell ill, apparently with cholera. Dr. Norris was summoned from Washington and, at Cincinnati, Seward was placed in a separate car and sent home ahead of the presidential party. When Johnson and his entourage reached Harrisburg, they were told that Seward was there, unable to travel and unlikely to live through the night. His family had been informed; Gus was on his way from Washington, and Will and Fanny from Auburn. The president and the secretary of the navy made their way to Seward's car, where they found him "low and weak." According to Welles, Seward took Johnson's hand and whispered: "My mind is clear, and I wish to say at this time that your course is right." Seward had sustained the president, "and if my life is spared I shall continue to do so."[10]

Fanny, herself in the final stage of tuberculosis, reached Harrisburg on September 15. She thought her father "desperately ill," his voice gone and his skin cold. Dr. Norris arranged a couch so that Fanny could be with her father without fatiguing herself unnecessarily. The train made its way slowly back to Washington, where Stanton had an army ambulance at the depot. Back in the Old Clubhouse, Seward began to recover. By September 23, only a week after Dr. Norris had despaired of his life, the secretary was coming downstairs for meals.[11]

Fanny Seward, not yet twenty-two, did not have her father's resilience. She had never been strong, and by the fall of 1866 her health had been declining for more than a year. She suffered periodically from chest pains and paroxysms of coughing. In the fashion of the day the family had moved her from Washington, first to Auburn and then to the Jersey shore, in the hope that she might benefit from a change in climate. Various physicians had attributed her symptoms to "over-exertion" or similar problems; not until August 1866 had she finally been diagnosed as suffering from tuberculosis. In September she had rushed to Harrisburg to tend to her father. A month later she was dead.

Seward, so optimistic about most things, had long feared for Fanny. Yet he was unprepared for the blow when it came. Fanny had to a considerable extent filled the void her mother had left, and Seward had taken to writing to her the long, detailed letters that he had once written to Frances. When an old friend, George Patterson, wrote his condolences, Seward apologized for not having included him in the services for Fanny:

> It would have gratified me to meet you at Auburn. But my child that I have lost was so retiring and unaffected in her life that I thought I must consonant with her character to make her obsequies as unpretentious as possible. I shall not doubt that you would have been with me if . . . human sympathy could assuage a sorrow that only God himself can heal.[12]

As if Seward were not already sorely oppressed, the autumn of 1866 saw his political fortunes at a nadir. Strong Radical gains in the November elections confirmed Johnson's "swing around the circle" as an unrelieved disaster. Once again, much of the onus for Johnson's policies rubbed off on his secretary of state. "I mourn over Andy," wrote Maine's Fessenden. "He began by meaning well, but I fear that Seward's evil counsels have carried him beyond the reach of salvation."[13] Thad Stevens held a similar view. Johnson had once spoken like a statesman, "but Seward entered into him, and ever since they have both been running down steep places into the sea."[14] The influential *Nation* wrote of Seward, "Distrusted by his old friends, he will never be taken to the bosom of his old enemies. . . . He wanders around like a ghost—a leader without a party."[15]

In Washington, the shadow of Ulysses S. Grant loomed large over Johnson's embattled administration. So popular was the Silent Soldier that all political factions—Democrats, moderate Republicans, Radical Republicans—seemed prepared to tender him the presidential nomination in 1868. Neither Johnson nor Seward had any confidence in Grant's loyalty to the administration, and in regard to the Mexican problem Grant was known to favor dispensing with Seward's diplomacy and sending Sheridan's army to take care of Maximilian. Between them Johnson and Seward came up with a plan under which Grant would accompany a new U.S. envoy, Lewis Campbell, on a mission to the migratory republican government of Mexico, somewhere in the hills north of Mexico City. Grant recognized the scheme as one designed to get him away from Washington, however, and declined the assignment.[16]

Altogether it was a traumatic year. In Washington, Fred Seward and George Baker supervised a move of the State Department from its location by the White House to a converted orphan asylum uptown on Fourteenth Street. Secretary Seward now had a carriage ride to his office, but the department as a whole gained considerable space as a result of the move. Department employees presented Seward with a cane carved from the bannister of the stairway leading to the secretary's office in the old building.

Henry Adams, home from London, found Seward showing the effects of war and violence, yet very much at peace with himself:

> Although his manner was as roughly kind as ever, and his talk as free, he appeared to have closed his account with the public; he no longer seemed to care; he asked for nothing, gave nothing, and invited no support; he talked little of himself or of others, and waited only for his discharge.[17]

John Hay, back from Paris, had a long conversation with his old mentor, which he described in his diary:

[Seward] never seemed to me to better advantage. His utter calmness and cheerfulness, whether natural or assumed, is most admirable. He seems not only free from any political wish or aspiration, but says distinctly that he cares nothing for the judgment of history, so [long as] he does his work well here.

He speaks utterly without bitterness of the opposition to him and the President. He thinks the issue before the country was not fairly put, but seems rather to admire the cleverness with which the Radical leaders misstated the question to carry the elections.[18]

Seward may not have been bitter, but neither was he the reform-minded statesman he had been in the decade before the war. Early in 1867 the cabinet met to consider the sensitive issue of black voting in the nation's capital. Congress had passed a bill that disenfranchised certain former rebels, while giving the vote to black citizens in Washington, D.C. Seward had earlier favored suffrage for blacks in New York State, where their numbers were negligible; now the question concerned a jurisdiction in which the black vote could be large or even preponderant. In Welles's account, Seward ruminated that in time universal suffrage would come to the entire world, but for the moment the thought that black men might control the nation's capital made him uneasy. A majority of the cabinet supported Johnson in his veto of the legislation, a veto that Congress promptly overrode.[19]

*   *   *

In the early hours of June 1, 1866, more than twelve hundred armed soldiers marched down the banks of the Niagara River near Buffalo, where they climbed aboard a motley collection of canal boats and barges. They were soldiers of the Fenian Brotherhood, one of the most powerful organizations in the country—an army of Irish militants determined to harass the British Empire wherever they could in the name of Irish independence. Now they were about to "invade" Canada. In a proclamation the Fenian "secretary of war" assured Canadians that they came as liberators.[20]

If an invasion of Canada by twelve hundred men seems ridiculous today, it was taken very seriously by Canadian authorities, who had the daunting task of defending a 4,000-mile frontier. The attitude of the U.S. government was for some time in doubt. In Washington, President Johnson, who needed all the friends he could muster, had no desire to offend Irish Americans. Seward, for his part, had encouraged Irish immigration to the United States during the Civil War, and the Fenians considered him a friend. Elsewhere, many Americans recalled the release by Canadian authorities of the Confederates who had launched raids into New England in 1864.

No one in Washington was eager to take the lead in action that would appear to favor Britain in an issue related to Irish independence, but Seward told the new British minister, Frederick Bruce, that he was as eager for peace along the Canadian border as the British were. In cabinet he argued successfully that a few hundred Irish militants did not qualify as belligerents in the legal sense. So when the Fenians trickled back across the border after clashing with Canadian militia they were promptly arrested. Others were captured in Canada. Seward, to Bruce, now urged clemency for the Fenian captives. Appreciative of Seward's role, Bruce sent a formal recommendation for clemency. Ultimately there would be no new Irish martyrs, but many Irish Americans felt let down by the president and his secretary of state.

* * *

The ill-conceived French occupation of Mexico worked toward its tragic end. Napoleon III, after agreeing to a three-stage withdrawal from Mexico, had second thoughts late in 1866, advising the U.S. minister, Bigelow, that he had decided to postpone the first withdrawal until the spring of 1867. Seward, his hand greatly strengthened by the presence of Gen. Philip Sheridan and thirty thousand troops on the U.S. side of the Rio Grande, flatly rejected any delay. Shortly thereafter the administration appointed Gen. John A. Logan, one of Sherman's corps commanders in the war and a bitter critic of France, as U.S. minister to Mexico. The appointment of "Black Jack" Logan was as clear a message concerning U.S. intentions as might have been sent. When it appeared that Austria was contemplating sending "volunteers" to Mexico, Seward told Motley to warn Austria that the United States would regard any such action as tantamount to a declaration of war against Mexico. If Vienna were to send a force anyway, Motley was instructed to leave Vienna.[21]

Napoleon III tried again, suggesting the formation of a Mexican provisional government that would exclude both Maximilian and his rival Juárez. But the United States had recognized the Juárez regime; Sheridan was providing the republicans with arms, and by the end of 1866 they had regained most of northeastern Mexico. Sheridan was also intercepting communications between Paris and Mexico City, and in January 1867 his headquarters deciphered a message in which Napoleon III instructed his commander not to compel Maximilian to abdicate but to begin the French withdrawal.[22] A month later the last French troops were on their way home.

Once Napoleon III returned to his earlier withdrawal schedule, relations between the United States and France improved. Whereas the British, in 1861, had regarded Seward as a loose cannon on the deck of Anglo-American relations, the French, in 1866, viewed him as a force for moderation and good sense. The French minister, Montholon, who had replaced Mercier in 1864, advised his government in April 1866 that Seward was so superior as a statesman, and so capable of seeing foreign affairs problems in their proper perspective, that there was no real danger of war with the United States.[23]

Maximilian, who should have left with the French army, chose instead to move his court from Mexico City north to Queretaro. Supported by a few Mexican irregulars he held out for several weeks, but his cause was hopeless. In April 1867 Seward telegraphed the U.S. minister to Mexico that, because Maximilian's capture appeared imminent, "You will communicate to President Juarez . . . the desires of this Government, that in case of [Maximilian's] capture, the Prince and his supporters may receive the humane treatment accorded by civilized nations to prisoners of war."[24] Seward could have saved his energy. The republican army captured Queretaro on May 14, and although the United States, along with France, Austria, and other European nations, interceded on Maximilian's behalf, the ill-fated "emperor" was tried and executed on June 19, 1867.

Throughout the four years of France's Mexican venture, Seward played a deft hand. He had emphasized from the outset that his government regarded France's actions as unacceptable. The fact that the United States was in no position to confront France during the Civil War gave Napoleon III several years in which to reassess his Mexican venture, but he refused to use this time to advantage. By the time he recognized his peril, the Civil War was over and the United States was actively supporting Juárez. The resulting debacle, played out far from France, proved costly to French prestige and fatal to the emperor's Austrian puppet.

Although praise did not often come Seward's way these days, his conduct of the Mexican affair generally received high marks. Napoleon III's foreign minister told visiting U.S. diplomat Henry Sanford that Seward would have a brilliant page in history. Charles XV of Sweden said that the result in Mexico showed Seward to be "the most wise and sagacious statesman of modern times." From Washington, the Russian minister, Stoeckl, informed his superiors that the United States was dependent on the talent, energy, and patriotism of its secretary of state. The liberal *London Daily News* praised Seward's patient diplomacy.[25] Among the few who had nothing positive to say was the irascible Gideon Welles. To him, Seward's part in the Maximilian affair was "shambling statesmanship."[26]

Notwithstanding this belated regard for Seward, the French at one time were eager to be rid of him. To this end, they appear to have hatched a plot employing his nephew, thirty-six-year-old Clarence, as bait. Clarence Seward had left his law practice in April 1865 to help out at the State Department while Fred recovered from the effects of Paine's attack. It was at this time that Clarence attracted the attention of Maximilian's French supporters and found himself up to his neck in intrigue.

Clarence was already somewhat compromised, having agreed, in his private legal capacity, to act as counsel for a French venture in Mexico, the Mexican Express Company. In September 1865, after Clarence had returned to New York City from Washington, "two gentlemen" invited him to take charge of a $100,000 fund to assure favorable press coverage of the Maximilian venture in Mexico. Clarence was to take the money and spend it as he saw fit; no accounting would be required.[27]

Clarence was noncommittal, but he mentioned the approach to Thurlow Weed. Weed in turn warned Seward that his nephew might have accepted money from Maximilian's agents—although in fact no money had yet changed hands. Secretary Seward instructed the U.S. attorney for southern New York to "diligently watch" the Mexican Express Company for evidence of illegal activity. He spoke to one of Clarence's law partners of being "ruined" by the incident, but he subsequently learned that Clarence had accepted no money and that the press had no inkling of Clarence's Mexican Express connection. Ultimately the story died away without ever becoming public knowledge.[28]

*   *   *

Seward had little time to rejoice over developments in Mexico. As the lines hardened between President Johnson and the Radicals in Congress, the Radicals sought means to prevent the president from removing officeholders critical of his reconstruction policies. One result was the Tenure of Office Act, which eventually would serve as the basis for Johnson's impeachment. This measure, passed by both houses in February 1867, provided that persons holding offices to which they were confirmed by the Senate could not be removed without the approval of the Senate. Moderate Republicans opposed the measure, but most Democrats—seeking to split the administration party—voted with the

Radicals. Johnson polled his cabinet, and his ministers were unanimous that the measure was unconstitutional. Even Edwin Stanton agreed, although Stanton was by then sufficiently close to the Radicals to embarrass Johnson and become a logical candidate for removal. Stanton rarely spoke in cabinet. Asked for his opinion, he generally said that the president should do as he pleased. But he made no attempt to conceal his disagreement with the president's policies and dutifully reported on cabinet proceedings to the president's enemies.

Johnson, seeking to pressure his secretary of war, asked Stanton to draft a veto message for the Tenure of Office Act. Stanton declined, citing work stress and his health, whereupon Johnson turned to his secretary of state. Seward agreed to provide a draft if Stanton would assist him. The end result was another presidential veto message, one that argued strongly that Congress had no legal basis for restricting a president's right to remove presidential appointees. James G. Blaine believed that Seward's hand "was evident in every paragraph."[29] Whatever the merits of his message, Johnson's veto was overturned.

Six months later Stanton would invoke the protection of the Tenure of Office Act in order to provoke a crisis that would bring about Johnson's impeachment. As for Seward, he continued to have an equivocal relationship with the colleague for whom he had found a portfolio in Lincoln's cabinet and with whom he had served so long. Although they differed politically, they maintained a degree of mutual rapport and exchanged small favors. When the secretary of war took a rare holiday in 1865, Seward maintained a watching brief for him in the cabinet, assuring him by telegraph that nothing was transpiring that required his early return. A year later it was Stanton who met Seward at the Washington railroad depot when Seward returned, sick and exhausted, from Johnson's "swing around the circle."

Although Seward's loyalty to Johnson was proving politically costly, at least the president was grateful. In June 1867 the president asked Seward to accompany him to the dedication of a monument to Johnson's father in Raleigh, North Carolina. Three weeks later Seward again accompanied Johnson on a trip, this time to Massachusetts. Seward's visit to the Adams home, and his evocation of John Quincy Adams in a speech there, fueled rumors that the New Yorker still aspired to the presidency—a reminder of how easily the rumor mills could be made to grind by an old pro like the secretary of state.[30]

In fact Seward appears to have been devoid of any personal ambition. Hay thought that one of his objectives was to "save" Lincoln appointees whose positions were at risk under Johnson—a reminder that Seward was, truly, a man without a party. He persistently sought to ease the contention between the president and Congress. When Johnson asked Seward to draft his second annual message to Congress, Seward painted a rosy picture of a restored Union. He found the country's foreign relations to be sound. The process of ratifying the Fourteenth Amendment was well under way. In a section of the speech explicitly designed to calm passions on Capitol Hill, Seward acknowledged a point long claimed by congressional Radicals: that Congress alone possessed the right to judge the credentials of its members.

Predictably, the president used Seward's section on foreign affairs but threw out the more conciliatory sections of his draft. There was no mention of the Fourteenth Amendment, and Johnson substituted a section haranguing Congress for its failure to admit representatives from the reconstructed states.[31]

As time went on, Seward wearied of his thankless role as middleman between a stubborn president and a hostile Congress. When he attempted to maintain the minimum necessary contacts with Johnson's opponents, he encountered only boorish behavior. Thaddeus Stevens, when Seward's name arose in conversation, complained, "What a bungler was Paine!"[32] Sumner announced that Seward had done "nothing but blunder" since 1860.[33] And, of course, there was Gideon Welles, who, though not opposed to the president, was incapable of recognizing that Seward's lobbying efforts were on the president's behalf. Welles complained in his diary that "Seward, relying on expedients, is dancing around Stevens, Sumner, [George] Boutwell, [Nathaniel] Banks and others. Runs to the Capitol and seats himself by Stevens in the House and by Sumner in the Senate. This makes comment in the galleries, and paragraphs in the newspapers."[34]

Seward was not engaged in a popularity contest: His own position required him to be on speaking terms with the power brokers in Congress. He still tried to maintain civil relations with Sumner and even with Stevens. Two of his closer senatorial allies were Edwin Morgan of New York and James Doolittle of Wisconsin. Seward's influence was waning, but it nevertheless remained a factor to be reckoned with. And he would need all the backing he could muster in pulling off one of the greatest territorial acquisitions in American history.

24

The Empire Builder

THE CIVIL WAR, with its repercussions in virtually every sector of American life, tended to obscure a national preoccupation that antedated the war and would continue after Appomattox: territorial expansion. Most Americans had come to accept the doctrine of manifest destiny—that the United States was destined to span the continent and dominate the Western Hemisphere. Many Americans, Seward included, considered the British presence in Canada an anachronism and believed that their northern neighbor would eventually become part of the United States. The American Indians were hardly considered at all. Neither war nor reconstruction had dulled Seward's keen interest in territorial expansion, so long as it could be accomplished by peaceful means. The Civil War, in fact, had whetted it. Fred Seward commented that during the war his father "had found the Government laboring under great disadvantage for the lack of advanced naval outposts in the West Indies and in the North Pacific."[1]

Seward's first target for acquisition was the Danish-owned Virgin Islands, which he believed would be useful as a naval base and a coaling station. Even before the war ended he made some preliminary inquiries of the Danish minister to Washington and learned that Denmark was in fact willing to sell these distant possessions. A visit to the islands in January 1866 confirmed Seward's belief that they would be a valuable outpost.

Returning to Washington, Seward convinced Johnson that purchase of the Virgin Islands was in the national interest. Although most of Johnson's cabinet officers were apathetic, Seward was eventually authorized to offer $5 million for the three islands. A long period of haggling over price followed; Denmark was asking $15 million but the United States was not prepared to pay more than $10 million. When Seward obtained approval for a formal offer of $7.5 million, Denmark insisted that for this amount it would sell only the islands of St. Thomas and St. John, not St. Croix. Seward, who feared that Denmark might sell the islands to one of the European powers, was prepared to proceed on this basis, but the Danes then brought up the subject of a plebiscite and the result was more delay.

Seward liked to operate in secret. He remarked to John Hay that when confidential negotiations become public, "obstacles spring up in an hour."[2] Indeed, by the summer of 1867, word of Seward's dealings with Denmark had leaked to the press, and much of the reaction was negative. Greeley's *Tribune* excoriated Seward's mania for "outlandish possessions." Even the *New York Times* was cool to the proposed purchase. Charles Francis Adams confided to his diary that he had "lost all confidence in the wisdom or judgment of Mr. Seward."[3] Meanwhile, the plebiscite on the islands went in favor of annexation.

Seward's cause was not helped when a tidal wave caught a U.S. gunboat, the *Monongahela,* off St. Thomas and deposited it in the town square. Mark Twain wrote a humorous story suggesting that hurricanes and earthquakes had reduced the value of West Indian real estate.[4] Seward submitted a treaty for the acquisition of the islands in December 1867, but the Senate declined to act. When the United States did ultimately purchase the three islands in 1917, the price was $25 million.

* * *

Even as his negotiations with Denmark continued, Seward was after bigger game: "Russian America," now known as Alaska. As early as 1846 he had predicted that America must expand "to the icy barriers of the North." While campaigning for Lincoln in 1860 he had predicted that the outpost settlements of Russian America would eventually become part of the United States. He saw the acquisition of the territory both as an end in itself and as a means of expediting a political union between the United States and Canada. He probably wanted also to forestall the sale of the territory to any other power, much as he had with the Virgin Islands. In the final months of the Civil War, when the Confederate raider *Shenandoah* was burning American whalers in the Bering Sea, Seward had had occasion to reflect that a U.S. naval presence in Russian America could have ended the *Shenandoah*'s rampage.

* * *

It was the fur trade that had brought the Russians to North America late in the eighteenth century; fur traders had leapfrogged eastward across the Aleutian Islands in search of seal, otter, and fox. These early traders led a precarious existence, for supply lines were long and the availability of provisions uncertain. In time the fur business became a monopoly of the Russian-American Company, but its ruthless exploitation of the animals took a toll, and by the middle of the nineteenth century the industry was in decline.

Meanwhile, in St. Petersburg, the czarist government was reconsidering its commitment to Russian America. The territory encompassed some 591,000 square miles, more than twice the size of Texas. Yet the czar's armies had been unable to defend even European Russia against Britain in the Crimean War. Considering its visible weaknesses at home, Russia was reluctant to invest more manpower and treasure in Russian America, particularly since the fur trade had become a losing proposition.

Russia first broached the subject of a possible sale of Russian America at the close of the Crimean War in 1856. Washington was preoccupied with internal problems at that time, and nothing came of the initiative. After the war, however, the atmosphere changed. The movement for confederation in Canada, formalized in 1867, underscored the permanence of the British presence in North America. What if the Union Jack, and not the Stars and Stripes, were to fly over Russian America? The United States might not be the dominant power in its own hemisphere. Alas, geopolitical wisdom was in short supply in postbellum Washington. The only lobby for the acquisition of Russian America consisted of fishermen in Washington Territory who wanted access to Alaskan harbors.

The dean of the diplomatic corps in Washington was fifty-eight-year-old Edouard de Stoeckl, with whom Seward had dealt throughout the Civil War. The Russian was truly a product of two worlds. He considered himself an aristocrat and liked to be addressed as "Baron." But he had married an American ("Protestant [and] without property," he reported to Czar Alexander II, but "stately as a queen") in 1856 and had come to enjoy life in Washington. More important, he had come to view Russian America as a liability to his own country. Returning to St. Petersburg on a visit in the autumn of 1866, he told the foreign minister, Prince Gorchakov, that Russian America was a "breeder of trouble" with the United States, and that the sooner it was disposed of the better. Gorchakov agreed, and Stoeckl was authorized to initiate negotiations for its sale. His instructions were to protect Russian commercial interests to the extent possible, but his principal instruction was not to accept a price less than $5 million.[5]

Stoeckl returned to Washington in March 1867. He called on Seward, ostensibly to discuss the trading rights sought by American fishermen. When Stoeckl indicated that the czar would not grant them, Seward asked whether he might consider selling his North American possessions outright. Stoeckl was encouraging but noncommittal.

Seward obtained authority from President Johnson to proceed with negotiations and soon the only question was one of price. Seward offered $5 million, but Stoeckl initially held out for double that amount. Seward raised his offer to $7 million, and, after an exchange of cables with St. Petersburg, the Russian confirmed that his government was prepared to compromise. A final sticking point concerned possible claims by the Russian-American Company. Seward agreed to add $200,000 to the price in order to liquidate any claims by the Russian trading company. Thus the price tentatively agreed on was $7.2 million—about 2¢ per acre.

On the evening of March 29, a Friday, Seward was at home playing whist when the doorman announced the Russian minister. Stoeckl, ushered into the parlor, had good news: The terms for the sale had been approved in St. Petersburg and he was prepared to sign the treaty the following day. Fred Seward described what followed:

> Seward, with a smile of satisfaction at the news, pushed away the whist table, saying:
> "Why wait till tomorrow, Mr. Stoeckl? Let us make the treaty to-night."
> "But your department is closed. You have no clerks, and my secretaries are scattered about the town."
> "Never mind that," responded Seward, "if you can muster your legation together before midnight, you will find me awaiting you at the department, which will be open and ready for business."[6]

The secretary was as good as his word: Throughout the small hours of March 30, lights flickered in the offices of the new State Department on Fourteenth Street. By 4:00 A.M., the documents were signed, sealed, and ready for transmission to St. Petersburg and to the U.S. Senate.

The negotiations had been carried out in the secrecy that Seward loved, probably because he feared that Britain might enter the bidding. In playing a lone hand, however, Seward ran a risk that the Senate might balk at being handed a monumental land transaction by an ad-

ministration that had few supporters on Capitol Hill. The secretary be-
latedly attempted to cover his tracks by inviting Sumner, chairman of
the Senate Foreign Relations Committee, to the signing. But Sumner
went to Seward's residence instead of the State Department and missed
the ceremony. In any case, he was suspicious of Seward's motives and
noncommittal as to whether he would support ratification.

Although the senator from Massachusetts was in the process of killing
Seward's treaty for the Virgin Islands, he recognized that Russian
America was a different matter. He disliked having the treaty sprung
on him, yet he was enough of an expansionist himself to share the secretary's vision. Seward rushed to the Capitol on the day of the signing
to urge immediate approval. Sumner, however, insisted that the treaty
be referred to his committee. He probably intended this move as a slap
at Seward, but Stoeckl later expressed his belief that if the treaty had
been voted on immediately it would have been rejected.[7]

The press, meanwhile, had a field day, ridiculing the acquisition of
"Seward's Folly" or "Walrussia." The *New York Herald* published a
mock advertisement:

CASH! CASH! CASH!—Cash paid for cast-off territory. Best price given
for old colonies, North or South. Any impoverished monarchs retiring
from the colonization business may find a good purchaser by addressing
W.H.S., Post Office, Washington, D.C.[8]

Harper's Weekly noted that the territory's climate was bracing, that the
fields were white with the harvest, the ice crop was most promising, and
that cattle sat cross-legged on the ice, giving ice cream instead of milk.
Much of the heckling was good humored—the *Herald* ultimately supported the purchase—but Greeley, in the *New York Tribune,* was furious:

Mr. Seward is engineering, with all his personal influence and the influence of his department, to win the vote of the Senate and to create a
public opinion that shall justify ratification. . . . Mr. Seward's dinner
table is spread regularly with roast treaty, boiled treaty, treaty in bottles,
treaty in decanters, treaty garnished with appointments to office . . .
treaty clad in furs, ornamented with walrus teeth, fringed with timber
and flopping with fish.[9]

On April 8 the Foreign Relations Committee voted in favor of the
purchase, and Sumner delivered a long speech to the full Senate recommending approval. The senator believed that the new territory should

have a name that was suitably indigenous and aboriginal; he suggested *Alaska,* an Aleut word for *mainland.* On April 9 the full Senate approved the treaty by a vote of 37 to 2.[10] Despite the lopsided final vote it had been a near thing, and success was owing as much to Sumner as to Seward's persistent lobbying.

The Senate vote should have brought the affair to a successful conclusion. It did not. Following the 1866 congressional elections, the House was even more anti-Johnson than the Senate, and it was the House that had to vote the funds for Alaska. Rumors persisted that the purchase was somehow a payoff for Russia's support during the Civil War, leading Ben Butler of Massachusetts to remark that if the United States desired to purchase Russia's friendship he would prefer to pay the $7.2 million and let the czar keep Alaska.[11]

While Congress argued, the Johnson administration took possession of its new territory. The formal transfer of sovereignty took place at Sitka on October 18, 1867. A company of U.S. Army troops and a Russian garrison stood at attention while the double eagle of czarist Russia was lowered and the Stars and Stripes raised. Batteries from both military units fired a salute, and Alaska joined the United States.

The matter of payment, however, remained. Seward assured Stoeckl that the money would be voted as soon as Congress convened in December, but he may have had doubts. The treaty with Denmark on the Virgin Islands was about to be defeated in the Senate. There were rumors that Grant—widely expected to be the next president—thought the Alaska purchase extravagant. On November 25, 1867, immediately after the House Judiciary Committee had voted to impeach President Johnson, the House, by a vote of 93 to 43, passed a resolution that it would vote no more money to fulfill Seward's expansionist dreams.[12]

In March 1868 the House decided to postpone consideration of the Alaska appropriation for two months. This action assured that no payment to Russia would be made before May and violated a stipulation in the treaty that payment would follow within ten months of ratification. Seward swung into action, demonstrating that he had not entirely lost his powers of persuasion. He won over Johnson's bitter enemy, Thad Stevens (whose conversion helped differentiate the Alaska purchase from the ongoing movement, led by Stevens, for the president's impeachment). A more likely ally was Nathaniel Banks, chairman of the House Committee on Foreign Relations, and Seward sent Banks a stream of documents attesting to the value of Alaska's resources. On July 14, 1868, the House finally appropriated the necessary funds by a vote of 113 to 43, with 44 members abstaining. The gold was loaded aboard a train bound for New York City; as a precaution against dynamite on the tracks, an engine and a flatcar preceded the train as Uncle Sam's gold began its long trip to St. Petersburg.[13]

Not the entire $7.2 million purchase price reached the Russian treasury, and for years there were rumors in Washington of improprieties in connection with the Alaska purchase. The *Worcester* (Mass.) *Spy* alleged that only $5 million had been paid to the czar, and that a lobbyist, Robert J. Walker, along with unnamed government officials, had received large sums. Where had the missing money gone? Seward was alleged to have taken $250,000, and Banks, who had championed the bill, the same amount. In January 1869 the House launched an investigation.

Testimony before the House committee on public expenditures confirmed that the amount of money transferred abroad was less than the total payment. The discrepancy, however, was nothing like what had been reported in the *Spy*. The full amount had been paid to Stoeckl, but he sent on only $7,035,000; the balance was credited to his own account. Of this amount $26,000 went to Walker (by Walker's own testimony), and another $4,000 to an editor-lobbyist, John W. Forney. What became of the remaining $135,000 the committee was unable to ascertain.[14]

Seward appeared before the committee on December 19, 1868. He roundly denied allegations that the State Department had spent extravagantly for press articles in support of the Alaska purchase, although he acknowledged that he had helped to circulate a speech of Sumner's and an article by Walker supporting the transaction. As for Stoeckl's expenditures, Seward testified, "I know nothing whatever of the use the Russian Minister made of the fund, I know of no payment to anybody, by him, or any application of the funds which he received."[15]

Actually, Seward knew more than he was telling. He had strong suspicions as to where the missing money had gone. In September 1868, two months after the funds for Alaska had been voted, Seward and President Johnson had taken a carriage ride into suburban Maryland, during which the Alaska purchase was a major topic of conversation. Johnson considered Seward's remarks on that occasion of sufficient importance that he penciled a memorandum on his return to the White House:

> The Secretary asked . . . if it had ever occurred to me how few members there were in Congress whose actions were entirely above and beyond pecuniary influence. I . . . regretted to confess that there was a much smaller number exempt than at one period of life I had supposed.

Seward then, according to Johnson's memorandum, recalled some of the events that had occurred while the Alaska appropriation was hung up in the House of Representatives. He told the president that the amount paid John Forney had been not $3,000 but $30,000. In Johnson's words:

> [Seward] also stated that $20,000 was paid to R. J. Walker and F. P. Stanton for their services—N. P. Banks, chairman of the Committee on Foreign Relations, $8,000, and that the incorruptible Thaddeus Stevens received as his "sop" the moderate sum of $10,000. All these sums were paid by the Russian minister directly and indirectly to the respective parties to secure appropriation of money the government had stipulated to pay the Russian Government.[16]*

Nothing in Johnson's memo indicates the source of the secretary of state's information. By the time Seward was called before the House committee, he had probably convinced himself that whatever suspicions he might have did not constitute official knowledge of Stoeckl's disbursements—particularly disbursements in such a good cause!

*   *   *

After Seward had retired to Auburn, one of his neighbors asked what he considered his greatest achievement as secretary of state. Seward replied that his greatest achievement was the Alaska purchase, "but it will take the country a generation to appreciate it."[17] Arguably, Alaska *was* Seward's greatest triumph, for it came at a time when he had comparatively little influence and relatively few powerful allies. In the *Trent* affair, his conciliatory line had been strongly supported by Sumner and others. His campaign to expel France from Mexico was popular both in Washington and in the country at large. But without Seward there would have been no Alaska purchase.

Alaska would prove to be Seward's one important territorial triumph. He was interested in acquiring San Domingo in the Caribbean—Spain had evacuated the island in 1865—but President Johnson's recommendation for annexation fell on deaf ears in Congress. Seward had come close to success with the Virgin Islands but had fallen short. A speck of land in the Pacific that no one seemed to own also interested Seward.

---

*Seward may have been careless with some of his figures. On another occasion he told John Bigelow that $1,000 was to have gone to Stevens, "but no one would undertake to give that to him, so I undertook it myself. The poor fellow died, and I have it now." See Fawn M. Brodie, *Thaddeus Stevens* (New York: W. W. Norton, 1966), 359.

At his suggestion the U.S. Navy occupied Midway Island in 1867, and no one seemed to mind.

As for Latin America, Seward had sought to maintain a policy of nonintervention. Still, he was intrigued by the commercial possibilities of a canal across Central America connecting the Atlantic and Pacific oceans. In 1867 he concluded a treaty with Nicaragua granting the United States the right to construct a canal across Nicaragua—the "great American route," as Seward termed it. But he also saw possibilities in a canal across Panama, and even after ratification of the treaty with Nicaragua, Seward attempted to interest New York financial barons in the route across Panama, then part of Colombia. Under Seward's prodding, the New York legislature passed a bill incorporating a Panama canal company. Prominent New Yorkers, including William H. Vanderbilt and Peter Cooper, began a campaign to raise $1 million for the project.

The next step was to obtain a treaty with Colombia comparable to that with Nicaragua, and Seward sent a veteran diplomat, Caleb Cushing, to Bogotá for negotiations. Although warned that the Colombians would be looking for payoffs, Cushing returned with a treaty permitting a U.S. company to construct a canal within a twenty-mile-wide zone that would be under U.S. control but Colombian sovereignty. Colombia would receive 10 percent of the company's net earnings until the investors had been reimbursed, 25 percent thereafter. Seward endorsed the treaty, telling potential investors that, with the Suez Canal approaching completion, a route across Central America was essential for America's commercial prosperity. All this took time, however, and the Colombian senate, apparently outraged that no American money was forthcoming, rejected the agreement. When word of this setback reached Washington, the U.S. Senate refused to act on Cushing's treaty. More than three decades would pass before the way was cleared for the Panama Canal.[18]

Asia was a foreign policy backwater during Seward's period as secretary of state. But with Asia as with Latin America, Seward was looking to the future. Anson Burlingame, the able U.S. minister in Peking, was under instructions to resist attempts by the great European trading corporations to erode Chinese sovereignty. His instructions put him at odds with the powerful trade tycoons who enjoyed quasi-sovereign status in the treaty ports. During the 1860s, however, Burlingame was able to persuade some of his diplomatic colleagues that all the powers would benefit from the emergence of a stable, united China.

Burlingame resigned as U.S. minister in 1867, but on Seward's suggestion he subsequently led an official Chinese mission to the United

States and Europe aimed at improving China's relations with the powers. On July 28, 1868, the Burlingame mission signed a new treaty with the United States in which the United States reiterated its support for China's sovereignty and stated that the existence of the treaty ports did not constitute a relinquishment of China's sovereignty. Under the treaty religious freedom was extended to Americans living in China, and the right of emigration was extended to all Chinese. The Burlingame Treaty was the basis for the subsequent importation of Chinese labor to California—a provision that, over time, would prove controversial in the United States.

* * *

For the country at large, the months of negotiations for the purchase of Alaska were completely overshadowed by maneuverings in connection with the impeachment of the president. *Harper's Weekly*, not exclusively a radical journal, spoke for many when it wrote in January 1867:

> The New Orleans massacre, the stumping and staggering orgy to the grave of Douglas, the exhortations to the late rebel States to reject the [Fourteenth] Amendment, the Copperhead society in which he loves to dwell, and the coarse vituperation of Senators and Representatives by name . . . have left Andrew Johnson morally impeached, and morally condemned.[19]

Following the rejection of his policies in the congressional elections of 1866, Johnson might have attempted to regroup and develop a working arrangement with Congress. This was probably what Seward urged. But Johnson was determined to defeat Radical reconstruction, and he was convinced that the people would eventually sustain him. White House policy continued to be one of confrontation.

On January 7, 1867, an obscure Radical congressman from Ohio, John M. Ashley, introduced a resolution for an investigation into whether Johnson was guilty of "high crimes and misdemeanors." For the next two months the House Judiciary Committee questioned reporters about the president's speeches, challenged actions such as his restoration of private property to ex-rebels, and dredged up gossip that had been circulating about his personal life. Tales of pardon brokers, prostitutes, and alcoholism leaked out of the committee hearings to an eager press.

The Judiciary Committee initially opposed impeachment on grounds of insufficient evidence. Then Congressman John Churchill, representing Seward's old congressional district, changed his position. By a 5-to-4 vote the committee recommended to the House that the president be impeached and held to answer before the Senate. When first submitted to the entire House, the impeachment recommendation was overwhelmingly defeated. Johnson then took an action that he should have taken earlier: He fired his disloyal secretary of war, Edwin Stanton. In so doing, however, he defied the Tenure of Office Act that had been passed over his own veto in March 1867 with just such an eventuality in mind.

Relations between the president and Stanton had been steadily worsening. Although Johnson knew that Stanton was informing key Radicals of deliberations in the Johnson cabinet, he was reluctant to believe the worst of the capable war secretary. But when Stanton failed to oppose the Reconstruction Acts, which effectively placed the South under military administration, the president was angered. In August he accused Stanton of having criticized the Alaska purchase after voting for it in cabinet. On August 12 the president dismissed Stanton and in so doing infused new life into the impeachment movement.

Stanton himself had thought the Tenure of Office Act unconstitutional and had concurred with Seward's earlier veto message. But when Lorenzo Thomas, Stanton's designated successor, sought to occupy his office, Stanton barricaded himself in the War Department. On February 24, 1868, the House voted to impeach the president, and within a week the Radicals had agreed on eleven articles of impeachment. Eight of the eleven related to Stanton's removal; one other charged the president with having delivered "inflammatory and scandalous harangues." The final article was a summary of the first ten. The trial itself began in the Senate on March 30.

Seward did Johnson a major service in urging that the president retain as his counsel William M. Evarts, a longtime Seward associate who was one of the leading trial lawyers in the country. In part because he was still dealing with Radicals like Ben Butler and Thaddeus Stevens on the Alaska appropriation, Seward was not initially in the forefront of the president's defenders. As the trial began, however, he put other concerns aside and openly supported the president's cause. When a mass rally on the president's behalf was held in Philadelphia, Seward wrote a letter testifying that the president had supported the constitution "with the singleness and fidelity of loyal and disinterested patriotism." Seward and Weed together raised more than $11,000 for the president's defense fund, most of it from wealthy New Yorkers.[20]

During the trial Seward arrived at his office to find one of the Radical senators, Fessenden of Maine, waiting to see him on some diplomatic business. "Why, Fessenden," Seward remarked, "I have not seen you since this [impeachment] business began. You are too good a lawyer not to see through such a case. Surely you don't believe the president is guilty of high crimes and misdemeanors, do you?"

"No," Fessenden replied. "But there's a feeling among the majority of the Senate like that of the jury who said they couldn't find the prisoner guilty of the crime he was indicted for, but they would like, if they could, to convict him of 'general cussedness.' "[21] Ultimately Fessenden voted for acquittal.

Recognizing that his own presence in the cabinet could be a liability to the president, Seward provided Johnson with a letter of resignation to take effect at the president's pleasure. Then unidentified Radicals sent word to Seward that if he would desert the president, Ben Wade—the president pro tem of the Senate, who would succeed to the presidency in the event of Johnson's impeachment—would keep him on as secretary of state. "I'll see them damned first," snapped Seward. "The impeachment of the president is the impeachment of his cabinet."[22]

Tuesday, May 12, was the day of the first Senate vote. It was clearly going to be close, and Johnson's cabinet was divided as to the probable outcome. Seward, between pinches of snuff, bet Secretary of the Interior Orville Browning two hampers of champagne that the president would be acquitted, but Browning declined the wager.[23] Notwithstanding his cool demeanor, Seward took the impeachment proceedings very seriously. He wrote one friend that if Johnson were to be convicted, "before the sun sets I shall retire from [a] public life now protracted too many years."[24]

The suspense continued when the Senate, because of the illness of one of the Radical senators, postponed the crucial vote until May 16. When a vote was finally taken on the catchall eleventh article, the tally of 35 to 19 fell one vote short of conviction. Seward put on his usual show of imperturbability, sending the president a brief note of congratulations. Privately, his relief was great. He had not wished to end his government service in association with a discredited president.

25

World Traveler

WITH THE COMING of the presidential election in November 1868, Seward had to make a difficult choice. The Republican candidate, Grant, had thrown in his lot with the Radicals and had broken completely with Andrew Johnson. At the same time the Democrats had nominated a ticket from their erstwhile "peace" wing, led by Gov. Horatio Seymour of New York. Seward doubtless longed for some grouping along the lines of the abortive Union party of 1866, but ultimately he bit the bullet and announced for Grant.

There was an air of unreality to the final months of the Johnson administration, as a president who had narrowly escaped impeachment attempted to maintain a facade of executive leadership. Johnson continued to send messages to Congress, which paid no attention to his appointments and recommendations. Having long favored a single six-year term for the president, Johnson had drafted a message to this effect. His cabinet opposed the proposal; Seward pointed out that had the six-year term been in effect that year, Johnson probably would have been convicted. The president nevertheless sent his message to the Capitol, where Congress pointedly ignored it.

Seward dreaded retirement, and he may have clung to a hope that President-elect Grant would ask him to stay on as secretary of state. The two men conferred on at least two occasions. Shortly after Grant's election they found themselves on the same train to New York, and Seward visited the president-elect in the latter's private car. Early in the new year Grant was a dinner guest at the Old Clubhouse. Such contacts fueled rumors that Seward would be asked to stay on, but Grant had no intention of retaining one of Andrew Johnson's closest associates.

Seward nevertheless hoped to bring off one final diplomatic coup before departing Washington. In 1865 he had instructed Charles Francis Adams to submit a claim for damages wrought by Confederate cruisers constructed in Britain, most notably the *Alabama*. Britain, however, refused to pay reparations and declined arbitration. Seward probably voiced a few expletives at London's stand, but he did nothing to exacerbate the improved atmosphere between Britain and the United States. He enjoyed good personal relations with the new British minister, David Bruce, who appreciated the fact that Seward had not sought to make political capital out of the Fenian raids into Canada.

In 1866, shortly after the Fenian furor, the Tories were voted into power in Britain and Lord Stanley became secretary of state for foreign affairs. Seward decided to reopen the *Alabama* claims, which by this time included not only direct but indirect damages—U.S. expenses growing out of Britain's recognition of Confederate belligerency. The British, in turn, had indicated that they would pursue the question of damages to British subjects who had lost ships and property as a result of the Union blockade. The issues were complex, but the attitude on both sides of the Atlantic was conducive to negotiations. On November 30, 1866, Stanley informed Seward that his government was prepared to accept the principle of arbitration.

During 1867 and much of 1868, Seward attempted to prod the British toward the conference table. Characteristically, he employed both the carrot and the stick. He told Bruce of the growing hostility toward Britain on Capitol Hill and threatened to turn the claims issue over to Congress. Shortly thereafter, however, Seward took an entirely different tack. In December 1867, he proposed the negotiation of all outstanding differences between Britain and the United States—issues that included naturalization problems, a minor territorial dispute in Puget Sound, private American backing for the Fenians, and fishing boundaries off Canada—as well as the crucial *Alabama* claims.[1]

The key personalities were changing on both sides of the Atlantic. John Bigelow, who had become minister to France following Dayton's death, had resigned in 1866. Charles Francis Adams had attempted repeatedly to give up his post in London, only to be told that his services could not be spared. In May 1868, after seven years of distinguished service, he resigned once and for all. His replacement was Reverdy Johnson, a seventy-two-year-old Unionist from Maryland who had served two terms in the U.S. Senate. Gideon Welles had attempted to have Seward himself exiled as minister to Britain, but Johnson chose to retain his secretary of state.[2]

In January 1869 Seward orchestrated a series of agreements signed in London that became known as the Johnson–Clarendon Convention. They dealt with naturalization problems and the border dispute in Puget Sound as well as the *Alabama* claims. The convention provided that all claims since 1853—including, of course, those relating to the *Alabama*—be submitted to arbitration, but made no mention of indirect damages resulting from the *Alabama*. The popular reaction in the United States to this omission was outrage, and when President Johnson sent the Johnson-Clarendon accords to the Senate, Sumner led the opposition. Further angered by the fact that Britain offered no statement of regret for the *Alabama*'s depredations, the Senate rejected the claims treaty by a vote of 54 to 1 and refused to act on the other two agreements.[3] A final resolution of the *Alabama* claims would require another three years of negotiations.

*   *   *

In October 1868, Gideon Welles turned his attention from matters in his department to record some intriguing observations in his diary:

> There is much gossip in relation to a projected marriage between Secretary Seward and a Miss Risley. He is in his sixty-eighth year and she in her twenty-eighth. I give the rumor no credit. Yet his conduct is calculated to make gossip. For the last six weeks he has passed my house daily to visit her.[4]

Olive Risley was the attractive brunette daughter of a New York political functionary, Hanson Risley, for whom Seward had found a position in the Treasury Department. Olive was almost the same age that Fanny Seward would have been, and she and her sister Hattie had known the Seward family for years. By 1868, two years after Fanny's death, Seward was infatuated with the daughter of his old friend. While the secretary did not lack companionship of the brandy-and-cigars variety, he was conscious that something had gone out of his life. Early in 1868 he wrote to Mrs. Henry Sanford, wife of the U.S. minister to Belgium, that the loss of his wife and daughter had left him "in want of a habitual support of life. . . . How I accept with thankfulness every expression of feminine respect and affection."[5] Seward's interest in Olive Risley may have been platonic, but it was certainly intense.

As tongues wagged about Seward's daily calls on the Risleys, the secretary prepared to leave Washington for the last time. His final weeks in the capital were a hectic round of social engagements that came to a climax on March 3. On that day the staff of the State Department called at Seward's residence, where they presented a letter expressing gratitude for his "courtesy toward subordinates, which renders official intercourse so gratifying" over his period as secretary of state.[6] That afternoon the diplomatic corps called at the State Department to say farewell.

The following day the Johnson cabinet gathered at the White House. Johnson had determined that, in view of Grant's hostility, he would not attend the general's inauguration that day, and as the morning ticked away he busied himself signing bills. Seward, who had recommended that Johnson observe the amenities, made one final attempt, walking into the White House, cigar in hand, and asking whether they should not be starting for the Capitol. The president replied that he would complete his work at the White House.[7] Johnson's brusque response to Seward's last piece of advice somehow seemed typical of their relationship. With Lincoln, Seward had reciprocated respect and affection; by contrast, his dealings with Johnson were reminiscent of a loveless marriage.

Seward's move from Washington back to Auburn was a major undertaking. Frederick supervised the packing of more than a hundred boxes containing furniture, papers, clothing, memorabilia, and enough wine and liquor, according to Seward, to last him for the rest of his life. The secretary himself could do little but observe. White haired, bent, and weary, he now required the assistance of a valet around the house. His legs were weak and his right arm was showing symptoms of the paralysis that would mark his final illness. But his hearing was excellent and his eyesight good; he normally wore glasses only for reading.

Fred and Anna were building a home overlooking the Hudson, and Gus's duties kept him in Washington. But Will and his wife, Janet, had returned to Auburn after the war and were living in the house on South Street while Will reestablished himself in the banking business. Will was now "the General," for his father had seen to it that his son's bravery at the Battle of Monocacy had not gone unrewarded. Will and his family were happy in Auburn. Seward was glad to share the house, but he warned Will that he did not want his residence cluttered with damask, rosewood, and gold like some of the more ostentatious Fifth Avenue mansions.[8]

John Bigelow, the former minister to France, visited Seward in Auburn only weeks after the secretary's return. He found his erstwhile chief already apprehensive regarding the Grant administration. Seward considered only three people fit to be secretary of state—Sumner, Charles Francis Adams, and himself—and he clearly regarded Grant's initial choice, Senator Elihu Washburne, as unsatisfactory. Seward confided to Bigelow that his personal relations with Grant had always been cordial, but that the new president had never indicated any interest in State Department business or expressed any desire for a briefing on foreign affairs before taking office. Grant, he believed, regarded his cabinet simply as staff officers, to be given orders and to assure that they were promptly carried out. Bigelow had not known Seward well; their earlier dealings had been almost entirely by correspondence. Bigelow now concluded that Seward was a "great man" who "talks more like a statesman and shows far more [vision] than any that I meet."[9]

Seward received a warm greeting from his neighbors in Auburn. He wrote Fred, "It is marvelous to see how popular it makes a man to retire from public life. . . . The most unrelenting critic I had is out this morning in full blast, raising a high voice in my defense."[10] Yet Seward seemed always to be *in* Auburn but not *of* it. When he had answered the last of the congratulatory letters and the bust of Lincoln had been placed in the library, he discovered he was restless. Of the forty-four months that he lived after retiring from the State Department, no fewer than twenty-one would be spent in travel.

Seward looked westward. He decided to visit Alaska and Mexico, and invited Fred and Anna to accompany him, along with Hanson Risley and his two daughters. Risley declined, pleading Hattie's poor health and the press of his own affairs. Seward left Auburn on June 7 in a special car provided by George Pullman, without Olive but accompanied by Fred and Anna, his valet John Butler, and an Auburn neighbor, Abijah Fitch. The Seward party went from Rochester to Chicago, Denver, and Salt Lake City. The transcontinental railroad, so long a pet project of Seward's, was now a fact and a source of pride to all Americans. In Salt Lake City, Seward met Brigham Young, the Mormon president, who asked whether it was true that he occupied the old Miller house in Auburn. When Seward answered in the affirmative, Young said that he had worked on the house many years before as a carpenter.[11]*

Although Seward missed Olive—he wrote her on one occasion, "Why did I ever allow myself to become dependent on you so entirely?"—the trip buoyed his spirits. After warm receptions in San Francisco and Sacramento, the Seward party boarded a steamer, the *Active,* for the voyage north to Alaska. At Sitka, on August 12, he extolled Alaska's

---

*The mantel in the front parlor of the Seward House is described as having been carved by the teenaged Brigham Young.

resources, and predicted that the territory would one day become a state of the Union.[12] At Portland, Oregon, on the return, there was a reception in Seward's honor and a new ship for the run back to San Francisco.

After a brief rest in San Francisco the travelers embarked for Mexico by way of Los Angeles. "The reception of William H. Seward in Southern California," wrote a correspondent for the *San Francisco Examiner,* "has been made a perfect ovation everywhere in that beautiful country." At a banquet in his honor on September 21, Seward touched on some favorite themes. He wanted to see railroads everywhere—north, south, east, and west. Much of the country was underpopulated, and railroads were the way to change that. Seward was still enamored of territorial expansion. He reminded his audience that Cuba lay but a stone's throw from the U.S. mainland. Should Cuba not become part of the United States?[13]

From southern California, Seward embarked for Mexico, where his hosts outdid themselves in hospitality for the man who had done so much for their country. From Mexico City he visited Popocatapetl and Chapultepec, where he was the guest of President Juárez. Responding to a welcoming speech at Chapultepec, Seward recalled the dark days when the United States was convulsed by civil war, when Spain had occupied San Domingo, and France was attempting to absorb Mexico. During that difficult time, Seward said, the United States had become the friend and ally of every American republic, and every American republic, he maintained, was the friend of the United States.[14]

When the travelers left Mexico, it was by ship across the Caribbean. They spent three weeks in Havana and did not dock at Baltimore until February 1870. After a few days receiving friends there and in New York City, Seward reached home on March 12. His travels had been wearying, but they had been far more stimulating than a winter passed in Auburn.

In Seward's absence Olive Risley had been stricken with typhoid fever, but in May she came to Auburn with her father for an extended visit. On warm days Seward and his friends would cross to a canal near their house and board a steam launch for an outing on Lake Owasco. At his summer house on Seward Point, the secretary would dictate letters to Olive and ruminate about his years in Albany and Washington. He was good company—fond of a good story and a good cigar.

In July, Seward had a visitor he had not seen for many years. Francis Carpenter, the painter who had spent six months in the White House memorializing the Emancipation Proclamation, visited Auburn for the

purpose of writing an article about Seward. The secretary had enjoyed
bantering with Carpenter in 1864, and now he engaged in several days
of reminiscences. Seward regretted that he had not actively opposed
McDowell's advance on Manassas in 1861. When Lincoln had asked
him in cabinet whether he supported the move, Seward had deferred to
Gen. Joseph Mansfield, McDowell's representative, a move Seward in
retrospect regretted.

The secretary considered his two most useful wartime services to have
been his persuasion of Lincoln to suspend the writ of habeas corpus and
his role in the *Trent* affair. As Seward told it, when Lincoln had first
declined to release Mason and Slidell, Seward had warned him that "it
is *surrender* or *war.*" Lincoln would make no decision until he had met
with his cabinet, and the entire cabinet was initially opposed to any
release of the prisoners.

Seward had no regrets on the subject of reconstruction. He told Carpenter, "History shows that the more generous and magnanimous the
conqueror to the conquered, the sooner victory has been followed by
conciliation and a lasting peace." He had personally favored the issuance of a universal amnesty in 1865.

Thurlow Weed and William Evarts were houseguests at the time of
Carpenter's visit, and the two joined Seward and Carpenter for portions
of the interview. At one point Weed made a disparaging remark about
Seward as a prophet: Had he not said publicly in December 1860 that
the sectional "flurry" would be resolved in sixty days? Seward was not
sure that he had ever said that. "You were so quoted," snorted the
Dictator. "If you did not say it, you were grossly misunderstood."
Seward, annoyed, insisted that he had only been attempting "to calm
the public pulse."[15]

*   *   *

Seward's thoughts turned again to travel. He considered a trip to
South America before settling on a grander design: a trip around the
world. To a late-twentieth-century traveling public made blasé by cheap
jet travel, such a trip might seem reasonable recreation for a retired statesman. To Seward's generation, however, for whom a trip to Europe was
an adventure, the idea was mind-boggling. Nevertheless, on August 9 the
Seward caravan set out once more. It consisted initially of five persons:
Seward, his valet, and three Risleys—Olive, Harriet, and their father. In
San Francisco they left Hanson Risley behind but were joined by two other
couples who would accompany the party as far as China.

In Japan, Seward was received in private audience by the emperor, an almost unprecedented tribute for a person not a head of state. In Olive's account, the emperor's "dark countenance is neither unintelligent nor particularly expressive. He was motionless as a statue. He held a sceptre in his right hand, and at his left side wore one richly-ornamented, straight sword."[16]

At Shanghai, Seward said farewell to a nephew, George Seward, who had accompanied the party from San Francisco to his posting as the U.S. consul in Shanghai. About this time Seward decided that something must be done to regularize his relationship with Olive Risley. He wrote to Hanson Risley that Olive "has ripened into a noble, impressive, intellectual and attractive" woman. Probably in Shanghai, Seward and Olive agreed that adoption was the best way of putting an end to gossip, and there they completed the formalities by which Olive Risley became Seward's adopted daughter. Seward rewrote his will, dividing his estate evenly among his three sons and Olive Risley Seward.[17]

When Seward's sons heard of the adoption arrangement, their principal reaction appears to have been one of relief. At least there would be no May-and-December marriage, and no young bride to inherit the bulk of Seward's estate. Will wrote his father that he and Janet were grateful to Olive for her care and affection, and anxious for his happiness "be the circumstances what they may." Privately, Seward's family appears to have been appalled by the Olive Risley affair. One of Seward's biographers wrote in 1967 that he had it on the best authority "that letters revealing more clearly the attitude of the Sewards toward Olive and her father were destroyed by relatives before the Seward Papers were donated to the University of Rochester."[18]

For the journey north to Peking, the Seward party picked up an escort from the U.S. Navy's Asiatic fleet, including Adm. John Rodgers, its commander. A company of Chinese militia met the Americans to lead them into the city, and Olive Risley Seward was much impressed:

[After the militia] followed the four chairs of Mr. Seward, the admiral, and the ladies, with a mounted escort composed of the gentlemen of the party, civil and military. Then the musicians and seamen mounted promiscuously on horses, mules and donkeys. . . . Having prudently determined not to shock the sensibilities of the Chinese by any display of banners or musical instruments, we came along quietly without accident or incident.[19]

From China the Seward party wended its way through Southeast Asia and India. At Calcutta the East India Railway Company furnished Seward with a special car in which he traveled north to within sight of the Himalayas. He and his group steamed across the Indian Ocean through the recently opened Suez Canal to Egypt. Then they traveled up the Nile from Cairo to Aswan as guests of the viceroy and the khedive of Egypt. From there they went to the Holy Land, last visited by Seward in 1859. After a week in Jerusalem they traveled to Athens and thence to Istanbul, where Seward was a guest of the Turkish government. The journey was taking a toll on Seward, who was gradually losing the use of both arms and who, by the final stages of the trip, required assistance from two servants. But his companions marveled at his stamina, good spirits, and unquenchable curiosity.

When the travelers reached Paris in August 1871, France was still reeling from the Franco-Prussian War, which had brought down Napoleon III. German troops were still quartered in the capital. Nonetheless, Seward arranged a meeting with Drouyn de Lhuys, who had been France's foreign minister for much of the period that Seward had been secretary of state, and the two exchanged reminiscences about the Maximilian episode.

Seward and his young companions arrived in New York City on October 2, 1871. The venerable statesman estimated that he had traveled some forty-four thousand miles in the course of his fourteen-month odyssey. Seward had an explanation for friends, remarking that he was convinced that "rest is rust," and that "nothing remained . . . but to keep in motion."[20] Historian George Bancroft wrote Seward that what he had accomplished would astonish the biblical psalmist, "if he should ever get news of it. When did a man of three score years and ten ever before go around the world?"[21] But when Seward arrived at Fred's new home on the Hudson, he slept in the library to avoid having to climb stairs.

Once back in Auburn, Seward turned to writing. His friends had long urged him to write his autobiography, and Seward himself was interested. He began putting in several hours a day on it, dictating to Fred or to a secretary, sometimes in his study, sometimes in the house on Lake Owasco. In the space of a few months he had reminisced about his boyhood in Florida, touched on his college-age capers, recalled his trip to Europe in 1833, and discussed his early political beginnings with the Anti-Masons. These charming early chapters suggest that Seward, had he stuck to his task, might have produced an important work of nineteenth-century autobiography, a work that would have compensated for his refusal to keep a diary during his years in Washington.

Alas, Seward allowed himself to be distracted. Olive proposed a travel book based on their trip around the world, and Seward encouraged her to make some inquiries. With several signs of interest on the part of publishers, Seward put aside his autobiography to collaborate with Olive on what would prove to be a lucrative if somewhat shallow literary project. They devoted most of 1872 to the travel book. Based on both Olive's journal and Seward's own recollections, its 720 pages and scores of photographs would hold considerable appeal to a generation of Americans just becoming conscious of the world beyond two oceans.

Seward continued to be an early riser, breakfasting at around eight, then turning to his correspondence and his writing. He would often work through the morning, breaking only for a walk in the garden. Lunch at one was followed by a brief nap, most often on his couch in the study. Afternoons were divided between visitors and writing. In late afternoon, in all except the most inclement weather, Seward went for a carriage ride or rowing on the lake. His mind was never at rest. After one ride he complained that around Auburn one no longer saw lovers' inscriptions on rocks in romantic places—only advertisements for bitters, ointment, or lotion. Seward concluded that if he did not live in an age of romance, he certainly lived in one of enterprise.[22] Dinner was usually followed by several rubbers of whist. Seward observed that if people would make time for a game like whist in the evening they would accomplish more during the day.[23]

Just as *William H. Seward's Travels Around the World* was approaching conclusion, a presidential election intruded. Grant's first term had been marked by scandal and incompetence. Seward was constantly receiving queries as to where he stood on Grant's reelection. The Democrats made his decision easy, however, for their presidential nominee was none other than Horace Greeley. The prospect of the erratic Greeley in the White House was unthinkable to Seward. On September 17, 1872, Seward gave Grant the most tepid possible endorsement, writing in an open letter that he saw "no sufficient reason" to withdraw his support from the Republican party.[24]

Meanwhile, Seward was growing weaker. He could walk and his mind remained clear, but he could eat only with the aid of attendants. It is likely that Seward was afflicted by amyotrophic lateral sclerosis (ALS), an impairment of the nervous system known today as Lou Gehrig's disease. ALS most often strikes men in their prime and kills within a year or two. It is also found in older people, however. In such instances the progress of the disease is much slower, as was the case with Seward.

On October 10, 1872, Seward arose as usual and put in a half day at his desk. After lunch he lay down on his couch but complained of difficulty breathing. The family sent for Seward's physician—the same Dr. Dimon who had brought the bad news from Chicago on the occasion of Lincoln's nomination twelve years before. Dimon advised that Seward was failing rapidly, and those of the family not in Auburn, including Fred and Gus, were summoned by telegram. No statesman of Seward's time could be allowed to die without last words, and late in the afternoon Janet asked her father-in-law if he had any final words for the family. Seward, still composed, whispered, "Love one another."[26]

A few days later Thurlow Weed, summoned to Auburn as a pall-bearer, looked on his old friend for the last time, tears streaming down his face. On a rainy autumn day, a parade of carriages wound from the Seward home to Fort Hill Cemetery, where Seward was buried next to Frances and Fanny. On the headstone were printed the words that Seward had requested from his defense of William Freeman: "He Was Faithful."

26

Seward and the Lincoln Legend

A STORY—PROBABLY apocryphal—that enjoyed considerable vogue during Seward's lifetime had Seward and Weed taking a carriage ride in New York City's Central Park. When they passed a bust of Lincoln, Seward ordered the carriage stopped. Had Weed done his job properly in 1860, Seward complained, the bust on the pedestal would be of himself, not Lincoln. To which Weed is said to have replied: "Yes, Henry, but wouldn't you rather be riding in Central Park with me?"

Whatever the provenance of this anecdote, it is a reminder that Seward's career and achievements were hostage to Lincoln's martyrdom. Seward himself felt this situation keenly. Once during the Johnson administration, Leonard Swett, a longtime Lincoln associate, called on Seward at the State Department. After some general conversation, Swett asked tentatively whether the secretary would let him see the scars left by Paine's knife. Seward obligingly removed his cravat, unbuttoned his collar, and showed Swett by how narrow a margin Paine had missed the great artery. He then remarked sadly that Providence had done him a bad turn in not allowing him to die with Lincoln: "I think I deserved the reward of dying there."[1]

Death initially brought Seward some of the acclaim he had been denied in life. When Olive Risley Seward brought out *William H. Seward's Travels Around the World* in 1873, the ponderous tome sold some sixty thousand copies—an immense sale for any book in nineteenth-century America. But even as readers admired the late statesman's stamina, he suffered from the zeal of some friends. In April 1873 Charles Francis Adams delivered a eulogy of Seward at the invitation of the New York legislature. In it, he spoke respectfully of Lincoln but managed to extol

Seward at the late president's expense. According to Adams, for all of Lincoln's virtues, the American people had never elected anyone with so little preparation for the presidency as the man from Illinois. In Adams's view, it had been Seward, with his grasp of both domestic politics and foreign affairs, who had carried Lincoln through the first difficult months of the war: "Mr. Lincoln could not fail soon to perceive the fact that, whatever estimate he might put on his own natural judgment, he had to deal [in Seward] with a superior in native intellectual power . . . in breadth of philosophical experience, and in the force of moral discipline."[2]

One person who dissented from this judgment with a vengeance was Gideon Welles. The former navy secretary approached the subject both as a critic of Seward and as a genuine admirer of Lincoln. Ignoring all strictures about speaking ill of the dead, Welles published a short book in 1874, *Lincoln and Seward,* which he acknowledged to be a rebuttal to Adams's eulogy. In Welles's account, Lincoln was an honest son of the West, wise beyond his years, the greatest president since Washington. Seward, in contrast, was a product of the Weed machine, "the most offensive lobby combination of that date." Seward had failed to understand the secession crisis, believing mistakenly that "time and the change of administrations" would make things right. Welles's comparison of Lincoln's and Seward's personal traits was damning. The president was "greatly superior in intellectual strength and vigor, had . . . more earnestness and sincerity, a greater grasp and comprehension, a more intuitive and far-seeing sagacity." Seward, though he had "the sustaining qualities" valuable in a subordinate and was skilled "in adapting himself to circumstances and exigencies which he could not control," lacked the self-reliance essential in a leader.[3]

Seward even took his lumps in the visual arts. Francis Carpenter's heroic painting, *First Reading of the Emancipation Proclamation of President Lincoln,* had been completed in July 1864. It was exhibited in several cities and became the subject of a popular engraving by Alexander Hay Richie. The painting, however, was not without its detractors. Chief Justice Chase complained to John Hay that Seward had been made the dominant figure, "while everyone else listens or stares into vacancy."[4] Chase had a point. In Carpenter's original painting, Seward dominates the center foreground, with papers on the table before him, quill pen at hand. The secretary of state may be addressing Lincoln across the table, who listens with deferential attention. While middle-class Americans framed their copies of Richie's engraving, Lincoln's friends fumed, and their complaints had some effect on the artist.

In 1878 Elizabeth Thompson of New York City purchased Carpenter's work for $25,000 with the intention of presenting it to Congress. When the painting was unveiled later that year before a joint session of the House and Senate, it had undergone a metamorphosis. The pen that for years had lain near Seward's hand was now held by Lincoln. A lightening of the background behind the president lent a haloed effect. The draft Emancipation Proclamation was in Lincoln's hand for all to see. Carpenter's changes were perhaps appropriate—Seward had been, after all, rather indifferent concerning the proclamation—but the episode was symbolic of the gilding of Lincoln's reputation at Seward's expense.

Through the 1870s and 1880s scores of maudlin books extolling the Great Emancipator were served up to the American public. Even without martyrdom, Lincoln had all the makings of a folk hero: humble birth, rugged honesty, the common touch. Some of Lincoln's personality seems even to have transcended the formal photographs of the day. Contemporary photographs of Seward, in contrast, are severe and even belligerent; none even hints at his puckish good humor.

To the extent that Lincoln was depicted as the quintessential American, the man who had almost single-handedly saved the Union, his associates in the Civil War years, particularly those who were not soldiers, were reduced to the status of bit players. But even as Seward languished in popular esteem, the influence of his tenure at the State Department grew. The policies he had espoused in the difficult years of the Johnson administration—peaceful expansion, good relations with Latin America, expanded commerce with Asia—were perpetuated by his successors. Hamilton Fish, Grant's secretary of state, brought the *Alabama* arbitration to a successful conclusion, in which Britain paid $15.5 million to the United States. Fish also attempted to negotiate agreements with Colombia and Nicaragua for an interocean canal but, like his predecessor, was unable to close any deals.

In Asia, Seward's diplomacy laid the groundwork for what John Hay would call the open-door policy, under which the industrialized nations would refrain from carving out spheres of influence on the Asian mainland. Writing in 1922, diplomatic historian Tyler Dennett concluded that "no new principles" had been added to U.S. policy in Asia from 1869 to the beginning of the present century.[5]

Even in terms of personalities, Seward's influence lived on. Grant's successor, Rutherford B. Hayes, selected as his secretary of state William M. Evarts, whose career had been furthered by Seward several times, most notably when he urged Johnson to engage Evarts as senior counsel in the impeachment trial. Evarts, in turn, chose Fred Seward to be his assistant secretary of state, and the total of twelve years that the younger Seward served in the second-ranking State Department post established a record that would not be challenged until the administration of Franklin Roosevelt, when Sumner Welles served in a number of senior positions.

At Montrose on the Hudson, Fred Seward attempted to keep his father's reputation alive. In 1891 he published a three-volume biography, picking up in 1834, where Seward had stopped in his autobiography, and carrying his father's life to its conclusion. Although clearly eulogistic, Fred's work incorporated hundreds of his father's letters and in so doing allowed the subject to speak for himself—something William Henry Seward had always done well. Unfortunately, Fred's magnum opus appeared shortly after the publication of a classic of Lincoln literature, the ten-volume Lincoln biography by his two secretaries, Nicolay and Hay, in the third volume of which the public learned for the first time of Seward's April 1, 1861, memorandum, "Some Thoughts for the President's Consideration." The two authors characterized it as "an extraordinary state paper, unlike anything to be found in the political history of the United States."[6] Most Americans agreed, and publication of the April 1 memorandum was a blow from which Seward's reputation never fully recovered. Henry Adams—probably recognizing a popular overreaction to the April 1 exchange—suggested to his friend Hay that he write a biography of Seward. But Hay, for whom Seward had done so much, declined.

The decades passed, with no dimming of popular interest in the Civil War. The focus, however, moved to the battlefield. The Civil War became the great American epic, the soldiers of each side equally brave and committed, the pious Lee the South's counterpart to Abraham Lincoln. At times, the political origins of the war tended to be submerged in battle reenactments; in any case, the fact that there had been a war at all was somehow an indictment of "the politicians." And William Henry Seward had certainly been one of the politicians.

A few books dealing with Seward occasionally surfaced in the flood of Lincolniana. In 1900 Frederic Bancroft, with cooperation from the Seward family, wrote a sonorous but substantial two-volume biography. John Bigelow, in a multivolume memoir published in 1909, characterized the appointment of Seward to the State Department as being as important to the nation as Lincoln's election to the presidency. In 1946, Burton Hendrick, a distinguished biographer, made Seward the centerpiece of an insightful work, *Lincoln's War Cabinet*. Nevertheless, not until

1967 was Seward the subject of a modern, full biography. The author, Professor Glyndon Van Deusen of the University of Rochester, was a leading authority on the politics of New York State. Van Deusen was less comfortable with Seward the diplomat than with Seward the politician, however, and the reader was overwhelmed with the minutiae of New York State politics.

*   *   *

From a late-twentieth-century perspective, Seward's political career can be divided into four phases of quite unequal duration. The first and longest period—from about 1830 to 1860—comprises his years as a reformist politician and presidential aspirant. The second, brief period encompasses the crucial three months of 1860–61 during which Seward sought to avert civil war. The third phase comprises the Civil War years, when Seward acted as both foreign minister and confidant to President Lincoln. The final period is Seward's tenure as secretary of state under Andrew Johnson. Although some might view Seward's eight years as secretary of state as a single phase, the problems and challenges he faced under Johnson were in fact very different from those under Lincoln.

The prewar years in Washington saw a maturing on Seward's part. On a personal level, he had reached an understanding with Frances that, notwithstanding her wish that he retire to Auburn, he was committed to a political career. The occasional instances of depression that marked his earlier years are not evident after 1855. In Washington he developed a political persona based on reasoned argument in support of a fervent nationalism. Seward's reputation as a political wizard, however, was greatly overstated by his contemporaries. The high visibility accorded the Seward-Weed alliance by both men was a political error; many Americans could not reconcile Seward's lofty ideals with his close association with Weed's Albany machine. Later, the break with Horace Greeley, the most influential editor in the country, proved devastating to Seward's presidential hopes. Seward's oratorical flights as senator, most notably his speeches referring to the "higher law" and the "irrepressible conflict," also were damaging to his long-term political aspirations.

Did Seward "use" the antislavery movement of the 1850s and subsequently betray its principles, as Sumner and others charged? That Seward was deeply opposed to slavery on humanitarian grounds is evident throughout his career, from his first contact with slavery in Virginia, through his controversial defense of William Freeman, to his insistence in the Senate that slavery must be contained and eventually eliminated. In a speech in 1844 Seward became one of the first American statesmen to use the term *human rights*. But during his second term in the Senate, Seward was compelled to recognize slavery as more than an issue crying for reform—it was the rock on which the entire Union might founder. This recognition, together with his own presidential ambitions, led Seward to blunt his rhetoric on the slavery issue in the period from 1858 to 1860.

With this qualification, however, Seward was remarkably persistent in his political agenda. He was a lifelong advocate of prison reform. He supported measures to facilitate immigration from Europe, in defiance of political logic. He was a strong advocate of territorial expansion by peaceful means. He was a friend to blacks, slave and free, until the black agenda came into conflict with the reconstruction of the Union. But there were occasions when Seward's rhetoric placed him further "in front" on the slavery issue than a prudent presidential aspirant should be. On these occasions the senator from New York trimmed his sails. He had a personal as well as an ideological agenda, and as a politician he had to consider what was politically attainable.

Seward's second phase, that of a crisis manager in 1860–61, has been fully explored earlier. There is no certainty that his policy of isolating the seceded states while cultivating the border states would have averted civil war. Moreover, even if Seward's strategy had succeeded, there is little reason to believe that the states of the Deep South would have returned to the fold. Yet how many Northerners would have followed Lincoln's course if they had known that a war to preserve the Union would cost 360,000 Northern lives? Seward at that time was clearly improvising. But the senator from New York had participated in many political compromises in his day, and he had heard threats of secession before. He believed that the 1860 crisis could be managed, and it is just possible that he was right. In any case, no one worked harder than he did to avert civil war.

Seward's penchant for improvisation infuriated ideologues like Chase and Sumner. They viewed his willingness to seek new paths as a reflection on his character. Yet Seward had never been one for nailing his flag to the mast. As governor of New York he had compromised on the issue of aid to parochial schools. Later he had supported a slaveholder, Zachary Taylor, for the presidency when the cause of the Liberty party was hopeless. When the threat of secession was imminent in the winter of 1860–61, Seward appears to have been prepared to open portions of the West to slavery if such action, as part of a broader compromise, would keep the peace.

Seward did not really begin to function as secretary of state until a month after Lincoln's inauguration. Only after the famous exchange of April 1, 1861, did Seward fully accept his subordinate role and move to make his relationship with the president one of effective partnership. Of his many roles during the war—military recruiter, political organizer, master of the "little bell"—not the least was his role as friend and confidant to Lincoln. Seward never doubted the eventual success of the Union cause, and his dogged optimism was probably a tonic to the often-melancholy Lincoln. The president, for his part, went to great pains to protect Seward from the wrath of the Radical Republicans in December 1862—as well he should have, for Seward was the one star in his lackluster cabinet.

As a diplomat Seward had a clear sense of priorities. The one imponderable in the Civil War was the possibility of foreign intervention by Britain or France, in the form of recognition of the Confederacy or major military aid. Seward seized the high ground. By his bellicose pronouncements in 1861, he caused the Palmerston government to fear for the safety of Britain's merchant marine and even its Canadian provinces if the United States should become sufficiently aroused. But when, with the *Trent* affair, he faced a true crisis, Seward was the essence of prudence. Thereafter he made skillful use of the carrot as well as the stick. He made clear that he sought to maintain cordial relations with London, and in matters like the confidentiality of international mails gave evidence of his good intentions. Thus when a new crisis arose— that of the Laird rams—Britain chose to give priority to the maintenance of correct relations with the United States.

As secretary of state Seward was blatantly opportunistic. Even while insisting that Britain adhere to the letter of the law with respect to its neutrality, Seward was dispatching agents to Ireland to recruit soldiers for the North. He played on Britain's and France's need for cotton, smoothly maintaining, however incorrectly, that their requirements could be met through ports under Federal control. He played the Russia card so as to remind both Britain and France that the United States was not without friends in Europe.

Because France did not control the seas as Britain did, Seward never regarded French intervention so seriously as he did the threat of British meddling. Yet Napoleon III's attempt to recolonize Mexico clearly trespassed against the Monroe Doctrine and posed a greater long-term threat than any wartime action by Britain. During the war, Seward built up a record of protests that France's activities in Mexico were unacceptable to the United States and would be addressed in due course. With Union victories on the battlefield, these implied threats took on substance, and the collapse of Maximilian's empire became only a matter of time.

Although Seward probably had more influence with Lincoln than any other member of his cabinet, his power was far less than his enemies suspected. The decision to accept civil war as the price for keeping the Union intact was Lincoln's, not Seward's. The president overruled his secretary of state on the relief of Fort Sumter. He dismissed Seward's proposal that he instigate a foreign crisis as a means of reuniting the nation. But he accepted Seward's counsel in the matter of the *Trent,* on the suspension of the writ of habeas corpus, and on a host of lesser issues. The suspension of habeas corpus underscores the "practical" Seward: The threat to the Constitution posed by secession justified the abrogation of one of its most sacred provisions.

Unlike Lincoln, Seward survived the war to grapple with the problems of reconstruction. By then he was no longer the liberal reformer of the 1850s, but there was much that he could have done for Lincoln's successor. Had Johnson attempted to cultivate moderate congressional Republicans in 1865 and 1866, as Seward recommended, he might have averted the breach with Congress that brought his impeachment. In practice, however, Johnson was far less receptive to Seward's counsel than Lincoln had been, and as a result he took Seward down with him. The secretary of state never recovered politically from his public support for Johnson's reconstruction policies.

Although Johnson would have improved his relations with Congress had he followed Seward's advice on matters like the 1865 Civil Rights Bill, the two men shared a view that the government had little responsibility for the freedmen. It is in his attitude toward the blacks that Seward made the sharpest turn after the Civil War. The same man who had advocated one man, one vote as senator opposed enfranchising blacks in 1865. Such a reversal might be justified, but it was symptomatic of Seward's attitude toward the freedmen: Having helped to end slavery, Seward washed his hands of the race problem. His attitude probably resulted from a combination of factors—annoyance with the Radicals in Congress who had long harassed him, physical fatigue, and preoccupation with the restoration to the Union of the erstwhile Confederate states. Still, it diminishes Seward's stature as a humanitarian.

Seward's greatest role under Johnson was, of course, that of territorial expansionist. In his other diplomatic triumphs Seward had had important allies, such as Lincoln, Sumner, and Charles Francis Adams. The *Trent* affair would probably have been peacefully resolved even without Seward's conciliatory role. Alaska, in contrast, was almost a personal coup. Seward alone had the vision and drive to see the purchase to its conclusion.

Seward did not have the ideal temperament for a secretary of state. In the early months of 1861, when he was engaged in sensitive negotiations, he talked incessantly, sometimes of peace, other times of war. His flippant remark to the Duke of Newcastle in 1860, to the effect that as secretary of state he would have a duty to insult Britain, haunted Seward during the war years. But the man from Auburn, on his good behavior, was an eloquent communicator; Burton Hendrick notes that "he spoke in the plainest of terms; his correspondence was 'shirt sleeves' diplomacy at its best."[7] And he could operate circumspectly when necessary, as in the negotiations leading up to the Alaska purchase.

Despite his loyalty to Lincoln and later to Johnson, Seward was not by instinct a team player. Prior to 1861 he had resolved many of his political problems in concert with Weed. In his years as a cabinet officer, however, he found no counterpart to the Dictator, and after 1865 he was denied the comfort represented by the regular exchange of letters with Frances. Confident of his own abilities, Seward tended to work problems out for himself. At best, as in his handling of the case of the *Trent* and of Napoleon III, the results were brilliant. On other occasions, he sometimes overintellectualized. Even today his insistence on defending Fort Pickens while evacuating Fort Sumter is a bit hard to rationalize. At worst, as with his "Some Thoughts for the President's Consideration," his reluctance to solicit counsel outside a small group of personal associates invited trouble. Yet few American statesmen have been as willing as Seward to take politically unpopular positions—including his suspension of the writ of habeas corpus, his support for the return of Mason and Slidell, his continuation of Lincoln's conciliatory design for reconstruction, and his campaign under Johnson for the acquisition of Alaska and the Virgin Islands.

American history affords few more complex figures than William Henry Seward, who at various times was shrewd, diligent, devious, tenacious, and indiscreet. As a person he was a model not only of rectitude but of warmth and charm. Although proud of his own achievements, he was easy and unaffected with others, treating servants and messengers with the same consideration that he showed foreign envoys. In the cut and thrust of Washington politics he was remarkable for his refusal to deal in personalities. When defeated for the presidency by someone he considered less qualified than himself, he not only became a trusted subordinate but a devoted friend. Small wonder that Lincoln called him "a man without gall."

For all these virtues, many of Seward's contemporaries were cautious in their praise. The anonymous diarist who wrote as the Public Man called Seward "one of the most perplexing men alive." He did not question Seward's integrity or patriotism, but thought that the New Yorker would countenance "the strangest and the most questionable operations imaginable."[8] Charles Francis Adams's two sons, Charles Francis, Jr., and Henry, both qualified in later years their youthful admiration for Seward. Henry Adams included in his famous autobiography a characteristic put-down: that Seward "had some means, unknown to other Senators, of producing the effect of unselfishness."[9] His brother Charles Francis wrote in 1916, long after his memorable 1860 campaign swing with Seward: "As I now see him, Seward was an able . . . adroit, and very versatile man; but he escaped being really great. . . . He was, after all, as men instinctively felt, more of a politician than a statesman."[10]

Part of Seward's problem was credibility. He was a bit too complicated for the lesser mortals with whom he dealt. For all his high-mindedness, he had risen to prominence in partnership with Thurlow Weed, and Weed was not everyone's choice as a used-carriage salesman. When the situation required, Seward was a master dissimulator. He blandly denied any knowledge of Weed's 1861 proposal to extend the Missouri Compromise line to the Pacific; he knew nothing of any money the Russians might have distributed in connection with the Alaska purchase. One of his contemporaries remarked that it was not fair to call Seward insincere: "We generally knew what hole he would go in, but we never felt quite sure as to where he would come out."[11]

One may question the place in history of a statesman whose judgment was sometimes flawed and whose credibility was occasionally suspect. What Seward had to compensate for these deficiencies was, simply, the quality called vision. He thought in broad terms—freedom, national unity, expansion. He felt instinctively that slavery was the one issue that the United States must confront if it was to achieve the greatness that awaited it. Similarly, he was convinced that the country, if it was to become a world power, must first assure that it was the dominant power in its own hemisphere—hence his continuing interest in projects as disparate as the transcontinental railroad, the Panama Canal, and the Alaska purchase, at a time when most of the country had lost interest in territorial expansion.

Seward was usually prepared to take a step backward in the pursuit of a political objective if the tactical situation so dictated. Because of this characteristic, and because he rarely lost his temper, Seward was said to lack commitment. But this sense of detachment was part of his personality. He viewed everything with a historical perspective and a dry wit. He could usually find a humorous side to the most serious question, as when he compared the Emancipation Proclamation to the raising of a liberty pole. As a hedge against disappointment, he reminded himself that politics was but a game, and politicians mere actors in a play. However avidly he sought the presidency, he was capable of recognizing that more was at stake in 1860 than the gratification of his personal ambitions.

Politically Seward was a nationalist. Temperamentally he was a healer. He sought to avoid confrontation, even when some of his speeches took on a confrontational tone. When he was unable to avert civil war, he determined to make the eventual reconciliation as painless as possible. In making harmony a political objective in its own right, Seward succeeded only in gaining a reputation for pragmatism, and Americans have always regarded pragmatism as one of the lesser virtues.

Even the inscription that Seward chose for his tombstone—"He Was Faithful"—strikes a slightly enigmatic note. To whom or what was he faithful? Is the reference to Frances, or to his political beliefs? Perhaps the quotation, from Seward's address in the William Freeman trial, refers to the slavery issue after all. Americans like their heroes to be unambiguous, and William Henry Seward steadfastly refused to oblige them.

APPENDIX

Seward's "Thoughts" and Lincoln's Response*

April 1, 1861

Some Thoughts for the President's Consideration:

1st. We are at the end of a month's administration and yet without a policy, either domestic or foreign.

2d. This, however, is not culpable, and it has been unavoidable. The presence of the Senate, with the need to meet applications for patronage, have prevented attention to other and more grave matters.

3d. But further delay to adopt and prosecute our policies for both domestic and foreign affairs would not only bring scandal on the Administration, but danger upon the country.

4th. To do this we must dismiss the applicants for office. But how? I suggest that we make the local appointments forthwith, leaving foreign or general ones for ulterior and occasional action.

5th. The policy—at home. I am aware that my views are singular, and perhaps not sufficiently explained. My system is built upon this *idea* as a ruling one, namely that we must *Change the question before the Public from one upon Slavery* for a question upon *Union or Disunion.*

*Seward's memorandum is in Frederick's hand, suggesting that it may have been drafted by Secretary Seward on March 30 or March 31 but copied on April 1. The envelope containing Lincoln's reply was addressed by Lincoln to "Hon. W. H. Seward/ Present." This, together with the fact that Lincoln's reply was found in the Lincoln rather than the Seward papers, indicates that although Lincoln may have shown Seward his reply, the president's letter was never formally sent. The editor of Lincoln's writings doubts whether Seward ever saw Lincoln's reply: "Having written it, Lincoln may have thought better of rebuking his secretary in writing and handled the matter orally." See Basler, *Collected Works of Abraham Lincoln,* vol. 4, 316–18.

In other words, from what would be regarded as a Party question to one of *Patriotism* or *Union.*

The occupation or evacuation of Fort Sumter, although not in fact a slavery or a party question, is so *regarded.* Witness the temper manifested by the Republicans in the Free States, and even by Union men in the South.

I would therefore terminate it as a safe means for changing the issue. I deem it fortunate that the last administration created the necessity.

For the rest, I would simultaneously defend and reinforce all the Forts in the Gulf, and have the Navy recalled from foreign stations to be prepared for a blockade. Put the Island of Key West under Martial Law.

This will raise distinctly the question of *Union* or *Disunion.* I would maintain every fort and possession in the South.

For Foreign Nations

I would demand explanations from Spain and France categorically, at once.

I would seek explanations from Great Britain and Russia, and send agents into Canada, Mexico, and Central America, to rouse a vigorous continental spirit of independence on this continent against European intervention, and if satisfactory explanations are not received from Spain and France, would convene Congress, and declare war against them.

But whatever policy we adopt, there must be an energetic prosecution of it. For this purpose, it must be somebody's business to pursue and direct it, incessantly.

Either the President must do it himself, and be all the while active in it, or devolve it on some member of his Cabinet. Once adopted, debate on it must end, and all agree, and abide. It is not my especial province; but I neither seek to evade, nor assume, responsibility.

*   *   *

Executive Mansion April 1, 1861

Hon. W. H. Seward:

My dear Sir:

Since parting with you I have been considering your paper dated this day, and entitled "Some thoughts for the President's consideration." The first proposition in it is, "1st. We are at the end of a month's administration, and yet without a policy, either domestic or foreign."

At the *beginning* of that month, in the inaugural, I said, "The power confided to me will be used to hold, occupy and possess the property and places belonging to the government, and to collect the duties and imposts.'' This had your distinct approval at the time; and, taken in connection with the order I immediately gave to General Scott, directing him to employ every means in his power to strengthen and hold the forts, comprises the exact domestic policy you now urge, with the single exception, that it does not propose to abandon Fort Sumter.

Again, I do not perceive how the re-inforcement of Fort Sumter would be done on a slavery, or party issue, while that of Fort Pickens would be on a more national, and patriotic one.

The news received yesterday in regard to St. Domingo, certainly brings a new item within the range of our foreign policy; but up to that time we have been preparing circulars, and instructions to ministers, and the like, all in perfect harmony, without even a suggestion that we had no foreign policy.

Upon your closing propositions, that ''whatever policy we adopt, there must be an energetic prosecution of it''

''For this purpose it must be somebody's business to pursue and direct it incessantly''

''Either the President must do it himself, and be all the while active in it, or devolve it on some member of his cabinet''

''Once adopted, debates on it must end, and all agree and abide.''

I remark that if this must be done, *I* must do it. When a general line of policy is adopted, I apprehend there is no danger of its being changed without good reason, or continuing to be a subject of unnecessary debate; still, upon points arising in its progress, I wish, and suppose I am entitled to have, the advice of all the cabinet. Your Obt. Servt.

A. Lincoln

NOTES

Chapter 1: A Convention in Chicago

1. Carl Sandburg, *Abraham Lincoln: The Prairie Years* (New York: Charles Scribner's Sons, 1937), vol.2, 335.
2. *New York Times*, May 12, 1860.
3. Henry Adams, *The Education of Henry Adams* (1907; reprint, Boston: Houghton Mifflin, 1974), 104.
4. Isaac Bromley, quoted in Peter Andrews, "How We Got Lincoln," *American Heritage*, November 1988.
5. Gamaliel Bradford, *Union Portraits* (Boston: Houghton Mifflin, 1916), 207.
6. Sandburg, *Abraham Lincoln: The Prairie Years*, vol. 2, 339–40.
7. David M. Potter, *The Impending Crisis* (New York: Harper & Row, 1976), 423.
8. *New York Times*, May 18, 1860.
9. Frederick W. Seward, *Seward* (New York: Derby and Miller, 1891), vol. 2, 445.
10. Quoted in William B. Hesseltine, ed., *The Tragic Conflict* (New York: George Braziller, 1962), 101.
11. Bruce Catton, *The Coming Fury* (Garden City, N.Y.: Doubleday, 1961), 61.
12. Hesseltine, *The Tragic Conflict*, 104.
13. Sandburg, *Abraham Lincoln: The Prairie Years*, vol. 2, 345.
14. Allan Nevins, *The Emergence of Lincoln* (New York: Charles Scribner's Sons, 1950), vol. 2, 260.
15. Sandburg, *Abraham Lincoln: The Prairie Years*, vol. 2, 345.
16. Ibid., 346.
17. Glyndon G. Van Deusen, *William Henry Seward* (New York: Oxford University Press, 1967), 225.

18. WHS to Thurlow Weed, May 18, 1860, Weed Papers, University of Rochester.
19. Alexander K. McClure, *Abraham Lincoln and Men of War-Time* (Philadelphia: Times Publishing Co., 1892), 22.
20. Quoted in *Lincoln Lore,* July 1968.
21. Andrews, "How We Got Lincoln."
22. WHS to John S. Gould, May 22, 1860, William R. Weiss Americana catalog no. 98, November 1989.
23. WHS to "The Managers," November 15, 1860, author's collection.

Chapter 2: "A Sweet Little Valley"

1. Seward, *Seward,* vol. 1, 20.
2. Ibid., 21.
3. Ibid.
4. Ibid., 26.
5. Ibid., 27–28.
6. WHS to Samuel Seward, November 22, 1816, Schaffer Library, Union College.
7. Van Deusen, *Seward,* 6.
8. Ibid., 5.
9. Ibid.
10. Noah Brooks, "William H. Seward," *Statesmen* (New York: Charles Scribner's Sons, 1904), 120.
11. General William H. Seward, "A Sketch of the Life of the Late William H. Seward," 1889, Seymour Library, Auburn, N.Y.
12. Brooks, "William H. Seward," *Statesmen,* 121.
13. Seward, *Seward,* vol. 1, 35.
14. Patricia C. Johnson, "Politics and the Seward Family," *University of Rochester Library Bulletin,* Autumn 1978.
15. Seward, *Seward,* vol. 1, 52.
16. WHS to S. S. Seward, August 5, 1824, Seward Papers, University of Rochester.
17. Seward, *Seward,* vol. 3, 479.
18. Leonard L. Richards, *The Life and Times of Congressman John Quincy Adams* (New York: Oxford University Press, 1986), 40–41.
19. WHS to Samuel Seward, December 9, 1824, Seward Papers.
20. WHS to S. S. Seward, May 11, 1825, Seward Papers.

Chapter 3: Anti-Masons and Whigs

1. Seward, *Seward,* vol. 1, 166.
2. WHS to Frances Seward, January 26, 1832, Seward Papers.
3. Harriet Weed, *Life of Thurlow Weed* (New York: Da Capo Press, 1970), 423.

4. Donald B. Cole, *Martin Van Buren and the American Political System* (Princeton, N.J.: Princeton University Press, 1984), 96.
5. Seward, *Seward*, vol. 1, 162.
6. Typescript, "Frederick W. Seward Recalls His Boyhood Home," Seymour Library, Auburn, N.Y.
7. Seward, *Seward,*, vol. 1, 169.
8. Ibid., 183.
9. Van Deusen, *Seward*, 18.
10. Seward, *Seward*, vol. 1, 205–6.
11. Ibid., 113.
12. Ibid., 138.

Chapter 4: "I Was the Criminal . . ."

1. Van Deusen, *Seward*, 33.
2. Ibid., 27.
3. WHS to William L. Stone, October 6, 1834, Seward Papers.
4. Weed to Seward, November 5, 1834, Seward Papers.
5. Van Deusen, *Seward*, 34.
6. WHS to Frances Seward, December 8, 1834, Seward Papers.
7. WHS to Frances Seward, December 5, 1834, Seward Papers.
8. WHS to Albert Tracy, December 29, 1834, Seward Papers.
9. WHS to Samuel Seward, July 25, 1834, Seward Collection, Goshen, N.Y., Historical Society.
10. WHS to Samuel Seward, October 23, 1834, Seward Collection, Goshen, N.Y., Historical Society.
11. Johnson, "Politics and the Seward Family," 47.
12. WHS to Samuel Seward, June 27, 1835, Seward Collection, Goshen, N.Y., Historical Society.
13. Van Deusen, *Seward*, 38.
14. Seward, *Seward*, vol. 1, 258.
15. Ibid., 325.
16. Locke Seward to Samuel Seward, n.d., author's collection.
17. Weed to WHS, October 28, 1838, Seward Papers.
18. WHS to Christopher Morgan, October 11, 1838, Seward Papers.
19. WHS to Mary Seward, November 11, 1838, Seward Collection, Goshen, N.Y., Historical Society.

Chapter 5: The Governor

1. Seward, *Seward*, vol. 1, 385.
2. George E. Baker, ed., *The Works of William H. Seward* (New York: Redfield Press, 1853), vol. 2, 199.
3. Ibid., 404.
4. Ibid., 453–54.

5. Quoted in Thornton L. Lothrop, *William Henry Seward* (Boston: Houghton Mifflin, 1899), 37.
6. Seward, *Seward,* vol. 1, 537.
7. Van Deusen, *Seward,* 75.
8. Seward, *Seward,* vol. 1, 502.
9. Ibid., 554.
10. n.d., Seward Papers.
11. Van Deusen, *Seward,* 87.
12. Seward, *Seward,* vol. 1, 547.
13. Bayard Tuckerman, ed., *The Diary of Philip Hone* (New York: Dodd, Mead, 1910), 153.
14. Seward, *Seward,* vol. 1, 642.

Chapter 6: "Our Conflict Is with Slavery"

1. Seward, *Seward,* vol. 1, 645.
2. Ibid., 705-6.
3. Ibid., 651-52.
4. Van Deusen, *Seward,* 31.
5. Seward, *Seward,* vol. 1, 657.
6. Van Deusen, *Seward,* 90.
7. Susan S. Smith, "Mr. Seward's Home," *University of Rochester Library Bulletin,* Autumn 1978.
8. Seward, *Seward,* vol. 1, 736.
9. Ibid., 682.
10. Richard B. Morris, ed., *Encyclopedia of American History* (New York: Harper & Row, 1965), 190.
11. Baker, *Seward's Works,* vol. 3, 251.
12. WHS to George Grier, October 7, 1844, Seward Papers.
13. WHS to E. A. Stanbury, September 2, 1844, Seward Papers.
14. WHS to Gerrit Smith, November 25, 1844, Seward Papers.
15. Seward, *Seward,* vol. 1, 742.
16. Ibid., 771.
17. Ibid., 779.
18. Baker, *Seward's Works,* vol. 3, 409.

Chapter 7: "Hold Him to Be a Man"

1. Earl Conrad, *Mr. Seward for the Defense* (New York: Rinehart, 1956), 56.
2. Seward, *Seward,* vol. 1, 810.
3. This and subsequent quotations from Seward's defense are from Baker, *Seward's Works,* vol. 1, 411-75.
4. Earl Conrad, *The Governor and His Lady* (New York: G. P. Putnam's, 1960), 282.

5. WHS to James Bowen, September 15, 1846, Seward Papers.
6. Seward, *Seward*, vol. 1, 822.
7. Van Deusen, *Seward*, 106.
8. Seward, *Seward*, vol. 2, 43.
9. WHS to Gerrit Smith, March 24, 1847, Seward Papers.
10. Seward, *Seward*, vol. 2, 41.
11. Clay to Horace Greeley, June 23, 1846, author's collection.
12. Seward, *Seward*, vol. 2, 37.
13. Glyndon G. Van Deusen, *Thurlow Weed* (Boston: Little, Brown, 1947), 156–57.
14. Seward, *Seward*, vol. 2, 77.
15. Ibid., 79.
16. Francis B. Carpenter, "A Day with Governor Seward at Auburn," July 1870, Seward Papers.
17. Ibid.
18. Seward, *Seward*, vol. 2, 99.

Chapter 8: A Higher Law

1. John M. Taylor, "Willard's of Washington," *American History Illustrated*, October 1979.
2. Thomas Froncek, ed., *The City of Washington* (New York: Alfred A. Knopf, 1979), 162.
3. WHS to Frances Seward, March 7, 1849, Seward Papers.
4. Merrill D. Peterson, *The Great Triumvirate* (New York: Oxford University Press, 1987), 236.
5. Johnson, "Politics and the Seward Family," 51.
6. Ibid., 53.
7. Ibid., 60.
8. Frances Seward to WHS, May 8, 1850, Seward Papers.
9. Holman Hamilton, *Prologue to Conflict* (Lexington: University of Kentucky Press, 1964), 84.
10. Burton J. Hendrick, *Lincoln's War Cabinet* (Boston: Little, Brown, 1946), 8.
11. WHS to Frances Seward, March 23, 1849, Seward Papers.
12. WHS to Frances Seward, March 9, 1949, Seward Papers.
13. Peterson, *The Great Triumvirate*, 459.
14. Paul I. Wellman, *The House Divides* (Garden City, N.Y.: Doubleday, 1966), 328.
15. Hamilton, *Prologue to Conflict*, 68.
16. WHS to George W. Patterson, February 9, 1850, Seward Papers.
17. This and subsequent speech excerpts are from Baker, *Seward's Works*, vol. 1, 65–75.
18. Seward, *Seward*, vol. 2, 127.
19. Van Deusen, *Seward*, 124.

20. Tuckerman, *The Diary of Philip Hone,* 376.
21. Seward, *Seward,* vol. 2, 129.
22. Van Deusen, *Seward,* 128.

Chapter 9: The Flames of Kansas

1. Seward, *Seward,* vol. 2, 139.
2. Ibid., 147.
3. Ibid., 156.
4. Van Deusen, *Seward,* 135.
5. WHS to George M. Grier, December 13, 1851, Seward Collection, Goshen, N.Y., Historical Society.
6. Frederic Bancroft, *William H. Seward* (New York: Harper and Brothers, 1900), vol. 1, 325–26.
7. Seward, *Seward,* vol. 2, 172.
8. Bradford, *Union Portraits,* 202.
9. Ishabel Ross, *Rebel Rose* (New York: Harper and Brothers, 1954), 74.
10. Hudson Strode, *Jefferson Davis: American Patriot* (New York: Harcourt, Brace, 1955), 293.
11. Gerry Van der Heuvel, *Crowns of Thorns and Glory* (New York: E. P. Dutton, 1988), 75.
12. David Donald, *Charles Sumner and the Coming of the Civil War* (New York: Alfred A. Knopf, 1960), 270–71.
13. Van Deusen, *Seward,* 133.
14. Harry J. Carman and Reinhard H. Luthin, ''The Seward-Fillmore Feud and the Crisis of 1850,'' *Proceedings of the New York State Historical Association,* no. 41, 1943.
15. James M. McPherson, *Battle Cry of Freedom* (New York: Oxford University Press, 1988), 121.
16. Seward, *Seward,* vol. 2, 216.
17. Van Deusen, *Seward,* 152.
18. Ibid., 153.
19. Ibid.
20. McPherson, *Battle Cry of Freedom,* 145.
21. Glyndon G. Van Deusen, *Horace Greeley* (Philadelphia: University of Pennsylvania Press, 1953), 190.
22. Van Deusen, *Seward,* 160.
23. Van Deusen, *Thurlow Weed,* 204.
24. Allan Nevins, *Hamilton Fish* (New York: Dodd, Mead, 1936), 34.
25. Seward, *Seward,* vol. 2, 245.

Chapter 10: "An Irrepressible Conflict"

1. WHS to Samuel Blatchford, ''Sunday Morning'' (1855), author's collection.

2. Michael F. Holt, *The Political Crisis of the 1850s* (New York: John Wiley and Sons, 1978), 149.
3. Van Deusen, *Seward*, 177.
4. Bancroft, *Seward*, vol. 1, 423.
5. Ibid., 406.
6. McPherson, *Battle Cry of Freedom*, 150.
7. Nevins, *Hamilton Fish*, 58.
8. Van Deusen, *Seward*, 171.
9. Ibid., 266–67.
10. McPherson, *Battle Cry of Freedom*, 160.
11. Ibid., 178.
12. Bancroft, *Seward*, vol. 1, 448.
13. Van Deusen, *Seward*, 185.
14. Ibid., 186.
15. Bancroft, *Seward*, vol. 1, 458–61.
16. Roy P. Basler, ed., *Collected Works of Abraham Lincoln* (New Brunswick, N.J.: Rutgers University Press, 1953), vol. 2, 461.
17. Seward, *Seward*, vol. 2, 353.
18. Van Deusen, *Seward*, 194.

Chapter 11: The Great Crusade

1. Elbert B. Smith, *The Presidency of James Buchanan* (Lawrence: University of Kansas Press, 1975), 5.
2. Bancroft, *Seward*, vol. 1, 539.
3. Nevins, *The Emergence of Lincoln*, vol. 2, 22.
4. Patricia C. Johnson, "Sensitivity and Civil War: The Selected Diaries and Papers, 1858–1866, of Frances Adeline [Fanny] Seward," Ph.D. diss., 2 vols. (processed), University of Rochester, 1964, vol. 1, 180.
5. WHS to Frances Seward, May 7, 1859, Seward Papers.
6. Frederick Seward to Frances Seward, May 8, 1859, Seward Papers.
7. Seward, *Seward*, vol. 2, 365, 370.
8. Van Deusen, *Seward*, 212.
9. WHS to Frances Seward, September 26, 1859, Seward Papers.
10. Quoted in Stephen B. Oates, *To Purge This Land with Blood* (New York: Harper & Row, 1970), 312.
11. Van Deusen, *Seward*, 214–15.
12. Nevins, *The Emergence of Lincoln*, vol. 2, 176.
13. Seward, *Seward*, vol. 2, 438.
14. Nevins, *Hamilton Fish*, 77.
15. WHS, "The Admission of Kansas," February 29, 1860, pamphlet by the *New York Tribune*.
16. Van Deusen, *Seward*, 219.
17. Hendrick, *Lincoln's War Cabinet*, 56.

18. Benjamin P. Thomas, *Abraham Lincoln* (New York: Alfred A. Knopf, 1952), 201.
19. Bancroft, *Seward,* vol. 1, 531.
20. Ibid., 519.

Chapter 12: Crisis

1. WHS to George W. Patterson, June 27, 1860, Seward Papers.
2. WHS to Eliza H. Schuyler, May 23, 1860, private collection.
3. Bancroft, *Seward,* vol. 2, 349.
4. Van Deusen, *Seward,* 267.
5. McPherson, *Battle Cry of Freedom,* 230.
6. Potter, *The Impending Crisis,* 432.
7. Charles Francis Adams, *Autobiography* (Boston: Houghton Mifflin, 1916), 62.
8. Nevins, *The Emergence of Lincoln,* vol. 2, 300–301.
9. David W. Blight, *Frederick Douglass' Civil War* (Baton Rouge: Louisiana University Press, 1989), 144.
10. Seward, *Seward,* vol. 2, 464.
11. Adams, *Autobiography,* 64.
12. Ibid., 65–66.
13. Basler, *Collected Works of Abraham Lincoln,* vol. 4, 127.
14. Smith, *James Buchanan,* 127.
15. Caleb S. Henry to WHS, November 10, 1860, Seward Papers.
16. William C. Davis, *The Deep Waters of the Proud* (Garden City, N.Y.: Doubleday, 1982), vol. 1, 33.
17. Wellman, *The House Divides,* 440.
18. James M. McPherson, *Ordeal by Fire* (New York: Alfred A. Knopf, 1982), 130.
19. Ibid., 129.
20. Daniel W. Crofts, *Reluctant Confederates* (Chapel Hill: University of North Carolina Press, 1989), 116.
21. Seward, *Seward,* vol. 2, 480.
22. Hendrick, *Lincoln's War Cabinet,* 132.
23. Ibid., 133.
24. Charles Francis Adams to WHS, November 11, 1860, Seward Papers.
25. Basler, *Collected Works of Abraham Lincoln,* vol. 4, 148.
26. Crofts, *Reluctant Confederates,* 221–22.
27. Van Deusen, *Seward,* 241.
28. McPherson, *Ordeal by Fire,* 134–35.
29. *New York Times,* December 24, 1860.
30. Seward, *Seward,* vol. 2, 485.
31. Van Deusen, *Seward,* 247.

32. Hendrick, *Lincoln's War Cabinet*, 137.
33. Newton Arvin, ed., *The Selected Letters of Henry Adams* (New York: Farrar, Straus and Young, 1951), 26.
34. Smith, *James Buchanan*, 179.
35. Seward, *Seward*, vol. 2, 489.
36. Ibid., 488.
37. Benjamin P. Thomas and Harold M. Hyman, *Stanton* (New York: Alfred A. Knopf, 1962), 100.
38. Van Deusen, *Seward*, 244.

Chapter 13: The Peacemaker

1. Thornton K. Lothrop, *William Henry Seward* (Boston: Houghton Mifflin, 1899), 222.
2. Hendrick, *Lincoln's War Cabinet*, 148.
3. Bancroft, *Seward*, vol. 2, 15.
4. Ibid.
5. Van Deusen, *Seward*, 245–46.
6. Crofts, *Reluctant Confederates*, 237.
7. Joseph T. Durkin, *Stephen R. Mallory* (Chapel Hill: University of North Carolina Press, 1954), 124.
8. Basler, *Collected Works of Abraham Lincoln*, vol. 4, 170.
9. Ibid., 198.
10. Van Deusen, *Seward*, 259.
11. Margaret Leech, *Reveille in Washington* (New York: Harper and Brothers, 1941), 36.
12. Crofts, *Reluctant Confederates*, 244.
13. Seward, *Seward*, vol. 2, 511.
14. WHS to Thurlow Weed, January 21, 1861, Weed Papers, University of Rochester.
15. "Sincere Friend" to WHS, April 5, 1861, Seward Papers.
16. Frederick L. Roberts to WHS, March 18, 1861, Seward Papers.
17. Edwards Pierrepoint to William Evarts, January 5, 1861, author's collection.
18. Van Deusen, *Seward*, 253.
19. Potter, *The Impending Crisis*, 565.
20. Basler, *Collected Works of Abraham Lincoln*, vol. 4, 261–62.
20. Seward, *Seward*, vol. 2, 516.
21. Basler, *Collected Works of Abraham Lincoln*, vol. 4, 271.
22. Carl Sandburg, *Abraham Lincoln: The War Years* (New York: Harcourt, Brace & World, 1939), vol. 1, 176.
23. Martin B. Duberman, *Charles Francis Adams* (Boston: Houghton Mifflin, 1961), 257.
24. William Russell, *My Diary North and South* (Boston, 1863), 17.

25. Ibid., 19.
26. Bancroft, *Seward*, vol. 1, 464.

Chapter 14: War

1. Bancroft, *Seward*, vol. 2, 118.
2. Lately Thomas, *Sam Ward* (Boston: Houghton Mifflin, 1965), 257.
3. Allan Nevins, *The War for the Union* (New York: Charles Scribner's Sons, 1959), vol. 1, 43.
4. Crofts, *Reluctant Confederates*, 275.
5. McPherson, *Ordeal by Fire*, 142.
6. Crofts, *Reluctant Confederates*, 258.
7. F. Lauriston Bullard, ed., *The Diary of a Public Man* (New Brunswick, N.J.: Rutgers University Press, 1946), 99–100.
8. Van Deusen, *Seward*, 280.
9. Catton, *The Coming Fury*, 286.
10. The full text of Seward's April 1, 1861, memorandum and Lincoln's draft response are in the Appendix.
11. Samuel E. Morison and Henry S. Commager, *The Growth of the American Republic* (New York: Oxford University Press, 1962), vol. 1, 678.
12. Davis, *The Deep Waters of the Proud*, vol. 1, 46.
13. See Basler, *Collected Works of Abraham Lincoln*, vol. 4, 317.
14. Frederick W. Seward, "After Thirty Years," Seward Papers.
15. Nevins, *The War for the Union*, vol. 1, 62.
16. Van Deusen, *Seward*, 292.
17. McPherson, *Battle Cry of Freedom*, 269.
18. Catton, *The Coming Fury*, 285.
19. Frederick L. Roberts to WHS, March 18, 1861, Seward Papers.
20. Joseph M. Churchill to WHS, April 13, 1861, Seward Papers.
21. "A Southerner" to WHS, April 20, 1861, Seward Papers.
22. Catton, *The Coming Fury*, 285.
23. Bancroft, *Seward*, vol. 2, 131.
24. C. Vann Woodward, ed., *Mary Chesnut's Civil War* (New Haven, Conn.: Yale University Press, 1981), 22.
25. Van Deusen, *Seward*, 289.
26. Gideon Welles, *Diary* (Boston: Houghton Mifflin, 1911), vol. 1, 24.
27. Undated memorandum, Seward Papers.
28. Sandburg, *Abraham Lincoln: The War Years*, vol. 1, 206.
29. Catton, *The Coming Fury*, 302.
30. Quoted in Crofts, *Reluctant Confederates*, 356.
31. Nevins, *The War for the Union*, vol. 1, 39, 72, 74.
32. Baker, *Seward's Works*, vol. 5, 613–14.
33. Bancroft, *Seward*, vol. 2, 121.
34. James G. Randall, *Lincoln the President* (New York: Dodd, Mead, 1945), vol. 1, 350.

35. Bancroft, *Seward,* vol. 2, 142.
36. Ralph H. Gabriel, *The Course of American Democratic Thought* (New York: Greenwood Press, 1986), 115.

Chapter 15: Mr. Seward's Little Bell

1. Fanny Seward to WHS, April 28, 1861, Seward Papers.
2. Sandburg, *Abraham Lincoln: The War Years,* vol. 1, 215.
3. Seward, *Seward,* vol. 2, 545.
4. Welles, *Diary,* vol. 1, 549.
5. Baker, *Seward's Works,* vol. 5, 42.
6. Johnson, "Politics and the Seward Family," 56–57.
7. Noah Brooks, *Washington, D.C., in Lincoln's Time* (New York: Times Books, 1971), 61.
8. Frank J. Merli, *Great Britain and the Confederate Navy* (Bloomington: Indiana University Press, 1970), 46.
9. Seward, *Seward,* vol. 2, 623.
10. Bancroft, *Seward,* vol. 2, 351.
11. Basler, *Lincoln's Works,* vol. 4, 360.
12. Ibid., vol. 5, 126.
13. Herbert Mitgang, "Garibaldi and Lincoln," *American Heritage,* October 1975.
14. Ibid.
15. Francis B. Carpenter, "A Day with Governor Seward at Auburn," July 1870, Seward Papers.
16. Dean Sprague, *Freedom Under Lincoln* (Boston: Houghton Mifflin, 1965), 159.
17. Van Deusen, *Seward,* 289.
18. Greenhow to WHS, April 9, 1861, Seward Papers.
19. Ross, *Rebel Rose,* 180–81.
20. Bancroft, *Seward,* vol. 2, 264–66.
21. Ibid., 272–74.
22. Jay Monaghan, *Diplomat in Carpet Slippers* (New York: Bobbs-Merrill, 1945), 148–49.
23. Catton, *The Coming Fury,* 357.
24. Bancroft, *Seward,* vol. 2, 279.
25. Sprague, *Freedom Under Lincoln,* 157.
26. Woodward, *Mary Chesnut's Civil War,* 176.
27. Jacob Mogelever, *Death to Traitors* (Garden City, N.Y.: Doubleday, 1960), 78.
28. Van Deusen, *Seward,* 296.
29. Thomas, *Sam Ward,* 273.
30. Welles, *Diary,* vol. 1, 124.
31. Rufus R. Wilson, ed., *Intimate Memories of Lincoln* (Elmira, N.Y.: Primavera Press, 1945), 374.

Chapter 16: Aggressive Diplomacy

1. Baker, *Seward's Works,* vol. 5, 43.
2. Bancroft, *Seward,* vol. 2, 151.
3. Ibid., 225.
4. Brian Jenkins, *Britain and the War for the Union* (Toronto: University of Toronto, 1980), vol. 1, 98.
5. Ibid.
6. Nevins, *The War for the Union,* vol. 2, 253.
7. Jenkins, *Britain and the War for the Union,* vol. 1, 26.
8. Van Deusen, *Seward,* 293.
9. Ibid.
10. Merli, *Great Britain and the Confederate Navy,* 21.
11. Ibid., 22.
12. Baker, *Seward's Works,* vol. 5, 213.
13. Jenkins, *Britain and the War for the Union,* vol. 1, 98.
14. McPherson, *Battle Cry of Freedom,* 388.
15. Basler, *Collected Works of Abraham Lincoln,* vol. 4, 376–80.
16. Ibid.
17. Duberman, *Charles Francis Adams,* 268–69.
18. Donald, *Charles Sumner and the Rights of Man,* 19.
19. Ibid., 23.
20. Seward, *Seward,* vol. 2, 590.
21. Woodward, *Mary Chesnut's Civil War,* 520.
22. Merli, *Great Britain and the Confederate Navy,* 75.
23. Ibid., 77.
24. Jenkins, *Britain and the War for the Union,* vol. 1, 198–99.
25. Donald, *Charles Sumner and the Rights of Man,* 35.
26. *Dublin Daily Express,* November 29, 1861, Seward Papers.
27. Merli, *Great Britain and the Confederate Navy,* 81.
28. Van Deusen, *Seward,* 310.
29. Carpenter, "A Day with Governor Seward at Auburn."
30. Seward, *Seward,* vol. 3, 25.
31. Ibid., 25–26.
32. Napier to WHS, January 17, 1862, Seward Papers.
33. Van Deusen, *Seward,* 316.
34. Russell, *Diary,* 262.
35. Jenkins, *Britain and the War for the Union,* vol. 1, 228.
36. Hendrick, *Lincoln's War Cabinet,* 209–10.

Chapter 17: "The Scenes are Unwritten"

1. Seward, *Seward,* vol. 3, 46.
2. Nevins, *The War for the Union,* vol. 2, 44.

3. Quoted in Wilson, *Intimate Memories of Lincoln* 520.

4. Van Deusen, *Seward,* 336–37.

5. George B. Lincoln to Gideon Welles, April 25, 1874, quoted in *Lincoln Lore,* April 1981.

6. Carl Sandburg, *Mary Lincoln* (New York: Harcourt, Brace, 1932), 268.

7. Hendrick, *Lincoln's War Cabinet,* 187.

8. Johnson, *"Fanny Seward Diary,"* vol. 1, 360.

9. Thomas, *Abraham Lincoln,* 351.

10. Johnson, *"Fanny Seward Diary,"* vol. 1, 137.

11. Frederick W. Seward, "Lincoln and Seward" quoted in *Obediah Seward of Long Island and His Descendants,* privately printed, 1948.

12. Wilson, *Intimate Memories of Lincoln,* 422.

13. Donald, *Charles Sumner and the Rights of Man,* 88.

14. Van Deusen, *Seward,* 323.

15. Bancroft, *Seward,* vol. 2, 328.

16. Frances Seward to WHS, March 11, 1862, Seward Papers.

17. Frances Seward to WHS, August 24, 1862, Seward Papers.

18. McPherson, *Battle Cry of Freedom,* 508.

19. Seward, *Seward,* vol. 3, 227.

20. Nevins, *The War for the Union,* vol. 2, 148.

21. Ibid., 148, 241.

22. Bancroft, *Seward,* vol. 2, 345.

23. Baker, *Seward's Works,* vol. 5, 9.

24. Bancroft, *Seward,* vol. 2, 326.

25. WHS to Thurlow Weed, April 7, 1862, Weed Papers, University of Rochester.

26. Welles, *Diary,* vol. 1, 39.

27. Fawn M. Brodie, *Thaddeus Stevens* (New York: W. W. Norton, 1966) 284.

28. Seward, *Seward,* vol. 3, 50.

29. Van Deusen, *Seward,* 336.

30. William R. Thayer, *John Hay* (New York: Kraus Reprint Co., 1969), vol. 1, 235.

31. Daniel Carroll, *Henri Mercier and the American Civil War* (Princeton, N.J.: Princeton University Press, 1971), 127.

32. WHS to Jerome Napoleon Bonaparte, December 13, 1861, Seward Papers.

33. Lynn M. Case and Warren F. Spencer, *The United States and France: Civil War Diplomacy* (Philadelphia: University of Pennsylvania, 1970), 278.

34. Ibid., 280.

35. Philip Van Doren Stern, *When the Guns Roared* (Garden City, N.Y.: Doubleday, 1965), 133.

36. Case and Spencer, *The United States and France,* 333.

37. Merli, *Great Britain and the Confederate Navy,* 100.

38. Albert A. Woldman, *Lincoln and the Russians* (New York: World, 1952), 98–99.
39. Merli, *Great Britain and the Confederate Navy*, 114–15.
40. Baker, *Seward's Works*, vol. 5, 49.

Chapter 18: *"Remove Him!"*

1. William Roscoe Thayer, *John Hay: American Statesman* (New York: Houghton, 1917), vol. 1, 137–38.
2. Seward, *Seward*, vol. 3, 104–5.
3. John Bigelow, *Retrospections of an Active Life* (New York: Doubleday, Page, 1909), vol. 1, 563.
4. Welles, *Diary*, vol. 1, 70.
5. Nevins, *The War for the Union*, vol. 2, 165.
6. John Niven, *Gideon Welles: Lincoln's Secretary of the Navy* (New York: Oxford University Press, 1973), 419–20.
7. Francis B. Carpenter, *Six Months at the White House* (New York: Hurd and Houghton, 1866), 72–73.
8. Van Deusen, *Seward*, 333.
9. McPherson, *Battle Cry of Freedom*, 507.
10. T. Harry Williams, *Lincoln and the Radicals* (Madison: University of Wisconsin Press, 1965), 217.
11. Hendrick, *Lincoln's War Cabinet*, 280.
12. Williams, *Lincoln and the Radicals*, 206.
13. Donald, *Charles Sumner and the Rights of Man*, 87.
14. Thomas, *Abraham Lincoln*, 352.
15. Hendrick, *Lincoln's War Cabinet*, 326.
16. Van Deusen, *Seward*, 343.
17. J. G. Randall and David Donald, *The Civil War and Reconstruction* (Boston: D.C. Heath, 1961), 462.
18. Van Deusen, *Seward*, 345.
19. Welles, *Diary*, vol. 1, 194–95.
20. Ibid., vol. 2, 359–60.
21. Ibid., vol. 1, 200–201.
22. Ibid., 201–2.
23. Thomas, *Abraham Lincoln*, 354.
24. WHS to Thurlow Weed, April 1, 1862, Weed Papers.
25. WHS draft statement, December 22, 1862, quoted in *Lincoln Lore*, September 1958.
26. Jenkins, *Britain and the War for the Union*, vol. 2, 191.
27. Donald, *Charles Sumner and the Rights of Man*, 100.
28. Van Deusen, *Seward*, 348.
29. *New York Times*, December 22, 1862.

Chapter 19: High Tide and Rebel Raiders

1. Seward, *Seward*, vol. 2, 521.
2. Welles, *Diary*, vol. 1, 398.
3. Ibid., 131.
4. Ibid., 205.
5. Niven, *Gideon Welles*, 441.
6. Jenkins, *Britain and the War for the Union*, vol. 2, 25.
7. Niven, *Gideon Welles*, 449.
8. Van Deusen, *Seward*, 353.
9. Donald, *Charles Sumner and the Rights of Man*, 110.
10. Welles, *Diary*, 273.
11. WHS, unsigned memorandum, August 1863, Seward Papers.
12. Duberman, *Charles Francis Adams*, 304.
13. Jenkins, *Britain and the War for the Union*, vol. 2, 267.
14. Stern, *When the Guns Roared*, 210.
15. Baker, *Seward's Works*, vol. 5, 387–88.
16. Duberman, *Charles Francis Adams*, 311.
17. William W. Wade, "The Man Who Stopped the Rams," *American Heritage*, April 1963.
18. Hendrick, *Lincoln's War Cabinet*, 213.
19. McPherson, *Ordeal by Fire*, 342.
20. Case and Spencer, *The United States and France*, 437–38.
21. Ibid., 441–42.
22. Stern, *When the Guns Roared*, 231.
23. Sandburg, *Abraham Lincoln: The War Years*, vol. 2, 524.
24. WHS to E. D. Morgan, May 6, 1863, Weed Papers.
25. Nevins, *The War for the Union*, vol. 3, 153.
26. WHS to Frances Seward, June 19, 1863, Seward Papers.
27. Seward, *Seward*, vol. 3, 173.
28. Van Deusen, *Seward*, 402.
29. Seward, *Seward*, vol. 3, 201.
30. W. Farquhar to——Boos, May 26, 1921. ADS Catalog, 1990.

Chapter 20: "Beyond the Pale of Human Envy"

1. Baker, *Seward's Works*, vol. 2, 208.
2. George S. Bryan, *The Great American Myth* (New York: Carrick & Evans, 1940), 6.
3. *Washington Star*, November 11, 1863.
4. Frederick W. Seward to Frances Seward, January 29, 1864, Seward Papers.
5. Benjamin Perley Poore, *Reminiscences* (Philadelphia: Hubbard Brothers, 1886), vol. 2, 148–49.

6. Van Deusen, *Seward*, 403.
7. Leech, *Reveille in Washington*, 313.
8. Nevins, *Hamilton Fish*, 77–78.
9. Bradford, *Union Portraits*, 225.
10. Wilson, *Intimate Memories of Lincoln*, 374.
11. Seward, *Seward*, vol. 3, 197.
12. Ibid., 196.
13. WHS to Frances Seward, June 13, 1864, Seward Papers.
14. Stern, *When the Guns Roared*, 268.
15. McPherson, *Ordeal by Fire*, 344.
16. Bancroft, *Seward*, vol. 2, 428–29.
17. Stern, *When the Guns Roared*, 273.
18. Harold Hyman, ed., *Heard Round the World* (New York: Alfred A. Knopf, 1969), 280–81.
19. Thomas, *Abraham Lincoln*, 410.
20. Van Deusen, *Thurlow Weed*, 307.
21. Ibid.
22. Van Deusen, *Seward*, 595.
23. Randall and Donald, *The Civil War and Reconstruction*, 473.
24. WHS to Frances Seward, April 20, 1864, Seward Papers.
25. Seward, *Seward*, vol. 3, 233.
26. Baker, *Seward's Works*, vol. 5, 502.
27. Ibid., 514.
28. Thayer, *John Hay*, vol. 1, 134.
29. Van Deusen, *Seward*, 399.
30. McPherson, *Battle Cry of Freedom*, 822.
31. James A. Garfield to Irvin McDowell, February 3, 1865, author's collection.
32. William S. McFeely, *Grant* (New York: W. W. Norton, 1981), 206–07.
33. Sandburg, *Abraham Lincoln: The War Years*, vol. 4, 46.
34. Hans L. Trefousse, *Andrew Johnson* (New York: W. W. Norton, 1989), 189–90.
35. Basler, *Collected Works of Abraham Lincoln*, vol. 8, 332–33.

Chapter 21: The Man in the Light Overcoat

1. Thayer, *John Hay*, vol. 1, 218.
2. Seward, *Seward*, vol. 3, 209.
3. Sandburg, *Abraham Lincoln: The War Years*, vol. 4, 175–76.
4. Bancroft, *Seward*, vol. 2, 418.
5. Seward, *Seward*, vol. 3, 271.
6. Ibid., 271–72.
7. Mark E. Neely, Jr., *The Abraham Lincoln Encyclopedia* (New York: Da Capo Press, 1982), 244.

8. Benn Pitman, ed., *The Assassination of President Lincoln and the Trial of the Conspirators* (New York and Cincinnati: Moore, Wilstach & Baldwin, 1865), 161.

9. Frederick W. Seward, *Reminiscences of a War-Time Diplomat and Statesman* (New York: 1916), 259.

10. Pitman, *The Assassination of President Lincoln*, 155.

11. Ibid., 156.

12. Thomas and Hyman, *Stanton*, 396.

13. Niven, *Gideon Welles*, 492–93.

14. Johnson, "Fanny Seward Diary," vol. 2, 890.

15. Pitman, *The Assassination of President Lincoln*, 157.

16. John K. Lattimer, *Kennedy and Lincoln* (New York: Harcourt Brace Jovanovich, 1980), 102.

17. Johnson, "Fanny Seward Diary," vol. 2, 891.

18. Van Deusen, *Seward*, 414.

19. George E. Baker to Mrs. Barnes, April 24, 1865, Weed Papers.

20. Van Deusen, *Seward*, 415.

21. Johnson, "Fanny Seward Diary," vol. 2, 893.

22. Seward, *Seward*, vol. 3, 286.

23. Ibid., 287.

24. Brooks, *Washington, D.C., in Lincoln's Time*, 61.

25. William E. Doster, *Lincoln and Episodes of the Civil War* (New York: G. P. Putnam's Sons, 1915), 260.

26. Ibid., 265.

27. Bryan, *The Great American Myth*, 302–3.

Chapter 22: President Johnson

1. Brooks, *Washington, D.C., in Lincoln's Time*, 458.

2. Lloyd Lewis, *Sherman: Fighting Prophet* (New York: Harcourt, Brace, 1958), 575.

3. WHS to George M. Grier, September 8, 1865, Grier Papers, University of Rochester.

4. WHS to James Watson Webb, August 9, 1865, private collection.

5. WHS to George W. Patterson, November 17, 1865, Patterson Papers, University of Rochester.

6. Van Deusen, *Seward*, 434.

7. Case and Spencer, *The United States and France*, 562.

8. Robert H. Ferrell, *American Diplomacy* (New York: W. W. Norton, 1969), 305.

9. Trefousse, *Andrew Johnson*, 197–98.

10. Van Deusen, *Seward*, 94.

11. Thomas and Hyman, *Stanton*, 445.

12. WHS to James Watson Webb, August 9, 1865, private collection.

13. Van Deusen, *Seward,* 426.
14. Seward, *Seward,* vol. 3, 296.
15. Van Deusen, *Seward,* 426–27.
16. Seward, *Seward,* vol. 3, 300.
17. Van Deusen, *Seward,* 437–38.
18. Michael Les Benedict, *A Compromise of Principle* (New York: W. W. Norton, 1974), 128–29.
19. Welles, *Diary,* vol. 2, 409.
20. Van Deusen, *Seward,* 442–43.
21. W. J. Branch to WHS, February 25, 1866, Seward Papers.
22. Joel Branham to WHS, March 1, 1866, Seward Papers.
23. Ransom Balcom to WHS, March 2, 1866, Seward Papers.
24. Welles, *Diary,* vol. 2, 463–64.
25. McPherson, *Ordeal by Fire,* 516.
26. Bancroft, *Seward,* vol. 2, 457.
27. Van Deusen, *Seward,* 427.
28. WHS to B. F. Perry, August 26, 1865, Seward Papers.
29. James G. Blaine, *Twenty Years of Congress* (Norwich, Conn.: Hill Publishing Co., 1886), vol. 2, 107.
30. Bancroft, *Seward,* 455–56.
31. Eli N. Evans, *Judah P. Benjamin* (New York: Free Press, 1988), 334.

Chapter 23: "He Wanders Around Like a Ghost"

1. Randall and Donald, *The Civil War and Reconstruction,* 634.
2. Van Deusen, *Seward,* 451.
3. Seward, *Seward,* vol. 3, 332.
4. Trefousse, *Andrew Johnson,* 256.
5. Benedict, *A Compromise of Principle,* 194.
6. Brodie, *Thaddeus Stevens,* 284.
7. Welles, *Diary,* vol. 2, 591.
8. Lately Thomas, *The First President Johnson* (New York: William Morrow, 1968), 493–94.
9. Van Deusen, *Seward,* 461.
10. Welles, *Diary,* vol. 2, 595.
11. Johnson, "Fanny Seward Diary," vol. 2, 990–91.
12. WHS to George W. Patterson, November 7, 1866, Patterson Papers.
13. Trefousse, *Andrew Johnson,* 267.
14. Brodie, *Thaddeus Stevens,* 285.
15. Bancroft, *Seward,* vol. 2, 462.
16. William B. Hesseltine, *Ulysses S. Grant: Politician* (New York: Dodd, Mead, 1935), 78–79.
17. Adams, *The Education of Henry Adams,* 246.
18. Thayer, *John Hay,* vol. 1, 250.

19. Welles, *Diary,* vol. 3, 4–5.
20. John M. Taylor, "Fenian Raids Against Canada," *American History Illustrated,* August 1978.
21. Bancroft, *Seward,* vol. 2, 440–41.
22. Philip H. Sheridan, *Personal Memoirs* (New York: Charles L. Webster Co., 1888), vol. 2, 226.
23. Van Deusen, *Seward,* 492–93.
24. Seward, *Seward,* vol. 3, 364.
25. Van Deusen, *Seward,* 464, 495.
26. Welles, *Diary,* vol. 2, 626.
27. Clarence A. Seward to Samuel Blatchford, November 14, 1865, author's collection.
28. John M. Taylor, "Dirty Tricks—A Forgotten Episode," *Wall Street Journal,* January 6, 1976.
29. Blaine, *Twenty Years of Congress,* vol. 2, 273.
30. Van Deusen, *Seward,* 473.
31. Ibid., 469.
32. Thomas, *The First President Johnson,* 513.
33. Donald, *Charles Sumner and the Rights of Man,* 280.
34. Welles, *Diary,* vol. 3, 25–26.

Chapter 24: The Empire Builder

1. Seward, *Seward,* vol. 3, 346.
2. Thayer, *John Hay,* vol. 1, 253.
3. Van Deusen, *Seward,* 527.
4. Ferrell, *American Diplomacy,* 316.
5. Albert A. Woldman, *Lincoln and the Russians* (New York: World, 1952), 280–81.
6. Seward, *Seward,* vol. 3, 348.
7. Donald, *Charles Sumner and the Rights of Man,* 305–6.
8. Ferrell, *American Diplomacy,* 312.
9. Robert L. Reynolds, "Seward's Wise Folly," *America and Russia* (New York: Simon & Schuster, 1962), 87.
10. Donald, *Charles Sumner and the Rights of Man,* 308–10.
11. Woldman, *Lincoln and the Russians,* 282–83.
12. Van Deusen, *Seward,* 545.
13. Roland T. Carr, *32 President's Square* (Washington, D.C.: Acropolis Books, 1980), 309.
14. William A. Dunning, "Paying for Alaska," *Political Science Quarterly,* September 1912.
15. Brodie, *Thaddeus Stevens,* 359.
16. Woldman, *Lincoln and the Russians,* 288–89.
17. Reynolds, "Seward's Wise Folly," *America and Russia,* 91.

18. Van Deusen, *Seward,* 517–18.
19. Brodie, *Thaddeus Stevens,* 325.
20. Van Deusen, *Seward,* 480.
21. Seward, *Seward,* vol. 3, 376–77.
22. Thomas, *The First President Johnson,* 586.
23. Ibid., 595.
24. Van Deusen, *Seward,* 481.

Chapter 25: World Traveler

1. Van Deusen, *Seward,* 504–5.
2. Welles, *Diary,* vol. 3, 256–57.
3. Donald, *The Civil War and Reconstruction,* 672.
4. Welles, *Diary,* vol. 3, 449.
5. Van Deusen, *Seward,* 554.
6. Seward, *Seward,* vol. 3, 398.
7. Trefousse, *Andrew Johnson,* 351.
8. Seward, *Seward,* vol. 3, 550.
9. Bigelow, *Retrospections of an Active Life,* vol. 4, 273–75.
10. Ibid., 401.
11. Ibid., 410.
12. Ibid., 432.
13. *San Francisco Examiner,* September 28, 1869.
14. Seward, *Seward,* vol. 3, 457.
15. Carpenter, "A Day with Governor Seward at Auburn."
16. Olive Risley Seward, ed., *William H. Seward's Travels Around the World* (New York: D. Appleton and Co., 1873), 83.
17. Van Deusen, *Seward,* 559–60.
18. Ibid., 558–59, 633.
19. Seward, *William H. Seward's Travels Around the World,* 140.
20. Bancroft, *Seward,* vol. 2, 524.
21. Van Deusen, *Seward,* 561.
22. Carpenter, "A Day with Governor Seward at Auburn."
23. Seward, *Seward,* vol. 3, 471.
24. Van Deusen, *Seward,* 564.
26. Seward, *Seward,* vol. 3, 508.

Chapter 26: Seward and the Lincoln Legend

1. Seward, *Seward,* vol. 3, 537–38.
2. Charles Francis Adams, *The Life, Character and Services of William H. Seward* (New York: D. Appleton and Co., 1873), 29–32.
3. Gideon Welles, *Lincoln and Seward* (New York: Sheldon & Co., 1874), 27–43.

4. Thayer, *John Hay*, vol. 1, 268.
5. Randall and Donald, *The Civil War and Reconstruction*, 650.
6. John Nicolay and John Hay, *Abraham Lincoln* (New York: Century Co., 1890), vol. 3, 445.
7. Hendrick, *Lincoln's War Cabinet*, 212.
8. Bullard, *The Diary of a Public Man*, 92.
9. Adams, *The Education of Henry Adams*, 104.
10. Charles Francis Adams, Jr., *Autobiography*, 89.
11. Bancroft, *Seward*, vol. 2, 528.

INDEX